A Short History of Renaissance Italy

From Giotto's artistic revolution at the dawn of the fourteenth century to the scientific discoveries of Galileo in the early seventeenth, this book explores the cultural developments of one of the most remarkable and vibrant periods of history—the Italian Renaissance. What makes the period all the more amazing is that this flowering of the visual arts, literature, and philosophy occurred against a turbulent backdrop of civic factionalism, foreign invasions, war, and pestilence.

The fifteen chapters move briskly from the Fall of the Roman Empire in the West through the growth of the Italian city-states, where, in the crucible of pandemic disease and social unrest, a new approach to learning known as humanism was forged, political and religious certainties challenged. Traversing the entire Italian Peninsula—Florence, Rome, Milan, Venice, Naples, and Sicily—this book examines the rich regional diversity of Renaissance cultural experience and considers men's and women's lives, their changing social attitudes and beliefs across three centuries. This second edition has been updated throughout; it now contains dozens of color images and timelines, as well as links to the author's new companion book of primary sources, *Voices from the Italian Renaissance*.

Readers will need no preliminary background on the subject matter, as the story is told in a lively, readable narrative. Interdisciplinary in nature, its characters are merchants, bankers, artists, saints, soldiers of fortune, poets, popes, and courtesans. With brief literary excerpts, first-hand accounts, maps, and illustrations that help bring the era to life, this is an ideal text for students in a college survey course, as well as for the interested general reader or traveler to Italy who is curious to learn more about the extraordinary heritage of the Renaissance.

Lisa Kaborycha holds a Ph.D. in Medieval and Early Modern European History from the University of California, Berkeley and has been the recipient of a Fulbright Fellowship; a National Endowment for the Humanities Fellowship with the Medici Archive Project; and Harvard's Villa I Tatti Fellowship in Italian Renaissance Studies. In addition to *A Short History of Renaissance Italy*, and *Voices from the Italian Renaissance*, she is the author of *A Corresponding Renaissance: Letters Written by Italian Women, 1375–1650* (2016). For years Kaborycha taught courses in Renaissance History for the University of California and currently works as adjunct professor at the University of New Haven Tuscany Campus and lecturer at the British Institute of Florence.

A Short History of Renaissance Italy

Second Edition

Lisa Kaborycha

LONDON AND NEW YORK

Designed cover image: Domenico Ghirlandaio, *Visitation*, detail.
Zip Lexing/Alamy Stock Photo R88PR7

Second edition published 2024
by Routledge
4 Park Square, Milton Park, Abingdon, Oxon, OX14 4RN

and by Routledge
605 Third Avenue, New York, NY 10158

Routledge is an imprint of the Taylor & Francis Group, an informa business

© 2024 Lisa Kaborycha

The right of Lisa Kaborycha to be identified as author of this work has been
asserted in accordance with sections 77 and 78 of the Copyright, Designs
and Patents Act 1988.

All rights reserved. No part of this book may be reprinted or reproduced or utilised
in any form or by any electronic, mechanical, or other means, now known or
hereafter invented, including photocopying and recording, or in any information
storage or retrieval system, without permission in writing from the publishers.

Trademark notice: Product or corporate names may be trademarks or registered trademarks,
and are used only for identification and explanation without intent to infringe.

First edition published by Pearson 2011

British Library Cataloguing-in-Publication Data
A catalogue record for this book is available from the British Library

ISBN: 978-1-032-21868-7 (hbk)
ISBN: 978-1-032-21869-4 (pbk)
ISBN: 978-1-003-27036-2 (ebk)

DOI: 10.4324/9781003270362

Typeset in Sabon
by Newgen Publishing UK

Contents

Figures	*xiv*
Tables	*xvi*
Maps	*xvii*
Preface	*xix*
Acknowledgments	*xxii*
Foreword by Dale Kent	*xxiii*
A note concerning dating	*xxviii*

1 Out of the Ashes: The Rise of the Communes and Florence in the Age of Dante   1

The grandeur that was Rome 1
The spread of Christianity 3
The empire returns? 4
The Commercial Revolution 5
Communal governments sprout up in Italy 6
Tensions between magnates and popolo *8*
The age of the popular commune, 1200–90 9
A "pullulation of little powers" 10
Florentines, the "fifth element of the world" 12
Dante Alighieri, Florentine poet and political exile 13
The Divine Comedy, *the first masterpiece of Italian literature 14*
"Those brand-new people and their sudden earnings" 15
Mendicant friars praised and corrupt popes punished 16
Dante and Marsilius of Padua on the powers of church and state 17
An explosion of naturalism in art: Giotto di Bondone 18
Developments in sculpture and architecture 20
Considerations: "Medieval" or "Renaissance"? 21
Sourcebook 22
Further reading 22

vi   *Contents*

2 The Crises of the Fourteenth Century: Climatic, Epidemic, Demographic Disasters   23

The "Little Ice Age," a time of global cooling 24
The Hundred Years' War and crash of international banking 24
1347: A devastating pandemic arrives in Europe 25
Boccaccio's account of the Black Death 27
The life of Giovanni Boccaccio 28
The Decameron, *100 tales of love, lust, and loss 29*
Society in the wake of the Black Death 30
Government and medicine respond to the crisis 31
Social mobility and unrest 32
The Ciompi Rebellion and the Florentine guilds 32
Town and country 34
"Motionless History" in the countryside 35
Hard times in the contado *35*
An age of new men 36
Painting in the early Trecento in Siena 37
Art in the wake of the Black Death 39
Recovery and renewal 40
Considerations: Just how calamitous was the fourteenth century? 41
Sourcebook 41
Further reading 41

3 Back to the Future: Italian Humanists Recover the Classical Past   43

Humanism, a cultural revolution led by notaries 44
The medieval scholastic heritage 45
Italian humanists restore ancient texts 46
The life of Petrarch, a passionate humanist 47
"Carried away by the fire of youth ..." 48
Petrarch's interiority: It's all about "me" 49
Scattered Rhymes 50
An "educational surge" in Italian cities 51
The flowering of Florentine vernacular culture 53
Rhetoric: How to speak with strength, impetuosity, and grace 54
The generation after Petrarch: Salutati, Bruni, and civic humanism 55
Women and humanism 58
Humanism, guilds, and the arts in quattrocento Florence 58
Ghiberti's gilded Gates of Paradise *59*
The sculpture of Donatello, a dazzling "mutation" 60
Brunelleschi's genius, ingenuity, and engineering 62
Masaccio, a youthful painter of dramatic realism 65
Considerations: Humanism, humanitarianism, and the humanities 67

Contents vii

Sourcebook 68
Further reading 68

4 *Caput Mundi* again? The City of Rome Reborn   69
The city of the Caesars becomes the city of popes 70
The papacy precariously balanced on a rock 71
Roman communal politics: A "monstrous thing" 72
Pope Boniface VIII clashes swords with the king of France 73
Rome widowed 74
The meteoric rise and fall of Cola di Rienzo 75
The "Babylonian Captivity" of the church, 1309–78 77
The popes return to Rome 78
The War of the Eight Saints, 1375–78 79
Antipopes and the Western Schism, 1378–1417 79
The conciliar movement, 1409–39 81
The birth of the Renaissance "papal prince" 82
Popes Martin V, Eugenius IV, and Nicholas V rebuild Rome 83
The amazing Leon Battista Alberti 85
Reinventing the role of the architect 87
Pope Pius II, a poet on St. Peter's chair 89
Considerations: Renaissance pope and Renaissance man 91
Sourcebook 93
Further reading 93

5 Hearth and Home: Lay Piety, Women, and the Family   94
Religion: A family affair 95
The saints: Christ's special friends 95
Confraternities: Organizations for prayer, good deeds, networking 96
Monastic reform and a third order for laypeople 97
Margaret of Cortona and Catherine of Siena, the saints next door 98
Female holiness in an age of living saints 99
Religion in women's daily lives 101
Who were Laura and Beatrice really? 101
"What's love got to do with it?" Marriage among elites 103
Governing the household: The woman's realm 105
A widow and her choices: Alessandra Strozzi 105
The nun in her cloister: Protected or imprisoned? 107
Working women: Domestic servants and wet nurses 108
Social outcasts: Prostitutes, outsiders, and slaves 109
Images of women in Renaissance art 109
Considerations: Renaissance for men, Dark Ages for women? 113
Sourcebook 114
Further reading 114

viii *Contents*

6 Lords of the Renaissance: The Medici, Visconti, and Sforza Dynasties through 1466 115

From commune to signoria 116
Dissatisfaction within the communes 116
Life under the signore 118
Milan: In the middle of it all 119
The Visconti: The clan of vipers 120
Giangaleazzo Visconti: A prince among tyrants? 122
An intermission between dynasties: The Ambrosian Republic 124
Francesco Sforza: From soldier of fortune to statesman 125
The Medici: Where did they come from? 126
Giovanni di Bicci and the foundations of the Medici banking fortune 127
Cosimo de' Medici: A moneychanger's son, father of his country 128
"Be careful not to draw attention to yourself" 128
1433: Arrest and exile 130
Cosimo's triumphal 1434 return 131
1454: Peace breaks out in Italy 132
Cosimo de' Medici: Patron of art, music, and learning 133
Medici projects, public and private 133
Cosimo's gift to the Convent of San Marco 135
Considerations: The Renaissance, cultural byproduct of the signori? 136
Sourcebook 137
Further reading 137

7 The *Mezzogiorno*: The "Other Renaissance" in Naples and Sicily 139

Land of myth and midday sun 139
Sicily: Bread-basket and lumber yard for Rome 140
Campania felix: *Naples under the Roman Empire 141*
Invasions: Vandals, Goths, Byzantines, Arabs 141
The south, economic powerhouse and cultural melting pot 143
Norman domination of the south 1059–1130 144
Frederick II: An emperor who was the wonder of the world 146
The Sicilian Vespers 147
Aragon and Anjou fight over the Two Sicilies 1282–1442 148
The Two Sicilies reunited under Alfonso of Aragon, 1442 149
Ferrante I: The "bastard" who brought stability to Naples 151
The Renaissance in Naples, 1443–94 152
Antonello da Messina: Meticulous realism and haunting mystery 153
Alfonso the Magnanimous and patronage of humanists 155
Lorenzo Valla: Humanist scholar and freethinker 156
Considerations: Was the south backward or ahead of its time? 157
Sourcebook 159
Further reading 159

Contents ix

8 *La Serenissima*: When Venice Ruled the Seas 160

"You live like sea birds, your homes scattered over the water" 161
The Venetians' battle for survival 163
Inventing a Venetian identity: The city of St. Mark takes wing 166
From the "Venetian Gulf" to "Beyond-the-Sea", 1000–1204 167
The Venetian commune comes of age, 1032–1297 170
The Great Council: Keystone of the Venetian Republic 171
The "aristocratic commune" closes ranks: The 1297 serrata *172*
The Council of Ten: The vigilant lion 173
The Doge of Venice: Prince or primus inter pares? *173*
"Lords of the Sea" 175
Expansion of the Venetian Empire into the terraferma *177*
Daily life in Renaissance Venice 178
Festivals, scuole, *and* venezianità *180*
Humanism, printing, the sciences 182
Venetian painting of the early Renaissance: Bellini and Carpaccio 183
Serenity expressed in the structure of buildings and political theory 184
Considerations: The myth and countermyth of Venice 186
Sourcebook 187
Further reading 187

9 Magnificent Florence: Life under Lorenzo de' Medici 188

The restlessness of the Florentine elites 1464–69 188
Lorenzo takes control 1469–77 189
"Brigades" of poets and jousts for love 190
Marsilio Ficino and Florentine Platonism 192
Vernacular magnificence: Lorenzo and literature 194
Luigi Pulci's Il Morgante *194*
Angelo Poliziano's Stanzas for Giuliano de' Medici *195*
The Renaissance on the streets 196
Lorenzo and Pope Sixtus IV collide 197
The Pazzi Conspiracy: Murder in the cathedral 198
Florence at war with the pope 199
Lorenzo as "boss of the shop" 200
Money and art in Renaissance Florence 201
Competition and innovation in the arts 202
The realism of Pollaiuolo and Verrocchio 203
The idealism of Botticelli 205
Depicting the here and now: Ghirlandaio 205
Building for posterity 206
The spiritual mood in late quattrocento Florence 208
Giovanni Pico della Mirandola's philosophical quest 209
Considerations: Golden Ages 209
Sourcebook 210
Further reading 210

x *Contents*

10 The Beginning of the Calamities of Italy 212

The Italian League unravels 213
Rodrigo Borgia becomes Pope Alexander VI 215
The French invasion of 1494 216
Savonarola: The rise of the "little friar" from Ferrara 218
The "New Jerusalem": The Florentine Republic renewed 219
Weepers, angry men, and ugly companions 219
The fiery end of Savonarola 220
Louis XII and the French Invasion of 1499 221
The meteoric career of Cesare Borgia 223
Julius II the "terrible" pope takes on Venice 225
The Holy League: A brief alliance born of mutual enmity 227
The Florentine Republic under Soderini gives way to Medici rule 227
Niccolò Machiavelli out of work 228
The Prince: *A mirror for the Medici? 229*
When virtù *is not virtuous and* fortuna *is not always fortunate 230*
Questions of morality and religion in The Prince *231*
Does Machiavelli advocate tyranny? 233
Considerations: Fortuna, providence, or chance? 234
Sourcebook 236
Further reading 236

**11 Paradoxes of the High Renaissance: Art in a
Time of Turmoil** 237

Leonardo: The pacifist artist who designed weapons for a prince 238
Mantua, Ferrara, Urbino: Small courts, big ambitions 241
Mantegna paints "The most beautiful chamber in the world" 241
Isabella d'Este's studiolo *of her own 242*
The dukes of Ferrara celebrated in poetry and music 242
Urbino: The condottiero's refined court, library, and art collection 244
Venice: Painters in a watery city dream of idyllic pastures 245
The visual poetry of Giorgione 246
Titian's bold colors, sensuality, triumphant images 247
The explosive Michelangelo: Extreme piety and extreme paganism 248
The David: *Bold symbol of the Florentine Republic 249*
Pope Julius II: A second Caesar 250
Bramante tears down St. Peter's 251
Michelangelo paints a "terrible" ceiling 253
Raphael creates majestic rooms for a pope 254
The School of Athens: *Antiquity alive and energized 255*
The banker's pleasure palace, talking statues, and risqué positions 255
Considerations: Terrible times and awesome art 257
Sourcebook 258
Further reading 258

Contents xi

12 The 1527 Sack of Rome and Its Aftermath 259
A New World and a new world order 260
The profligate papacy of Leo X 1513–21 262
Francesco Guicciardini's career as papal governor in the Romagna 264
The tragically indecisive Pope Clement VII 264
On the brink of disaster, 1526 265
The Sack 267
A traumatized Christendom takes stock 269
Baldassarre Castiglione's instant bestseller 270
Contradictions and tensions within The Courtier 272
The Machiavellian courtier? 273
Gender-bending at court and the changing role of women 273
Courtiers, court ladies, and courtesans 274
Women's distinctive voice in literature 275
Ariosto and Sannazaro's escapist fantasies 275
Considerations: Accepting defeat with grazia 276
Sourcebook 278
Further reading 278

13 Reformations: Political, Religious, and Artistic Upheaval 279
The Last Florentine Republic, 1527–30 280
1532 The Medici principate established 281
The teenaged Cosimo becomes duke of Florence 281
Michelangelo and the Medici, 1516–34 282
Martin Luther: A German friar protests 284
Humanist origins of the Reformation: "Christian humanism" 284
Catholic reformations before the Reformation 285
The Church reacts: Catholic versus Protestant 286
The Council of Trent, 1545–63 287
The Vulgate Bible: "No one is to dare or presume to reject it" 288
The Sacraments and the role of the priest reaffirmed 288
Social consequences of Trent 289
Clerical reform and full enclosure of nuns 289
Michelangelo in Rome 1534–64 290
Florentine mannerism: Pontormo and Rosso's avant-garde 292
The artist as courtier: Agnolo Bronzino and others 294
The Lives of the Artists: *Vasari invents art history 295*
Benvenuto Cellini's Autobiography: *The artist invents himself 297*
Considerations: Sixteenth-century reformations in perspective 297
Sourcebook 300
Further reading 300

xii   *Contents*

14 The "Imperial Renaissance": Italy during the Spanish Peace   301

The Habsburgs: A spectacular matrimonial conglomerate 301
Keeping the troublesome republics subdued 303
The rule of Spanish viceroys 303
Pax hispanica *304*
Learning that was not strictly academic 305
Print culture: Read all about it 306
The epic poetry of Torquato Tasso 307
Women speaking out: Veronica Franco and others 307
Birth of Renaissance theater 308
Words and music come together: Madrigals, motets, and masses 309
Architecture: Perfection of classical forms and experimentation 311
Palladio shapes Western architecture 311
Rome gloriously rebuilt 313
Venetian masters: Titian's late style, Tintoretto, and Veronese 314
Women artists: Sofonisba Anguissola and Lavinia Fontana 316
The anti-mannerists: Annibale, Agostino, and Ludovico Carracci 318
The Michelangelo from Caravaggio 318
Considerations: The late sixteenth century, a Siglo de Oro *for Italy? 320*
Sourcebook 321
Further reading 321

15 Celestial Revolutions: Heaven and Earth Collide at the Turn of the Seventeenth Century   323

Inquistions 325
The Roman Inquisition: Myth and reality 325
Persecution of Jews, Protestants, Muslims, and witches 326
The Index of Prohibited Books *327*
Missionaries to the mezzogiorno: *"The Indies down here" 328*
Natural philosophers reading the book of nature 330
Italian scientific revolutions 331
A flowering of the natural sciences 332
The sciences put to work: Engineers and artists go to war 335
Anatomy: Physicians and artists look inside the human body 336
Astrology, astronomy, cosmology: The sixteenth-century view 337
Measuring the heavens: Mathematicians invade outer space 339
Galileo and the "new science" 341
Galileo takes a spyglass and turns it into a telescope 342
The Starry Messenger: *The Medici become moons, the scientist a star 344*
The conflict between the new science and religion 345
The trial of the century: Galileo before the Inquisition in 1633 347
Considerations: What would the Greeks and Romans have said? 348

Sourcebook 348
Further reading 349

Epilogue: The End of the Renaissance?   350

Figure credits   355
Index   358

Figures

1.1	Giotto di Bondone, *Visitation*, Scrovegni Chapel, Padua	19
1.2	Giovanni Pisano, *Massacre of the Innocents*, Church of Sant'Andrea, Pistoia	21
2.1	Simone Martini, *Annunciation*, detail, Uffizi	38
2.2	Ambrogio Lorenzetti, *The Effects of Good Government*, Palazzo Pubblico, Siena	39
3.1	Lorenzo Ghiberti, *Jacob and Esau*, Opera del Duomo, Florence	60
3.2	Donatello, *St. George*, Bargello, Florence	62
3.3	Filippo Brunelleschi, *Cupola of Santa Maria del Fiore*, Duomo of Florence	64
3.4	Masaccio, *Distribution of Alms and Death of Ananias*, Brancacci Chapel, Florence	66
4.1	Fra Angelico, *St. Lawrence Distributes Alms*, Chapel of Nicholas V, Vatican Palace	84
4.2	Leon Battista Alberti, *Façade of Church of Santa Maria Novella*, Florence	88
5.1	Lo Scheggia, *Adimari Wedding Cassone*, Accademia, Florence	103
5.2	Domenico Ghirlandaio, *Birth of John the Baptist*, Cappella Tornabuoni, Florence	110
5.3	Piero della Francesca, *Madonna del Parto*, Monterchi	112
6.1	Giovannino de' Grassi, *Visconti Book of Hours*, Biblioteca Nazionale, Florence	124
6.2	Benozzo Gozzoli, *Journey of the Magi*, detail, Palazzo Medici-Riccardi, Florence	135
7.1	*Cappella Palatina*, Norman Palace, Palermo	145
7.2	Antonello da Messina, *Virgin Annunciate*, Museo Nazionale, Palermo	154
8.1	Vittore Carpaccio, *Hunting on the Lagoon*, Getty Museum, Los Angeles	163
8.2	Giovanni Bellini, *Portrait of Doge Loredan*, National Gallery, London	174
8.3	Jacopo Sansovino, *Loggetta*, detail, Piazza San Marco, Venice	185

Figures   xv

9.1 Sandro Botticelli, *Young Man with Medal of Cosimo de' Medici*, Uffizi   191

9.2 Andrea del Verrocchio, *Christ and St. Thomas*, Orsanmichele, Florence   204

9.3 Giuliano da Sangallo and others, *Palazzo Strozzi*, Florence   207

10.1 Giorgione, *The Tempest*, Accademia, Venice   217

10.2 Luca Signorelli, *Rule of the Antichrist*, detail, Chapel of San Brizio, Orvieto   222

11.1 Leonardo da Vinci, *Vitruvian Man*, Accademia, Venice   240

11.2 Andrea Mantegna, *Camera degli Sposi*, detail, Palazzo Ducale, Mantua   243

11.3 Giuliano da Maiano, *Bookshelves, Lute, and Sword*, Palazzo Ducale, Urbino   245

11.4 Giorgione/Titian, *Sleeping Venus*, Gemäldegalerie, Dresden   247

12.1 Raphael, *Portrait of Pope Leo X with Giulio de' Medici and Luigi de' Rossi*, Uffizi   263

12.2 Titian, *Equestrian Portrait of Charles V*, Museo del Prado, Madrid   269

13.1 Michelangelo, *Night*, New Sacristy, Basilica of San Lorenzo, Florence   283

13.2 Jacopo Pontormo, *Capponi Chapel Altarpiece*, Church of Santa Felicita, Florence   293

14.1 Andrea Palladio, *Villa La Rotonda*, Vicenza; *Pantheon*, Rome   312

14.2 Paolo Veronese, *Wedding Feast at Cana*, detail, Louvre   316

14.3 Sofonisba Anguissola, *Portrait of the Artist's Sister*, City Art Gallery, Southampton   317

15.1 Caravaggio, *The Calling of St. Matthew*, Church of San Luigi dei Francesi, Rome   324

15.2 Giovanna Garzoni, *Ranunculus*, Uffizi   333

15.3 Anatomical theater, Palazzo Bo, Padua   337

16.1 Michelangelo et al. *St. Peter's*, Vatican; United States Capitol Building, Washington D.C.   353

Tables

1.1	Population of Italian cities *c.*1300	12
3.1	Partial list of ancient texts and dates when they appear in Italy	57
5.1	Percentage of female saints	99

Maps

1.1	Principal Italian communes *c.*1250	7
2.1	Spread of the Black Death in Europe	26
2.2	Social unrest in Europe during the fourteenth century	33
3.1	Education in Renaissance Italy	52
4.1	Western Schism 1378–1417	80
6.1	Communes and signories in Italy *c.*1250	117
6.2	Communes and signories in Italy *c.*1450	117
6.3	Milanese territory under the Visconti	121
6.4	Cosimo the Elder's banking empire	129
7.1	Southern Italy and the Mediterranean *c.*600 CE	142
8.1	Ancient Roman regions of northern and central Italy	162
8.2	The early settlement of Venice and trade routes through the mainland	165
8.3	Venice and the Eastern Mediterranean 1140–1204	168
8.4	Venetian merchant fleets in the fifteenth century	176
10.1	Italian states in 1494	214
10.2	Expansion of the Papal States in the sixteenth century	226
12.1	The Empire of Charles V in Europe	261
14.1	Italy in 1559	302
15.1	Changing concepts of the cosmos	340

Preface

"Why a new edition of this book?" a reader might very well ask.

This is a reasonable question. After all, the Italian Renaissance ended centuries ago, so everything described in the earlier edition should still be fine, right? Well, yes and no. Of course, there is the usual need to correct errors that slipped into the first edition (no one's perfect!) and to update with references to recent scholarship; however, there are other more pressing reasons for a Renaissance reconsideration.

Let's start by looking at the Black Death.

In 2010 when the text of this book was just being sent to the typesetter, one crucial passage read: "Paleopathologists have begun to extract DNA material from the remains of epidemic victims from the past, and undoubtedly in the coming years we will learn much more about the exact nature of the disease."

Then, just the following year, in 2011 scientists sequenced the entire genome of the pathogen. It is now a certainty that the disease was caused by *yersinia pestis*, and in addition to "paleopathology," the historian must become acquainted with the field of "paleogenetics," and familiarize herself with research on "aDNA" (ancient DNA). These discoveries, while fascinating to specialists, would hardly have registered a blip in public attention, had not a certain modern health emergency occurred: Covid 19. Suddenly, awareness of factors involving transmission, strains, variants, public health measures, socio-economic and cultural impact of pandemics has become a foremost concern. Thus, much of the material concerning the 1348 pandemic, even the information that has remained unchanged, has had to be re-written.

Here is one example: in 2010, references to the practice of quarantine were limited to a definition of the term and a brief mention of its employment in Milan under Bernabò Visconti. Who would have known back in 2010 how interested readers a decade later would be in the history of this and other sanitary measures? Thus, not only does the current edition address the first establishment of quarantine facilities in territories under Venetian dominion, but the accompanying sourcebook also includes a document outlining health

xx *Preface*

precautions adopted by the Commune of Pistoia in 1348 to prevent spread of the disease.

It quickly becomes apparent that it is not so much an issue of how much the Renaissance itself has changed—excluding new facts coming to light, the past itself does not change—but how the lens through which we observe history changes, and does so constantly, under our very eyes. There is yet more evidence of our ever-changing historical perspectives in the need to revisit issues of gender and sexuality, as well as marginalized communities, including heretics, foreigners, slaves, religious minorities, and witches. The current edition has more coverage of these topics with new sections on topics such as contributions of women to humanist studies, and the impact of the New World on Renaissance science and cultural outlook.

Nevertheless, in order to continue to deserve the words "a short history" in its title, the present book must by necessity be limited in length. This textbook has been adopted in a variety of courses over the past decade, functioning very well as a clear, concise, introductory outline of the period. In order to supplement that basic material, I have created a companion volume entitled *Voices from the Italian Renaissance*, a sourcebook containing primary documents and eyewitness accounts that provides more depth and richer context as a background for *A Short History*. Either volume can be read alone, but when read together, a fuller, more complex picture develops of the worldview of the men and women who lived during that time.

Permit me to give another example: in the first edition there was a section devoted to humanist Giovanni Pico della Mirandola and his well-known *Oration on the Dignity of Man*. Sometimes referred to as a "manifesto" of the Italian Renaissance, the *Oration* has traditionally been considered a centerpiece of Renaissance studies that demonstrates a new, inquiring philosophical approach. The second edition still contains that material, but in the sourcebook, a selection by another Pico della Mirandola has been added—the nephew Gianfrancesco who was the first to publish his uncle's work. Gianfrancesco, also a humanist scholar, himself wrote a popular work on witchcraft, in which he questions the most fundamental sources of knowledge—science, reasoning, and ancient philosophical learning—favoring instead superstitious belief supported by confessions extracted under torture.

Thus, reading the textbook alongside selections in the sourcebook adds subtlety and nuance to understanding of this fascinating period of history, as well as shedding light on our current understanding of the world, a time when, as in Pico's day, traditional belief structures are being challenged. Of course, this textbook can stand alone as a guide to the Italian Renaissance, as it has always done, but for those wishing to dive a little deeper, there is now the sourcebook as well. Throughout the margins of this textbook there are magnifying glass icons calling the reader's attention to corresponding selections in the sourcebook that illuminate, expand upon, or in some way problematize the material. In addition, at the end of every chapter there is a

Preface xxi

list of related primary source material in *Voices from the Italian Renaissance* so they can be easily cross-referenced.

And at the end of each chapter there is a short, very select list of secondary sources under "further reading." There has been no attempt to provide an exhaustive bibliography; the sheer quantity of material that has been written, and continues to be written, on the Renaissance is staggering. In the interests of space, I have tried to provide examples of the finest scholarship—maintaining a balance between the most recent research, alongside older classic studies; between scholarly monographs, and more accessible books—but I have had to leave out many excellent resources and apologize in advance to colleagues whose work was not included. There are additional resources provided at the end of each section in *Voices from the Italian Renaissance.*

For readers who want more information, two useful in-depth guides to scholarship on the Italian Renaissance are: *Oxford Bibliographies Online—Renaissance and Reformation* and *Routledge Resources Online—The Renaissance World.* There are also many concise articles written by specialists in the six-volume *Encyclopedia of the Renaissance* (Paul F. Grendler, editor in chief, published by Scribner's in association with the Renaissance Society of America, 1999). For general art historical background, two fundamental resources are: Paoletti and Radke, *Art in Renaissance Italy* and Hartt and Wilkins, *History of Italian Renaissance Art*; both volumes available in multiple printings. I also post many useful articles, images, and links on my website: www.lisakaborycha.com

Acknowledgments

As Bernard of Chartres would have it, I've had to perch on the shoulders of giants to write this book. Among those who have born my weight during the writing of the current edition are Maurizio Arfaioli, Mary Beard, Lynn Catterson, Jessica Goldberg, Monica Green, Allen Grieco, Peggy Haines, Dale Kent, John Nadas, and Stefano Villani, all of whom gave me crucial advice that has vastly improved this volume and the accompanying sourcebook. I have also benefitted immeasurably from the scholarly input of those professors who have used the first edition in their teaching; in particular thanks are due to Jeremy Boudreau, Nathan Crick, Kevin Murphy, Mary O'Neil, and the numerous anonymous advance readers who provided suggestions and encouragement. For their help and guidance on the first edition I will always be grateful to Eve Borsook, Sam Cohn, Margaret Fisher, Richard Goldthwaite, Michaela Paasche Grudin, John Marino, Maureen Miller, Laura Smoller, Randy Starn, John Paoletti, Janet Robson, and Ron Witt. I also thank my former colleagues at the Medici Archive Project who contributed in ways great and small: Alessio Assonitis, Sheila Barker, Elena Brizio, Stefano dall'Aglio, Francesca Funis, Piergabriele Mancuso, Roberta Piccinelli, Mark Rosen, and Julia Vicioso. After all the assistance and generous advice from such colleagues and renowned experts, it goes without saying that any inadvertent omissions or inaccuracies are my fault alone. Over the years Nicholas Hassitt, Marissa Moss, and Francie Starn have read infinite drafts of my writing; their wise comments and warm encouragement have sustained me and vastly improved this book. Finally, I am deeply indebted to teachers no longer with us, who forever shaped my historical outlook and whom I will always hold dear: Robert Brentano, Gerard Caspary, Armando Petrucci, Ruggero Stefanini, and most of all Gene Brucker, for whom no words of gratitude will ever be sufficient.

Foreword by Dale Kent

For more than three centuries from the age of Dante and Giotto to that of Copernicus and Galileo, Italy made a vital and distinctive contribution to Western civilization, quite disproportionate to the size of its territory and population. It endures today in our cultural and political life, in many of our most iconic and beloved works of literature and art, and in ideas and ideals that continue to shape a now global world, especially the aspiration to democratic government. This was a product of the cities of the ancient world, originating in the Greek *polis* and developed in the archetypal *urbs* of republican Rome, over the last five centuries BCE, in the first age of a remarkable Italian contribution to world history. After the fall of Rome to the "barbarian" invasions, a largely feudal agrarian society prevailed for almost a millennium, in which Christianity was the chief engine of cultural creativity. But from the thirteenth century, Mediterranean trade and the cities it nourished started to revive; classical urban culture began once again to seem sharply relevant to the inhabitants of cities. They described their self-conscious revival of it as a Renaissance.

For too long Western European culture, its values and achievements exported in the seventeenth century to the New World of North America, was the main object of historical study in institutions of learning in the United States, Europe, and countries in their spheres of economic, political, and cultural influence. Only recently has this cultural myopia given way to an appropriate recognition of the many other great civilizations and cultures long dominated and suppressed by the colonialism of Western Europe. Scholars and students have rightly rushed to redress the former imbalance by cultivating new and exciting fields of study; of Asia, Africa, the Middle East, and the Islamic world. However, this is not a reason to abandon or neglect Western civilization, but rather an opportunity to put it in perspective, to view it with fresh eyes, pursuing new questions with which to interrogate its meaning and value.

Writing and teaching about the Renaissance has long been shaped by the interpretation of the nineteenth-century Swiss historian Jacob Burckhardt, who proposed it as a distinct period of history that he characterized as more

xxiv *Foreword*

secular and individualistic than that of the "Middle Ages," and whose political and social innovations ushered in "the modern state." Whether a term coined by those who instigated the revival of ancient texts, of classical literature, languages, and artistic vocabulary, to refer specifically to this learned movement, can be extended to embrace change in areas such as the economy, politics, religion, and the fabric of social life, or what "modern" might mean now, are interesting questions, but a continuing focus on them has risked embalming the Renaissance in its own historiography.

The author of *A Short History of Renaissance Italy*, Dr. Lisa Kaborycha, received her BA from the University of California, Berkeley, majoring in comparative literature, Italian, and French. Her MA from Berkeley was in Italian Studies, and her PhD in History. A Fulbright fellowship initially supported her research in Italian libraries and archives, and she went on to become a Fellow of the Harvard University Center for Italian Renaissance Studies in Florence, regarded as the leading institution for the advanced study of the Italian Renaissance. She also worked on the Medici Archive Project to digitize the correspondence of the sixteenth-century Medici grand dukes. Kaborycha's experience in teaching interdisciplinary courses including Italian studies, literature, history, and art is broad and varied, beginning with a Visiting Lectureship at Berkeley. She now lives in Florence, where for some years she has been a Lecturer at the British Institute, and Visiting Professor lecturing in education abroad programs for several American universities, particularly the University of California.

Kaborycha's mastery of current scholarship provides a firm foundation on which teachers can rely in building their own and students' understanding of Renaissance Italy. Her narrative of the grand sweep of this period is enlivened by telling detail in tables and lists, showing the size of the most important Italian cities, or naming the major Greek texts restored in the fifteenth century, along with the dates they appeared in Italy, so we can see what "the recovery of ancient learning" actually meant. There are many evocative images and helpful maps; comparing the number of communes and signories in 1250 with those in 1450, or charting the establishment of branches throughout Europe of the Medici family's international bank. This book is an unusually rich, multilayered, multifaceted, interdisciplinary resource; for formal courses, or for anyone simply interested in learning more about Renaissance Italy. At the end of each chapter are judicious suggestions for additional reading, and of course there are virtually infinite possibilities for further exploration via the internet, especially of works of art that bring the Renaissance to life.

In her comprehensive coverage of the numerous interwoven aspects of Renaissance society, Kaborycha raises many fresh questions arising from recent research or driven by current concerns; about the experience of women, long considered marginal to the Renaissance; the roles of outsiders like Jews, Muslims, and witches, previously largely overlooked; Italy's interactions with the New World, which appropriated and elaborated upon

Foreword xxv

the republican communes' political thought and practice. The past does not change, but our perception of it is altered by new discoveries and experiences. Beside Boccaccio's *Decameron*, Kaborycha discusses the latest investigations of genome sequencing and quarantine measures, while our own experience of Covid 19 now allows us to see the Black Death that wiped out a third of Europe's inhabitants in the mid fourteenth century in an entirely new light.

In lieu of conclusions to each chapter that wrap them up with cut and dried answers, Kaborycha proposes "Considerations" that invite further enquiry. Chapter 3, "Back to the Future: Italian Humanists Recover the Classical Past," ends with the vexed question of how Renaissance humanism might relate to modern interest in the role of the humanities, and notes how obscurantist and pedantic studies involving close examination of texts in fact paved the way for the critical thinking crucial to the advancement of all human knowledge. And at the end of the final chapter we are asked to consider, in the words of the poet Tassoni in 1620, "What would the ancient Greeks and Romans have said" of the invention of the printing press, the telescope, or the circumnavigation of the globe?

Perhaps the outstanding quality of Kaborycha's history of Renaissance Italy is its focus on a brilliant selection of original sources; contemporary documents recording the voices of people from the past directly describing their own experiences and perceptions. A distinguished professor of history once advised his students to "go on reading until you can hear people talking." Understanding other people, from the past—as indeed the present—involves listening; recognizing our shared humanity and respecting differences in assumptions about the way the world works. The ancient Roman writer Terence declared: "I am human, and regard nothing human as alien to me." Like travel, the study of history offers opportunities, through the exploration of alien worlds, to add new dimensions to one's self, to expand through learning the bounds of time and space, the narrow limits within which most of our individual lives are constrained.

Kaborycha, with her witty and cultured conversational style and her infectious enthusiasm for the study of this period, offers us the excitement of new encounters in strange places often associated with travel, but seldom with history. Quotations from key sources set the tone of every chapter, beginning with the immediate shock of a letter from Pelagius to a friend in 413 CE. "It happened only recently, and you heard it yourself. Rome, the mistress of the world shivered, crushed with fear, at the sound of the blaring trumpets and the howling of the Goths." Supplementing the passages included in this textbook, there are links to Kaborycha's companion collection of sources, signaled by the symbol of a magnifying glass in the margin, so the readers of this book can go on and on reading as they want.

I would certainly encourage them to do so. Renaissance Italy was an extraordinary place; dynamic, exciting, breathtakingly creative in so many ways. When we first encounter its inhabitants around 1300, experiencing an explosion of economic activity and population, they are bursting with civic pride,

xxvi *Foreword*

writing paeans of patriotic praise for their cities, marveling at their own achievements: the unceasing construction of new and beautiful buildings—churches, palaces, and hospitals; the proliferation of occupations—international merchants and skilled artisans, judges and notaries to serve the needs of increasingly sophisticated commerce and government; the provision of secular schools to achieve an unprecedented level of literacy required for citizen participation in business, political, and cultural life. This frenetic activity, the creative intensity of Italian cities, is celebrated in Ambrogio Lorenzetti's frescoes of "Good Government" for the town hall of Siena, and the bronze plaques adorning Giotto's imposing bell tower for the cathedral of Florence. At the height of that city's expansion, 100,000 people crowded together within its walls, in a space that could be crossed from north to south or east to west in less than half an hour.

Over the next three centuries there was considerable change, but the Renaissance saw no simple transition from the "Middle Ages"—a period that also appears more complex and ambiguous the more we learn of it—to "modernity," a constantly evolving concept. As Gene Brucker pointed out, classical, Christian, civic, and feudal ideals all contributed to the dynamism of Renaissance culture and society. Revered Rome represented both classical republicanism and imperial power, and was not only the "head of the world," but also of the church. As the Renaissance progressed, classical secular ideas and forms were increasingly admired and cultivated, but Christian ideals remained transcendent. Classical and Christian "authorities" were customarily cited in tandem. Petrarch wrote letters to "his friend" Cicero, and during his challenging ascent of Mont Ventoux in Provence, while reflecting in a new way on the natural world around him, was prompted to consider his own nature by a companion he carried always with him—a copy of the *Confessions* of Saint Augustine. The paintings of Raphael and Titian depicted the same sacred subjects and figures as those of Duccio and Giotto, but in more classicizing and naturalistic forms, more humanized and personalized, along with classical and secular subjects, especially portraits, that were added to the artist's repertoire during the Renaissance.

Creativity ultimately defies explanation, but the extraordinary concentration of great artists in Italy during the Renaissance suggests that the distinctive culture of the Italian cities provided particularly favorable conditions for it to flourish. In artists' workshops masters passed on skills to their apprentices, who were stimulated by both collaboration and competition with their fellows. Wealthy patrons' commissions posed problems of execution that artists solved creatively; Leonardo da Vinci's voluminous notebooks are evidence of his practical genius for figuring out how to represent the mists of the landscape around Milan or the dust motes that conveyed the heat of a battle. Michelangelo's poems reflected more philosophically on the nature of creativity, that "The greatest artist has no single concept which a rough block of marble does not contain already in its core; *that* can attain only the hand that serves the intellect." Patrons like the Florentine bankers Cosimo de'

Foreword xxvii

Medici and Giovanni Rucellai competed for the services of such gifted artists to express their own passions and allegiances in the supremely eloquent medium of art; Rucellai spoke for most great patrons of the Renaissance in declaring that he had far less pleasure in getting his fortune than in spending it, building his family palace and embellishing the churches of his neighborhood "for the glory of God and the honor of the city, and the commemoration of me." This delicate balance in the civilization of Renaissance Italy between tradition and innovation, secular and sacred, individual and collective, continues to fascinate across the centuries.

Dale Kent

A note concerning dating

The dating system in this book uses BCE in place of BC, and CE in place of AD. BCE means "Before the Common Era" and CE the "Common Era." They stand for exactly the same dates as BC "Before Christ" and AD "Anno Domini" or "the year of the lord." The BC/AD dating was established by a medieval monk who wanted to establish the birth of Jesus as the central reference point for recorded history (although the year he calculated for Jesus' birth is probably off by as much as ten years). The BCE/CE system is widely accepted by historians throughout the world, as it is religiously neutral.

Dates that are approximate or uncertain are preceded by the abbreviation "*c.*" short for *circa* meaning "around.". Often the years given for kings or popes are prefaced by the letter "r.", which refers only to the years in which that person ruled, rather than their entire lifetime.

The Italian dating system refers to the 1200s or thirteenth century as the "Duecento" (pronounced: "DOO-eh CHEN-toh"), the 1300s or fourteenth century as the "Trecento" (pronounced: "TRAY CHEN-toh"), the 1400s or fifteenth century as the "Quattrocento" (pronounced: "KWA-troh CHEN-toh"), the 1500s or sixteenth century as the "Cinquecento" (pronounced: "CHIN-kweh CHEN-toh"), and the 1600s or seventeenth century as the "Seicento" (pronounced: "SAY CHEN-toh"). Particularly in the field of Art History the Italian names for the centuries are commonly used. The terms are here used interchangeably.

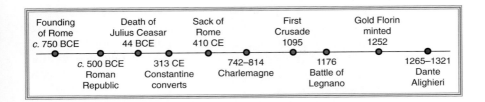

1 Out of the Ashes

The Rise of the Communes and Florence in the Age of Dante

> It happened only recently, and you heard it yourself. Rome, the mistress of the world shivered, crushed with fear, at the sound of the blaring trumpets and the howling of the Goths. Where, then, was the nobility? Where were the certain and distinct ranks of dignity? Everyone was mingled together and shaken with fear; every household had its grief and an all-pervading terror gripped us. Slave and noble were one. The same spectre of death stalked before us all.[1]
>
> Pelagius, *Letter to Demetrias*, 413 CE

> My voice sticks in my throat; and, as I dictate, sobs choke my utterance. The City which had taken the whole world was itself taken.
>
> Jerome, *Letter to Principia*, 412 CE

The grandeur that was Rome

Rome had seemed invincible. For 800 years, no invading force had entered the city walls. Rather, for centuries, vanquished enemy soldiers were paraded in triumphal victory parades, while tribute from distant lands poured into her treasury. With over a million inhabitants at its height, the metropolis was the marvel of the ancient world; her many magnificent villas dominated the seven

---

1 Peter Brown, *Augustine of Hippo*, Faber & Faber, 1967, p. 289.

DOI: 10.4324/9781003270362-1

2 Out of the Ashes

hills, while below lay narrow streets with teeming slums. The Colosseum attracted huge audiences, holding 50,000 people for sporting events featuring gladiators and exotic beasts. Above all, the Forum with its gleaming marble temples, towering monuments, sculptures, and public buildings, was the epicenter of power and crossroads for peoples from around the world. Rome, the object of both admiration and fierce hatred, was spoken of with awe from Scotland to Samarkand.

The people who built this city were determined and resourceful. Around 750 BCE they began settling the area known as Latium, hence the name "Latin" for the language they spoke. Their village was located on a rather unpromising patch of land surrounded by seven hills, snaked through by the Tiber River; their legendary founder was Romulus, and they became known as Romans. While Romulus was a mythical figure whom they recognized as their own and held as their first king, most of the kings who ruled for the next 200 years were outsiders. Eventually, around 500 BCE the Romans overthrew the monarchy; in its place they established a constitution, presided over by elected officials, known as senators and consuls, who passed legislation within a political structure based on a set of checks and balances. The name they gave to the state was the *res publica* (the republic), literally meaning the "public thing." Though never a true democracy, but rather an oligarchy controlled by influential families, the Republic was successful because it was run with a sense of rigid military discipline, under which every Roman was compelled to contribute to the public good.

During the tumultuous first century BCE the republican government collapsed and gave way to rule by one man, an emperor. From this point on, Rome was ruled by emperors and its vast political and cultural network became known as the Roman Empire. The Senate remained intact; however, its function became largely symbolic, rubber-stamping the decisions of the emperor who acted essentially as a dictator. The Romans had long dominated the Italian Peninsula and established settlements abroad, but under the empire, Rome was able to expand its influence even further. By the third century CE the Roman Empire encompassed almost all of Europe, including Britain; the Mediterranean; all of the lands of North Africa; Egypt; and much of the Middle East, as far as present-day Iraq. Individual Romans amassed vast fortunes by exploiting these territories and Roman control was assured by the military presence of its well-disciplined legions. There were advantages that came with Roman occupation: wherever Romans went, they built roads, aqueducts, theaters, and baths, bringing with them their customs and laws. The Latin language and its rich written culture, encompassing literature, history, natural sciences, and philosophy spread from one end of the Empire to the other. Perhaps most important, Roman military presence brought stability to war-torn regions, making it possible to enjoy the so-called *pax romana* (Roman peace).

Despite such benefits, people in Roman-occupied lands resented ever-increasing taxes imposed by a distant, impersonal imperial authority, as

Out of the Ashes 3

well as the widespread corruption and profiteering of local officials. There were frequent uprisings against the Roman forces in the provinces and the empire became increasingly incapable of governing its immense territories. In particular, Roman forces never managed to subdue the restless, warlike tribes known as Goths, who lived in the region of modern-day Germany. After years of emperors' broken promises and abuses at the hands of Roman officials, armed warriors and masses of hungry, ragged people descended from northern Europe toward Rome. When one summer day in 410 CE, under the leadership of Alaric, the Goths broke through its walls and sacked the city, the world was shocked. Jerome (*c.*340–420 CE) summed up the general feeling of despair: "If Rome can perish, what can be safe?"

The spread of Christianity

Though things would never be the same, Rome did not in fact perish. For one thing, nearly a hundred years earlier, another capital of the Roman Empire had been established in the east, where it would continue to thrive in Constantinople for another millennium. And as for the city of Rome itself, though the sack was shocking, the damage was less than the devastation and carnage that the invading troops of Charles V would inflict on Rome a thousand years later (Chapter 12). The Goths looted, taking precious metals and treasures, destroying some pagan statuary in the process; but the invading "barbarians" by and large did not commit atrocities and left the city largely intact; these invaders were Christians and respected Rome as a sacred site. The Christian faith, which had begun in the Roman colony of Judea in the first century CE had gradually spread throughout the empire, by this time reaching even the remote forests north of the Danube. The days of the official persecutions of Christians had ended nearly a century earlier, among the worst those ordered by the emperors Nero (64 CE), Decius (249–251 CE), and Diocletian (303–311 CE). By the time the Emperor Constantine converted in 313 CE, declaring official toleration of the religion, Christianity can be said to have triumphed, the followers of Jesus having gone from the original twelve Apostles to an estimated six million believers in just three centuries.

How can we account for the stunning success of this new religion? The late antique world was swarming with cults and esoteric religious practices, yet Christianity stood out from the rest. Christianity not only offered anyone, regardless of their sex, ethnic background, or social position, personal salvation in the afterlife, but also extended material help in this world. Christians practiced charity, providing assistance to widows, orphans, and the poor in their community. In a vast impersonal system such as the Roman Empire, without regular safety nets for the poor, this was obviously appealing. Equally appealing was the idea of a caring God, who did not demand burnt offerings or sacrifices made at a temple, but was concerned with intimate matters of each human's soul. This was especially irresistible in an era in which pagan

4   *Out of the Ashes*

religious practices had become so ritualized and arcane that they had lost their meaning for many.

The bloody Roman persecutions of Christians were largely political acts, used to single out Christians as scapegoats for the many troubles which beset the Empire, rather than the reflection of a general hostility to the new faith in Rome. As opposed to the elite, average Romans did not feel threatened by a creed that taught that all were equal in the eyes of a single, compassionate Creator. Whereas official avenues for advancement were closed to all but the upper echelon of Roman society, the portals of Heaven would welcome even cobblers and slaves. Gradually, Romans had become Christians. And precisely because there had been official persecutions in the city of Rome, believers venerated the many Christians killed there as martyrs and saints. The very fact that so much blood of these early Christians was spilled in Rome, sanctifying the ground itself, gave the city yet another claim to pre-eminence. Not only had Rome been the capital of the empire, it was also now the capital of the Christian faith in the West.

By the fifth century CE, much of Europe was Christian, but that was all that unified the fractured, de-centralized continent in the years following the invasion of Rome. In 455 CE, yet another barbarian tribe, the Vandals, had sacked the city; and after Romulus Augustus, the last Roman Emperor, was deposed in 476 CE, the formal organization of the empire vanished. Not only had political and economic stability disappeared, but the actual physical infrastructure of the continent was shattered. The roads, of which the Romans were once so proud, became overgrown with weeds and unsafe to travel, as bandits prowled the countryside. City-dwellers, who once would have taken refuge within city walls, fled to the countryside as cities became indefensible. They put themselves under the protection of powerful lords who ruled from heavily fortified country estates.

The church, too, provided security and organization for frightened, defenseless peoples. As in its earliest days, Christianity was not only a set of beliefs, but also a community of believers, which provided social assistance. To guide laypeople there was a structure of clergy, consisting of a variety of priests and deacons, and above all of them stood the bishop. In each region the principal city had a bishop, and his power often rivaled or surpassed that of secular overlords. One of the most important, the bishop of Rome, came to be known as the pope. Whereas today we think of figures such as priests and bishops as individuals with only spiritual authority, possessing little or no influence in the secular world, in this period there was no such clear division between secular and temporal powers. Bishops effectively wielded great political power, while lords often exerted influence over church matters.

The empire returns?

After nearly four centuries of fragmentation, a powerful secular leader arose who was able to unite all of Europe for a time. Charlemagne (742–814 CE), the descendent of Frankish kings, who inherited the lands of Francia (present day France, Belgium, the Netherlands, Austria, Switzerland, Denmark, and portions of Germany) viewed himself as successor to the emperors of ancient Rome. Like a Roman emperor, he waged incessant war, increasing the borders of his territories in all directions until the Carolingian empire stretched 800 miles from east to west. From his court in Aachen he commissioned building and artistic projects, issued laws, and received ambassadors from as far away as Constantinople and Baghdad.

However, there were some important differences between this emperor and those of antiquity. Though he understood Latin and Greek, Charlemagne could neither read nor write. He proudly wore Frankish trousers and personally supervised his entire empire, galloping back and forth on horseback. He commanded no standing army; rather his subjects had to be mobilized for each campaign, providing their own weapons. Most important, his central role was that of champion and defender of the Holy Roman Church. Early on, Charlemagne established close ties with the pope in Rome, thereby legitimizing his territorial ambitions in Europe in the name of Christendom. The pope benefited from this relationship, because without military support the papacy was all too vulnerable. Pope Leo III, who placed the imperial crown on Charlemagne's head on Christmas Day in the year 800 CE, had been in danger of his life and forced to flee Rome just the year before. Furthermore, by choosing the defender for his church and bestowing a crown on him, the pope increased his own power, effectively placing himself above the emperor. Though the Carolingian dynasty was short-lived, the uneasy relationship created between pope and emperor, with its ensuing debate over the separate realms of church and state would endure in Europe for centuries.

After Charlemagne's death, the empire he had forged swiftly disintegrated due to internal discord as well as from increasing hostilities from Magyar tribes from the east, Vikings from the north, and Arabs from the south. In 843 Charlemagne's grandsons split the empire three ways. One received the western portion that would become France, another, the eastern portion that would become Germany. The third took the "Middle Kingdom" and the title of emperor, ruling over a portion of Germany as well as the Italian Peninsula—in 774, Charlemagne had invaded the northern Italian Kingdom of the Lombards, adding Italy to his domain, and over the course of the following centuries, the Holy Roman Emperor, as he came to be called, would figure significantly in the fortunes of Italy.

The Commercial Revolution

It was not until the so-called Commercial Revolution, which began around 1000 CE, that Europe would begin to recover, and it was in the northern Italian territories of the Empire that dynamic change took place. When we think of the Middle Ages we think of the lords and ladies in the courts of northern Europe and the peasants who plowed their fields. The great castles

6 Out of the Ashes

of England and France come to mind. Italy also had its lords, castles, and peasants working the land, but in significant ways it developed very differently from the rest of medieval Europe, under conditions especially favorable to economic growth. For unlike most of the rest of Europe, after the fall of the Roman Empire, the Italian Peninsula still had around forty inhabited cities, located on former Roman sites. Though these cities were greatly depopulated compared with ancient times, they were lively centers of commerce. Whereas in other parts of Europe people had to depend on periodic fairs or traveling peddlers for their goods, the vibrant little Italian cities were like year-round fairs for their inhabitants. This was because, in spite of dangers on the roads, there was constant trade and travel through Italy.

Rome's location in the heart of the Italian Peninsula was decisive, as the church affected all aspects of cultural, political, and economic life in Italy over these centuries. In economic terms, the church brought business to Italy. Whether on their way to Rome or to the Holy Land on pilgrimage or crusade, medieval travelers passed through Italy. People and goods flowed through the Italian Peninsula by land, along the pilgrimage route of the Via Francigena (Map 1.1), and traversed the ports of Genoa, Pisa, and Venice. Thriving communities of merchants trading goods, and craftsmen manufacturing products for export developed. Inns sprang up to cater to travelers, and the feeding and clothing of these foreigners further stimulated local economies. The population of Italian cities doubled between the tenth and fourteenth centuries as people increasingly moved from the country into towns, where economic opportunities abounded.

Communal governments sprout up in Italy

Just as their cities' economies expanded, so too did their political clout, and gradually city-dwellers in Italy began to form organizations known as communes. A commune was not so much the city itself, as the association of individuals who lived there gathered together through common interests to govern themselves. In the very earliest phase in the growth of the communes (c.1080–1140), aristocrats dominated these organizations, banding together in order to enact civic legislation. The members of these early communes called themselves consuls, taking the same name as the patrician representatives in the ancient Roman Republic. Though these were not broad-based democracies in any sense, the citizens in Italian communes were forging a unique form of representative government that did not exist anywhere else in Europe at the time.

Though they were largely self-governing, the Italian consular communes were not independent, but subjects of a distant monarch. The emperors in Germany who had jurisdiction over the Italian Peninsula occasionally visited their territories south of the Alps, but generally preferred to govern through agents. This was a workable arrangement in which communes paid their taxes and in return received a measure of autonomy, but the

Map 1.1 Principal Italian communes c.1250

growing conflict between the emperor and the pope complicated the political situation. As protectors of the faith, the emperors felt entitled to grant church offices and lands in Italy to favored vassals. The popes, on the other hand, claimed that not only ecclesiastical offices, but much of the Italian Peninsula itself belonged to the church, citing the so-called "Donation of Constantine" (Chapter 7).

8 Out of the Ashes

Emperor Henry IV (1050–1106) and Pope Gregory VII (r.1073–85) disagreed openly over who had the right to invest (literally "to dress" in his official garb or appoint) the archbishop of Milan, as it had become custom for lay authorities to appoint bishops. Controversy over the issue of lay investiture escalated: in 1076 Henry summoned his bishops and had them declare Gregory's election invalid; the pope retaliated by excommunicating Henry and denying his right to rule over Germany and Italy, giving his subjects, in effect, permission to rebel. In January of 1077, Henry crossed the Alps to reach the Castle of Canossa where the pope was the guest of the powerful Countess Matilda of Tuscany (1046–1115), an ardent supporter of the papacy. The emperor kneeled in the snow for three days asking forgiveness, and promised allegiance to the pope, but soon after it was granted and the excommunication lifted, literal war broke out between the two sides. After many years of fierce battles, Matilda's forces eventually triumphed in 1092. Meanwhile, in order to garner local support, each side had been making concessions to the communes, gradually increasing their independence.

The Investiture Conflict was officially settled in 1122, when it was agreed that the two powers were equivalent. The pope argued that there were two swords: the emperor wielded a temporal sword, the pope a spiritual sword. Imperial claims, however, were hardly resolved with a metaphor. Matters came to a head again in the twelfth century when Henry's great-grandson, the Emperor Frederick I "Barbarossa" (r.1152–90) insisted on his supreme control over Italy. Barbarossa had difficulties ruling the Italian city-states; the men he put in charge often spoke only German and were unpopular because of their insensitivity to local customs. By 1167 most northern Italian cities had joined in the Lombard League (Chapter 6) with Pope Alexander III (r.1159–81) against the emperor, defeating him at the Battle of Legnano in 1176. The Peace of Constance (1183) set the stage for the independence of the Italian communes. The citizens agreed to swear an oath of allegiance to the emperor, continuing to pay taxes to him, while being allowed to elect their own consuls, govern their own territories, and make their own local laws. From this point on, the Holy Roman Emperor was ruler of Italy in little more than name alone.

Tensions between magnates and *popolo*

The image of determined little city-states banded together in a struggle against the emperor presents in many ways an unrealistic image of solidarity and cooperation that in fact rarely, if ever, existed. Nobles, knights, or magnates, as they are most frequently referred to in documents from this period, were constantly fighting with one another. Fierce blood feuds like the one depicted in Shakespeare's *Romeo and Juliet* were common. Italian cities suffered from incessant violence between powerful clans, as they and their thugs menaced one another and passersby in the streets. And they fought not only on the ground; from the mid-twelfth century, the magnate clans had filled Italian cities with their towers, from which they waged battles with one another. The oppressive effect that these immense constructions once had on residents can be felt today in the Tuscan town of San Gimignano, which still bristles with towers.

Eventually a group of citizens stood up to the dangerously uncivil behavior of the magnates. Known as the *popolo*, these city-dwellers earned their living through trade, banking, or crafts. Though the word *popolo* comes from the same root as the English word people, it does not mean "the people" in the sense of "the masses," but indicates all city-dwellers who were not members of the arrogant, warlike nobility. The more prosperous were known as the *popolo grasso* (fat people), and the poorest, such as cloth workers and leather tanners as the *popolo minuto* (little people). Groups of these citizens had begun to form individual trade guilds toward the end of the twelfth century, and as they became more and more prosperous the guilds banded together against their common enemies, the magnates. Throughout Italy armed companies of the *popolo* rose up to defend themselves.

Their rebellion against the nobles, however, ought not to be romanticized. The leaders of the *popolo* were no Robin Hoods, battling injustice to give to the poor. Rather, they recognized that civic unrest interfered with business; private quarrels between local strongmen only made city streets unsafe and were in no one's best interests. Moreover, the richest of the merchant class now outstripped the wealth of the landed nobility, giving them greater political clout. The origins of powerful banking families such as the Florentine Peruzzi and Medici were from the *popolo*. Indeed, as we will see, there was much conflict within the *popolo* between the less politically powerful minor guilds and the wealthy influential major guilds, all of whom nevertheless participated in city government.

The age of the popular commune, 1200–90

The Duecento was the golden age of the *popolo*. Throughout the peninsula, popular regimes had succeeded in overthrowing the ruling elite, thus the so-called "consular communes" governed by nobles were replaced by "popular communes," led by tradesmen, artisans, and members of various guilds. As the *popolo* gained in power and experience, the citizens experimented with various ways of governing their republics. From the outset they wanted a form of representational government and recognized the need to have a central executive figure to direct their corporate interests. But who should lead them? If one powerful citizen were chosen, this could lead to factional fighting within the city, or worse. If that person became too powerful he might make himself signore (Chapter 6), become a tyrant, and destroy the commonwealth altogether. Thus, most communes during this period decided upon a *podestà* as the chief executive. The *podestà* was always an outsider, the citizen of another commune, as long as it was a distant one. He was a respected nobleman, often trained in law, who was hired for six months to

10   *Out of the Ashes*

two years, varying by city. He brought with him a team of notaries, police, and administrative assistants. The *podestà* was well paid, but always accountable to the city council and subject to strict audits when he left office.

The first government entirely ruled by the *popolo* was in Florence, the so-called *primo popolo* of 1250. One of its first decrees was to lop off the tops of all towers over 96 feet high. The extent to which they were successful can be seen in Florence today where very few towers stand out, whereas once the skyline was crowded with over a hundred of them, some as high as 230 feet. By the 1290s when the *popolo* was firmly established, the Florentine priors approved the building of their new headquarters, the Palazzo dei Priori (now called the Palazzo Vecchio), which with its solid fortress-like appearance projected an image of stability and strength. Where once there had been scores of individual towers, now the single, enormous campanile, or bell tower, would dominate the skyline of Florence, representing the power of the Republic.

The new regime did not stop with symbolic gestures against the former ruling class. It now officially excluded members of magnate clans from participation in city politics and applied severe penalties to any misbehavior. In Florence, for example, the Ordinances of Justice were passed in 1293, in which magnates were prohibited from joining guilds and from holding civic offices. A new office was created, called the standardbearer of justice (*gonfaloniere di giustizia*), specifically to enforce these regulations.

The *popolo* enacted other laws that reflected their own, rather than the magnates' interests. Tax legislation was a central issue in popular communes. Property and income taxes were introduced, assessing each household proportional to its wealth; the exemptions formerly enjoyed by the nobility were done away with. And now that violent crime was being systematically prosecuted, criminal law grew and developed.

Structural changes were made in the organization of city government as well. The office of the *podestà* was replaced by that of the *capitano del popolo*. The role of the *capitano del popolo* was very similar to that of the *podestà*; his term was short (six months to a year), and he had to know law in order to pass judgments. Significantly, he controlled an armed citizen militia, and in times of emergency he set the city bells clanging in a general call to arms. The *capitano* was answerable to a city council of twelve elders (*anziani*, later known as *priori* or priors). They were members of major guilds who were elected for six-month terms of office, and who, to pass laws, had to have the approval of legislative committees. Though the numbers of the members of these councils, their names and terms of office varied by commune, by the end of the century not only Florence but most Italian city-states had adopted this system of government.

A "pullulation of little powers"

By the Duecento, central and northern Italy was made up of dozens of these city-states, thriving centers of commercial and cultural energy. The Italian

Peninsula was dotted with these tiny city-republics, each proudly self-governed, each eyeing the others with suspicion and ever on the lookout for an opportunity to conquer its neighbor. From the very earliest time of their foundation, this "pullulation of little powers" in the words of historian Chris Wickham, warred not only against each other, but with the people in their surrounding countryside or *contado*. It seems absurd to us today to imagine a "Republic of New York City" declaring war on a "Republic of New Jersey," or a "Republic of Oakland" sending ambassadors to a "Republic of Berkeley," in alliance against San Francisco, but these were precisely the kinds of situations the Italian city-states found themselves in during the thirteenth century, except of course that most of them had populations between only 10,000 and 40,000.

The allegiances of these city-states in the thirteenth century became polarized around the Guelf and Ghibelline political parties. The Guelfs, named after the Welf family, who were dukes of Bavaria, supported the pope. The Ghibellines were supporters of the emperor, and the name derives from the castle of Waibling, which belonged to the emperor. There is a colorful story related by the chronicler Dino Compagni (*c.*1260–1324), who gives a somewhat different version of the origins of Guelf and Ghibelline factions in Florence in 1215:

> In Florence a young, noble citizen by the name of Buondelmonte de' Buondelmonti had promised to marry the daughter of Oderigo Giantruffetti. He was going by the home of the Donati, when a gentlewoman by the name of Madonna Aldruda, the wife of Messer Forteguerra Donati, who had two very lovely daughters, was on the balcony and saw him. She was standing there and called to him, pointing to one of these daughters: "Who have you chosen for a wife? I've been saving this one for you!"

Compagni goes on to explain that the young man married the daughter of Donati and the jilted girl's family was so enraged that they began a feud that spread throughout all of Italy.

Though it is improbable that hostilities throughout the peninsula were ignited because of a thwarted love affair, this passage does indicate that there was more than political ideology involved in the Guelf/Ghibelline conflict. Class divisions cannot totally account for the discord either; though Guelfs tended to be more prominent in banking and commerce and Ghibellines were more likely to be associated with landed wealth, both essentially came from the same class. Economic interests as well as traditional clan allegiances played probably the most important part in determining which side people would belong to. Those whose business benefited from a strong connection with the papacy naturally sided with the Guelf party; thus, the Florentine bankers who lent vast sums to the pope were devoted Guelf adherents. On the other hand, those who resided in cities such as Pisa, whose leading family the Gambacorti, derived their authority from the emperor, sided with the Ghibellines.

Further complicating the political situation was that, with the victory of one party over another, the losers would be exiled from their city. The exiles would go to a nearby city that was in the hands of their faction, plotting and preparing to return and regain power. If exiled Florentine Ghibellines rallied in Pisa, for instance, Pisa became the de facto enemy of Florence; hostilities would be declared and war between the two cities became a certainty. Allegiances were formed and broken with alarming rapidity; the only certainty was constant strife. Even when the Florentine Guelfs eventually crushed the Ghibellines at the Battle of Campaldino in 1289, there was to be no peace. The Florentine Guelfs then broke into two factions, known as the Whites and the Blacks, who proceeded to combat each other with a ferocity equal to that with which the Guelfs had formerly fought the Ghibellines.

Florentines, the "fifth element of the world"

If Florence was remarkable for its violent politics, it was equally renowned for its vigorous economy. Among all the communes, the most stunning economic growth took place in Florence. Around the middle of the thirteenth century, it was an important center of trade and banking, but its population was only around 45,000. By 1300, Florence had become one of the largest, most important cities in Europe, with a population of more than 100,000, making it, along with Paris, Venice, Milan, and Genoa, one of the five most populous cities in Europe (Table 1.1). Its commercial and financial interests extended to England, Constantinople, and beyond. Pope Boniface VIII was so impressed with how widely Florentines traveled that he allegedly once exclaimed: "Florentines are the fifth element of the world!" Like earth, air, water, and fire, Florentines seemed to be everywhere. Indeed, it is tempting to

Table 1.1 Population of Italian cities *c.*1300

80,000–100,000	Florence, Genoa, Milan, Venice
c. 50,000	Bologna, Brescia, Naples, Palermo, Pisa, Siena, Verona
20,000–40,000	Agrigento, Ancona, Ascoli, Barletta, Catania, Cremona, Fano, Lucca, Mantua, Melfi, Messina, Padua, Parma, Pavia, Perugia, Piacenza, Rome, Salerno, Siracusa
c. 10,0000	Alessandria, Aversa, Arezzo, Asti, Bari, Bergamo, Bitonto, Brindisi, Capua, Catania, Cesena, Chieri, Chioggia, Como, Cortona, Crema, Fabriano, Faenza, Ferrara, Fermo, Forlì, Gubbio, Imola, Moderna, Monopoli, Orvieto, Pistoia, Prato, Ravenna, Recanati, Reggio, Rimini, Savona, Spoleto, Taranto, Todi, Trani, Trapani, Treviso, Vercelli, Vicenza, Viterbo, Volterra

Out of the Ashes 13

attribute their success to the enterprising spirit of the Florentines themselves, for the city would seem to have little to recommend itself as a future metropolis. It is located inland, with inconvenient access to the sea, and was not on the main pilgrimage route, the Via Francigena. The Arno River, which runs through the city, is so shallow that it is hardly navigable, and the city is subject to periodic catastrophic flooding.

The Arno, however, did prove to be a source of profit to Florentines, as it provided the plentiful water the textile industry needed for the dying of cloth. For this reason, wool-finishing and silk industries developed early in Florence. Demand for Florentine cloth soon outstripped the raw materials available in the region, and Florentine merchants ranged always farther away to buy their wool, purchasing much of it in England. The initiative and willingness to embark on long-distance trade that characterized Florentine business endeavors also created a need for ways of transferring money to far-away lands, and so international banking developed. In 1252 the florin was minted, the first gold coin produced in large amounts in Western Europe since Carolingian times. Like the Florentines who minted it, the florin rapidly began to circulate everywhere; within several years it was to be found not only all over Tuscany, but throughout Italy, at the fairs in Champagne, and as far away as the Levant. When other governments began to mint coins, they imitated the size, weight, purity, and sometimes even the design of the Florentine coin. Rivaled only by the Venetian ducat, which was introduced in 1284, by the end of the thirteenth century the florin became the standard currency for international commercial and financial markets throughout Europe and the Mediterranean.

Florence was a boom town by the second half of the Duecento. The city walls, built in 1072, had to be expanded in 1172 to enclose an area three times the size; then in 1284, building was begun on walls which would enclose eight times the original size of the city. These years saw the beginning of many building projects; the landmarks that a visitor in Florence to this day recognizes were initiated during this time. The Dominican monastery of Santa Maria Novella was begun in 1279 and the Franciscan monastery of Santa Croce expanded in 1295. The plan for Santa Maria del Fiore (the Duomo) was made in 1294, and work began two years later. Across from it, the Baptistery of San Giovanni was completely renovated in the 1290s.

Dante Alighieri, Florentine poet and political exile

This was the world that the poet Dante Alighieri (1265–1321) grew up in. He lived through a time of great conflict and change, which he vividly describes in his masterpiece, the *Divine Comedy*. Born into a genteel, but not wealthy, family, Dante was nevertheless raised and educated along with the elite of Florentine society, reading classical Latin authors, attending lectures on theology at the Dominican school at Santa Maria Novella, and listening to Provençal troubadour love songs. He had a precociously romantic nature,

14   *Out of the Ashes*

falling in love at age nine with a little girl his own age. Her name was Beatrice, and she would remain his muse for his whole life.

Dante's interests, however, were not entirely engrossed in love and poetic pursuits; he was a fascinated observer of the world around him and was passionate about politics. Nor was he content to be a bystander to political events, but actively took part in city government. By this time the Ghibellines had been defeated, and Dante is believed to have belonged to the party of the White Guelfs; indeed, he held public office between 1295 and 1300, serving as *priore* while the Whites were in power. Dante was on an ambassadorial mission to Rome in 1301 when the Black Guelfs took over control of Florence, having swiftly executed or exiled the remaining members of the Whites. Dante was condemned, in absentia, first to exile and then to death.

Dante never returned to Florence. Exile became a central theme of his poetry, and he could never write of Florence without expressing either fierce anger or intense nostalgia. The proud former citizen of the Florentine Republic wandered from place to place for the rest of his life, relying on the hospitality of the mighty. Dante came to know, in his own words, "how salty is the bread of others and how hard it is to go up and down their stairs." Dante died in exile in Ravenna in 1321, already recognized throughout Italy as the greatest writer of his day.

The *Divine Comedy*, the first masterpiece of Italian literature

Dante's *Divine Comedy* is famous both for its content and for its vigorous poetic language. Dante was the first poet to choose to write in *volgare*, in Italian vernacular, or more precisely in Tuscan vernacular. There was as yet no formal Italian language, no grammars or dictionaries; indeed, at this time there was no single vernacular Italian language, but many versions. A traveler going from one region to another, sometimes even from one town to the next, would have had a difficult time understanding the local tongues. Learned people communicated in Latin, and though popular songs, legends, and poetry existed in *volgare*, it was a radical move for Dante to write a serious work in the spoken language of Tuscany.

Dante's genius was in sounding all the registers of the Tuscan dialect, from the roughest street slang to the most sublime expressions of divine love. And when there were no words to express exactly what he meant, he created them. Like Shakespeare, more than 200 years later, Dante enriched his language with hundreds of colorful new words and expressions. The Italian language spoken and studied today is the direct descendent of Dante's elaboration of the spoken Florentine dialect of his day.

Dante envisioned a poem on a grand scale that would explain the place of humankind in the cosmos and represent man's dilemma on earth: his difficult choices between good and evil and his paradoxical striving for perfect love in an imperfect world. It is a narrative poem of 14,233 lines, composed in the interlocking rhyme scheme known as *terza rima*. The poem is divided into three books, each describing a realm of the afterlife according to contemporary Christian theology: *Inferno* (Hell), *Purgatorio* (Purgatory), and *Paradiso* (Heaven). The story is told in the first person, as Dante/the pilgrim is lost in a forest of doubt and confusion, unable to scale the mountain representing virtue. Tempted by sin, Dante's soul is in mortal danger, causing Beatrice to send the Roman poet Virgil (70–19 BCE) to guide him first through Hell, then through Purgatory. In the final book Dante visits Heaven, where he at last encounters Beatrice.

In the *Inferno*, the poet employs all his poetic invention and fantasy to punish evil-doers in horrible, yet imaginative ways. Dante devises a system of *contrappasso*, in which, to paraphrase Gilbert and Sullivan, the "punishment fits the crime." The lustful, who were carried away by passion on earth, in the afterlife are incessantly blown and battered by powerful winds. The suicides, who had willfully stripped themselves of their earthly lives, are turned into trees, from which branches are painfully ripped off. Flatterers who once spewed disgustingly false praise are immersed in pools of excrement.

"Those brand-new people and their sudden earnings"

Although it is obviously impossible to give an idea in English of the sheer beauty of the sound of Dante's poetry, the content of the *Divine Comedy* communicates directly. Dante closely observed the world around him and his critical gaze missed nothing. Witness to the unprecedented economic boom that was taking place in Florence during his lifetime, he denounced "those brand-new people and their sudden earnings" who "have brought to Florence excess and arrogance." He was disgusted with the unheard-of opulence of rich Florentines. Many sumptuary laws were introduced at this time, to reduce the extravagance of dress among the wealthy, while the amount of money spent on dowries and lavish wedding banquets skyrocketed. In the *Comedy*, Dante condemns what he considers the immoral, decadent atmosphere in Florence. He compares Florence of his day with that of his great-great grandfather:

> Florence within her ancient circle of walls,
> from which the bells still ring the hours,
> was at peace, modest and sober.
> They did not wear golden chains, crowns
> or embroidered dresses, nor belts
> that attracted more attention than the wearer.
> Fathers were not frightened at the birth of a daughter,
> as dowries were not yet beyond measure.

Dante does not stop here with his condemnation. He places many prominent Florentines in Hell both for their greedy accumulation of wealth and for their squandering of it, and especially for moneylending. Usury, as it was called, was a sin according to the church, yet if banks never lent money at interest, there would be no banking. As we know, banking flourished in Florence; the moneylender sitting at his counter or *banco* (hence the term "bank" in English), was a common sight in the city, so Dante's Hell is full of Florentines. "Be joyous, Florence," the poet exclaims, "you are great indeed, for over sea and land you beat your wings; through every part of Hell your name extends!"

Mendicant friars praised and corrupt popes punished

Dante's depiction of the wealth of his contemporaries is real enough, and so was its corollary: poverty. The very poorest Florentines lived in urban squalor. From the earliest days of the wool industry, the Arno had been used for cleansing dyes from cloth and dumping both household and industrial waste byproducts; the indigent came in daily contact with these noxious fumes and filth. Where was Christian charity, when fellow Florentines were allowed to live in these conditions? This was a city where the words of St. Francis of Assisi (*c.*1181–1226) still echoed. The son of a wealthy Umbrian cloth merchant, Francesco (Francis), was horrified by the greedy consumerism he saw around him and rejected the accumulation of material goods. Begging for food in bare feet, Francesco and his disciples practiced absolute poverty. *Il Poverello* (the little pauper) as he came to be called, had preached on these very streets, where enormous fortunes were amassed off the labor of others.

St. Francis touched his listeners by directly appealing to the emotions; he used images drawn from nature in his sermons; and his chivalric romance with "Lady Poverty," captured the spirit of the age. The Franciscans became enormously popular, and as they caught on, so did another important mendicant order created at the same time, the Dominicans. They were known as mendicants (from the Latin *mendicans* meaning "to beg"), because the friars renounced material possessions, living only on charity. Their popularity with the laity was due less to a discomfort with wealth in general—for indeed most people desired to be wealthy—but as a reaction to the widespread corruption among the clergy. Bejeweled, richly dressed bishops were losing their credibility with the faithful. Here Dante gives voice to the outrage people felt, for instance, at greedy popes who sold church offices, a practice known as simony. These popes appointed bishops and other clerics not for their spirituality, but on the basis of how much money candidates could pay. Dante and Virgil walk past a simonist buried upside down, with legs flailing in the air; this is Pope Nicholas III (1216–1277), who was well known for this practice. The pope calls out: "Is that you standing there, Boniface?" meaning Pope Boniface VIII (*c.*1235–1303). After Dante identifies himself, Nicholas recognizes his mistake, but expresses his assurance that both Boniface and his successor Pope Clement V (1264–1314) will be coming to join him soon. Thus, in one stroke, the author has condemned three popes to Hell.

Dante and Marsilius of Padua on the separate powers of church and state

It is often confusing to modern sensibilities how a person could so openly criticize the most powerful figure in the Catholic Church and "get away with it." Though obviously no pope would have been pleased to be consigned to Dante's literary Hell, we must keep in mind that the period of the vast spy network of the Roman Inquisition (Chapter 15), which held the Italian populace in its iron grip, would not come into being until several centuries later. Equally confounding to today's readers of the *Commedia* is Dante's attitude toward religion. Though he lashed out at the church, Dante was a devout Christian. He wanted to see the church return to a purer, less worldly form of religion; specifically, he believed the pope should renounce all temporal power. Harking back to the Investiture Conflict, this was still a burning issue in Dante's day. Indeed, Boniface VIII, one of the simonists Dante condemns to Hell, was a forceful pope who envisioned vast control for himself over all of Europe (Chapter 4).

The need to wrest political control from the papacy was taken up by Marsilius of Padua (Marsilio dei Mainardini *c*.1275–1343), who blamed the popes for all of Italy's political troubles. In his 1324 treatise *Defensor pacis* (*Defender of the Peace*), Marsilio used classical models to argue in favor of a separation of powers of church and state, although unlike Dante, the Paduan was optimistic about self-government among city-states. As he grew older, Dante became convinced that the only solution for the incessant discord in Italy was to have the entire peninsula, indeed all of Europe united under one monarch, the Holy Roman Emperor Henry VII of Luxembourg (*c*.1275–1313). Dante expounded these views at length in his political treatise *De monarchia* (*On Monarchy c*.1314). Long gone were his republican ideals; Dante no longer had faith in the ability of citizens to govern themselves. He ridiculed Florence's ever-changing legislation, sarcastically comparing the politically troubled city to an invalid:

> How often, over time within recent memory,
> have you changed your laws, money, offices, and customs,
> changing and revising your citizens!
> And if you recall with clarity,
> You will see you resemble a sick woman,
> who cannot be comforted in her feather-bed,
> but constantly tosses and turns to relieve her pain.

Though Dante's shift from staunch republican to reactionary monarchist seems like a step back, he was actually anticipating the political direction that Florence would take 200 years later. It is also important to remember that he felt driven to this stance by the violent factionalism around him: a strong authority figure, he believed, could be counted on to maintain law and order. Dante reserves the lowest levels of the *Inferno* for those who disturb the peace and sow discord. The deepest part of the pit is for traitors, and to describe these most vile sinners, the poet lets loose his most powerful language. Dante's poetic style becomes increasingly brutal and realistic as his journey takes him to the lowest reaches of Hell. The characters brawl, sling insults at one another, and make obscene gestures. His writing reaches such a pitch of naturalism here that you can almost hear echoes of the streets of Florence of his day. When, toward the very bottom pit, Dante meets a traitor to the Guelf party, Dante grabs him by the scruff of the neck, shouting: "Tell me your name or I'll rip every hair from your head!"

An explosion of naturalism in art: Giotto di Bondone

Before Cimabue was the top, now Giotto is all the rage ...

With these words, Dante sums up the artistic revolution that was being created by his contemporary, Giotto di Bondone (*c.*1266–1337), who pioneered naturalism in painting. Giotto had broken away from the style of his predecessor, Cimabue (*c.*1240–1302), who painted intensely expressive figures, but stylized in the older Byzantine manner. Giotto's figures, on the other hand, vibrate with life. At times they dance with joy, musicians swaying to a tune, trumpeters puffing out their cheeks. At other times his characters exude intolerable sorrow, as in his *Death of St. Francis* (Bardi Chapel, Santa Croce, Florence).

In addition to movement, however, his forms have weight, unlike earlier paintings where figures sometimes seem to float in space. In contrast to the two-dimensional, flat figures of earlier paintings, Giotto's men and women have very real, solid bodies that move convincingly through the seemingly three-dimensional spaces they inhabit. In his *Ognissanti Madonna and Child* (Uffizi), the infant Jesus holds up his chubby little hand in benediction, against the background of his mother's swelling breasts and solid thigh; one cannot doubt that her feet are planted firmly on the ground.

Dante and Giotto may have met while Giotto was working on his frescoes for the Scrovegni Chapel in Padua, as the two men were both there at the same time. Even if the two never met, however, their work, the scope and scale of their vision is comparable. The chapel (also known as the Arena Chapel) was built by Enrico Scrovegni, the son of a wealthy moneylender whom Dante had placed with the usurers in the *Inferno*. As a kind of spiritual money laundering scheme, Scrovegni hired Giotto, already recognized as the greatest living painter, to decorate its walls with biblical scenes. Giotto's *Last Judgment* is a powerful, vivid depiction of the last day, when according to Scripture the dead will rise up and be judged. God presides, as the elect are led to heaven (Giotto's patron is featured prominently among these) and the damned are grotesquely tortured. At the bottom of the fresco sits an immense, bloated, hairy Satan, crushing and devouring sinners.

Out of the Ashes 19

Figure 1.1 Giotto di Bondone, *Visitation*, 1304–06, detail, Scrovegni Chapel, Padua

Though the vision of his *Last Judgment* is a dark one, Giotto, like Dante knew how to represent all the registers of the human condition. In the same chapel, in the *Visitation* (Figure 1.1), the artist depicts an aged St. Elizabeth painfully bent in homage to Mary, who gazes compassionately down at the older woman, embracing, as well as supporting her, with her arms. In the scene of the *Wedding at Cana*, in which Jesus miraculously produced plentiful wine, off to one side Giotto playfully includes a well-fed citizen, one of those "brand-new men" so odious to Dante. The man stares off vaguely into the distance, unconcerned with the miraculous event happening around him; instead, he placidly guzzles wine, surrounded by jugs as round and bulging as his belly. Though we look at his paintings today and notice "medieval" elements, such as imprecise spatial perspective, for

20   *Out of the Ashes*

instance in *The Expulsion of Joachim from the Temple* (Scrovegni Chapel, Padua), Giotto's fresh use of color, his figures' dramatic gestures, and realistic emotions were entirely new and would lead the way to even greater artistic innovations.

Developments in sculpture and architecture

In addition to painting, Giotto also worked as an architect, designing the Campanile (bell tower) beside the cathedral in Florence. At this time there were not always clear distinctions among expertise in fields of painting, sculpture, architecture, and engineering. Arnolfo di Cambio (*c.*1240–1302) was a gifted sculptor who also designed the Basilica of Santa Croce, the Palazzo Vecchio, as well as the circuit of walls that surrounded Florence. As we will see, throughout the Renaissance, men of genius were recognized as valuable resources and their talents employed in a variety of artistic, literary, and engineering enterprises. Giotto began work on the Campanile in 1334, working on it until his death in 1337, after which he was replaced with the goldsmith and sculptor Andrea Pisano (Andrea d'Ugolino da Pontedera *c.*1295–1348) who also cast the gilt bronze panels on the south doors of the Baptistry (1330–36).

The graceful simplicity of Andrea Pisano's sculptures in stone and his realistic, yet stylized reliefs on the Baptistry doors owed much to Giotto's compositions, dramatic poses, and the monumentality of the painter's figures. Moreover, Andrea followed in the tradition of the great innovators in sculpture during the Duecento and early Trecento, who came from the Tuscan city of Pisa. Nicola Pisano (*c.*1220–1284) and his son Giovanni (*c.*1250–1314) created works that at once incorporated elements of ancient Roman statuary and infused new realism into the Gothic style of sculpture of their day. For the marble pulpits in the Pisan Baptistry, Giovanni Pisano drew inspiration directly from classical figures on Roman sarcophagi, which to this day can be viewed in Pisa. In his *Adoration of the Magi* (Baptistry, Pisa) the Madonna sits nobly upright, gazing into the distance, with the features and bearing of a Roman goddess. This trend of artists, especially sculptors harkening back to the ancient world for inspiration, would become one of the key elements of Renaissance art.

The realism the Pisanos introduced in sculpture can be seen vividly in Giovanni Pisano's 1301 *Massacre of the Innocents* on the pulpit of the Church of Sant'Andrea, in Pistoia (Figure 1.2). In the upper corner, Herod coldly commands his soldiers to murder the male infants. The work vibrates with frantic activity and pathos, mothers desperately trying to protect their newborns as soldiers wrench the children away and slice them open. A woman cowers in horror watching as a soldier in one hand holds her baby by the ankles like a slab of meat, his other raised to strike. In the lower corner a mother reclines on the ground and stares at her child, whose neck is bent in a grotesque angle like a broken doll.

Figure 1.2 Giovanni Pisano, *Massacre of the Innocents*, 1301, detail of pulpit in Church of Sant'Andrea, Pistoia

Considerations: "Medieval" or "Renaissance"?

Though the events described in this chapter took place before the period generally referred to as the Renaissance, they are crucial for understanding the cultural innovations that would develop later. The story of the rise and fall of ancient Rome is important not only because it helps us understand the creation of medieval Europe, but also because the events that took place many centuries earlier on Italian soil formed a legacy for future generations. Renaissance Italians could never forget the grandeur of their past; they self-consciously looked back to ancient Rome, measuring themselves against Cicero, Seneca, and Livy. Ancient Rome is the "Re" in "Renaissance."

Renaissance Italians compared not only contemporary arts and literature, but also their political structures to that of ancient Rome. The question of how a state is best governed, whether through democracy or by an individual, whether emperor, lord, or prince—is one that Renaissance Italians debated continuously. In this light, the political backdrop of communal Italy is fundamental, because it was there that Italians first experimented with an innovative form of representative government while the rest of Europe was still immersed in feudalism. Moreover, the vigorous debate taking place in the Italian communes over the separate realms of church and state, ideas expressed by Dante and by his even more radical

22 *Out of the Ashes*

contemporary Marsilius of Padua, heralded a new belief in the legitimacy of secular government.

Dante's *Divine Comedy* is often considered the perfect synthesis of the medieval world view, incorporating the theology of Aquinas, Bonaventure, and Augustine with the philosophy of Aristotle. He presents us with a severe and inflexible system of judgment ordered by a merciless God. In some ways his masterpiece is like a towering Gothic cathedral, complex, intricate, embellished with monstrous gargoyles. Coined by the sixteenth-century artist and historian Giorgio Vasari (Chapter 13), the term alone, which refers to the Gothic invaders from the north, conjures up dark, medieval images. However, there is another way to look at Dante's work. The sheer breadth of his vision and the scope of his monumental undertaking looks forward to the achievements of Michelangelo, who 200 years later would splash the ceiling of the Sistine Chapel with his equally vast vision of man's place in the universe. The vigor of Dante's language, his poetic naturalism, and artistic daring place him at the threshold of a new, exciting period in the history of Western Europe.

Sourcebook

Francis of Assisi, "Canticle of the Creatures"
Dante Alighieri, *Inferno* X
Marsilius of Padua, *Defender of the Peace*
Giotto, *Ognissanti Madonna*, Uffizi

Further reading

Borsook, Eve. *The Mural Painters of Tuscany from Cimabue to Andrea del Sarto*, Oxford, 2nd edition, 1980.
Little, Lester. *Religious Poverty and the Profit Economy in Medieval Europe*, Cornell, 1978.
Najemy, John. *A History of Florence 1200–1575*, Blackwell, 2006.
Waley, Daniel and Trevor Dean. *The Italian City-Republics*, 4th edition, Taylor & Francis, 2013.
White, John. *Art and Architecture in Italy 1250–1400*, Yale, 1966.
Wickham, Chris. *Early Medieval Italy: Central Power and Local Society 400–1000*, University of Michigan Press, 1989.

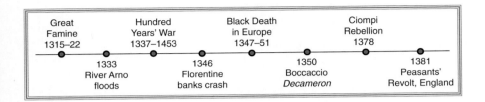

2 The Crises of the Fourteenth Century
Climatic, Epidemic, Demographic Disasters

> In the Year of Our Lord 1333, at the beginning of November, it pleased God that the city of Florence was powerful, happy, and prosperous, more than ever since 1300 ... On All Saints' Day it began to rain.
>
> Giovanni Villani, *Chronicle of Florence*

In the early years of the fourteenth century, not only Florence, but most of Italy was enjoying prosperity and unprecedented well-being. Living conditions throughout the peninsula were better than they had been for centuries, and the outlook for the future was good. Then over the course of the century, a series of unprecedented catastrophes, both natural and human-made, occurred. One of the most densely populated regions in Europe, Italy in 1300 supported around 12,500,000 inhabitants; fifty years later that number fell to 9,000,000. By 1400 the total population of the Italian Peninsula was 7,300,000. In the passage above, Giovanni Villani (c.1275–1348) records the onset of these troubles as he observed them in his city of Florence. In November of 1333 torrential rains caused the River Arno to overflow its banks, sweeping away bridges and creating massive destruction in Florence that would not be equaled until the flood of 1966. As bad as this series of storms and flooding were, there was much worse in store, but Villani would not be able to write about it. He died in 1348 during a terrifying pandemic that spread through Europe, North Africa, the Middle East, and Western Asia—the Black Death.

DOI: 10.4324/9781003270362-2

24   *The Crises of the Fourteenth Century*

The "Little Ice Age," a time of global cooling

Before addressing the Black Death, it is worthwhile examining the many factors which led historian Barbara Tuchman to refer to this era as "the calamitous fourteenth century," for these disasters helped shape the world of the Renaissance. For one thing, though extreme, the flooding in Florence Villani described was not an isolated event. From 1311 torrential rains had begun to occur throughout the continent and temperatures everywhere dropped. There is evidence that there were long-term climate changes at work throughout Europe. The "Little Ice Age," as it is sometimes called, was a period of global cooling. Though obviously there were no accurate measurements of temperature in the fourteenth century, scientists today have determined that glaciers advanced, and by measuring tree lines and types of crops produced at various latitudes during this time, they have concluded that the world cooled several degrees roughly between the fourteenth and sixteenth centuries. Under the best of conditions, contemporary farming methods could barely sustain Europe's population. The prosperity of the medieval Commercial Revolution led to a dramatic population explosion, which taxed the continent's agricultural capacity to its maximum, so even the slightest weather changes inevitably led to crop failure and the "Great Famine" of Europe that began in the 1310s.

The Hundred Years' War and crash of international banking

Adding to the human suffering due to natural causes, was war. The Hundred Years' War (1337–1453) between England and France devastated the coun-tryside and weakened the economies in much of Europe. Moreover, the eco-nomic effects of this war were broad, reaching south to Italy. In order to finance military operations in Aquitaine and Flanders, the king of France, Philip IV ("the Fair" 1268–1314), had borrowed vast sums from Italian bankers. He then imposed heavy taxes on the banks, seizing their goods (in 1303 and 1311). Some Italian banking houses, especially that of the Franzesi brothers, were hit very hard. Others, such as the Florentine Bardi and Peruzzi banks had large networks of offices stretching from England to Cyprus and initially were not seriously affected, even managing to keep their Paris branch offices open.

In the 1340s it began to look like the king of England was not going to pay back the enormous sums he had borrowed. These loans, amounting to approximately 1,365,000 florins, were financed primarily by Italian bankers. When, between 1343 and 1346 King Edward III (1312–1377) did default on his loans, the respected Bardi and Peruzzi were forced into bankruptcy, setting off shock waves in the Florentine economy and throughout Italy. Though it has been argued that the boom economy in Italy was showing cracks before this disaster occurred, the blow was severe: members of the urban elite lost their investments, slowing production of finished goods and creating unemployment among workers in cloth factories and other industries. However, despite this economic setback and climate change, life could have gone on essentially unchanged if, on the heels of these events, an even greater natural disaster had not struck.

1347: A devastating pandemic arrives in Europe

What changed everything in the fourteenth century was the Black Death, the most devastating pandemic in world history. It is possible that the disease had been circulating a century earlier, spread by Mongol troops throughout the steppes of Central Asia, where it continued to exist in less populous areas without noticeably affecting human societies. Afterward, the pestilence spread westwards via the trade routes exploited by industrious entrepreneurs such as the father and uncle of Marco Polo (c.1254–1324), and was carried along the Silk Roads through India, Syria, and Mesopotamia, reaching the city of Kaffa in 1346. A major port on the Crimean Peninsula, which controlled trade in the Black Sea, Kaffa (modern-day Feodosia) was in the hands of the Republic of Genoa. When Genoese and Venetian sailors and merchants returned home from the Black Sea region in late 1347, they brought the disease back with them to Europe. The population, already weakened by years of famine, may have had a lowered resistance to infection. In any case they succumbed swiftly; in its first wave the plague killed off somewhere between one-third to one-half of the people of Europe. By 1420 almost two-thirds of Europe's population had died of it, and densely populated Italian cities were reduced by as much as 80%(Map 2.1).

What was the disease that caused such devastation? Thanks to recent developments in the field of paleogenetics, in which aDNA (ancient DNA) is extracted from teeth of skeletons buried in plague pits, we have learned much about the origins and genesis of this terrifying disease. In 2011 the full genome of *Yersinia pestis* DNA was reconstructed from human remains buried in a 1348–50 plague pit in East Smithfield, London. It provided conclusive evidence that the pandemic, which first struck Europe between 1346 and 1353, was caused by *Yersinia pestis*, descended from the same bacterium responsible for the Justinianic Plague, which broke out during the reign of the Byzantine Emperor Justinian and ravaged the whole Mediterranean area, the Middle East, Western Europe, and the British Isles between 541 and 750 CE. Endemic to rodents, who carry it in fleas in their fur, at various points the disease crossed species to human carriers. One of the ways *Yersinia pestis* affects humans is known as bubonic plague, from the swellings called buboes that develop in the victim's neck, underarm, and groin, so vividly described by fourteenth-century chroniclers.

Today we refer to it as the "Black Death," but this term was not coined until the eighteenth century. When it first appeared in the fourteenth century, Italians called the illness *la grande mortalità* (the great mortality), or simply la *morìa* (the dying-off), words indicative of the fear inspired by

26   *The Crises of the Fourteenth Century*

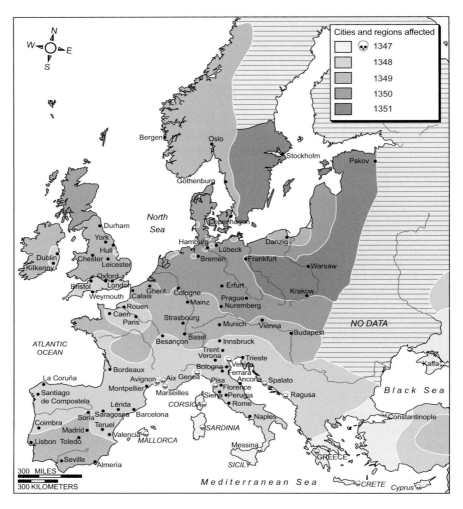

Map 2.1 Spread of the Black Death in Europe

its extraordinarily high mortality rate. When it struck, Europeans had no living memory of anything as fatal as this. They were not unfamiliar with early death, whether from contagious disease or other causes. This was an era, after all, that had an extremely high infant mortality rate and short life expectancy. Throughout the Middle Ages, already before the Black Death, three out of five children died before the age of four from illnesses like dysentery or worms, or simply of malnutrition. Perhaps half of those children survived to the age of twenty; overall, average life expectancy was thirty-five years. Yet when it appeared, Europeans were awed and terrified by this disease. The Black Death had nearly a 90% mortality rate, killing young and old, rich and poor, emptying entire villages. Although many medical remedies were tried, doctors were essentially powerless in the face of this pandemic during its first wave. As Matteo Villani (*c.*1285–1363) wrote, taking up the chronicle at the point where death had silenced his brother Giovanni: "No doctor in the world could cure this pestilence. Neither through science, medicine, nor any astrological art could they come up with a hint of any kind of cure."

In the Tuscan city of Siena, as many as 80,000 people—three-quarters of the population—died between April and October of 1348. One Sienese eyewitness, Agnolo di Tura, captures the sense of terrified awe the disease inspired and the rapidity with which it carried away its victims:

> During this time in Siena the Great Mortality began, the largest, most mysterious and most horrible disease you could speak of or imagine ... men and women died almost immediately. There were swellings in the groin and the armpit and no sooner could you speak of it than they died ... This illness was transmitted through the gaze and through the breath. And truly so many people died in the months of May, June, July, and August that no one could be found to bury them for any amount of money. And I, Agnolo di Tura, known as Il Grasso, buried my five children in a pit with my own hands, as did many others.

The people's immediate reaction was one of shock and panic that often led to mass hysteria. Italians, like other Europeans, viewed this pestilence as God's punishment for their sins. Just as Villani had attributed the flooding in Florence to divine causes, so too did a devoutly religious society believe the fault for this disaster lay within its own community. Groups of flagellants tramped through city streets and down country lanes whipping themselves in an effort to expiate the sins that had brought this scourge down upon them. Marginalized groups such as foreigners, prostitutes, and vagabonds were also blamed. Throughout Europe, Jews and lepers who were accused of poisoning wells to spread the contagion were killed as scapegoats. Nothing helped; people listened in dread as preachers thundered that the Apocalypse had arrived. As Agnolo di Tura wrote:

> The bells did not ring and no one wept ... each awaited death and things went in such a way that people believed that no one would be left and many men believed and went about saying it was the end of the world.

Boccaccio's account of the Black Death

The most celebrated account of the Black Death was written by Giovanni Boccaccio (1313–1375) in his Introduction to *The Decameron*. Although the disease spread everywhere, it has often been referred to as "the plague of

28   *The Crises of the Fourteenth Century*

Florence" because of the vividness of Boccaccio's description of its effects in his city:

> each citizen was repulsed by the other and hardly anyone cared for their neighbor, relatives rarely visiting each other, and only at a distance. Such was the terror that had entered men and women's hearts that brother abandoned brother, the uncle his nephew, the sister her brother, and often women abandoned their husbands. What is even worse, and almost unbelievable, fathers and mothers abandoned their children, as if they were not their own, so disgusted were they to touch or wait on them ... And thus the sick were abandoned by neighbors, family, and friends ... For the great multitude of bodies exposed, brought every day and at all hours to churches, there was not enough consecrated ground to bury them all. Wanting to give them all proper burial, according to tradition, the churches were turned into cemeteries; then, when all those were filled, enormous pits were dug into which hundreds of the stricken were thrown. And they were placed there as merchandise is loaded on a ship layer upon layer, each covered with very little earth until they reached the top of the pit and it would hold no more.

The life of Giovanni Boccaccio

It is difficult to imagine when reading the previous passage on its own, that it is part of a large, rollicking collection of stories, ingeniously crafted to amuse, delight, and move. One of the greatest writers in the Italian language, Boccaccio was widely admired and his writings imitated throughout Europe. Geoffrey Chaucer (*c.*1340–1400), author of *The Canterbury Tales*, was heavily influenced by Boccaccio, in particular by *The Decameron*. This complex work, full of contrast and paradox, was created by a man who in many ways embodied the times in which he lived. Giovanni Boccaccio was born the illegitimate son of a prosperous Florentine merchant. As a boy, he was provided with a good education, studying Latin and accounting, as he was being groomed for a business career. When he was thirteen years old, Boccaccio was sent to apprentice at the Bardi bank in Naples, which lent money to the king of Naples, Robert of Anjou. In 1327 he was joined by his father, who was given the prestigious position of chamberlain to the king, and the young man was catapulted into colorful Neapolitan court life.

The atmosphere was cosmopolitan, and the young man's impressionable imagination was entranced by the exotic foreign beauties, musicians, and performers at the Angevin court. His mind was also stimulated by the many poets, astrologers, and philosophers who lived in Naples. By this point Boccaccio had convinced his father that he was not suited to banking. His father agreed under condition that he study canon law, and become a lawyer. At the university Boccaccio studied with the great jurist Cino da Pistoia, who had been a friend of Dante, and with the celebrated Augustinian friar Dionigi da Borgo San Sepolcro. However, the young man was more interested in literature and humanistic studies than the law, which he abandoned as soon as his father left for France in 1332. Boccaccio threw himself into literature, writing love stories and epic poems based on mythological subjects and French courtly romances. He experimented in different styles, mixing genres and devising innovative poetic meters, in both vernacular and Latin. His literary fantasy apparently had no limits.

In 1340 everything changed for the brilliant young Boccaccio. After the crash of the Bardi bank he was forced to return home to Florence, a dull, business-like place compared with the glittering Neapolitan environment he had known. Nonetheless, Boccaccio continued writing, producing many works in poetry and prose. When the Black Death struck in 1348, he watched helplessly as the disease took the lives of his father and step-mother and innumerable friends. Rather than giving in to despair, however, Boccaccio was moved by these events to create his greatest work, *The Decameron*.

The Decameron, 100 tales of love, lust, and loss

The Decameron (1349–51) has as its frame the narrative that ten young people, seven women and three men, have decided to flee the city of Florence at the height of the Black Death. Together they take refuge in a rural villa where they can breathe the healthier country air, as many privileged city-dwellers indeed did in an attempt to protect themselves from the disease. For entertainment and to distract their thoughts from the loved ones they have lost; they sing, dance, and tell stories. The book is a collection of one hundred stories told over a period of ten days—the title *Decameron* means "ten days" in Greek—artfully arranged by theme and told in distinctive narrators' voices.

The central theme of these stories is love, both sublime and earthy, and everything in between. There are tales of first love, conjugal love, adulterous love, thwarted love, exuberantly requited love, and tragically doomed love. Boccaccio recounts the loves of queens, merchants, peasants, and priests; the book is full of lusty clerics, especially friars. Though the ribald stories and anti-clerical attitudes are often heralded as new to the Renaissance, indicative of a secular cast of mind, the stories themselves were not new. While shaping and embroidering them, Boccaccio drew the majority of his stories from tales that had been in circulation throughout the Middle Ages. Criticism of the clergy was nothing new either, as we have seen with Dante.

What is new in Boccaccio is the vibrant way he tells these tales; there is little in the way of judgment or moralizing. The author presents the full spectrum of human behavior as he finds it and encourages the reader to sit back and enjoy the spectacle. We are meant to admire the cleverness of slick con artists, marvel at the virility of monks, guffaw at adulterous housewives hiding their lovers in unlikely places. Because Boccaccio cleverly sets the story within the frame of a society whose morals have been broken down by the

30   *The Crises of the Fourteenth Century*

plague, he allows readers to suspend judgment on the transgressive behavior of the characters. In his Introduction he writes:

> What with the scarcity of servants, unheard-of behavior began to occur. It no longer made a difference to any woman, no matter how lovely, beautiful or refined, once she became sick, if she were cared for by a male servant. Whether he was young or not, with no sense of shame she would expose any part of her body to him, as if to a woman, because the illness demanded it.

Thus when coming upon the tale of a convent of nuns having sex with their handsome young gardener, or of Alibech, the pretty young convert to Christianity enthusiastically learning from a lustful hermit "how to put the devil back into Hell," the reader accepts that the ten well-brought-up young people would repeat such tales in mixed company as a product of extraordinary circumstances.

Because of Boccaccio's great artistry, when reading *The Decameron* we must be careful not to take everything he tells us at face value; as a skillful writer he knew how to manipulate facts to make an artistic impression. Though there is no doubt whatsoever that Boccaccio was an eyewitness to the Black Death in Florence, his account draws heavily on ancient sources. In Boccaccio's writing, there are echoes of the descriptions of plagues from ancient sources such as the Greek historian Thucydides (*c.*460–404 BCE) and others. Did the structure of society break down as completely as Boccaccio indicated (and Thucydides before him)? Though many parents undoubtedly abandoned their children during the Black Death as Boccaccio describes in the Introduction, for instance, what do we make of the real-life account of Agnolo di Tura who buried his five children "with his own hands"?

Society in the wake of the Black Death

Nonetheless, though caution must be exercised when trying to read any work of art directly as history, we can learn much of Italian, specifically Tuscan, society in the Trecento (fourteenth century) by reading *The Decameron*. Boccaccio was acutely aware of social issues of his time. In his description of the Black Death, he is careful to note not only what he perceives as dramatic shifts in social behavior caused by the plague, such as women losing their sense of modesty, family and community ties breaking down, and so on, but also subtle distinctions of class. Boccaccio draws distinctions between the types of people, for instance, who bury the dead:

> It was rare for a corpse to be accompanied by more than ten or twelve neighbors to a church, and these were no dear or honorable citizens, but a kind of gravedigger dredged up from the lowest elements (they called themselves gravediggers, but they were really servants for hire) who carried the bier.

Furthermore, though Boccaccio describes the universal suffering caused by the disease, he indicates how its effects varied, depending on people's social stations:

> The poor people and, perhaps, in large part even the ones in the middle, were in a much more miserable state, so much that these, whether out of hope or poverty had remained in their homes, staying in their neighborhoods. They fell sick by the thousands each day, and not cared for, nor helped in any way, all died. And many there were who ended up dead in the street.

The most powerful social message from the tales in *The Decameron* is that of a resourceful and resilient merchant class. There are many stories that mock the figure of the ignorant country bumpkin, who is often outwitted by a clever city-slicker. It is the quick-thinking entrepreneur, who triumphs through his or her shrewdness and perseverance, not to mention dishonesty, that is the hero of *The Decameron*. As we shall see, this vigorous group bounced back swiftly from the misfortunes of 1348. The world that Boccaccio seems to be describing is one of moral decay, breakdown in civic virtues, and total inefficacy of medical science. However, the very fact that he reworked the writings of ancient authors to do so and transformed the literature of his day demonstrate the vitality not only of Boccaccio himself, but also of the culture in which he thrived.

Government and medicine respond to the crisis

Despite the panicked first reaction, people began to adjust and respond to the disease in measured, thoughtful ways. City governments, which had seemed primarily skilled in waging continual wars on their neighbors and bickering among themselves, rose to the occasion, attempting to control the effects of the disease. The city of Florence, for instance, swiftly passed legislation to recruit more officials to run the government, extra troops to guard the city, and experienced craftsmen to operate the mint. To ensure the food supply, the government forbade peasants from leaving their farms and instituted measures to encourage agriculture in the surrounding countryside. Because the crisis caused costs to rise, the priors imposed new tariffs on goods entering Florence. As people often died before they had a chance to write a will, the government passed inheritance laws to protect the property of those who died intestate. Sanitary measures such as those enacted in May of 1348 in the Tuscan city of Pistoia were not uncommon. An effective system of quarantine was also devised. From the word *quaranta*, meaning forty, it was literally a forty-day isolation period for individuals suspected of exposure to disease. Quarantine was first practiced in 1377 in the Venetian colony of Ragusa (modern-day Dubrovnic), and was soon adopted throughout the Italian Peninsula. Notably, the duke of Milan was able to control the spread of the disease through enactment of a city-wide quarantine. The Republic of Venice established two permanent island facilities to treat victims of the disease and

32   The Crises of the Fourteenth Century

to quarantine those suspected of carrying it: the Lazzaretto Vecchio in 1423 and the Lazzaretto Nuovo in 1463. In short, while nothing could stem the tide of the pestilence, government could be relied on to control and direct human activity so that society did not lapse into chaos.

And, although there was no cure for the disease, gradually medical science began to respond in developing effective treatments. Unlike Matteo Villani and others who reported that doctors were completely ineffectual in treating the first wave of the disease, later sources show that medicine was improving. After the first outbreak, the Black Death recurred on average about every ten years, and over the course of the next 200 years hardly a generation passed that was not affected. Physicians began to do away with old, ineffectual remedies, and little by little, through direct observation, developed strategies to combat the disease. Rather than blindly following the prescriptions of Aristotle and Galen, medicine was gradually becoming an empirical science.

Social mobility and unrest

Because entire families had been wiped out, and whole villages emptied, opportunities were created for survivors and wealth was redistributed. During the second half of the fourteenth century, the demand for workers outstripped the supply, and wages rose. Agricultural products were plentiful as there were now fewer mouths to feed, so prices of food dropped. Despite, or perhaps because of, improved conditions, the humblest members of society now expected more. The Black Death had temporarily reshuffled the deck of social rank and entitlements.

A "contagion of revolts," as it has been described, followed the Black Death between the years 1355 and 1382 (Map 2.2). Throughout Europe, from the French Jacquerie of 1358 to the English Peasants' Revolt of 1381, peasants and workers rose up to protest their poor social conditions. A series of workers' revolts shook Italy during the latter half of the fourteenth century: the cities of Lucca, Siena, Perugia, Florence, Genoa, and Verona were among those that experienced rioting and rebellions of workers on the lowest rungs of the social ladder, the so-called *popolo minuto*.

The Ciompi Rebellion and the Florentine guilds

The most well known of these outbreaks, the Ciompi Rebellion, occurred in Florence in the summer of 1378 when 13,000 laborers from the cloth industry rose up and took control of the city government. The Ciompi were mostly unskilled cloth workers who felt disenfranchised. More than merely demanding changes such as tax reforms, they sought greater participation in city government. Specifically, they demanded recognition in the strictly hierarchical guild system.

There were twenty-one officially recognized guilds in Florence, but they did not play equal political roles. Most priors were elected from the largest,

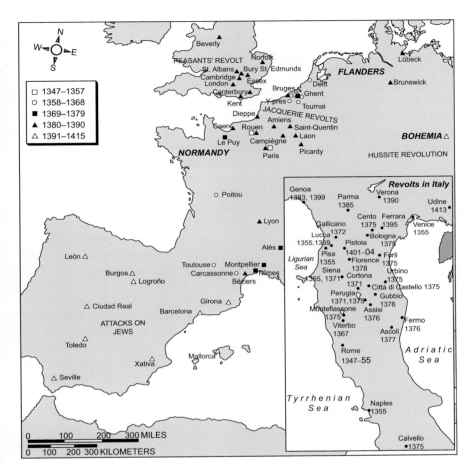

Map 2.2 Social unrest in Europe during the fourteenth century

wealthiest guilds, the *Calimala* (cloth importers and finishers), *Lana* (wool cloth manufacturers), *Cambio* (money changers), and *Giudici e Notai* (judges and notaries). Also important were the *Seta* (silk weavers) *Medici e Speziali* (physicians and pharmacists), and *Vaiai e Pellicciai* (furriers). Without membership in one of these major "arts"[1] (*arti maggiori*) as they were called, a citizen could not hold public office. Thus, Dante had joined the physicians and pharmacists' guild, in order to participate in city government. Lower in

---

1 The Italian word *arte* translates into English as "art," but also as "craft," "skill," or "profession." See references to Cennino Cennini's *Libro dell'arte* (*Craftsman's Handbook*) and the theater tradition of commedia dell'arte.

34   *The Crises of the Fourteenth Century*

social status were the minor guilds (*arti minori*), which included butchers, blacksmiths, shoe makers, carpenters, tavern keepers, hotel keepers, tanners, cheese merchants, linen manufactures, harness makers, armorers, locksmiths, and bakers. The members of these guilds had little clout compared to the powerful major guilds, yet they were allowed to express their views, often banding together to increase their influence. Moreover, alongside the major guilds, they contributed to highly visible civic projects, notably the decoration of Orsanmichele (Chapter 3). The up-and-coming artists they hired produced some of the most striking, innovative work of the early Renaissance: for instance, the guild of stonemasons and carpenters commissioned a sculptural group from Nanni di Banco (*Four Crowned Saints*), while the linen makers and the armorers each commissioned sculptures from Donatello (*St. Mark* and the *St. George*, respectively). Such contributions to the city's political and cultural landscape added to the guilds' prestige.

The Ciompi, however, belonged to no guild and were entirely lacking in prestige. These were the workers who beat and carded the wool, the most menial jobs, and lowest on the pecking order of the wool industry. Carding involved straightening the fibers of raw wool between two combs; fulling was a laborious process of washing, rinsing, beating, and stretching the wool. The legions of workers who carried out these necessary but lowly tasks were considered unskilled and were excluded from political office. In July of 1378 the Ciompi seized control of the seat of government, the Palazzo dei Priori (Palazzo Vecchio), and for five and a half weeks Florence was ruled by manual laborers. The impact of that revolt was felt for several years thereafter when broader participation was allowed in the city's government, but eventually Florence returned to an oligarchy ever more tightly controlled by the major guilds.

Town and country

As indicated earlier, this was a time not only of workers' revolts, but also of unrest among the peasantry. Though in Italy there were no rural uprisings on the scale of those in France or England, there were long-standing tensions between city and country that came to the fore during this period. City and country were physically very closely linked; one needed only to walk a few footsteps outside the walls of any city to see orchards and fields. Indeed, even within city limits it was not uncommon to observe livestock grazing, vegetables growing, and chickens clucking. Much of the land in the surrounding *contado* (country) was owned by city-dwellers. Although from the times of the earliest development of the communes there was a tendency for landed aristocracy to move into cities, where they became involved in mercantile and other business enterprises, they never thoroughly abandoned their rural estates. The prosperous urban elite always kept a foothold in the country, enjoying their villas for short getaways, as well as during extended summer holidays. However, more than mere vacation homes, the property

The Crises of the Fourteenth Century 35

on which these villas were located was usually working farms, producing significant quantities of grain, beans, olive oil, wine, fruits, and vegetables. The income, as well as the extra security that these rural holdings provided urban landlords during times of scarcity cannot be underestimated.

To keep these farms working, it was clearly not feasible for busy merchants or bankers to be constantly involved in the plowing, sowing, and harvesting of fields, so over time landlords and peasants worked out a system of sharecropping known as *mezzadria*. The term derives from the word *mezzo* (half); in the *mezzadria* system the landlord provided equipment and oxen, often lending money or seeds to the farmer, or *mezzadro*, who in exchange would give him half the harvest. Eventually *mezzadria* became the dominant model for farming in Italy, lasting through the twentieth century. Though the system could be mutually beneficial, the sharecroppers were often exploited and they resented their wealthy urban landlords.

"Motionless History" in the countryside

What was life like for the sharecropper? The story of Renaissance Italy is usually told in terms of urban developments, yet in the entire peninsula the number of people living in rural areas greatly outnumbered those living in cities. This was true not only in the south, but also in central and northern Italy; in Tuscany there were roughly three times as many peasants as city-dwellers during this period. Why is it, then, that one rarely hears about the peasants? For one thing, of course, the great cultural developments in art, architecture, letters, and science were produced in cities or court environments. Even merchants and artisans who lived in cities left behind documents that attest to their experience. However, since by and large peasants do not leave traces of their individual existence in the historical record, it is difficult to study them. Above all, historians like to observe changes in a society over time, pinpointing exact moments when ideas or values began to alter. In a sense, rural life can be said to have remained essentially unchanged for hundreds of years. French historian Emmanuel LeRoy Ladurrie coined the term "motionless history" to describe a world in which day-to-day existence is governed more by changes in the seasons than by political or cultural events.

Hard times in the *contado*

What can be said then about the life of rural people, who made up the vast majority of the population of the Italian Peninsula during this period? Decades of poor harvests had led to famines, driving many peasants to seek a living in the cities. There they joined the numerous urban poor who lived in crowded slums, working as manual laborers, prostitutes, and beggars. Though it is true that those who remained in the country did not fare as badly when the Black Death struck as did those in densely populated urban areas, nevertheless they experienced enormous hardship. Obligated to pay taxes

36   *The Crises of the Fourteenth Century*

and bound by the laws of the commune, inhabitants of the *contado* were not citizens of the city that controlled their region and were not entitled to many of the privileges that citizens enjoyed. When military crises occurred, it was the rural peasantry who were called upon to serve as foot soldiers; when cash was needed to fund those wars, their taxes were raised. Generally, city-dwellers looked upon the people in the *contado* as a resource to be exploited, like the beasts of burden that farmed their lands.

Considered ignorant, inferior, and often barely human by their urban counterparts, peasants would fall victim to crimes of violence committed by unscrupulous city-dwellers. Women were particularly vulnerable, and many instances of country girls raped by men from the city were recorded. On the other hand, people in the cities lived in fear of bandits who inhabited the remote mountainous hinterlands. Living essentially under no city's jurisdiction, these were people who lived mostly by hunting and harvesting chestnuts. Dante had referred to these mountain dwellers as "foul swine, more fit for acorns than food eaten by men." In short, city and country were bound together, but often eyed one another with suspicion and mistrust.

During the Black Death, the burden of supporting the cities fell especially heavily on those in the country, as communal governments squeezed the surrounding *contado* for all available resources. In the decades following, the countryside was ravaged by an equally devastating affliction. Bands of mercenary soldiers, known as *condottieri* (singular *condottiero*, from the contract or *condotta* that bound them to their employers) roamed the countryside. Though in the early days of the communes battles tended to be fought by citizen militias, by the fourteenth century most cities hired paid professionals to fight their wars for them. These soldiers of fortune were often foreigners, younger sons of noble families who were trained as knights but lacked the means to support themselves, so they took their military expertise on the road. Some rose to great prominence such as the Englishman Sir John Hawkwood (1320–1394 called "Giovanni Acuto" in the Italianized version of his name) who fought so valiantly for the city of Florence that his portrait is painted in a fresco by Paolo Uccello on the wall of the city's cathedral. With the advent of the Black Death, however, the need for their services dropped off, and marauding bands of unemployed soldiers continually plundered the countryside during the 1350s to 1360s, terrorizing the inhabitants.

An age of new men

For those who survived the Black Death, there were opportunities; some peasants were able to take advantage of the moment of social flux, becoming wealthy landowners. Others moved to the cities, accepting citizenship that was now being widely offered, as cities strove to repopulate. Likewise, because so many professionals had died during the epidemic, lawyers, notaries, doctors, priests, as well as artisans and craftsmen were

The Crises of the Fourteenth Century   37

in high demand. People who were uncertified or formerly ineligible were now called upon to step into these jobs. Guilds were forced to accept new members; laypeople carried out many tasks formerly reserved for priests. The people who stepped into these roles often brought with them a brand-new approach, invigorating their professions, leading historian David Herlihy to dub this an "age of new men." It has even been argued that, because there was a shortage of university professors, the new scholars who stepped in brought with them an entirely fresh approach, unseating medieval scholastic methods and opening the way for humanism (Chapter 3). This was also a time when, especially in response to crisis, many cities began to shift from the communal style of government to leadership by a single man, or signore. Already by 1300 many republics had given way to rule by a single lord, and by the end of the century, signorial, rather than republican government became the dominant political model on the peninsula (Chapter 6).

Painting in the early Trecento in Siena

Though the convulsions of the fourteenth century created opportunities for individuals in the professions and led to growth and the vigorous development of fields like medical science, law, and humanistic studies, the social upheaval, at least initially did not have a positive effect on art. Indeed, the century that began with the stunning new art of Giotto that seemed to herald the beginning of the Renaissance in painting was cut short by the disasters that befell Italy.

In the early part of the century in Florence there were painters such as Bernardo Daddi (active 1312–48) and Taddeo Gaddi (active 1328–66) who created works that were inspired by Giotto's naturalism. But it was in Siena that an original, especially dynamic school of painting was flourishing by the early 1340s. There, painters followed in the footsteps of the master Duccio di Buoninsegna (active 1278–1318), a contemporary of Giotto, who, however, developed his own highly distinctive manner. His style incorporates the older Byzantine style of painting, with formal poses and gold backgrounds, but throughout, Duccio's paintings are infused with vitality through innovative use of color and delicate human expression. Though the composition is traditional, naturalistic details, such as the lifelike angels surrounding the Virgin's throne in the *Rucellai Madonna* (Uffizi), enliven the painting. Each angel crouches near the seated Virgin, the folds of their subtly colored robes hanging gracefully over bent knees. Their faces respond alternately with sorrow, wonder, and concern to the affecting scene of mother and child who sit solemnly in the center. The emotion is powerful but muted. Though four of the six angels are kneeling in mid-air and the position of the throne is slightly askew, the viewer, entranced, tends to forget the unrealistic or supernatural elements of the painting.

In Duccio's masterpiece, the monumental *Maestà* (Museo dell'Opera del Duomo, Siena) begun in 1308, the Virgin Mary is regally enthroned, surrounded by a court of angels, saints, and martyrs. The city of Siena had always had a special devotion to the Virgin Mary, which intensified after the 1289 Battle of Montaperti: Sienese Ghibellines triumphed over Florentine Guelfs and they credited their victory to the Virgin. Duccio's massive panel, painted front and back with biblical scenes was carried in procession through the city of Siena on June 9, 1311 into the cathedral. Art enhanced both sacred and civic messages as the Sienese joyfully celebrated the glories of all three.

Simone Martini (c.1280–1344) and the brothers Ambrogio Lorenzetti (c.1290–1348) and Pietro Lorenzetti (c.1280–1348) all created works for the Palazzo Pubblico, or city hall of Siena. Like Duccio, Martini, in his *Maestà* (Palazzo Pubblico, Siena) fresco painted in 1315, grouped many figures around an enthroned Madonna and Child, yet he added visual depth to the tableau by the addition of a canopy, creating an illusion of perspective. Martini would travel to Assisi and Avignon, and his later works display an ever-increasing delicacy and gracefulness of line, demonstrated in his enchanting *Annunciation* (Uffizi, Figure 2.1).

Figure 2.1 Simone Martini, *Annunciation*, 1333, detail, Uffizi

A high point of this Sienese school was Ambrogio Lorenzetti's fresco cycle *Allegory of Good and Bad Government* (1338–40, Palazzo Pubblico, Siena) painted on the walls of the council chamber where the priors of Siena met (Figure 2.2). Intended to inspire the city fathers as they met to decide matters of state, on one wall Lorenzetti represents the effects of good government in the city; shopkeepers can be seen doing business, a teacher instructing his students, and young women freely dancing in the street. Beside the images of life in the city is a panorama of the effects of good government in the country. There are plentiful harvests and healthy peasants tending their well-fed livestock. In counterpoint to these cheerful images, on the opposite side the artist represents the damage wrought by bad government, portraying the city almost as a ghost town, its walls shattered, and a corpse lying in the foreground beside an angry group of men. In the *contado*, armed individuals roam a barren, apocalyptic landscape. The effect of the whole fresco cycle is the vigorous representation of the aspirations of a society, displaying the citizens' pride and absolute belief in republicanism as the ideal form of government.

Figure 2.2 Ambrogio Lorenzetti, *The Effects of Good Government*, 1338–40, Palazzo Pubblico, Siena

Art in the wake of the Black Death

Much of this vibrant artistic activity died out with the demise not only of artists themselves (of the above-mentioned artists, only Gaddi survived the

40   *The Crises of the Fourteenth Century*

Black Death), but of the patrons who commissioned their works. As a consequence, the latter half of the fourteenth century presents nothing like the flourishing, innovative works of the early Trecento. Even a cursory comparison of the works of painters like Orcagna (Andrea di Cione, 1308–1368) and Andrea da Firenze (Andrea Bonaiuti, active 1343–77) with works of artists of the previous generation reveal a more remote, less naturalistic style of painting. The works from this later period are much more formalistic and seemingly medieval both in subject matter and in treatment. There have been various explanations for this shift. It has been suggested that the tastes of the "new men" who now patronized art were more old-fashioned than those of their predecessors. Some art historians have maintained that the somber mood following the Black Death caused a turning back towards more traditional forms of artistic representation. Buffalmacco's macabre *Triumph of Death* fresco in the Camposanto in Pisa has been used as proof of the indelible impression left on art by the Black Death: it depicts young people playfully chatting in a garden while death mows down crowds of people, who are thrown into mass graves with decomposing bodies. These frescoes were considered a visual representation of the traumatic after-effects of the 1348 epidemic, until it was definitively proven that they were painted decades earlier.

There is no simple explanation for changes that came over the arts during this time, though it can be said that with one-half or more of the population dead from the epidemic, and an equal number of artists who lost their lives, those who managed to survive no longer created works of art within the lively, competitive atmosphere prior to the Black Death. Innovation in the arts depends largely on the stimulus that individuals receive from working with others, playing off their ideas, and experimenting with new ones, and this cannot occur in a vacuum.

Recovery and renewal

Nevertheless, these troubled years did ultimately have positive effects on art. Churches and religious orders were flooded with bequests, both from the dying, many of whom left all their money to the church, and from the living, who made pious donations in hopes of saving themselves from the pestilence or to aid their departed loved ones in the afterlife. Much of this money was spent on building new altars and chapels, all of which would need to be decorated. Paintings and sculpture were commissioned on an unprecedented scale, with a new emphasis on portraiture, especially as a way to remember the dead. Throughout Italy, large building projects that had begun at the end of the thirteenth century or beginning of the fourteenth and had been brought to an abrupt halt by the advent of the Black Death were suddenly being worked on again. The Duomo and Santa Croce in Florence, the cathedrals in Orvieto and Milan, all were impressive structures, which would

The Crises of the Fourteenth Century   41

now be carried to completion. This vast infusion of wealth into the church would impact succeeding generations of artists and would pave the way for the unprecedented flowering of the arts that would take place in fifteenth-century Italy.

Considerations: Just how calamitous was the fourteenth century?

While not denying the severity of conditions at the time, lately scholars have tended to ask just how "calamitous" was the fourteenth century? After all, what century has been without its toll of human suffering caused by disease? In addition to the 1917 Influenza and the 2019 Coronavirus pandemics, outbreaks of diseases such as smallpox, syphilis, typhoid, cholera, and AIDS have been responsible for millions of deaths that have devastated humanity. As for warfare, there has never been a generation that has not known the ravages of war. And if any century has to be singled out for the sheer loss of life due to military aggression, the twentieth century with its two world wars dwarfs all others; whilst in terms of climate change, scientists have determined that changes in today's climate are more dramatic than anything in recorded history.

What then should we make of the events of the 1300s? Regardless of our view in hindsight, contemporaries were awed by the relentlessness of the disasters that struck them. And it is impossible to deny the dramatic impact, especially of the Black Death, on Italian culture. There would be a very long pause before Masaccio would come along and take over where Giotto left off. Culture apparently does not always march forward, progressing from one momentous achievement to the next; sometimes there must be a pause, and a backward glance, before advances are made. And we must ask ourselves, is it really productive to try to quantify and compare human misery in this way? One thing is certain; the vigorous, resilient society described by Boccaccio emerged more dynamic than ever after the hardships of the fourteenth century: medical science would make advances, governments would coalesce, art would blossom, and shortly Italian humanists would revolutionize the way Europeans viewed the ancient world and themselves.

Sourcebook

Marco Polo, *Description of the World*
Sanitary Ordinances of Pistoia City Council, May 2, 1348
Boccaccio, *Decameron*, Introduction to Day IV
Nanni di Banco, *Sculptor's Workshop*, Orsanmichele, Florence

Further reading

Benedictow, Ole J. *The Black Death, 1346–1353: The Complete History*, Boydell Press, 2004.

42 The Crises of the Fourteenth Century

Cohn, Samuel Kline, Jr. *Popular Protest in Late-Medieval Europe: Italy, France and Flanders*, Manchester University Press, 2004.

Green, Monica. "The Four Black Deaths," in *The American Historical Review*, vol. 125, no. 5, December 2020, pp. 1601–31.

Grove, Jean. *Little Ice Ages: Ancient and Modern*, Routledge, 2004; orig. pub. 1988.

Hyman, Timothy. *Sienese Painting: The Art of a City-republic (1278–1477)*, Thames & Hudson, 2003.

Meiss, Millard. *Painting in Florence and Siena After the Black Death: The Arts, Religion and Society in the Mid-Fourteenth Century*, Princeton University Press, 1951.

Norman, Diana (Ed.). *Siena, Florence, and Padua: Art, Society, and Religion 1280–1400*, Yale University Press, in association with the Open University, 1995.

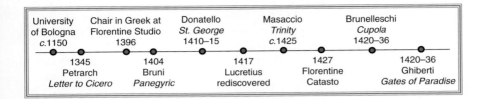

3 Back to the Future

Italian Humanists Recover the Classical Past

> The children should not wander about aimlessly, ignorant of letters due to an absence of teachers, rather under a teacher's rod they ought to succeed in attaining the glory of learning.
>
> City Council of Lucca, August 14, 1348

In August of 1348, while the Black Death was raging, a schoolteacher in the Tuscan town of Lucca wrote asking the city council to pay his salary; so many of his pupils had died that he was unable to support himself through his private wages. Surrounded by the dead and dying, it would have been understandable had the city council ignored the teacher's petition. Instead, the city fathers granted the request, agreeing to pay him three lire a month to continue teaching. The schoolchildren in Lucca may just have been repeating rote lessons of Latin, but this episode is indicative of an exciting, new emphasis on learning that grew out of the barren landscape of the fourteenth century. Rather than fall back on fear and superstition, citizens of Italian communes responded to the crisis with vibrant intellectual activity, seeking solutions to their troubles through a new learning. A dynamic cultural movement was blossoming in the cities of Italy, which eventually spread throughout all of Europe and revolutionized society, inspiring people to reshape their governments, to create startling new art, and to reinvent themselves.

This movement has come to be called humanism. The Renaissance, the era this book covers, means literally "rebirth" and refers to the rebirth of antiquity introduced by the humanists. Humanists were literary scholars who recognized the elegant style of the ancient Roman authors and consciously imitated them

DOI: 10.4324/9781003270362-3

44 *Back to the Future*

in their own Latin writings. The process began in the Latin language in the fourteenth century and later in Greek when Italian humanists began to study that language in the following century. But they went further than merely imitating the style of writing. Humanists were deeply interested in the content of classical writings as well. Amidst the suffering and death of the fourteenth century, Italians were looking for answers beyond those provided by the church. While not rejecting Christian doctrine on the afterlife, the survivors focused on improving peoples' lives here, in this world, supplementing Christian ethical ideas with those of the ancients. As Italian citizens began to think about modeling their own lives on those of ancient pagan philosophers, they began to develop an ethical structure for society, distinct from that offered by religion. Many humanists began to view their communes as republics similar to those of Ancient Greece and Rome and began to develop theories about why an elected government was superior to all other political systems. Artists, sculptors, and architects were also affected by this admiration for antiquity and began to imitate classical models. Rather than being a sterile act of copying, however, all this imitation led to cultural innovation, a burst of creative energy that in all of history has never been surpassed.

Humanism, a cultural revolution led by notaries

Why did humanism begin in Italy rather than elsewhere? Why at this time in history and in this place did rediscovery of antiquity, not only occur, but have meaning in peoples' lives? In contrast to much of Europe, which at the time was predominantly rural, communal Italy was full of cities, as we have seen. In this document-based society there was a demand for secretaries to record minutes of meetings; lawyers to argue cases before the civil courts; and above all, notaries to draft nuptial agreements, wills, business contracts, sales of land, and to write official letters. These official legal documents had to be written in Latin, and thus in the thirteenth and fourteenth centuries Italian cities began to have large numbers of professionals trained in both Latin and law. The number of notaries in particular is impressive: in Florence in 1280 the Judges and Notaries' Guild had 65 judges and 374 notaries, in 1338 there were 66 judges and 880 notaries. Such a large segment of the lay population educated in Latin was rare in Europe at the time. Throughout the rest of the continent, Latin education, indeed learning of any kind, was generally limited to the clergy. As we shall see, the perspectives that educated laypeople such as notaries brought to the reading of classical authors was very different from those of priests or monks.

Among the earliest humanists were a group of notaries from the city of Padua, including poets Lovato Lovati (*c.*1240–1309) and Albertino Mussato (1261–1329), the first writers since antiquity to compose poetry in classical Latin. Innovative thinkers emerged from this circle, such as the political theorist Marsilius of Padua (Chapter 1). A portion of the legal training for their profession involved the study of Roman law. The Justinianic Code, named after the Emperor Justinian who had ancient Roman law codified in 529 CE, became the basis for legal studies in Italy. Since the early thirteenth century, the University of Bologna was recognized throughout Europe as the premier institution for study of law. The need to reconcile the rights of the communes with those of the Emperor originally drove this great emphasis on law.[1]

However, while studying Roman Law, these notary–scholars developed interests far beyond what was provided in the academic environment of their day. Their interests in the classics, sparked by their study of Latin, developed along entirely different lines than their clerical predecessors. Reading the works of ancient poets, orators, and historians on their own, they rebelled against the teaching in the universities, and it is not mere coincidence that Florence, the city that came to be most identified with humanism, had no major university. Founded in 1321, the Florentine Studio, as it was called, was constantly beset by problems, and it never rivaled the universities of Bologna or Padua. The *studia humanitatis* (study of the humanities) emphasizing literature and history grew up outside of the universities and came to challenge the accepted medieval scholastic curriculum taught in such institutions.

The medieval scholastic heritage

> We are like dwarves perched on the shoulders of giants; thus, we can see more and farther than they, not because our vision is more acute, or our capacities greater, but because we are carried up and raised to greater heights.

With these words, Bernard of Chartres, a French philosopher and theologian at the cathedral school in Chartres during the early twelfth century, acknowledged the debt that medieval scholars owed to the ancients. Only by being "perched on the shoulders" of great thinkers of antiquity like Aristotle and Plato could human knowledge progress. Contrary to popular belief, the Middle Ages were not a time of ignorance. Medieval people did not, in the historian Jakob Burckhardt's words, "lay dreaming or half-awake beneath a common veil," to be awakened only when the Renaissance brought the light of learning to Europe.[2] It is largely because of generations of medieval monks and nuns bent over their writing desks in their *scriptoria* (writing workshops) painstakingly copying and lovingly decorating precious Latin manuscripts that so much of classical antiquity survived. In the twelfth century, after the Commercial Revolution had begun, and once cities began to grow and flourish, the great European universities at Bologna, Paris, and Oxford were

---

1 The body of Roman civil law known as the *Corpus Iuris Civilis* was first applied in Medieval Italy in 1076 in the "Placito di Marturi," a legal case initiated by Beatrice of Tuscany, mother of the Countess Matilda.

2 Jacob Burckhardt (1818–1897) was the author of *The Civilization of the Renaissance in Italy* (1860), a highly influential work, which for more than a century shaped historians' thinking about the period.

46 *Back to the Future*

founded. Within the medieval scholastic system, as it was called, students not only pored over the Bible and works of the Church Fathers, but also studied classical texts. The students had to be fluent in Latin, as all lectures and texts were in that language; just as today scholarly publications and information on the internet are predominantly in English, Latin was then the common language for learned people across Europe. By the fourteenth century the scholastic system was widespread and functioned well, churning out educated professionals throughout Europe.

Italian humanists restore ancient texts

Renaissance humanists were not the first to recognize the value of the ancients. Dante, a generation earlier, had enormous reverence especially for the poets of classical antiquity. Not only did he select Virgil as his poetic mentor and guide through the afterlife, everywhere in the *Comedy* Dante cites classical history and mythology, describing with special tenderness the great philosophers and poets of antiquity who dwell in the noble castle of Limbo (*Inferno* IV). Most important, the poem's entire structure is shaped largely on moral principles from Aristotle's *Nicomachean Ethics*. But there was an important difference in how Renaissance and medieval scholars viewed the writings of the ancients. In the Middle Ages—and in this regard, Dante is very medieval—theology was known as the Queen of the Sciences; the ultimate purpose of the study of any subject was to praise and exalt God. Writers drew upon ancient texts for ideas that could be grafted onto Christian theology, often distorting those ideas in the process. The practice of superimposing one culture on another is known as syncretism, as in the way Dante substitutes the name of the Greek god "Jove" for the Christian "God." Medieval scholars often merged pagan and Christian world views, overlooking any inconsistencies that could not be reconciled. Humanists recognized the need to view the classical world within its historical context and to accept the ancients on their own terms.

Free of university constraints, the humanists brought a radically new approach to the classical authors. Like restorers removing yellowed varnish from antique furniture, they stripped away layers of accumulated medieval interpretations, in order to reveal the original works in all their freshness and vigor. They scoffed at the clumsy grammar and syntax of medieval writers of Latin, and in their quest for perfect Latin style the humanists began to discover how the Latin language grew and evolved over time. The field they pioneered is known as philology, which shows how the uses and meanings of words have changed in specific historical contexts and under precise conditions. To get at the meanings of texts, however, first they had to assemble accurate editions of the classical authors' works. Medieval scribes, over centuries of copying manuscripts had made mistakes, which were often copied and recopied. By comparing various versions, humanists were able to assemble purer editions of known texts, and in the process of their research discovered "new" texts from antiquity. While digging through collections of manuscripts in remote monastic libraries, the humanists uncovered many ancient works that had been believed to be lost, adding enormously to our knowledge of the ancient world.

The life of Petrarch, a passionate humanist

> Your letters I sought for long and diligently; and finally, where I least expected it, I found them. At once I read them, over and over, with the utmost eagerness. And as I read, I seemed to hear your bodily voice, O Marcus Tullius, saying many things, uttering many lamentations, ranging through many phases of thought and feeling.
>
> Petrarch, *Lettter to Cicero* June 16, 1345

These words were written by the man whose life and literary activities best embody this early phase of humanism, Francesco Petrarca (1304–1374), or as he preferred to be called, in the Latinized version of his name, Petrarch. He wrote these words in one of his letters to the ancient Roman author Marcus Tullius Cicero (106–143 BCE). Petrarch proceeds to chide the ancient Roman orator as one would a dear friend who has made a serious mistake. "What insanity led you to hurl yourself upon Antony?" writes Petrarch, as if just yesterday his friend Cicero had insulted Marc Antony, setting in motion events that would lead to his conviction and death. The tone of these letters may appear odd or stilted to us today, and the very idea of "corresponding" with someone who has been dead for centuries seems absurd. However, in a sense Petrarch was responding to a fresh work of Cicero's—the letter *Ad Atticum* had been lost since antiquity—and he himself had only just discovered it several years before. Petrarch speaks for many humanists of his generation when he declares to "his friend" Cicero, "You, we freely acknowledge, are the leader who marshals us; yours are the words of encouragement that sustain us; yours is the light that illumines the path before us."

Petrarch was born in Arezzo, the son of a Florentine notary named Ser Petracco who had been exiled along with Dante in 1302. He grew up in Pisa, and moved to Avignon when his father went to work there in 1312. In Provence the boy studied with a notary from the Tuscan town of Prato. In 1316 he began to study law in Montpellier and later went on to attend the University of Bologna. However, when his father died in 1326 Petrarch decided to give up law, taking up minor church orders[3] to pursue a career in letters. Woven together in his life are the many familiar strands that contributed to humanist culture: the connection with Florence, the theme

---

3 Petrarch was not a priest; taking "minor orders" in the Catholic Church entitled a cleric to perform certain ecclesiastical rituals, without being bound to celibacy, and most important from a financial point of view, the individual was entitled to receive an income from church benefices. During Petrarch's time this was a common career path for educated men.

of exile, an interest in antiquarianism, book collecting, exposure to notarial culture and immersion in legal studies, as well as his rejection of a career in law with its traditional scholastic education. Despite these elements that he shared with other Italian humanists, Petrarch was atypical in one important aspect. Though his family was Florentine and he would ennoble the Florentine dialect by using it to write some of the most passionate verse ever written, Petrarch actually spent very little time in Florence, or indeed in any one part of Italy. Much of his life was spent traveling and living abroad.

Petrarch, recognized as exceptional from an early age, was an unusually brilliant and well-spoken young man. In addition, he had the good fortune to attract a series of wealthy and powerful patrons to sponsor his literary activities. In his *Letter to Posterity* Petrarch tells us—for he wrote not only back to people in the past, but also forward to those in the future—about himself as a youth:

> In my prime I was blessed with a quick and active body, although not exceptionally strong; and while I do not lay claim to remarkable personal beauty, I was comely enough in my best days. I was possessed of a clear complexion, between light and dark, lively eyes, and for long years a keen vision, which however deserted me, contrary to my hopes, after I reached my sixtieth birthday, and forced me, to my great annoyance, to resort to glasses.

"Carried away by the fire of youth ..."

After giving up his legal studies and returning to Avignon, the handsome young Petrarch, still without need of eyeglasses, found two things: an employer, Cardinal Giovanni Colonna, and his lifelong love, Laura. Passionate by nature, Petrarch tells us that he was often "carried away by the fire of youth or by my ardent temperament," and he fell in love with Laura at first sight. However, his amorous passion was matched, if not exceeded, by his appetite for literary glory. During these years he began a monumental Latin epic, modeled on Virgil's *Aeneid*, and wrote many shorter Latin works, especially letters. Formally composed literary set pieces, these letters, or epistles as they are more appropriately called, were copied and re-copied, circulating all over Europe.

Perhaps his most well-known letter is *The Ascent of Mount Ventoux* (1336), in which Petrarch tells of how in his youthful exuberance he was inspired to climb the highest peak near his home in southern France and achieved a spiritual epiphany. Through works such as the *Ascent of Mount Ventoux*, Petrarch, not yet forty years old, had become famous. In his *Letter to Posterity*, Petrarch makes it seem as if he was taken unawares when he was offered the highest poetic award, to be crowned poet laureate. He actually had lobbied for years for this prize. After he was examined by

Robert of Anjou, king of Naples—an exam that he obviously passed with honors—in 1341 Petrarch was crowned in Rome like the ancient god of poetry, Apollo with branches of laurel (the word "laureate" derives from the word "laurel"). In that same letter, Petrarch, dispenses with false modesty to inform us that "this royal estimate was, indeed, quite in accord with that of many others, and especially with my own." He had become a celebrity. Now well known as a man of letters, Petrarch never lacked for patrons, and throughout his career he was sent on diplomatic missions to represent them.

Petrarch's interiority: It's all about "me"

During the 1340s Petrarch continued writing Latin prose, studying the classics—he personally owned the largest library in Europe at this time—until he, like everyone else on the continent, was left desolate by the Black Death. In another epistle, appropriately titled *Ad se ipsum* (*To Himself*), Petrarch describes his response to the horrors of the disease in terms that are almost entirely subjective:

> O what has come over me? Where are the violent fates pushing me back to? I see passing by, in headlong flight, time which makes the world a fleeting place. I observe about me dying throngs of both young and old, and nowhere is there a refuge.

He considers with sadness his loved ones who have died:

> The last hour of life comes to mind, and, obliged to recollect my misfortunes, I recall the flocks of dear ones who have departed, and the conversations of friends, the sweet faces, which suddenly vanished.

But most of all, the sight of so much death forces Petrarch to think with terror of his own mortality:

> Just thinking of these things, I confess I am frightened and I see before me the snares of imminent death. For where could I hide my head, when neither the sea nor the land nor the rocks full of dark caves show themselves to the one who flees, because death, rushing impetuously into even safe hiding-places, overcomes all things.

Though he appears excessively self-centered, by exposing the fears and yearnings of his own soul, Petrarch draws the reader closer to him. Petrarch's literary self-awareness is known as interiority and it was something brand new at the time. It was unheard of for an individual to refract the joys and sorrows of the human experience so starkly through the lens of his own emotions.

50   *Back to the Future*

Scattered Rhymes

Nowhere is Petrarch's quality of interiority more evident than in his vernacular poems. Although Petrarch wrote thousands of pages of verse and prose in Latin (over 90% of his works) he also composed around 10,000 lines of Italian verse. The most well known of these are gathered in a collection sometimes referred to as *Rime sparse* (Scattered Rhymes), the *Rerum vulgarium fragmenta* (Fragments of Vernacular Works), or most often as the *Canzoniere* (Songbook). Petrarch worked on this collection of poetry over the course of his entire life. The poems are divided into those written before the death of Laura during the Black Death in 1348 and those written afterward. In all, there are 366 poems, of which 317 are sonnets.

Though Petrarch did not invent the sonnet form, which originated in the thirteenth century among notary–poets in Sicily (Chapter 7), he raised it to such a level of prominence that it caught on everywhere in Europe. Literary scholar Stephen Minta has called the sonnet "the single most important Italian contribution to the development of the European lyric," and Petrarch was its master. His poetic style inspired generations of Spanish, French, even English poets after him, many of whom were known as *petrarchisti* (Petrarchans).

So what was so new about Petrarch's poetry that it revolutionized the European vernacular lyric tradition? Let us look at one of his sonnets:

> Peace I find not, yet I cannot wage war
> I fear and hope; I burn and yet I freeze
> I soar above the heavens and lay prostrate on earth
> I grasp nothing, yet embrace the entire world
> The one who imprisons me neither opens nor locks me in
> Neither holding me, nor loosening my bonds;
> Love does not kill me, nor does he release me,
> He neither desires that I live, nor removes me from these troubles.
> I see without eyes, and without a tongue I scream;
> And I yearn to perish, and beg for help,
> Hating myself, while loving another.
> I feed on pain, while weeping I laugh,
> Equally displeasing to me are both death and life:
> I am in this state, my lady, because of you.

This poem demonstrates some of Petrarch's most characteristic motifs. He loves to use contradictions (anti-thesis) to describe the extreme psychological conditions of the lover: he sees without eyes, screams without a tongue, and most famously of all, burns and freezes at the same time. The extreme cruelty of the situation is represented by images of bondage and a prison, with doors and locks shutting the lover away. Yet while suffering such agonies, he is also nourished ("I feed on pain") and cheered ("while weeping I laugh"). The cause of all this suffering, the lady herself, only appears at the very end of the poem; the most important element in Petrarch's love poetry is not Laura, who is the object of his love. He describes her in vague, idealized terms; for example, her golden hair stirring in the breeze as he compares her to a mythological nymph or a Christian angel. Rather, the subject of Petrarch's poetry is love itself, or more precisely, the effects that love has on the poet. All nature mirrors and responds to the poet's interior state (pathetic fallacy); the storms at sea torment him, while the delightful shade of a laurel tree comforts him.

There were many imitators of Petrarch's style of poetry, and even those who chose to break away are often termed anti-Petrarchan because of their conscious attempt to avoid his influence. In one of his sonnets, William Shakespeare (1564–1616) openly mocks Petrarchan style. Petrarch had written: "Her golden hair was loosened in the breeze, / Swirling in a thousand sweet knots, / And lovely sunlight burned beyond measure in her beautiful eyes," which the English poet parodies: "My mistress' eyes are nothing like the sun / Coral is far more red than her lips' red / If snow be white, why then her breasts are dun / If hairs be wires, black wires grow on her head." Even in modern times it is difficult to avoid Petrarchan motifs, as the lyrics from a 1957 Elvis Presley song demonstrate: "Ah well bless my soul / What's wrong with me? / I'm itching like a man on a fuzzy tree / My friends say I'm actin' wild as a bug / I'm in love I'm all shook up." Petrarch indeed cast a long shadow throughout the Renaissance and beyond.

An "educational surge" in Italian cities

Petrarch's excellence in both Latin and the Florentine vernacular points to yet another reason that humanism took off in Florence. There was a crucial link between education in the vernacular and the origins of Florentine humanism. Ironically, the stage was set there for the Renaissance rediscovery of the classics through a heavy emphasis not on Latin, but rather on vernacular learning. Throughout the Italian cities during this period, education was given a high priority. Though few records are available for the preceding century, by the fourteenth century, all over Italy, students were learning to read and write, a phenomenon historian Paul Grendler has defined as an "educational surge." Public schools that provided free education to the children of taxpayers began to sprout up all over the peninsula (Map 3.1). These schools mostly concentrated on teaching Latin grammar using traditional methods and provided students with the skills they would need for professional careers.

Oddly enough, the exceptions to this rule were Florence and Venice, the two economic powerhouses of Renaissance Italy. Neither of these two prosperous mercantile cities provided free public education to their populaces. This was partially because the elite preferred to arrange private instruction for their children, but it was also because the upwardly mobile businessmen of these cities preferred a more practical education than the study of Latin

52 *Back to the Future*

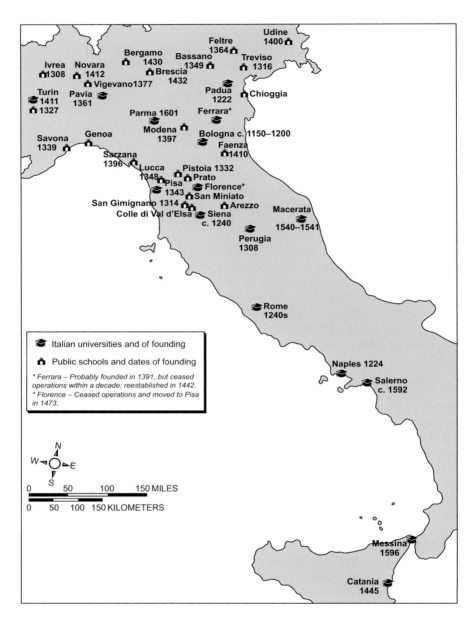

Map 3.1 Education in Renaissance Italy

grammar. To a merchant it was more important that his son could balance the account books than master Latin declensions. Italian merchants had used sophisticated accounting methods such as double-entry bookkeeping since the thirteenth century, and as can be imagined, the study of arithmetic was an educational priority to businessmen. Boys were sent at an early age to so-called abacus schools where they learned the basics of computation. Unlike grammar schools, which taught Latin grammar using Latin textbooks, Florentine abacus lessons were taught in the local vernacular using vernacular texts. Though Italian was not officially recognized or formally taught as a language at the time, businessmen with their eyes on the bottom line were increasingly having their sons skip Latin, and having them educated in the *volgare* instead. A teaching contract drawn up in Florence in 1313 demonstrates the practical focus of education there. In this document the teacher commits himself to instructing his pupil "how to be able to read and write all his letters and to do his figures so that he would know enough to work in an apothecary's workshop."

The result of this practical approach to education in Florence was a more, rather than a less, educated populace. While the overall elementary adult vernacular literacy rates throughout Europe at the time have been calculated to be around 5% of the population, (with higher rates in cities than in rural areas), in Florence the adult-male literacy rate was an astounding 69–80% by the fifteenth century, with women's literacy close to the same. The chronicler Giovanni Villani wrote toward the end of the 1330s that in Florence from "8,000 to 10,000 boys and girls are learning to read." By 1427, when the Florentine Catasto (graduated income tax) was introduced, and the head of every household was required to fill out a precise accounting of all the family's assets, four out of five Florentines filled this out in their own hand.

The flowering of Florentine vernacular culture

Vernacular literacy was more than a by-product of instruction in the abacus schools, however. In Florentine merchant culture the ability to read and write in a commonly understood, spoken language was crucial. A Florentine merchant or banker living in London would write home frequently. If the price of wool rose, if the king placed an embargo on foreign imports, if a galley was sunk in a tempest, or pirates raided one of their ships, he had to describe all of this in writing. Based on such communications, the agent would receive detailed instructions from the main office on how to proceed with investments, transfers of funds, and so on. This type of detailed written report called for more than a passing ability to handle pen and paper; the success or failure of business enterprises depended on exchanging subtle nuances of information. To give an idea of how much writing went on, a collection of business records of one merchant from the town of Prato between the years 1384 to 1411 includes 125,549 commercial letters, 8,049 personal letters, and including

54 *Back to the Future*

miscellaneous correspondence, the number reaches 152,648 letters, covering approximately 600,000 pages.

The result of the Florentine emphasis on reading and writing *volgare* is that the Florentine vernacular became an ever more rich and expressive language. Florentines did not limit themselves to business correspondence; they voraciously read vernacular stories of saints' lives, poetry, chivalric romances, sermons, city chronicles, and anything they could get their hands on. And they wrote as well; not only did they compose poems and stories, but they kept diaries—over 500 Florentine *ricordi* (memoirs) written during the fourteenth and fifteenth centuries exist today. In these diaries, private Florentine citizens record the ups and downs of their businesses, marriages, the births and deaths of family members, and so on, while revealing a fascination with language. One such memoirist, Giovanni Morelli, in his grief at the death of his sister Mea, recalls her hands that "were like ivory, so well made that they seemed to have been painted by the hand of Giotto." The sensitivity to Florentine vernacular and grasp of its expressive potential is a current that runs through the Italian Renaissance. The *volgare* runs parallel to humanist interest in the classics, and as we will see, there will be rich exchanges between Latin and vernacular literary cultures.

Rhetoric: How to speak with strength, impetuosity, and grace

We have seen why, for practical concerns of business, it was important for Florentines to master the vernacular, but there was yet another crucial reason to be literate—to participate in government. At this time in most of Europe the noble ruling class had little need to read or write in any language, and indeed many were illiterate, content to have scribes write for them and affix their seal to decrees, contracts, or testaments; the peasants who farmed their lands could not read or write at all. However, to participate in their collective city government, Florentine citizens had to be able not only to read and write, but to speak well. The new humanist education, offered mostly by notaries moonlighting as teachers, had a very practical application in that it taught the ancient art of rhetoric. Florentines, even those who knew little or no Latin, readily understood the practical value of such instruction. Brunetto Latini (*c.*1220–1294), whom Dante refers to in the *Inferno* as his teacher, had written a work on rhetoric widely read in the vernacular, and there were dozens of other Tuscan adaptations of classical works on oratory that were popularly studied.

Today the practice of rhetoric seems an obscure or even shady endeavor; the term carries a negative connotation. We say for instance: "I don't trust that politician—his speeches are nothing but rhetoric." Rhetoric has come to be viewed as a kind of underhanded trick, but originally the aim of rhetoric was an exalted one. The Roman advocate Quintilian (Marcus Fabius Quintilianus *c.*35–*c.*100 CE) wrote: "The orator's duty is not merely to instruct, but also to move and delight his audience; and to succeed in doing this he needs strength, impetuosity and grace as well." These skills—strength, impetuosity, and grace—were precisely the ones needed to survive in communal Italy. To citizens of Italian republics riven by civic antagonism, good public speaking was crucial to reaching consensus; those who could speak well and persuasively could reap rich political rewards. Conversely, those who failed to persuade could end up exiled or worse. Rhetoric could be a life or death issue to them, as it had been for the orator Cicero who was executed for his outspoken criticism of Mark Antony. Afterward, Cicero's head and hands were cut off and mounted on the speaker's rostrum in the Roman Senate. Florentines needed no convincing that rhetoric was a vital skill to succeed in a career in the public sphere.

The generation after Petrarch: Salutati, Bruni, and civic humanism

Although he grew up abroad and spent most of his life far from Florence, Petrarch retained close ties with the city that had exiled his father. One of his closest friends there was Giovanni Boccaccio. For years before they actually met, the two kept up a lively correspondence, developing a lifelong friendship. Boccaccio frankly adored Petrarch, referring to himself in one of those letters as "the most insignificant of your disciples." It was not until 1350 that they first met face to face, and by that time Boccaccio was regarded as the leader of the Florentine literary scene. Boccaccio managed to arrange a post for his friend with the Florentine university that was just being formed, but Petrarch did not accept it. Rather than be employed by a tumultuous republican government, such as the one that had exiled his father, Petrarch chose instead to work for "tyrants," the Visconti lords of Milan (Chapter 6), where he remained for the next eight years. He felt that the work was more steady; there was no chance of a new regime upsetting his appointment; and with fewer demands on him, the scholar would be able to study in quiet, master of his own time.

While Petrarch was greatly admired in Florence, choice of a life of quiet study over civic involvement was not approved by all humanists. The tide was beginning to turn in the long-standing debate over which was better, the *vita contemplativa* (contemplative life) or the *vita activa* (active life). Throughout the Middle Ages the quiet life of contemplation was generally held to be more virtuous and appropriate to a thoughtful person. The reclusive life of a monk absorbed in prayer had been universally esteemed, while the busy life of a merchant, city councilman, or notary was looked down upon. Now humanists would change all that, raising the service of one's republic to among the noblest of occupations.

Whereas Petrarch had criticized his hero Cicero for dirtying his hands in politics, many humanists of the next generation, such as Coluccio Salutati (1331–1406) felt it an honor to participate in the political sphere. Salutati was born in the village of Stignano, his father having been exiled when he was an infant. He was educated and worked as a notary for many years, then was employed as secretary for various communes. In 1375 Florence asked Salutati to serve as chancellor of the Republic, a job that he held for the rest of his life. This position was one of the most prestigious in the city, as the chancellor was responsible for writing official letters within Florence, to neighboring Italian states, to the Papacy, and to foreign governments. These letters had to be composed in elegant language, some in vernacular, some in Latin, depending on the context. For example, in a letter to the city of Ancona, Salutati urges them to take arms: "Do you wish to always remain in shadowy servitude? Do you consider not, oh most excellent men, how sweet liberty is?" Salutati's elegant letters brought him fame throughout Europe, and his well-paid job gave him the ability to collect a sizeable library. Soon, largely because of Salutati's cultural preeminence, humanist scholars were converging upon Florence.

It was Salutati who arranged in 1396 to give Emmanuel Chrysoloras (1350–1415) a ten-year appointment teaching Greek at the Florentine Studio. Up until this point, recovering the classics involved reading Latin works, or Greek writings translated into Latin, sometimes by way of Arabic, but European scholars had very little direct access to the Greek language. All this was about to change dramatically, and the study of ancient Greek in Florence would soon make it the center of an exciting new school of thought known as Florentine Platonism (Chapter 9). Salutati's example inspired the younger generation of humanists, including Niccolò Niccoli (1364–1437), who used his private wealth to travel throughout Europe hunting down classical manuscripts. The humanist booklover uncovered over 800 volumes—and bankrupted himself in the process. Poggio Bracciolini (1380–1459), a friend of Niccoli, worked as papal secretary, and later, he too became chancellor of Florence. In his travels, Poggio also discovered many lost classical texts in monasteries. During the century between Petrarch's earliest discoveries of Cicero's letters, and Poggio's last discoveries, most of the texts that would be recovered from the ancient world had been found; and they first reappeared in Italy (Table 3.1).

The leader among the generation of Florentine scholars inspired by Salutati was Leonardo Bruni (1370–1444). Originally trained in law, Bruni had a masterly command of Latin and threw himself into the study of Greek, producing translations of Xenophon and Aristotle. A disciple of Salutati who also went on to serve as chancellor, Bruni shared Salutati's admiration for the values of ancient Rome, studying its history to learn how human affairs should be conducted. Many humanists in Florence began to view their republic as a reflection, or continuation of the ancient Roman Republic. They regarded Julius Caesar as a tyrant, whose intention to make himself emperor betrayed the liberty of the Roman people. The Florentine civic humanists, as they are known, championed liberty and believed that their learning was most nobly employed in the service of their own present-day republic.

Back to the Future 57

Table 3.1 Partial list of ancient texts and dates when they appear in Italy

Date	Ancient texts
1400	Homer *Odyssey*; Demosthenes *Orations*; Isocrates *Orations*; Plutarch *Lives*; Thucydides *History of the Peloponnesian War*
1402	Aristotle *On the Soul*
1405	Plato *Gorgias, Cratylus, Phaedo*; Ptolemy *The Geography*
1407	Aristotle *Physics*
1408	Aristophanes *Plutus, The Clouds, The Frogs*
1413	Demosthenes *On the Crown, Philippics I* and *II, On the Peace*; Sophocles *Ajax, Electra, Oedipus Rex*; Euripides *Hecuba, Orestes, Phoenissae*
1415	Aristotle *On the Parts of Animals, On the Universe*; Lucian *Dialogues of the Gods*
1416	Aristotle *Nicomachean Ethics*; Diogenes Laertius *Lives of the Philosophers*
1417	Lucretius *On the Nature of Things*; Philostratus *The Life of Apollonius of Tyana*
1418	Plato *Protagorus*
1419	Aristotle *Economics*
1421	Aristarchus *Commentary on the Iliad*; Dio Cassius *Roman History*; Herodotus *Histories*
1421	Polybius *Histories*; Theophrastus *Opuscula*
1423	Plato *Apology, Crito, Phaedrus*; Apollonius Rhodius *Argonautica*; Callimachus *Hymns*; Hesiod *Theogony, Works and Days*; Pindar *Odes*; Theocritus *Idylls*
1424	Diodorus Siculus *Historical Library*; Dionysus of Halicarnassus *Attic Lexicon*; Hephaestion *Manual on Metrical Verse*; *Homeric Hymns*; Plato *Republic*; Plotinus *Complete Works*; Xenophon *Oeconomicus*
1425	Aristotle *Rhetoric*; Homer *Illiad*; Aeschylus *Prometheus, Persians, Seven Against Thebes*; Pindar *Complete Works*; Hermogenes *Rhetorical Exercises*
1427	Hippocrates *Letters*
1433	Galen *Method of Medicine*; Ptolemy *Harmonics*
1436	Euripides *Medea, Alcestis, Andromache, Rhesus*
1438	Aristotle *Politics*
1440	Ptolemy *On Astrology*
1454	Plato *Symposium*; Pausanius *Description of Greece*; Aratus *Phaenomena*
1455	Aristides Rhetorica; Aristotle *Logic*; Dioscorides *On Medical Material*; Diophantus *Mathematics*; Euclid *Elements*; Heliodorus *Ethiopian Stories*; Ptolemy *Almagest*
1460	Plato *Timaeus*
1464	Callimachus *Hymns*
1468	Archimedes *Various Works on Geometry*; Josephus *The Jewish War*; Longinus *On the Sublime*; Strabo *Geography*
1480	Euripides *Iphigenia, Bacchae, Cyclops, Electra*
1489	Epictetus *Enchiridion*
1490	Solon *Verses*; Theognis *Elegies*

Source: data abridged and selected, taken from R. R. Bolgar, *The Classical Heritage and Its Beneficiaries*, London, Cambridge University Press, 1954/1973, pp. 455–505.

Women and humanism

Although many girls in Florence learned to read and write, it was mostly in the vernacular; they hardly ever studied Latin. In the Italian republics humanism was closely linked to public life, from which women were almost entirely excluded. Forbidden from even setting foot in Florence's Palazzo dei Priori, the seat of government, much less holding public office or serving as chancellor, women, it was believed, had no need for a humanist education (Chapter 5). This did not mean there were no women who excelled in humanist studies, but they were mostly women from wealthy or noble backgrounds, often with family members who supported and guided their studies at home.

There was for instance, Costanza Varano (1428–1447) whose grandmother Battista Montefeltro Malatesta (1383–1450) was accomplished in humanist studies. The sisters Isotta (1418–1466) and Ginevra Nogarola (1417–1464) from Verona followed in the footsteps of their learned aunt Angela Nogarola (c.1360–c.1436), an author of Latin verse. Both sisters excelled in Greek and Latin and corresponded with members of Guarino Guarini's humanist circle. While her brothers were sent to study at a prestigious humanist school, Brescian humanist Laura Cereta (1469–1499) learned her Latin with a nun in a convent. Cassandra Fedele (1465–1558) from Venice, also learned Latin from a nun, and went on to study Greek, rhetoric, history, philosophy, and theology with the learned Servite monk and astronomer Gasparino Borro.

These female humanists wrote eloquent Latin letters, poems, and orations that circulated widely. The orations, or speeches, which these learned women often delivered publicly before university rectors, popes, doges and other rulers, brought them fame. Many of them took advantage of their celebrity to draw attention to the inequalities suffered by women, especially with regard to education, adding significant contributions to the *querelle des femmes* debate (Chapter 12).

Humanism, guilds, and the arts in quattrocento Florence

Humanism must be viewed within its social context, as we have seen in the case of female scholars. Similarly, Florentine artists did not live in a bubble. By the beginning of the Quattrocento (fifteenth century) the humanists' rediscovery of the classical world was being reflected in the visual arts, in sculpture, architecture, and painting. It is not always easy or appropriate to draw direct lines from developments in literature or philosophy to the visual arts, but the early Quattrocento in Florence was one of those moments in history where scholars, poets, sculptors, architects, and painters were inspired by a common source; they in turn inspired one another, creating a new cultural ideal. As the most talented Italian artists and artisans flocked to the wealthy city of Florence looking for commissions, the new aesthetic grew rapidly.

The civic spirit promoted by Florentine humanists was reflected in the public works of art and architecture in the city. A great number were carried out under the supervision of the major guilds in the first three decades of the fifteenth century. The government assigned a project to a particular guild, which then established a committee, known as an *opera* (from the Latin for "work") and the members of these committees were known as *operai*. The *operai* oversaw the allocation of funds, made payments to contractors, and very importantly, selected painters, sculptors, masons, and others who would be able to project this glorious image of the city.

And during this same time, with the support of public and private patronage, the role of the artist began to evolve. When the painter Cennino Cennini (*c*.1370–*c*.1440) first wrote his *Il Libro dell'arte* around the beginning of the century, the status of the artist was that of a skilled craftsman, indeed the title is generally translated as *The Craftsman's Handbook*. By the end of the century artists would come to be recognized for the greatness of their innovations and the originality of their minds; four Florentine trailblazers—Ghiberti, Donatello, Brunelleschi, and Masaccio—led the way.

Ghiberti's gilded *Gates of Paradise*

The Opera of the Calimala Guild, which had been responsible for works on the Baptistry of San Giovanni since the twelfth century, in 1401 announced a competition for a set of modeled bronze panels in high relief, complementing those made by Andrea Pisano almost a century earlier. The finest Tuscan sculptors vied for this major commission and submitted competition panels, only two of which survive (today in the Bargello Museum, Florence), those of the finalists, Filippo Brunelleschi (1377–1446) and Lorenzo Ghiberti (1378–1455). Though the artistic merits of the two panels were (and still are) hotly debated, ultimately the guild awarded the job to Ghiberti. Though the contract stipulated that the doors be completed in ten years, it took Ghiberti twenty-one years to carry out the project. He employed a huge workshop of the most talented craftsmen in Florence, so difficult and labor-intensive was the process of casting and finishing the bronze panels. No sooner were the twenty-eight panels on New Testament themes finished, than the guild decided in 1425 to give Ghiberti a new commission for another pair of doors depicting scenes from the Old Testament. Combined, these two projects took up the greater part of Ghiberti's adult life; he completed the second commission in 1452, just three years before his death.

With this second set of doors, known as the *Gates of Paradise*, because Michelangelo commented that they were beautiful enough to grace the entrance to Heaven, Ghiberti broke entirely new artistic ground. In these gilded bronze panels Ghiberti employs the rules of linear perspective—only

Figure 3.1 Lorenzo Ghiberti, *Jacob and Esau*, c.1435, panel of *Gates of Paradise*, Opera del Duomo, Florence

recently established by Florentine artists—to impart a persuasive impression of depth to the shallow reliefs. In a single panel depicting the story of *Jacob and Esau*, the artist manages to tell the complex biblical narrative of seven scenes side by side (polychronic narration), from the moment God informs Rebeka that she is pregnant with twins, through a grown Jacob receiving his father Isaac's blessing. Rather than appearing cluttered and chaotic, the scene has a sense of panoramic space. The overall effect of Ghiberti's panel is lyrical; the story is told with freshness and realism, within a masterly perspectival representation of the architectural setting (Figure 3.1).

The sculpture of Donatello, a dazzling "mutation"

Among the constellation of goldsmiths and sculptors employed in Ghiberti's workshop on his first set of Baptistry doors was the young

Donatello (Donato di Niccolò di Betto Bardi *c.*1386–1466). The art historian H.W. Janson would characterize Donatello's sculpture as "a mutation among works of art," because of the way it broke away from the work of his contemporaries and dramatically altered the course of Western art. Janson was referring to *St. Mark* (1411–13), one of two of Donatello's early masterpieces displayed on the façade of Orsanmichele, the oratory and civic granary of Florence, where niches held statues of patron saints of the various guilds. In his *St. Mark*, made for the Linen-weavers' and Second-hand Clothing Merchants' Guild, the sculptor portrays the Apostle with the somber, noble features and clothing customarily associated with statues of ancient Roman philosophers. In the company of a fellow Florentine artist, in 1402 the young Donatello made a trip to Rome, where the two closely studied such ancient statuary. Like one of those ancient philosophers, Donatello's Mark is an elderly, yet vigorous man, with hands that reveal his strength of purpose, the veins and tendons carved naturalistically. Donatello employs meticulous realism in depicting both the elegant drapery of the figure's robes and the cushion on which he stands, serving incidentally as advertisements for products sold by the guild that employed the artist. This realism is extended all the way to the depression caused by the Apostle's feet on the carved cushion. The pose itself is the classically inspired contrapposto (counter-posed) stance, in which the weight of the figure rests on one straight leg and the other bends; this stance is dynamic, imparting the illusion of potential energy as the torso twists gently from the hips to counterbalance the weight.

The artist's *St. George* (1410–15) (Figure 3.2), for the Armorers' and Sword-makers' Guild, wears armor and holds a shield. The right hand is balled into a fist, which originally grasped a sword or lance, also advertising the merchandise of the guild that paid for it. St. George slaying the dragon was a popular subject for art during the Middle Ages, but here, rather than a medieval knight, Donatello has carved an idealized youthful figure dressed in what seems to be ancient Roman armor, with a cloak slung naturalistically over his shoulders. The head, turned slightly at a graceful angle, and the whole figure exude elegance, while at the same time transmitting focus and determination. The feet are spread apart, planted firmly, yet a pose which might be static is energized by the fixed determination on the face. Located on the main thoroughfare that connects the Duomo and the Palazzo dei Priori, both the august *St. Mark* and the intrepid *St. George* gazed out over the heads of Florentines as they went about their business in the city. These statues convey a message of strength, not only of the city's influential guilds, but of the mission and determination of the Florentine Republic, which had only recently escaped the threat of invasion by the Duke of Milan. Without the innovations introduced by Donatello it is impossible to imagine the artistic triumph and powerful civic icon, Michelangelo's *David*, created a century later.

Figure 3.2 Donatello, *St. George*, 1410–15, Bargello, Florence. This is the original; the statue on the exterior north side of Orsanmichele today is a copy

Brunelleschi's genius, ingenuity, and engineering

The friend who went with Donatello to Rome in 1402 was Filippo Brunelleschi, disappointed after losing the competition for the Baptistry doors to his rival Ghiberti. Though he trained as a goldsmith and sculptor, it was when he turned his attention to engineering and architecture that Brunelleschi won the biggest competition of all, to design the *cupola*, or dome of Florence's Cathedral of Santa Maria del Fiore. The Opera del Duomo (Works Committee of the Cathedral) had been managed by the powerful Wool Guild since 1296, when work began on an immense new cathedral for the growing metropolis.

The proud Florentines, in a gesture that did not go unnoticed by the pope, had decided to erect a building even larger than St. Peter's in Rome; it was to be large enough to accommodate the entire population of Florence. The problem was that once the main structure was finished, there was seemingly no way to complete the vast dome, intended to be the largest and highest since antiquity.

In Rome, Brunelleschi had closely studied the construction of the Pantheon (originally built in 27 BCE, destroyed in fire, rebuilt 125 CE Figure 14.2b); however, the dome in Florence posed unique challenges. It was to rise higher than the Pantheon, and the *operai* required that it be shaped not as a hemisphere, but a pointed fifth. Moreover, Brunelleschi could not use wooden centering to build the dome—this would have necessitated a forest's worth of wood—and the plan forbid the use of external supports such as flying buttresses employed in Gothic architecture. Brunelleschi came up with innovative responses to all these problems. He devised scaffolding suspended from the inside wall of the dome, to be shifted upward as it rose, and he invented a rotating hoist to raise tons of building material to the dizzying heights of the construction site. His design incorporated a pair of inner and outer shells made from lightweight bricks laid in herringbone pattern to strengthen the structure, which was anchored with lateral "chains" to offset outward pressure, to be topped with a graceful lantern stabilizing and unifying the whole.

Brunelleschi was able to pull off this extraordinary achievement through a combination of artistic vision and use of precise mathematical calculations. The Florentine astronomer, physician, and mathematician Paolo Toscanelli (1397–1482) was good friends with both Leon Battista Alberti (Chapter 4) and Brunelleschi, instructing the latter in the principles of Euclid. Brunelleschi constructed the cupola of the Florence cathedral (Figure 3.3) by incorporating Euclidian geometry, as well as inventing practical engineering solutions involving pulleys, gears, and cranes. In Italian the word for engineer, *ingegniere*, derives from *ingegno*, meaning "intelligence," "mind," or "talent," and has the same root as the word "genius." The Renaissance concept of genius is linked to the ingenuity and precision of an engineer added to a craftsman's process of tinkering, the whole inspired with an artist's sense of beauty.

Though the Wool Guild imposed the various above-mentioned design restrictions when he worked on the dome, Brunelleschi was not hindered by a pre-existing plan when designing the Ospedale degli Innocenti foundling home in Florence (begun 1419). Here Brunelleschi was able to start from the ground up, and he pioneered an entirely new Renaissance aesthetic. He introduced a new order and symmetry by using the vocabulary of classical Roman architecture—columns, pediments, pilasters, entablatures—on the façade. The *loggia*, or covered walkway, features an arcade of delicate Corinthian columns with wide semicircular arches. Based on Pythagoras's

Figure 3.3 Filippo Brunelleschi, *Cupola of Santa Maria del Fiore*, Duomo of Florence

(*c*.569–*c*.500 BCE) ratios observed from nature, the proportions of this new Renaissance style convey an intrinsically satisfying sense of balance. The interiors of the Florentine churches of San Lorenzo, Santo Spirito, and the Pazzi Chapel, designed by Brunelleschi in the1420s and 1430s, all display a harmonious regularity of classical forms, and give an impression of simplicity and lightness in contrast to more intricate shadowy Gothic structures.

But Brunelleschi's most important contribution to the history of art was undoubtedly his invention of single-point perspective sometime between 1410 and 1420. During his studies, while measuring classical buildings and making sketches of them, Brunelleschi devised the means of representing three-dimensional objects on a flat plane. This was a major contribution to architecture, suddenly making it simple for the designer to express his vision

Back to the Future 65

to others; in painting it constituted a revolution. Previously, artists—Giotto in particular—had experimented with representing three-dimensional objects realistically in their paintings, but not until Brunelleschi worked out the mathematical relations of all the visual elements to a single vanishing-point could an artist portray a convincing illusion of three-dimensional reality.

Masaccio, a youthful painter of dramatic realism

This effect of heightened realism was first achieved in painting by Brunelleschi's younger friend, Masaccio (Tommaso di Giovanni di Simone Guidi 1401–1428). Though barely twenty-seven years old at the time of his death, during his brief lifetime Masaccio blazed new paths for all Renaissance painters to come. He adopted Brunelleschi's formula for perspective, and most clearly demonstrated it in the fresco[4] of the *Trinity* (Santa Maria Novella, Florence). Painted sometime between 1425 and 1428, this painting is the first instance of a completely realized use of single-point perspective in the history of painting. In Masaccio's *Trinity*, the figure of God the Father with arms outstretched stands behind the crucified Christ, while a dove representing the Holy Spirit hovers above his head. Christ is flanked by two saints, Mary and John the Evangelist, and beneath them, closer to the viewer, a man and a woman—the two donors who commissioned the work—kneel in devotion before the scene. What keeps this from being a stiff, hieratical image is the painfully realistic depiction of the body of Christ suspended in what appears to be real three-dimensional space. The spatial illusion is created by a painted architectural vaulting that recedes into the background from behind an arch set on a pair of classical columns. The two donors, Domenico Lenzi and his wife, are placed on either side of a ledge in front of the columns, on the same plane as the viewer. Rather than shut us out of the picture, Masaccio intentionally draws us in. Though the other figures appear lost in contemplation, one turns her gaze toward the viewer: the Virgin, gesturing mutely, beckons us to take part in the drama.

Masaccio's fresco cycle in the Brancacci Chapel of the Carmine Church, carried out along with the painter Masolino da Panicale (Tommaso di Cristofano Fini *c.*1383–1447), likewise moves us, through a combination of technical mastery and raw emotional power. In *St. Peter Healing with His Shadow* (Brancacci Chapel, Florence) we witness a moment that is both miraculous and mundane. The setting is real enough: in front of the rusticated stone exterior of a medieval building is a line of disabled people begging, a common scene in quattrocento Florence. However, suffused in an eerie light

---

4 The word "fresco" literally means "fresh" and refers to the technique of painting directly onto fresh plaster walls.

the saint glides silently forward, as if in trance. As Peter's shadow falls upon them, each of the men rises, cured; only the man with the misshapen limbs lies on the ground propped up on some pieces of wood, looking up expectantly at the mysterious passerby. The moment is pregnant with hope and wonder as, with a single step, the life of one disabled man is about to change forever.

Moreover, Masaccio pioneered the effect in painting known as chiaroscuro (literally "light–dark"). He did away with outlines by employing subtle gradations of light and shadows to enhance the naturalistic illusion of three-dimensional modeling of the figures. Thus, when we look at a painting such as his *Distribution of Alms and the Death of Ananias* that depicts the gritty realities of quattrocento life, we are as if transported to the streets of Masaccio's Florence (Figure 3.4).

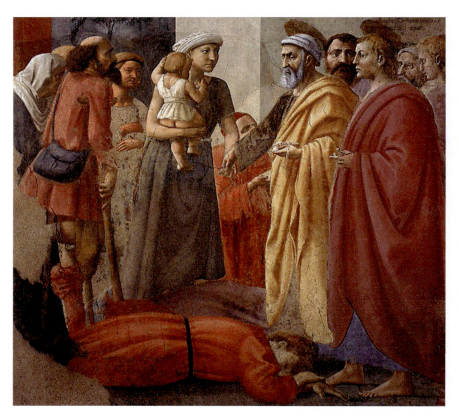

Figure 3.4 Masaccio, *The Distribution of Alms and the Death of Ananias*, 1427–28, detail, Brancacci Chapel, Florence

Considerations: Humanism, humanitarianism, and the humanities

Though the Renaissance was a rebirth and rediscovery of classical techniques and aesthetics, we can also see a strain of powerful emotional content that owes little to classical influences. Indeed, in a sense the rebirth that is most powerfully sensed in Masaccio's work is a rebirth of Giotto's severe, restrained gestures, his expressive power. This new movement in art was not merely a technical exercise motivated by an antiquarian impulse. It was a living, deeply felt means of expression, reflected in that strand of humanism in which Petrarch cries out, exposing his interior joys and anguish to the world. And Petrarch in many ways embodies humanism—the notarial culture he was raised in, his antiquarianism, his expressiveness in both Latin and Florentine languages—but most of all in his passion for the literature of pagan antiquity. It is easy to think of humanism as a dry academic pursuit, but it was a vital, exciting movement. Artists too, were caught up in the fever, though most never saw the inside of a university classroom. Many did not even know Latin, but in their workshops they discussed the thrilling new concepts with one another and conversed with the humanists of their day. They absorbed new ideas rapidly, competing and striving to outdo one another, and in the process, they began a chain-reactive explosion of creative activity.

By the beginning of the fifteenth century in Italy, a cultural revolution was in full swing. A new classical aesthetic in the arts and literature was born, and the traditional medieval educational system was overthrown in favor of the *studia humanitatis* (study of the humanities). Most important of all, perhaps, was the revolution in thinking that humanism made possible. Humanism in itself was never an ideology or unified set of beliefs; it is essential not to confuse the term humanist with humanitarian. We will see, for instance, how the humanist Gianfrancesco Pico della Mirandola (Chapter 15) actively participated in witchcraft trials and executions, whereas his more famous uncle Giovanni Pico della Mirandola (Chapter 9) was a humanist deeply committed to harmonizing Christian beliefs with Jewish, Muslim, and ancient pagan traditions. Humanists did not have a unified program for the betterment of humankind; rather, they contributed something even more valuable. Through their critical inquiries into the nature of language and exploration of history, the humanists opened the way for a questioning of every widely held belief. The very fact that we now generally accept that societies governed by the people themselves are superior to rule by an individual, whether king or dictator, we owe to the humanists. That we are able to recognize human beings not as passive instruments of fate, that through our powers of reason we are capable of choosing for ourselves what we would be, we also owe to them. Renaissance humanism has had lasting effects, as did the art it inspired. The aesthetic standards set in Italy during this time would guide Western art for the next 400 years, and the humanist educational program, study of "the humanities," has dominated our educational systems to the present day.

68 *Back to the Future*

Sourcebook

Petrarch, *Letter on the Ascent of Mount Ventoux*; *Sonnet 162*
Leonardo Bruni, *Panegyric to the City of Florence*
Giovanni di Pagolo Morelli, *Memoirs*
Margherita Datini, *Letter to Francesco Datini*
Gregorio Dati, *Diary*; *La Sfera*
Isotta Nogarola, *Letter to Antonio Borromeo*
Laura Cereta, *Letter to Lucilia Vernacula*
Cassandra Fedele, *In Praise of Learning*
Cennino Cennini, *The Craftsman's Handbook*
Lorenzo Ghiberti, *Commentary II*

Further reading

Battisti, Eugenio. *Brunelleschi: The Complete Work*, Thames & Hudson, 1981.
Baxandall, Michael. *Painting and Experience in Fifteenth-Century Italy*. Oxford University Press, 1988.
Black, Robert. "Education and the Emergence of a Literate Society" in *Italy in the Age of the Renaissance*, ed. John Najemy, Oxford University Press, 2004.
Galluzzi, Paolo. *Renaissance Engineers: From Brunelleschi to Leonardo da Vinci*, Giunti, 2001.
Grendler, Paul. *Schooling in Renaissance Italy: Literacy and Learning, 1300–1600*, Johns Hopkins Press, 1989.
Krautheimer, Richard in collaboration with Trude Krautheimer-Hess. *Lorenzo Ghiberti*, Princeton University Press, 1956.
Kristeller, Paul Oskar. *Renaissance Thought and Its Sources*, Columbia University Press, 1979.
Minta, Stephen. *Petrarch and Petrarchism: The English and French Traditions*, Manchester University Press, 1980.
Pope-Hennessy, John. *Donatello: Sculptor*, Abbeville Press, 1993.
White, John. *The Birth and Rebirth of Pictorial Space*, Faber & Faber, 1957.
Witt, Ronald. *In the Footsteps of the Ancients: The Origins of Humanism from Lovati to Bruni*, Brill, 2003.

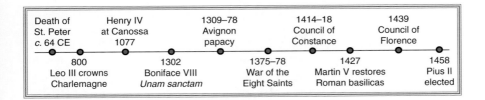

4 *Caput Mundi* again?
The City of Rome Reborn

> After wearing ourselves out wandering the immense city, we often used to visit the Baths of Diocletian. Sometimes we even climbed to the top of the vaulted shell of that once-great building ... And as we walked along the walls of the shattered city, or sat in that place, the fragments of ruins were before our eyes. What then did we speak about? We had many conversations about history.
>
> Petrarch, *Familiarum Rerum Libri* 6.2

Petrarch and Giovanni Colonna were inspired with noble thoughts as they gazed out over the city of Rome, but as the two sat high atop the ruins of Diocletian's Baths in 1343, what did they see? As they looked in the direction of the river, there would have been the terracotta-tiled roofs of a sleepy little town mostly clustered around the low-lying area known as the *abitato* (inhabited area) on the banks of the Tiber River. It was in this area of Rome, the first encampment of the early Latin-speaking tribes, where most Romans now lived in modest homes, the more prosperous in bigger ones built largely from stone scavenged from ancient ruins. Gone were the monumental villas; in 1257 noblemen's towers, 140 in all, were razed by a city ordinance, and with them many of the ancient villas they were built upon. When new buildings were constructed, they were often made of stucco created by melting a mixture of crushed lime and pieces of ancient marble. At the same time as Donatello and Brunelleschi were wandering around collecting treasured fragments of architecture, builders were eagerly smashing marble columns to make cement.

DOI: 10.4324/9781003270362-4

70   Caput Mundi *again?*

Yet, against this sparsely inhabited landscape, the noble ruins—the Arch of Constantine, the Colosseum, Trajan's Column, the Mausoleum of Hadrian, the Pantheon, and others—stood out in stark relief. Over time Romans had stopped living on the seven hills; the hills were now used mostly as gardens and vineyards. Indeed, Petrarch and his friend would have looked down at a city composed largely of vegetable gardens, orchards, and pastures. Busy streets where once toga-clad senators strolled, making way for noble matrons in diaphanous robes riding in litters, these thoroughfares formerly thronged with foreigners from everywhere in the known world were now deserted. The Forum was now known as the *Campo Vaccino* (cow pasture), and where once there had been a deafening babble of languages, haggling, arguing, laughter, the only sound now was the clanging of cowbells as shepherds herded their cows between fallen marble columns.

While other Italian cities were exploding with economic and artistic energy, Rome was largely stagnant. In the centuries following the fall of the ancient empire, Rome itself, the *caput mundi* (capital of the world), had fallen into a long, dismal decline. The metropolis, which at its peak had been home to over a million people, numbered only 35,000 by the early thirteenth century. The entire population could easily have, in the words of historian Robert Brentano, "sat down in the Colosseum, if it too had not crumbled and gradually fallen, if it had not turned itself into an exotic wildflower garden (still perhaps nurturing seeds from the paws and fur and fodder of ancient beasts)."

The city of the Caesars becomes the city of popes

How could Rome have decayed like this, while so many cities in Italy not only had recovered, but were prospering by the fourteenth century? To answer this question, we must first look at the city's relationship with the papacy. Rome's unique destiny, both its glory and its curse from the beginning of the Christian era, was that it was the site of the Holy See, from the Latin *sancta sedes*, literally the holy seat of the bishop of Rome. During the period of the disintegration of the Roman Empire, bishops had emerged as strong, central figures of authority. Every major urban center had a bishop, yet from the beginning, the bishop of Rome, or pope as he came to be called (in Italian *papa* from the Greek word *pappas*, meaning father), held a place of special importance, for a number of reasons. Firstly, though it had suffered indignity and disgrace, even after waves of invasions, Rome still occupied a privileged place in the eyes of the Western world. Its glamour was enhanced for Christians by the fact that the very ground of Rome was infused with sanctity and drenched with the blood of Christian martyrs, making Rome the second holiest city in the world to them, after Jerusalem. Furthermore, the Apostle Peter (died *c.*64 CE) was widely considered to have been the first pope, appointed by Christ to rule from Rome. This belief derived from a phrase in the Bible, in which Christ declares, "Thou art Peter and upon this rock I will build my church." Based on a play on words (Peter's name, *Petrus*, in Greek means rock), this sentence was taken quite literally to mean that Christ intended all his believers to be led by a central authority, beginning with the Apostle. Furthermore, tradition has it that Apostles Peter and Paul established the bishopric of Rome, before they were martyred there. Thus, to many in the West, it seemed clear that God's anointed shepherd ought to lead all of Christianity from Rome.

The papacy precariously balanced on a rock

Despite such seemingly impeccable credentials, successors to Peter's chair did not progress along a simple, unimpeded course to supreme authority. To begin with, the job description was unclear. What did it mean precisely to lead the church? It became obvious from an early date, given the power vacuum following the fall of the Roman Empire, that among the tasks of the pope were to arrange defenses for the city of Rome, to maintain the city's law and order, to raise vast sums of money, and to conduct diplomacy with foreign powers. From the mid-eighth century the papacy laid claim to lordship over a large swathe of land in central Italy, known as the Papal States or "Patrimony of St. Peter" based on a forged document known as the *Donation of Constantine* (Chapter 7 and also Chapter 10, Map 10.2). Where ought the pope's territories and powers to end? In the words of Pope Innocent III (r.1198–1216): "The Lord left Peter not only the church to rule, but the whole world as well." Yet despite such grandiose notions of papal authority, the pontiff had no army at his command and no authority except the trust he inspired in the faithful. He was not even universally accepted as the leader of Christendom, as the Eastern Church, based in Constantinople, had split from the West (Great Schism), and the powerful Byzantine Empire refused to acknowledge the Roman bishop's supremacy.

Individual popes were forced to come up with solutions to political dilemmas using what means they had at their disposal; the strongest of them succeeded seemingly through sheer power of will. Pope Leo I the Great (r.440–61) negotiated with Attila the Hun, preventing him from invading Rome; later Pope Gregory I the Great (r.590–604) arranged a peace treaty with the Lombard invaders. The reason these particular popes received the sobriquet "the Great" after their names was that they were extraordinary men. By contrast, many popes were weak and inefficient, and the papacy faltered under their rule. Throughout the Middle Ages, popes were often deposed, murdered, or challenged by other candidates. There were many so-called antipopes throughout history, men claiming to be the legitimate bishop of Rome and desiring to unseat the official pope. Being pope was often a dangerous and precarious vocation, and when Pope Leo III crowned the Emperor Charlemagne (800 CE), he tacitly admitted the papacy's desperate need to be defended by a strong temporal power.

72 Caput Mundi *again?*

For a period, the popes were caught in a delicate pas-de-deux with the Holy Roman Emperors, which led, as we have seen, to the Investiture Conflict. When the emperor absolutely opposed him, however, Pope Urban IV (r.1261–64) reached out to the royal house of France, seeking to offset imperial power in the Italian Peninsula (Chapter 7). This triangulated diplomatic relationship between the papacy, France, and the empire would come to a head, with disastrous consequences, in the early sixteenth century.

Roman communal politics: A "monstrous thing"

How did the government of the city of Rome itself develop under these circumstances, dominated as it was by the imposing figure of the pope, whose politics were intertwined with those of the empire and France? It was a chaotic state of affairs at best; the same antagonisms between supporters of the emperor and the pope that were being played out in cities throughout the peninsula were intensified in Rome, taking place, as it were, on the pope's home turf. So complex and contentious were Roman politics that the jurist Bartolo da Sassoferrato (1314–1357) referred to it as a *res monstruosa* (monstrous thing).

Like other Italian cities, Rome had established a commune, and fairly early, in 1083. Conscious of their unique historical legacy, the Romans chose to call the members governing their commune senators, taking the name from the ancient Roman legislative body. They had coins minted with the legend *caput mundi* on one side and on the other, the letters S.P.Q.R., an abbreviation for *Senatus populusque Romanus* (the Senate and people of Rome). These same initials had been carried into battle atop the standards of the legions of Julius Caesar and inscribed on public monuments still visible throughout Rome. Yet despite such grand aspirations, the Roman commune never attained the autonomy of other Italian communes, or achieved even a modicum of stability.

From its inception, the Roman commune struggled with the papacy over control of the city. In 1140, tensions exploded when the Romans, who had been besieging the nearby town of Tivoli, succeeded in taking it, but Pope Innocent II (r.1130–43) forbade them to destroy it. The Romans rose up in revolt against the pope, and hostilities had still not cooled when several years later Pope Lucius II (r.1144–5) took up arms against the populace (and died after being wounded in battle). The next pope, Eugenius III (r.1145–53), was driven out of Rome by the people who were inspired by the powerful speaker Arnold of Brescia (*c.*1090–1155), a monk who preached clerical reform. The Romans signed a treaty with Pope Clement III in 1188. By 1205, Pope Innocent III gained absolute control of the Senate; yet tensions were never completely resolved, and popular uprisings in Rome continued.

Power shifted rapidly in Rome. Popes are usually elected when they are elderly; thus, each individual pope's term is usually rather short. For example, there were eighteen popes during the thirteenth century, making the average reign of each pope five and a half years. Thus, agreements hammered out with one pope could easily be undermined by his successor. By contrast, the one constant in Rome was the iron fist of the powerful families known as *baroni* (from medieval Latin *baro*, meaning warrior), who had become the city's ruling elite. These families, the Orsini, Colonna, Savelli, and a dozen or so others controlled not only city politics but the papacy itself, as the names of senators and popes were over and over drawn from the ranks of these clans. Whereas by the same time in other communes the *popolo* had already gained the upper hand, the struggle between magnates and *popolo* in Rome was still raging in the late thirteenth century. Romans were attempting to unsettle the *baroni* by bringing in foreigners to serve as senators, notably Brancaleone degli Andalò (served 1252–8) who had the magnates' towers knocked down. In 1266 there was yet another attempt to establish a government led by the *popolo*, but it only lasted ten years.

Pope Boniface VIII clashes swords with the king of France

The politics of the city of Rome and that of the papal court were closely tied. Romans loved to gossip, as they still do, about the latest news from the Roman Curia (the governing structure of the Catholic Church). When the nobleman Benedetto Caetani (1235–1303) was elected Pope Boniface VIII in 1294, rumors flew. It was claimed that Boniface had tricked his predecessor Celestine V into abdicating by whispering into pipes in the Lateran Palace, pretending to be a heavenly voice urging Celestine's resignation. The new pontiff was well known as a bon vivant, who enjoyed rich foods and wines, and had lovers of both genders. He was also corrupt, channeling vast wealth into his family's coffers as soon as he was elected. Dante was a vocal critic who named Boniface among the souls in his *Inferno* before the pope had even died. Despite all this, it was not the pope's corruption, but his intractable personality that would change the course of history.

Boniface was fifty-nine years old—aged for the time—and in ill health when he became pope. He was no doddering old pontiff, however: the man was full of energy and irascible, given to terrifying fits of rage when contradicted. A renowned jurist, Boniface argued in favor of the absolute power of the papacy over all secular rulers, exceeding even the wildest dreams of Innocent III, the most powerful medieval pope before him. Boniface was unbending; he rapidly alienated both the German Emperor and the powerful Colonna Family in Rome. He was to meet his match in an equally inflexible opponent, King Philip IV of France. No sooner had Boniface become pope than he lashed out at Philip for proposing taxation of the clergy in France to finance his war with England. Boniface issued the bull[1] *Clericis laicos* in 1294, insisting that only the pope could authorize the taxation of clerics, and he threatened to excommunicate[2] kings who taxed members of clergy without papal permission. Boniface was forced to back down from this position, but several years later, in 1300, he rallied and declared a Jubilee year.[3] Cheered by the exuberant attendance of tens of thousands of pilgrims (described by Dante in *Inf.* XVIII 28–32), not to mention the wealth they brought into the papal treasury, and enjoying improved health, Boniface once again struck out against the king of France in a series of caustic bulls.

In 1302 Boniface issued the bull *Unam sanctam*, the most powerful statement of absolute papal authority ever written, asserting that the pope reigns supreme above all earthly rulers, including the king of France. This was not a cannonade that Philip was going to take lying down. The following summer of 1303 while Boniface was relaxing in his family's villa in Anagni preparing a decree of excommunication against the French king, troops sent by Philip arrived. Philip's men seized the pontiff and, while keeping him in custody, treated him roughly. Several weeks later, shocked and humiliated, Boniface died.

Rome widowed

> How doth the city sit solitary, that was full of people! how is she become as a widow! she that was great among the nations, and princess among the provinces, how is she become tributary!
>
> *Lamentations* 1:1

The above words from the Bible referred to Jerusalem, but by the Trecento (fourteenth century) they were being used to describe Rome, because for the greater part of the century there would be no pope in Rome. Soon after the death of Boniface VIII, Philip managed to have a French pope elected,

---

1 A papal "bull" is an official document, stating papal policy on a given issue. The name comes from the Latin *bulla* for "bubble," which is what the lead seal affixed to the document looked like. The name of each individual bull comes from the first line of its Latin text.
2 "Excommunication" means "exclusion from communion" and is the harshest form of censure used by the Catholic Church, a punishment that excludes an individual from taking Holy Communion and participating in the other sacraments of the Church, endangering his salvation.
3 A jubilee is an anniversary commemoration. Though there is evidence of other similar papal celebrations, Boniface is recognized as inaugurating the first papal jubilee with his bull "Antiquorum fida relatio" in 1300, in which the faithful were offered remission of their sins if, in a true spirit of penance they made confession, and visited the Roman basilicas of St. Peter and St. Paul at least once a day for a determined period of time. Although the frequency of jubilees and conditions required of participants has varied over time, the custom continues to the present day. The most recent papal jubilees were held in 2000 by Pope John Paul II, in 2008 by Benedict XVI, and in 2016 by Pope Francis.

Clement V (r.1305–14), who in 1309 moved the papacy out of Italy entirely, to Avignon in the south of modern-day France. Sparsely inhabited, without the glory of the papacy, not to mention the income it generated, Rome became a backwater. Without her lord, Rome was a desolate and lawless place. Though the presence of the Holy See had caused problems for the city, its absence created a power vacuum that the *baroni* were quick to fill. No longer restrained, even nominally, by the presence of papal authority, the great families openly warred with one another; their thugs roamed the streets, terrorizing the population. A Roman chronicler writing in the mid 1350s describes the anarchic condition of the city:

> In the city of Rome there was great suffering. There was no one to rule; every day there was fighting and thieves were everywhere. Virgins and widows were violated, wives taken right from their husbands' beds. No place was safe. Laborers, when they went to work, were robbed. Where? At the very gates of Rome. Pilgrims, who went to the holy churches for the sake of their souls were not defended, but attacked and robbed. Even priests committed crime. Nothing could be done, for without justice there was no restraint and all over there was lust, and every kind of evil; everyone was perishing. The person who wielded a sword was the one in the right. Unless you had relatives and friends to defend you, you were not safe. Every day groups of armed men gathered.

The phrase "calamitous fourteenth century" indeed has special poignancy in Rome.

The meteoric rise and fall of Cola di Rienzo

From this chaos emerged an unlikely hero, an extraordinary, mercurial character, who for a brief time captured the imagination of the Roman people. The son of a tavern keeper and a washer-woman, Cola di Rienzo (*c*.1313–1354) was educated in Latin and trained as a notary. Consumed with the humanist passion for ancient Rome, he read the works of Cicero, Livy, and Seneca. The young man was fascinated by his city's classical past and delighted in wandering her streets reading the Latin inscriptions on ancient monuments. Cola was a passionate speaker and became known for his embrace of the values of republican Rome. He soon became active with a group known as the "Thirteen Good Men," an organization attempting to revive the Roman commune. The group sent the handsome and well-spoken Cola as ambassador to Avignon in 1342 to persuade Pope Clement VI (r.1342–52) to support their project. In Avignon Cola met Petrarch, and the two became devoted friends. The younger man inspired the poet, who shared his passion for ancient Rome and burned with a desire to restore the actual city to its former glory. One of the many letters Petrarch wrote to the young politician is characteristic of the excitement Cola inspired:

76   Caput Mundi *again?*

As I recall that most holy and serious discussion of ours two days ago, when we stood at the portals of that famous ancient temple, I burn with such ardor that I feel as if an oracle had spoken to me from the depths of that sanctuary. I believed that I was listening not to a man, but to a god!

Cola also charmed Clement VI, who recognized an opportunity to use this charismatic young man for his own political ends. Clement rewarded Cola with the lucrative post of papal notary to the Apostolic Camera (the financial board of papal administration) and sent him back to Rome. When he returned, Cola continued to agitate on behalf of the people against the interests of the *baroni*, urging a return to ancient Roman republican ideals. He succeeded in organizing a coup, and on May 30, 1347, Cola di Rienzo seized control of the government. He drove the Roman crowds wild with his speeches, promising to rid them of the hated *baroni* while appealing to their *romanitas* (Latin for "Roman-ness") and their pride in being the descendants of the great Roman civilization. The people cheered as Cola, dressed in classical robes, declared himself their leader, taking the name of tribune, a title used during the ancient Roman Republic.

Cola wrote letters to all the city-states of Italy, urging them to join him in an Italian confederation, and soon ambassadors from all over the peninsula began appearing in Rome to pay their respects. He instituted tax reforms, enforced justice evenly, and staged flamboyant spectacles that were popular with the public. Despite these successes, he remained in power as tribune for only seven months. His project was doomed to failure by a combination of factors. Cola demanded that Pope Clement VI return to Rome and insisted that popes henceforward be elected by the people of Rome. He issued an edict on August 1, 1347, proclaiming Rome once again the capital of the known world. By insisting that all rulers submit to Rome, Cola in one stroke challenged the power of both the pope and the emperor. He had gone too far, angering the pope, as well as his curia. Many of the cardinals, the pope's closest advisors, were also members of the powerful Roman families who hated Cola's regime and had been plotting against him for some time. Finally, certain disturbing megalomaniacal tendencies that began to show in his character the longer he was in office hastened his downfall. As the pope prepared a bull denouncing him as a heretic and the tide of public feeling began to turn against the tribune, Cola fled Rome. He did, amazingly, manage to return to power on August 1, 1354. By this time desperate for funds, Cola made the crucial error of raising taxes, in particular on wine—this was more than Romans would tolerate. There was rioting in the streets, and once more Cola was forced to escape, but this time he did not get away. On October 8, 1354, he tried to slip out of the Palace of the Campidoglio disguised as a peasant. He shaved his beard, blackened his face with soot, and covered himself with a filthy cloth, but he was recognized. He was seized by the crowd; members of the angry mob repeatedly stabbed him and then dragged along the ground. What was left of the tribune's body was hung from a balcony to bloat in the sun.

The "Babylonian Captivity" of the church, 1309–78

Meanwhile, as Rome was in the throes of revolution, the pope lived in luxury in the elegant and secure fortress of the Papal Palace in Avignon. There were seven popes who resided in Avignon during the years 1309–78, a period often referred to as the "Babylonian Captivity." The Biblical image recalls the time when the Israelites, in exile from their homeland, were forced from their homeland to live in servitude in Babylon. Because the papacy had left Italy and all seven Avignon popes were French, the term implies that the church is being held prisoner by foreigners, in a foreign land. The expression also criticizes the morality of the Avignon papacy by equating it with the decadent ancient city of Babylon. Once again it is Petrarch who gives voice to the feeling of the age; in a letter to a friend, the poet condemns the Avignonese papal court:

> Now I am living in France, in the Babylon of the West ... Here reign the successors of the poor fishermen of Galilee; they have strangely forgotten their origin. I am astounded, as I recall their predecessors, to see these men loaded with gold and clad in purple, boasting of the spoils of princes and nations; to see luxurious palaces and heights crowned with fortifications.

The papal court in Avignon was indeed splendid. The magnificent Palace of the Popes was built during this time on the site of the former Bishop's Palace, and the crenellated walls and towers of the fortress could be seen from miles around. The interior of the Palace of the Popes was adorned with paintings by some of the finest artists of the day, among them Simone Martini and Matteo Giovanetti (1300–1368). When he lay down in his silken bed, the pope could gaze at the walls of his bedchamber adorned with brightly colored frescoes of gardens and graceful birds perched on branches, reminiscent of the frescoes in the ancient villas of Roman emperors. In his private study, the pope surrounded himself with lively painted country scenes of fishing and of stags pursued through forests by hounds and hunters. In the splendid vaulted halls of this palace the elite of the church entertained princes and foreign ambassadors. In order to write all the correspondence, bulls, and dispensations, not to mention simply keeping accounts, a veritable army of scribes and notaries (among them Petrarch's father) was kept constantly employed. Intellectuals from all over Europe were drawn to the papal court in Avignon, creating a unique and cosmopolitan, if not exactly religious, atmosphere.

How was all of this luxury paid for? In addition to charitable bequests, popes had hitherto relied largely on taxation for their revenues. Parishes paid 10% of their income as tithes, and bishoprics were made to contribute their first year's income or annates (from the Latin *annata* meaning "a year's work"). Papal tax collectors circulated throughout Europe collecting these and other taxes; additionally, revenues were due from the Papal States

78   Caput Mundi *again?*

in Italy and from papal vassals in cities such as Bologna, Verona, Parma, Vicenza, and Piacenza. Nevertheless, the fourteenth century was a time of economic recession on the continent, and the pope often had a hard time collecting from countries that resented the French influence on the papacy. In particular, the Italian cities that comprised the Papal States resisted, and the Avignon popes sent troops there to bring them to obedience. To fund these wars, as well as to maintain their costly court in southern France, the popes had to come up with other sources of income. Additional taxes were devised, and in the name of reform, under Avignon popes Clement V and John XXII, papal bureaucracy was centralized and made more efficient. The popes seized the right to appoint bishops and abbots of monasteries, sweeping aside the traditional local elections, thus opening the way for corruption. Simony, the selling of church offices—a sin harshly punished in Dante's *Inferno*—became the order of the day, and the papal treasury began to swell as every church appointment now came with a price tag. Moreover, the church also raised money through the increased practice of selling indulgences that would incur much criticism during the Reformation (Chapter 13).

The popes return to Rome

The popes had settled in comfortably in their new palace and it seemed to many that they would never leave, yet they were under pressure to return to Italy. Though bishops were not always obliged to live in the city where their episcopal see was located, how long could the bishop of Rome be absent from the city of the Apostle Peter and still claim to rule the church? The longer the popes remained in Avignon, the more they damaged their credibility with the faithful. Furthermore, a papacy submissive to the French monarchy lost prestige as an autonomous spiritual authority. The saying *Ubi papa, ibi Roma* (Wherever the pope is, there is Rome) that had been used to justify papal absence was wearing thin; it was time for the pope to return to Rome.

When on June 4, 1367, the French pope Urban V (r.1362–70) stepped off his ship onto Italian soil, he was greeted by joyous crowds. With great pomp the representatives of the city of Rome handed him keys to the city and, with them, complete control of its defenses. Urban entered Rome mounted on a humble mule, led on foot by the German emperor as a sign of reverence. The Romans cheered madly; seemingly all was set right: here was spiritual power in proper relationship with temporal power. The pope began to receive visits from royalty, no less a personage than Byzantine Emperor John V Palaeologus (1332–1391) making the journey to see him; with the pope, Rome's glory had returned. However, it was not to last, as Urban and his French cardinals were never comfortable in Rome. The papal living quarters were in a disastrous condition after being long uninhabited, and Urban had to make do with various temporary living arrangements. Furthermore, the climate did not agree with him; he was afraid of catching malaria, a perennial problem in the damp, marshy air of Rome. But, most seriously, Urban feared the populace. Despite the initially warm welcome, rebellion was in the air. Weary and frightened, in 1370, the pope returned to Avignon, where he died later that year.

The War of the Eight Saints, 1375–78

For the first five years of his papacy Gregory XI (Pierre Roger de Beaufort, r.1370–78) aggressively intervened in peninsular politics in the cities of Milan, Ferrara, and Perugia, posing a threat to Florentine foreign policy, as well as antagonizing them by placing papal supporters in key strategic locations within Tuscany. By 1374 when plague and famine struck, the Florentines asked to import grain from Bologna, then in papal control, and the pope refused unless the Florentines made political concessions. Additionally, behind the Florentines' back Gregory made peace with their common enemy, the duke of Milan, and the *condottiero* (mercenary captain) John Hawkwood, who had been leading papal troops, was released from service. Now the Florentines, in addition to feeling betrayed by the pope, were suddenly afraid the English mercenary would attack their city, and were obliged to raise the huge sum of 130,000 florins to pay him off. To offset the cost, a commission of eight Florentine citizens known as the "Eight Saints" was created, whose job was to tax the clergy, and the Tuscan cities of Pisa and Siena, who had likewise been forced to pay Hawkwood, did the same. Meanwhile, in nearby Prato a plot had been discovered involving members of the clergy working on behalf of the pope, who had intended to turn the city over to papal troops. The plotters were executed, and in order to fund what came to be known as the War of the Eight Saints (1375–78), vast amounts of church lands were seized and sold to Florentine citizens. An antipapal league was formed among the cities of Tuscany, eventually joined by many cities in the Papal States, including Viterbo, Perugia, and Bologna as well. The pope responded by issuing interdicts against rebel governments and excommunicated many individuals. But he did not limit himself to spiritual retaliation. The goods of Florentines residing in Avignon were confiscated, many Florentines expelled or imprisoned. The pope used military force as well: he employed Breton mercenary troops, who terrorized the countryside in the Romagna, leading to such infamous episodes as the massacre of civilians, including women and children in the town of Cesena.

Antipopes and the Western Schism, 1378–1417

It took another seven years for Gregory XI to move the seat of the papacy back to Rome, urged by, among others, Catherine of Siena (Chapter 5). When Gregory entered Rome on January 17, 1377, it was with great fanfare of trumpets, accompanied by dancers and jugglers. However, the atmosphere in Rome had cooled toward the pontiff, and as the War of the Eight Saints

80 Caput Mundi *again?*

still raged, he brought 2,000 troops to guard him. Relations between the pope and the Romans were still in this tense and apprehensive mood when Gregory died the next year, making the election of a new pontiff necessary. The College of Cardinals elected popes then, as now, in a practice that dates back to the eleventh century. Though the number of cardinals has grown over time, in 1378 there were twenty-three, of which sixteen cardinals assembled to choose a pope (six were in Avignon and another one was away at Sarzana). As the Roman crowds rioted outside their chambers, noisily demanding that an Italian be elected, the cardinals duly elected the Neapolitan, Bartolomeo Prignano, who was crowned Pope Urban VI in April, 1378. Four months later, however, eleven of the French cardinals gathered together in Anagni and, claiming that they had been forced against their will to elect an Italian pope, decided to choose a different one. On August 2, joined by one

Map 4.1 Western Schism 1378–1417

more cardinal, a Spaniard, they elected Robert of Geneva, a cousin of the French king, as Clement VII.[4] The French returned with their pope to Avignon, while the Italians had installed their pope in Rome.

As both popes had been elected by a majority of cardinals, the Western world was divided over whom to recognize as the actual pope. The allies of France (Scotland, Naples, Aragon, and Castile) backed the pope in Avignon, while the allies of England (the Holy Roman Empire, Bohemia, Hungary, and Poland) supported the Roman pontiff (Map 4.1). For years, the two sides were locked in a stalemate, unable to resolve the problem. Each pope issued edicts, bulls, and sentences, but neither was universally recognized as authoritative. One of the two men had to be deposed, but who had the authority to depose a properly elected successor to St. Peter? The situation was absurd and intolerable, calling into question the very validity of the institution of the papacy. Something had to be done.

The conciliar movement, 1409–39

The situation continued for decades, neither side agreeing to step down. Even the death of the two popes did not resolve the schism, as successors to both the Roman pope (Boniface IX r.1389–1404; Innocent VII r.1404–06; Gregory XII r.1406–15) and the Avignon pope (Benedict XIII r.1394–1417) were elected by their supporters. A general church council was called, according to a provision in canon law that provided for the meeting of such a council in the event that a pope acted against the interests of the faith. The theologians and jurists who agreed to resolve the controversy through the meeting of a council are known as conciliarists. In 1409 these conciliarists, joined by cardinals from both sides who had left the Roman and Avignon pope, met in a council at Pisa to try to settle the dispute. They deposed both popes and elected yet a third pope, Alexander V (r.1409–10), who in turn would be succeeded by Pope John XXIII (r.1410–15). Now with three popes concurrently in office, drastic measures had to be taken, and so in November 1414 the German emperor called for another council to be held in Constance (Konstanz, the city in the southwest corner of modern-day Germany bordering Switzerland).

The Council of Constance, held from 1414 to 1418, marked the high point in the conciliar movement. After deposing two popes, and accepting the abdication of the third, the council ended the schism with the election of Pope Martin V (r.1417–31). Martin agreed to a decree passed by the council that the church would hold regular conciliar meetings every five to ten years to oversee papal policy and initiate reform. The conciliarists were concerned with more than just resolving the schism; they recognized underlying

---

4 This antipope is not to be confused with Giulio de' Medici, who was Pope Clement VII (r.1523–34).

82 Caput Mundi *again?*

weaknesses in the structure of the church and sought to remedy problems of corruption, nepotism, and absenteeism among the clergy; to legislate doctrine; and to restrict the absolute power of the pope.

Martin presided at the council at Pavia (1423–24), but died before the opening of the subsequent Council of Basel, Switzerland, in 1431. The popes increasingly came to resent conciliar interference with their authority. Martin's successor, Eugenius IV (r.1431–49) was angered by the limitations that the Council of Basel placed on papal power outside Italy, such as its decree that no more than a third of cardinals come from any one country and the decision to reduce papal revenues from outside Italy. He was further outraged to see the council deciding on issues of doctrine and infringing on papal privileges, such as granting indulgences and dispensations.

The birth of the Renaissance "papal prince"

In September 1437 Eugenius dissolved the Council of Basel and moved it first to Ferrara, then to Florence; it was thereafter known as the Council of Florence (January 1439). The move was a shrewd one, as the pope's power base was strongest in Italy. Furthermore, the focus of this council was not on internal reform but on reaching out to heal a much older schism. Since 1054 there had been a break between the Western and Eastern churches (sometimes referred to as the Great Schism) that Eugenius hoped to mend.[5] Instead of meekly accepting decrees issued by canonists in Switzerland, this historic negotiation with the Byzantine emperor presented Eugenius with an opportunity to display extraordinary statesmanship, and on his own turf, thus enhancing, rather than diminishing, papal authority. Many conciliarists refused to leave Basel, which Eugenius now declared a schismatic council. Rather than controlling the Church, the conciliarists suddenly found themselves excluded from it.

Eugenius IV, and the other popes of the first half of the Quattrocento were not only restoring authority to the office of the pope, they were laying the groundwork for a new kind of papacy. Since the return from Avignon, popes found they had lost both prestige and financial support. From the mid-fifteenth century popes worked not only on consolidating their territories, but on increasing them. Renaissance popes expended vast sums hiring mercenary armies to wage war. Around this time, it becomes increasingly difficult to distinguish between the role of the pope and a secular ruler, prompting historian Paolo Prodi to coin the term "papal prince." The pope held court, levied

---

5 Prior to 1054, the term Catholic (meaning "universal" in Greek) was applied to believers in both the East and West who adhered to basic doctrine established at church councils. After the schism, the Western Christian church retained the name Catholic, while the Eastern Christian church in Byzantium took the name Orthodox or Greek Orthodox. After the Protestant Reformation in the sixteenth century the Catholic Church began to be referred to also as the Roman Catholic Church.

Caput Mundi *again?* 83

taxes, and waged war, ruling his people with something like the authority of an absolute ruler. Just as most communes had given way by this time to the rule of the signore, so too Romans and all those people who lived in the lands of the Papal States were increasingly ruled by their lord, the pope. The difference between the pope and other signori, however, was that the pope's right to rule was believed to derive directly from God, thus making his claim to power seemingly all the more legitimate.

Popes Martin V, Eugenius IV, and Nicholas V rebuild Rome, 1417–55

After returning to Rome, quattrocento popes began to rebuild not only the papacy, but Rome itself, which was in shambles. The Lateran Palace, which had been home to former popes, was dilapidated and had suffered from fires, earthquakes, and flood. Consequently, the popes moved their residence to the Leonine City, an area named after Pope Leo IV, who had built upon and fortified it in the ninth century, when it was outside the borders of the city of Rome. Located on the west bank of the Tiber, the area of land on which St. Peter's Basilica was built is known as the Vatican. The Vatican Palace, adjacent to St. Peter's, which popes had used when presiding at the basilica, would become the permanent home of the pontiff from the fifteenth century to the present.

In addition to work on the papal residence, Martin V in 1427 ordered restoration work to begin on the Roman basilicas, the four great churches of St. John Lateran (San Giovanni Laterano), St. Paul's Outside the Walls (San Paolo Fuori le Mura), Santa Maria Maggiore, and on the portico of St. Peter's. All at once not only bricklayers and stonemasons, but painters, sculptors, goldsmiths, and mosaic artists were needed to carry out the new papal projects. The absence of the papacy during the previous century had deprived Rome of its largest employer and patron of the arts. Unlike other Italian cities, Rome did not have well-developed trade, banking, or manufacture to support it, and for its livelihood relied largely on the business that came with papal bureaucrats and pilgrims. By the beginning of the fifteenth century, the population of Rome had dwindled to 17,000, roughly half its size during the thirteenth century. Now that there was so much employment, workers and artists from all of Italy were flooding back into Rome. As testament to this frenzied activity is Masolino's *Founding of Santa Maria Maggiore* (1428–32 Museo di Capodimonte, Naples) portraying Pope Liberius (r.352–66) clearing the ground with a hoe for construction of the basilica. The painting was commissioned by Martin V, and commemorates Martin's own role in restoring the same basilica.

Martin's successor, Eugenius IV, commissioned Filarete (Antonio Averlino *c.*1400–1469) to cast impressive bronze doors for the entrance to St. Peter's. These doors, begun *c.*1435 around the same time as Ghiberti's *Jacob and Esau* panel, are very different from the Florentine's groundbreaking work. Rather than innovating, the artist was aiming to re-establish a link with the

84 Caput Mundi *again?*

past; Filarete not only matches early medieval style, expressing his patron's wish to emphasize continuity with the long tradition of popes in Rome, but also incorporates elements of Roman imperial sculpture. By drawing on the kind of decoration used on Trajan's Column, the sculptor links the papacy with the grandeur of ancient Rome, as in the frieze representing Eugenius IV and the Holy Roman Emperor re-entering Rome. The two figures are mounted on horseback, Eugenius slightly in advance, extending his arm in

Figure 4.1 Fra Angelico, *St. Lawrence Distributes Alms*, 1447–49, Chapel of Nicholas V, Vatican Palace

benediction, the castellan (or governor of the palace) poised to lead them into the Vatican. The program of these doors, the threshold for the most sacred Christian site in Europe, was intended to glorify Eugenius IV and the newly restored Roman papacy.

After Eugenius, Pope Nicholas V had the painter Fra Angelico (Giovanni da Fiesole; Guido di Piero c.1395–1455) brought from Florence in 1447 to paint frescoes on the walls of his private chapel in the Vatican. A Dominican monk who was later beatified (thus he is also known as "Beato Angelico"),[6] Fra Angelico had spent the greater part of the last decade covering the walls of his monastery of San Marco with paintings infused with light, emanating a quietly intense spirituality. For the pope, the artist painted a series of imposing frescoes in sparkling jewel-like tones. In one of them, *St Lawrence Distributes Alms* (1447–49, Chapel of Nicholas V, Vatican Palace, Figure 4.1), the sumptuously-garbed saint gives coins to a group of beggars, framed by grandiose classically inspired architecture. Papal munificence is suggested in these scenes, as well as Nicholas's ambitious building plans for the Vatican.

Of these three popes, Nicholas V had the most far-reaching architectural vision; he carried out extensive renovations on St. Peter's, rebuilt the Vatican Palace, and undertook many urban renewal projects. On his deathbed in 1455, according to his biographer, Giannozzo Mannetti, the pope told his cardinals: "The power of the Holy See should be displayed in noble buildings, which are perpetual monuments, seemingly made by the hand of God." Of course, to carry out such plans, Renaissance popes needed more than the will or money; they would need architects, men of genius to make such visions a reality.

The amazing Leon Battista Alberti

> [A] man of my same age, Battista Alberti, whose intellect seems so worthy of praise as to be beyond comparison with others. I admire him so much that I do not mind if my name is not passed down equally to posterity. He is so gifted that whatever discipline he applies himself to, with ease and rapidity he excels everyone else.
>
> Lapo da Castiglionchio, (1406–1438)

Many years before becoming Pope Nicholas V in 1447, Tommaso Parentucelli had been a student in Bologna, where like so many other young people he had caught the fever for humanism. When he became pope, he collected classical manuscripts from all over Europe, founding the Vatican Library. He also reached out to humanists, drawing many talented men to Rome. Leon Battista Alberti (1404–1472) was an old friend of Nicholas V from his student days, who had come to Rome to work in the papal chancery, the office concerned

---

6 An individual is "beatified" or declared "blessed" by the pope in recognition of his or her holy life. It is often a step that leads to canonization, that is, being made a saint (see Chapter 5). Fra Angelico was officially beatified in 1982 by Pope John Paul II.

86   Caput Mundi *again?*

with records, archives, and official correspondence. As the largest, busiest bureaucracy in Europe, the chancery employed upwards of a hundred secretaries. Here rhetorical skills and classical training were highly prized, and many humanists who went on to important literary careers began by writing briefs and other documents for the pope. Among them were historian Flavio Biondo (1392–1463) and satirist and essayist Poggio Bracciolini (1380–1459).

Even among extraordinarily gifted scholars, Alberti stood out. It was not merely that he excelled in Greek and Latin; he possessed a brilliant, many-faceted mind and boundless curiosity. Over the course of his life he wrote books on a seemingly endless range of topics from philosophy to horsemanship and from geometry to household management. Linguistics, cryptography, painting, and architecture—the man wrote on all of these subjects as well. The extent to which Alberti impressed his contemporaries is reflected in the impossible tales they told about him. Some said Alberti possessed superhuman powers, that he could jump over the shoulders of ten men in a single bound, tame the most indomitable horses, and throw a coin so high inside the Duomo that it would hit the ceiling.

The brilliance of the man's mind was no less astonishing than the fantastic legends he inspired. Born the illegitimate son of Lorenzo Alberti, Leon Battista was descended from one of the most influential families in Florence, though they had been exiled for political reasons. As a boy, Alberti was sent to a boarding school in Padua to study with the humanist Gasparino Barzizza (1360–1431), from whom he received an exquisite education in the Latin classics. As a student of law at the University of Bologna, he endured severe poverty due to his family's condition and his own illegitimacy; nevertheless, he avidly pursued the study of mathematics and literature, earning his doctorate in 1428. Unable to rely on a family income, the young Alberti made his way to Rome to earn a living as a papal secretary in 1432, taking holy orders to further his career. During this time in Rome, in addition to his official duties, Alberti pursued his interest in cartography by surveying and mapping Rome. He also experimented with the *camera oscura* (an optical device that led to the discovery of photography), studying the effects of images and light rays. The young man's brilliance soon won him the attention of Pope Eugenius IV, who recognized his exceptional talents and rewarded Alberti with a church benefice[7] that would provide him with a small but steady income throughout his life.

Alberti was thirty years old in 1434 when he accompanied Eugenius to Florence, setting foot in his family's native city for the first time. The

---

7 Deriving from the Latin *beneficium*, meaning "benefit," a benefice was the grant of a piece of church land, along with money paid by local residents of that parish in the form of tithes and from income earned from agriculture cultivated there. Though there were also ecclesiastical duties involved, many holders of benefices never set foot on their land, but subcontracted to local priests to carry out those tasks. In principle no one was to hold more than one benefice, but in reality wealthy churchmen often held dozens of such lucrative incomes. In Alberti's case the pope had to issue two special bulls to make this happen, due to Alberti's illegitimate birth.

atmosphere in Florence was heady for Alberti. It was during this two-year stay that he met all the major artists working there, and he was inspired to write his study entitled *Della pittura (On Painting)*, dedicated to Filippo Brunelleschi. The excitement he felt is palpable in his prologue to this book:

> I used to both marvel and sorrow at the fact that so many splendid arts and sciences of the ancient past had been missing or were lost to us … But since I have come back here from exile … I have understood that in many men, but especially in you, Filippo, in our dear friend Donato [Donatello], as well as in Nencio [Ghiberti], Luca [della Robbia], and Masaccio there is genius worthy of praise, that by no means should be given second place behind works of antiquity.

In this treatise Alberti outlines the theory and practice of perspective, codifying rules Brunelleschi developed. He also discusses at length suitable subject matter for paintings, as well as the most graceful and appropriate treatment of figures and landscapes. Most important, he expresses an admiration for the nobility of the art of painting. The relative status of the various arts was a longstanding Renaissance debate, and here Alberti passionately defends painting. Alberti insists that rather than being a hired craftsman, slavishly carrying out a commission, a painter is a unique creative agent who draws upon both technical expertise and a wide range of knowledge, and preferably should be educated in all the liberal arts, which included geometry.

Reinventing the role of the architect

After the death of his patron Eugenius IV in 1447, Alberti was appointed architectural advisor by his old friend, now Pope Nicholas V. Nicholas dreamed of rebuilding Rome and set Alberti to surveying the streets of the city and studying its ancient architecture. Rarely have the wishes of patron and artist coincided more felicitously. Alberti now focused his attention on architecture, not only observing examples of classical architecture around him in Rome but also studying the only surviving ancient work on architecture, *De architectura* written by Vitruvius (*c*.80 BCE–*c*.15 BCE). In 1452 Alberti presented the pope with his volume *De re aedificatoria (On the Art of Building)*, the first modern treatise on architecture. In this book, Alberti re-established rules of classical architecture, advocating balance and harmony as essential elements in well-designed buildings and public spaces, though he was not able to carry out any significant work for Nicholas who died in 1455.

Over the next twenty years, between 1452 and 1472, Alberti created the majority of his architectural works, putting into practice the theories expounded in his treatise. In the simple, harmonious geometry of the façade of Santa Maria Novella in Florence, Alberti incorporated elements of the pre-existing fourteenth-century façade of the church, but did away with

Figure 4.2 Leon Battista Alberti, *Façade of Santa Maria Novella*, completed in 1470

intricate Gothic tracery and statuary (Figure 4.2). Rather than a cold exercise in mathematical precision, however, the building is elegant, the higher portion flanked by two graceful upended volutes (scrollwork that traditionally adorns capitals of classical columns) that impart movement, drawing the eye upwards to the top of the building, which is capped by a satisfying isosceles triangle (the tympanum).

In a narrow band beneath the tympanum of Santa Maria Novella is an inscription bearing the name of Alberti's patron who was footing the bill for this project, Giovanni di Paolo Rucellai (1403–1481). Alberti designed a number of structures in Florence for the wealthy wool merchant, notably his home, the Palazzo Rucellai (1452–58), which set the standard for the Renaissance palazzo.[8] The building is covered in protruding rough-hewn stone work (rustication) and is composed of three stories of equal height.

---

8 *Palazzo* in Italian means both "palace" and more generally "building." In this period, the term is most often used to refer to a large civic building, often the private residence of a prosperous merchant or noble.

Overall, the palazzo gives an impression of fortress-like solidity; however, by adopting elements of classical architecture in its façade, Alberti adds elements of grace to its otherwise forbidding appearance. Following ancient Roman building technique—as seen for example on the exterior of the Colosseum—Alberti framed the arched windows with a different type of column for each level. The ground level façade is decorated with a series of simple Doric columns, and each subsequent floor has a more complex style of column. The contrast between the uneven stonework and the elegantly carved columns adds interesting variety to the building, which as a whole communicates a sense of power and noble restraint.

Aside from his many buildings, which revolutionized architecture, Alberti contributed something more intangible but nonetheless significant—the idea of the architect as an original, creative genius. Throughout the Middle Ages impressive works of architecture were constructed—Chartres, Cologne, and York are only a few of the many medieval cathedrals that still soar above city skylines—however, none of these were designed and supervised by a single architect. These large-scale projects often took several generations to complete, and no one individual was solely responsible for a building's design. Rather, teams of skilled masons, under the direction of a master mason, would carry out the plans as dictated by the bishop and city fathers. Indeed, the title assigned to Filippo Brunelleschi for his role in the construction of the Duomo was that of *capomaestro* (chief master builder). Though the original design for the *cupola* had been determined long before Brunelleschi came to the project, his ingenuity and artistry have forever identified him as its architect. Although not a mason, but a goldsmith by trade, Brunelleschi was recognized as an accomplished craftsman and was admitted into the mason's guild for his work on the Duomo. Alberti's background, however, was entirely different. He was not trained in any manual art; his skills rather were in mathematics and aesthetics. He was a capable draftsman and through his drawings was able to communicate his designs to builders, but unlike the hands-on Brunelleschi, he had little or no involvement with the actual construction of his buildings.

Over the course of these twenty years (1452–72), Alberti designed many buildings throughout Italy, spreading the new Renaissance architectural aesthetic that he had developed in Rome. And it was in Rome that he chose to live most of his life. Even after the death of his patron and friend Nicholas V, and after being dismissed from the office of the papal chancery, Alberti found himself most at home in Rome, surrounded by the ruins of antiquity, and among the cultivated members of the papal court. He lived his final years in Rome, where he died at the age of sixty-eight.

Pope Pius II, a poet on St. Peter's chair

Not only did the Renaissance papacy attract brilliant humanists to work as secretaries in Rome, but many of the popes themselves were men of exceptional learning and refined taste, as we have seen in the case of Nicholas

90 Caput Mundi *again?*

V. The one pope who embodies this more than any other is Pius II (Enea Silvio Piccolomini 1405–1464). The oldest of eighteen children of noble Sienese parents who had fallen on hard times, as a young man Piccolomini grew up in relative poverty in the countryside. Sent to study law and humanities at the University of Siena, Piccolomini later went to Florence to study Greek with the renowned humanist Francesco Filelfo (1398–1481). Skilled in the finer points of Latin style and being a talented speaker, it was only natural that the young man would make his career in the church. In his youth he traveled widely throughout Europe, going as far as France, England, Scotland, Switzerland, Austria, and Germany on church business. The future pope enjoyed good food and wine, loved women, wrote dramas in Latin—one of them a comedy set in a brothel—as well as an erotic "best-seller" entitled *The Story of Two Lovers*.

Piccolomini rose to prominence as an eloquent spokesman for the reforms of the conciliar movement, attending the Council of Basel, where he served as secretary to the antipope Felix V. After the defeat of the council, Piccolomini went to work as secretary to the Holy Roman Emperor, before being reconciled with Pope Eugenius IV. Afterward he worked as papal secretary to both Eugenius and Nicholas V. Aware of having had a unique career, Piccolomini would later write: "I don't know if any other man has ever happened to have the good fortune to be secretary to two popes, as well as an emperor and an antipope." As his position within the curia grew, Piccolomini became an ordained priest, was made a cardinal and a bishop, and was eventually elected Pope Pius II in 1458.

A man of many contradictions, Pius is especially known to us because he is the only Renaissance pope who wrote a memoir. His *Commentaries*, composed in Latin prose and modeled on Julius Caesar's autobiographic work, is written in the second person. However, in spite of this literary device, the man's personal experiences and character sparkle on every page. Where a lesser man might have avoided, for instance, mentioning the scene in which he meets Eugenius and repudiates his own former activities at the Council of Basil, Pius revels in describing his success with the Pope. Fearing the pope's wrath, his family tearfully tried to persuade him not to meet with Eugenius, but the young prelate instead boldly spoke the following words to the pope:

> I know that much has come to your ears about me that is neither good, nor worthy to be repeated, nor have those who told you these things lied. I did, said, and wrote many things against you in Basel. I deny nothing. I did not think to harm you, but to advance the Church of God. I was wrong (why deny it?) but there were not a few others with me, men of no mean importance.

Indeed, the year after he became pope, Pius went on to completely denounce the conciliar movement in his bull *Execrabilis* in 1459.

Caput Mundi *again?* 91

In the *Commentaries*, Pius also gives a vivid account of the backroom politics involved in the conclave[9] that assembled after the death of Pope Calixtus III (r.1455–58), which resulted in his own election. During the conclave, one of Pius's enemies exclaims: "He has just come back from Germany; maybe he will want to move the curia there. And what about his writing? Should we put a poet in St. Peter's chair and rule the Church by pagan laws?"

When they elected Enea Piccolomini pope, the cardinals did indeed put a poet on St. Peter's throne. In addition to descriptions of papal politics and ceremony within the Vatican, in the startlingly candid self-portrait that Pius paints in the *Commentaries* the picture emerges of a man who is not particularly devout, but who has a consuming passion for life, sensual pleasures, and an extraordinary love of nature.

Considerations: Renaissance pope and Renaissance man

In this chapter we have explored the distinctive traits of the Renaissance as it took shape in Rome, characterized at once by the omnipresence of its antique past and papal present. We have also been introduced to three types of Renaissance individuals whom we will repeatedly encounter throughout the course of this history: the charismatic self-made secular ruler here represented by Cola di Rienzo; the multi-talented genius in the person of Leon Battista Alberti; and the forceful figure of the pope, in the guises of Boniface VIII, Nicholas V, and Pius II.

At moments of political and social turmoil, Italians sought a strong leader to unify them, just as Dante had looked to Henry VII. Sometimes this leader was of noble extraction or often a self-made man, who like Cola knew how to seize power at the right moment. Giangaleazzo Visconti (Chapter 6) and Cesare Borgia (Chapter 10) are just two of the dynamic Renaissance figures we will meet who captured the public imagination and for a time seemed capable of uniting the peninsula. Nor did this type of Italian leader end with the Renaissance. Cola's dream of a united Italy brings to mind the unification of Italy in 1870 under Garibaldi; Cola's demagogic appeal to ancient glories recalls Mussolini. Men like Cola did not appeal solely to the populace; the force of his personality was such that he was able to stir an intellectual like Petrarch. Similarly, the humanist Machiavelli was taken with the brash and ruthless Cesare Borgia, proposing him in *The Prince* as a model leader to bring together all of Italy in a time of crisis.

The stereotype of the polymath genius, the universal or Renaissance man, has become so widespread as to take on the proportions of a myth. In the past, historians following the lead of Burckhardt represented Italy

---

9 "Conclave" from the Latin *cum clavis* meaning "with a key" refers to the ceremony of electing a pope, in which the College of Cardinals assembles in a large hall and are locked in until such time as they arrive at a decision. This was initiated in order to prevent long drawn-out proceedings as well as to attempt to reduce outside influence on cardinals' votes.

during the Renaissance as swarming with individuals of superhuman intellectual and artistic abilities. Modern scholarship tends to take a more critical look at individuals such as Alberti, examining ways that he consciously promoted this self-image. To a certain extent Alberti was engaged in Renaissance "self-fashioning." A term introduced by literary historian Stephen Greenblatt, self-fashioning describes the way people during this time began to reinvent themselves and represent their accomplishments to the world. Furthermore, in taking a closer look at Alberti's actual contributions in various fields, scholars have at times charged Alberti and other humanists like him, with dilettantism—historian Anthony Grafton going so far as to refer to Alberti's "catastrophic lack of artistic talent." Nonetheless, even if we discount some of the overblown claims of humanist polymaths, there is no doubting the accomplishments of such acknowledged multifaceted geniuses as Michelangelo, Galileo, and most of all, Leonardo, all products of Renaissance culture.

Finally, the figure of the papal monarch looms over the Renaissance. Sometimes these were men of uncontrollable rages and passions like Boniface, at times discerning artistic patrons like Nicholas, or themselves learned humanist scholars like Nicholas and Pius. Many of the Renaissance popes combined all three qualities. Consciously promoting their role as prince and patron, these popes would physically transform Rome with building and urban planning projects into the most magnificent city in Christendom. The territorial aspirations, short-sighted policies, and stubborn arrogance of Renaissance popes would also be the destruction of the city of Rome (Chapter 12). Was it inevitable that the papacy would assume the form it did? What would have happened if the conciliarists had succeeded in reforming the papacy? Would there have been a Protestant Reformation?

Of course, there is no answer for such questions. It is easy to judge the actions of individual popes, but it is important to keep in mind that the papacy is an institution that grew and developed in response to circumstances over time. And the man who sat on the throne of St. Peter was caught in a double-bind. On the one hand he was expected to maintain spiritual authority, guiding his flock by his example of Christian love and mercy; on the other it was his responsibility to defend the community, often physically, against outside threats. If a pope commanded too aggressively, he was accused of worldliness and could lose spiritual credibility; if he devoted too much attention to spiritual matters and neglected politics, the consequences could be disastrous. The lives of Renaissance Italians were often directly influenced by the political actions and doctrinal decisions of the pope; yet although he was the titular head of the Western church this did not mean he could dictate the way men and women experienced spirituality or every aspect of their everyday lives. Not yet. By the sixteenth century, autocratic popes reacting to the Protestant threat would clamp down on the moral behavior of every man, woman, and child in Italy. But until then, to most people, the pope was a distant, if powerful, representative of God on earth.

Caput Mundi *again?* 93

Sourcebook

Boniface VIII, *Unam sanctam*
Anonymous, *Letter from Avignon*, 1343
Catherine of Siena, *Letter to Gregory XI*
Leon Battista Alberti, *On Painting*
Pius II Piccolomini, *The Story of Two Lovers*
Fra Angelico, *Annunciation*, Convent of San Marco, Florence

Further reading

Brentano, Robert. *Rome Before Avignon: A Social History of Thirteenth-Century Rome*, University of California Press, 1974.

Dey, Hendrik. *The Making of Medieval Rome: A New Profile of the City, 400–1450* Cambridge University Press, 2021.

Gadol, Joan. *Leon Battista Alberti, Universal Man of the Early Renaissance*, University of Chicago Press, 1969.

Grafton, Anthony. *Alberti Master Builder of the Italian Renaissance*, Cambridge University Press, 2002.

McCahill, Elizabeth. *Reviving the Eternal City: Rome and the Papal Court, 1420–1447*, Harvard University Press, 2014.

Musto, Ronald G. *Apocalypse in Rome: Cola di Rienzo and the Politics of the New Age*, University of California Press, 2003.

O'Brien, Emily. *The "Commentaries" of Pope Pius II (1458–1464) and the Crisis of the Fifteenth-Century Papacy*, University of Toronto Press, 2018.

Rollo-Koster, Joëlle. *Avignon and Its Papacy, 1309–1417: Popes, Institutions, and Society*, Rowman & Littlefield, 2015.

Wickham, Chris. *Medieval Rome: Stability and Crisis of a City, 900–1150*, Oxford University Press, 2014.

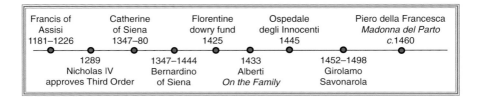

5 Hearth and Home
Lay Piety, Women, and the Family

> I thought I could convert him, but if he goes to the papal court and sees the wicked, depraved lives led by the clergy, he will never become a Christian.
> — Giovanni Boccaccio, *Decameron* Day 1, Story 2

Even as the prestige and grandeur of the papacy rose, popular feeling was growing increasingly critical of the excesses and corruption of the popes, a strong anti-clericalism that is echoed in the writings of Dante, Petrarch, and Boccaccio. In the story quoted above, Boccaccio tells of a Christian merchant who wants to convert a Jewish friend named Abraham, but he despairs when his friend goes to Rome, afraid that Abraham will be disgusted by what he finds there. We have looked until now at the history of the papacy, focusing on the larger-than-life individuals who wore the papal tiara. But what did people in Italy make of the comings and goings of popes and all their pomp and splendor? This chapter takes a look at the everyday lives of men and women in Italy during this period, with special attention to the part religion played in their lives.

Renaissance Italians were cynical not only about the papacy but also about the corrupt and often ignorant clergy. It was not uncommon for village priests to have female "housekeepers," in reality their concubines, who gave birth to children fathered by the priest. Many priests mouthed the words of the Mass but knew little or no Latin, or were actually illiterate. An equally serious problem was that prelates frequently did not even reside in their parish. Leon Battista Alberti, for instance, probably rarely, if ever, put in an appearance at the village church that was given to him as a benefice. Absentee priests would hire someone else to say Mass and attend to the needs

DOI: 10.4324/9781003270362-5

of parishioners, but often these substitutes neglected their duties. The family of a dying man often searched in vain for the village priest to administer the Last Rites (Extreme Unction), without which it was believed that it would be difficult for him to enter Heaven. Church doctrine insisted upon the importance of the priest administering not only this rite, but officiating over the other Sacraments[1] to aid in their salvation. But people asked themselves: If religious rituals were performed by a sinful priest in a careless way, how efficacious could they be in interceding with God? (Chapter 13 on Protestantism and the Donatist heresy).

Historians used to believe that this extreme cynicism indicated a society that was becoming increasingly anti-religious; however, the Renaissance was a time of, if anything, deepening faith. As the historian Denys Hay puts it: "Anti-clericalism in a sense is only possible to true believers. The church satisfies their spiritual craving; the clergy inflame their hatred and contempt." In other words, if Renaissance Italians had been less deeply religious, they might not have minded the corrupt clergy so much.

Religion: A family affair

Religion indeed played a central role in the everyday lives of Italians during the Renaissance. They began their letters with the words: "In the Name of the Lord"; the merchants Francesco di Marco Datini (*c.*1335–1410) and Goro Dati (1362–1435) frequently invoked God in their private writings. Datini headed each page of his account book with the words: "In the Name of God and Profit." Most homes, even the humblest, had a painted image of the Virgin or one of the saints; nearly every street corner and village crossroad had a shrine or a cross. People were surrounded with painted, carved, and sculpted images of Christ's story; there were vivid depictions of his last hours on the cross, his life ebbing away as his mother and friends wept. There were also joyful renderings of a girlish Mary dandling her chubby baby while his grandmother (St. Anne) proudly looks on, or of the Virgin nursing him tenderly at her breast. A popular practice initiated by St. Francis of Assisi was setting up a *presepio* (nativity scene) at Christmas time. With the image of the manger scene at Bethlehem before their eyes, it was easy to imagine that Christ had just now been born, a tiny squirming infant in a crib surrounded by admiring family and friends.

The saints: Christ's special friends

People were accustomed to thinking of the divine in very down-to-earth terms; just as when they had troubles they turned to their human friends

---

1 The Seven Sacraments of the Catholic Church as defined at the Council of Trent in 1547: Baptism, Confirmation, the Eucharist, Penance, Extreme Unction, Holy Orders, and Matrimony.

96   *Hearth and Home*

for assistance, they would ask for help from their divine friends. God, who might appear too awesome to be approached directly, could be appealed to through one of His family members or any number of His saints. In addition to the Holy Family and the twelve Apostles, legends of hundreds of saints had accumulated over the centuries. Among these saints were men and women who had been courageously martyred for their faith, hermits who lived devout lives of solitude, and other holy people who even long after their death were capable of working miracles. Churches kept relics of parts of the bodies or bones of the saints displayed in precious containers known as reliquaries. People sought favors from these influential individuals whom historian Peter Brown has called "Christ's special friends." The lives of most of these saints were not found in the Bible, but could be read about in books known as hagiographies (stories of saints' lives), especially the very popular *Golden Legend* of Jacopo de Voragine (*c.*1230–1298) and *Lives of the Holy Fathers* of Domenico Cavalca (1266–1342). These familiar tales were told and re-told and acted out in sacred dramas known as *sacre rappresentazioni*, the popular theater of the day (Chapter 9).

In addition to interceding on your behalf with God, certain saints had specialties: a prayer to Santa Lucia (St. Lucy), a martyr who had had her eyes gouged out, could cure blindness, and one to San Sebastiano (St. Sebastian), who survived being shot full of arrows, could cure the plague. A man about to embark on a long sea voyage would make a vow to San Nicola (St. Nicholas), patron saint of mariners, promising a gift to the church if he returned safely; a nursing mother who wanted to produce more milk would offer a medallion to Sant'Agata (St. Agatha), whose breasts were torn off during her martyrdom. People vowed to make an offering if their wishes were granted and churches were often hung with medals, known as ex-votos (meaning "in fulfillment of a vow"), representing the various body parts that saints had cured. They had faith in the power of the saints to improve their lives and prayed fervently for their help. It was believed that certain prayers, if recited regularly, could prevent sudden death while on a journey and other prayers, if written on a slip of paper and bound to a woman's abdomen, could ease her childbirth.

Confraternities: Organizations for prayer, good deeds, networking

The populace, then, which did not feel entirely reliant on clergy and formal ritual, and experienced deeply imaginative and personal responses to religion, also began to express their spiritual yearning in more active and personally meaningful ways. Religious devotion in the Renaissance took many forms. In urban centers in Italy, where citizens had the custom of reacting cooperatively by forming trade guilds for increasing their economic strength, or neighborhood organizations for safety, it was natural for them to look for religious well-being in group settings. Known as confraternities (brotherhoods), these groups were rather similar to clubs. Confraternities sprang up all over Italy during the thirteenth century; after the Black Death

Hearth and Home 97

there was an explosion in their numbers so that by the 1450s there were over one hundred in Florence alone. Some of these pious clubs were organized around quiet devotional activities such as prayer or meditation, while others focused on the penitential activity of flagellation.[2] Many groups concentrated on singing hymns and performing dramas based on biblical stories[3] or the lives of the saints. Fundraising for improvements to local churches or charitable causes, including hospitals and orphanages, were important functions of confraternities. In these organizations, Renaissance Italians from all walks of life, from wool carders to bankers, would gather, worshipping and doing good deeds which, it was believed, would help them achieve salvation in the afterlife.

Monastic reform and a third order for laypeople

The popular enthusiasm for the mendicant orders that swept through Italy in the thirteenth century had not died out by the fourteenth and fifteenth centuries; 572 Franciscan monasteries had been founded in Italy, roughly one half of those in all of Europe. Likewise, the Dominicans had firmly established themselves throughout the peninsula, building schools and convents in over one hundred Italian cities. As they prospered, however, these orders that claimed to espouse evangelical poverty came under harsh criticism. There were efforts to reform from within; during the mid-fourteenth century a group of Franciscans broke off to form the "Spirituals."[4] Toward the end of the century the Franciscans, Dominicans, and Augustinians were all divided into "Conventual" and "Observant" factions. The Conventuals were those who believed it was appropriate for their orders to become wealthy and established, while the Observants believed their orders needed reform and a return to the simplicity intended by their founders.

The public was by no means unaware of the incongruity between friars who went begging for food and an order that built lavish churches decorated with the finest art, the altars adorned with precious brocaded altar cloths and golden chalices. Nonetheless, large crowds gathered in piazzas and street corners to listen to fiery sermons given by wandering friars wearing austere, tattered robes. There were also famous preachers who would travel from city to city filling enormous cathedrals to overflowing as listeners strained to catch every word. The Franciscan St. Bernardino of Siena (1380–1444) and Dominicans Giordano da Rivalto (*c.*1260–1311), Giovanni Domenici

---

2 From the Latin *flagellus* (whip), this ritual self-inflicted whipping was a common practice among monastic orders and used to punish the body, subdue physical desire, and atone for sins.

3 See pp. 135–36 on the Confraternity of the Magi.

4 Members of the most radical wing of the Spiritual Franciscans, known as the Fraticelli, were denounced as heretics and the group was effectively destroyed by the Inquisition. Reform-minded Franciscans thereafter were known as Observants.

98   *Hearth and Home*

(1356–1420), St. Antoninus (Antonino Pierozzi 1389–1459), and, most well known of all, Girolamo Savonarola (1452–1498; Chapter 10) mesmerized listeners, inspiring them to lead better lives according to the teachings of the Gospels.

Many laypeople wanted to do more than attend Mass and go to Confession; they felt the urge to perform works of Christian charity, feed the poor, and tend the sick—in short to do many of the things that monks and nuns did—but while still leading their secular lives. In addition to the First Order comprised of monks, and Second Order of nuns, beginning in the thirteenth century, a so-called Third Order of laypeople (tertiaries) appeared, and was officially approved by Pope Nicholas IV in 1289. Affiliated with a particular religious house, these men and women sometimes wore the monastic garb of that order, took vows similar to those taken by monks and nuns, but could live in their own homes. Male monastic orders were divided into those whose members were obliged to stay within the monastery—Benedictines, Vallombrosans, Cistercians, Carthusians, Camaldolese—and those who wandered the cities and countryside begging for alms, preaching, and helping the poor. These latter, known as friars, belonged to the Franciscan, Augustinian, Dominican, Carmelite, and Servite orders. Women were especially attracted to the Third Order, because unlike their male counterparts, ever since Boniface VIII's 1298 bull *Periculoso*, all nuns were forbidden from leaving their convent walls; tertiaries, however, were exempt. Moreover, for women of the lower classes who felt a religious calling, but who were unable to afford the dowry required to join a convent, the Third Order provided an outlet for their devotion. Among these female tertiaries who played a prominent role in their communities from the thirteenth through sixteenth centuries were the *Pinzochere*, named after the grey color of their robes, and the *Mantellate* who took their name from the distinctive mantles, or cloaks they wore.

Margaret of Cortona and Catherine of Siena, saints who lived next door

Some tertiaries rose to fame and were canonized for the holiness of their lives, such as St. Margaret of Cortona, who was attached to the Franciscan order, and St. Catherine of Siena, who was connected with the Dominicans. As a teenager, Margaret (1247–1297) ran away from home to live as the mistress of a nobleman for nine years in his castle, bearing him a son. She later repented, forming a group of Franciscan tertiaries known as Poverelle, and founded a hospital. Renowned for her devotion, in her last years she moved to a cell on a hilltop where she lived in solitude, devoting herself to contemplation.

Catherine of Siena (Caterina di Iacopo di Benincasa 1347–1380) became even more prominent. One of a Sienese dyer's twenty-five children, many of whom died in childhood, Catherine from a very early age showed signs of saintliness, refusing to marry and instead lived a hermit-like existence in a small upper room in the family house. She fasted rigorously, subsisting at times on nothing but the wafer taken at communion, and experienced visions, most famously of her mystic marriage with Christ. When she was not engrossed in personal spiritual exercises, Catherine turned her attention to the outside world, caring for the sick in the public hospital in Siena. Around 1364 she became a *Mantellata*, a Dominican tertiary, and was actively engaged in charitable deeds for the poor and sick. Catherine became a prominent figure in her community, sent by the government of Siena to negotiate peace treaties with political enemies and went on several occasions as an emissary to the pope in Avignon.

Female holiness in an age of living saints

Catherine and Margaret were not alone; they were part of a long line of "living saints," as historian Gabriella Zarri has called them. These were not people from long-ago legends, but contemporaries known for exceptional piety, who might be living down the street or in the next village. Though both Italian men and women achieved sainthood in unprecedented numbers during the Renaissance, the thirteenth through early sixteenth centuries was a kind of golden age of female holiness. Male saints have always outnumbered female saints, but in Italy during the period between 1200 and 1500 more Christian holy women were recognized than during any other period in history (Table 5.1). Not all were ecstatic virgins like Catherine or scandalously "fallen women" like Margaret; many led everyday lives as wives and mothers. Umiliana de' Cerchi (1219–1246), born of a prominent family of Florentine

Table 5.1 Percentage of female saints

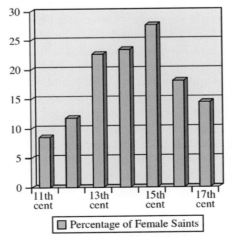

Source: Data from Bell and Weinstein, *Saints and Society*.

100   *Hearth and Home*

merchants, was a Franciscan tertiary, who had two children by her brutish, greedy husband. Elena Valentini da Udine (1396–1458) had been married to a nobleman and gave birth to six children. Also mothers, were these married saints from noble families: Francesca of Rome (Bussa dei Ponziani 1384–1440) and Catherine of Genoa (Fieschi Adorno 1447–1510). Some holy women were wives who managed to live chastely such as Elena Duglioli (1472–1520), who lived with her husband for twenty-nine years without ever having sexual intercourse. They came from many walks of life: Zita of Lucca (1218–1271) worked as the servant for a wealthy family in Lucca for fifty years; Veronica Negroni of Binasco (1445–1497) was a peasant who grew up in the countryside outside Milan; Caterina Mattei of Racconigi (1486–1547) was the daughter of a blacksmith.

Aside from their piety, these women were known for their exceptional spiritual experiences. Denying sensual pleasures through abstinence and fasting was common among them, as was the practice of various forms of "mortification of the flesh." Blessed Elena Valentini da Udine (1396-1458), who walked with thirty-three stones in her shoes (thirty-three was the age of Christ when he died) and wore an iron barbed-wire band around her head in simulation of Christ's crown of thorns. Colomba da Rieti (1467–1501), a Dominican tertiary well-known as a mystic and prophet, wore spiked chains underneath her hair shirt. Some, such as Lucia Broccadelli da Narni (1476–1544), experienced the stigmata of Christ, reliving his crucifixion by miraculously bleeding from their palms, feet, and often the sides of their chests. Stefana Quinzani (1457–1530), a Dominican tertiary from a peasant family, regularly experienced not only the stigmata, but the entire Passion of Christ every Friday for forty years.

There were secular men too, who were recognized for their holy lives. There was for instance, Giovanni Colombini (1304–1367). One day the rich Sienese merchant came home for lunch and was angered when his wife told him that the food was not yet ready. "I have to get back to the shop—I don't have all day to wait here!" he shouted. His wife Mona Biagia calmly put a book of saints' lives into his hands and told him to improve his soul while he waited. In a fury Giovanni threw the book to the ground, but then feeling guilty, he picked it up and began to read the legend of St. Mary the Egyptian. He became so absorbed in reading that he did not even pay attention when the food came, and from that point on he changed his life. Giovanni began to go to church regularly, and becoming very devout, he would flagellate himself and wear a hair shirt under his clothing. He even convinced his wife that they should live chastely from then on. He eventually renounced all his wealth, and founded the mendicant order of the Gesuati.

The story of St. Mary the Egyptian, who inspired Giovanni Colombini to alter his life, was widely known. Born in the fourth century CE, Mary lived a wild youth in Alexandria, where she indulged in every kind of sexual excess, but after her conversion she repented, living for many years as an anchorite in the deserts of Egypt. Average men and women who led lives dedicated to making money and enjoying sensual pleasures learned from her example, as well as that of St. Mary Magdalene, that they too could be saved. Giovanni Colombini is only one of the many pious men and women from all walks of life and from all over Italy who imitated the lives of the saints during this period. They were known within their communities for their holiness, and many were officially recognized as saints by the pope. Out of 190 new cults of saints created during the period 1300–1500, 127 were Italian.

The church approved and promoted the veneration of the saints. It was impossible to stem the tide of all the stories of miraculous cures and holy deeds that circulated during this period, but before officially acknowledging a man or woman as a saint the church needed to verify that the stories were true. There was (and still is) a long process of investigation of the life and miracles of a candidate for sainthood, which is known as canonization. First the candidate must be approved for beatification, and only when their deeds have been verified is the way open for being officially declared a saint. Giovanni Colombini, for instance, was beatified, but never canonized.

Religion in women's daily lives

Though men could be extraordinarily pious, it was the woman who often set the religious tone of the household. (Note how in the story of Giovanni Colombini it is his wife who places the book of saints' lives in his hand.) What is striking in the painting of *St. Bernardino Preaching in the Piazza del Campo*, by Sano di Pietro (*c*.1445, Museo dell' Opera del Duomo, Siena), is the sea of veiled women kneeling in the foreground intently listening to the preacher. Women were exceptionally devout, and they attended Bernardino's sermons in large numbers. Many of the sermons he delivered in Siena and Florence in the years 1424 through 1427 were written down, and a number of their titles indicate the importance of women in his audience: "How a husband should love his wife, and the wife her husband," "The proper love that should exist between husband and wife," "How marriage should be considered," and "How widows should be respected." In these sermons the Franciscan preacher explains to women, especially, how they can integrate the teachings of the Bible into their daily lives. Throughout the Middle Ages, women were told that they were evil, tainted with the sin of Eve. Only through renunciation of the world, maintaining their virginity as nuns, could they expect to enter Heaven. Instead, Bernardino told women that their conjugal lives did not necessarily exclude them from salvation; indeed, the everyday nurturing of others is, in itself, holy.

Who were Laura and Beatrice really?

All this raises the question: What do we really know about the inner lives of women in the Renaissance? Two of the well-known women mentioned in the previous chapters are Dante's love, Beatrice, and Petrarch's muse, Laura.

102   *Hearth and Home*

Nonetheless, we do not have any substantial information about either of these women. Beatrice is generally assumed to have been Beatrice or "Bice" Portinari (1266–1290), who was married to the Florentine banker Simone de' Bardi. About Laura we know even less; as Petrarch scholar Robert Durling has written: "We do not know who she was ... or even whether she really existed." One of Petrarch's friends even teased him that Laura was a figment of the poet's imagination, a play on the word *lauro*, his beloved laurel wreath, which was the symbol of his fame. Because of a reference in one of Petrarch's writings to Laura as a woman "worn out with frequent childbearing," it has been assumed that she was married and had children, of course, by someone other than the poet.[5] Apart from their idealized loves, both Petrarch and Dante had physical relations with very real women who bore them real children as well. Dante's wife's name was Gemma; she a member of the powerful Donati clan. Beyond her name and the fact that she bore him four children, we know nothing else, because Dante never wrote a single word about her. Likewise, Petrarch had liaisons with a number of women, and had children with one of them. The boy was called Giovanni and the girl Francesca; we have no clue as to the name of their mother.

Though we know little about these women of high social extraction, who prominently featured in the lives of famous poets, we usually know even less about those further down the social ladder. One of the greatest challenges in studying the history of women from other ages is uncovering even the most basic details of their biographies. An even greater challenge is finding out about these women's feelings and inner beliefs. Did Gemma love her husband? Was Beatrice as deeply devout as Dante portrayed her? Did Laura appreciate the sonnets written in her honor, or even know how to read? We will never have the answers to these questions, but fortunately, the historical record does contain documents recording the lives and feelings of other women during the Renaissance (see below on Alessandra Strozzi's letters). Some of these documents, written by the women themselves, reveal what feminist scholars have termed the "female voice." To study women's experience during this, or any period, we must explore what women have to say, not only the things men write about women. Known as the "male gaze," men's representations of women, whether in art, literature, or other writings, may idealize women's beauty, condemn their sensuality, or praise their spirituality, but they inevitably distort and distance us from women's real experience. The many Renaissance paintings that hang in galleries with the customary title

---

5 Laura has sometimes been identified as Laura de Noves (*c.*1308–1348), married to Hugues de Sade, an ancestor of the Marquis de Sade (1740–1814), an identification that has never been definitively proved. That she actually lived, however, seems likely, as on a page of a volume of Virgil in which Petrarch noted the deaths of relatives and friends, he wrote: "Laura, illustrious through her own virtues, and long famed through my verses, first appeared to my eyes in my youth in the year of the Lord 1327 on the sixth day of the month of April, in the church of St. Clare in Avignon at matins; and in the same city, in the same month of April, on the same sixth day, at the same first hour, in the year 1348, her light was withdrawn from the light of day."

Portrait of a Young Woman, or *Portrait of a Lady*, reveal almost nothing of the inner life of their subjects. These female portraits in profile are static. The faces display no more expression than that of mannequins, and aside from their flawless complexions, the main focus of the paintings seems to be the young women's elaborate hairstyles richly woven with jewels and their opulent brocaded gowns.

"What's love got to do with it?": Marriage among Renaissance elites

The pomp and splendor of such nuptial rituals—exchanges of lavish gifts, music, banqueting, and public processions—cemented the alliance of two important families, while exalting their social standing (Figure 5.1). Marriage, as practiced among the elite in Renaissance Italy in many ways resembled a corporate merger rather than the romantic or spiritual linking of a man and a woman. Matches were arranged based on a set of carefully calculated criteria that had nothing to do with love.

The following conditions had to be satisfied: First, was the family well established and respectable? Given that merchant fortunes often rose (and fell) swiftly, the fact that the family was "new" wealth was not necessarily a deal-breaker. It was important, however, that the family was not too rough around the edges. Girls from the wealthy classes were expected to have perfect comportment; speak well; and often to play a musical instrument, dance, or sing. The girl's appearance and manners would be closely scrutinized. A very fair complexion was desirable, and a high forehead set off by a single pearl, with which it vied in whiteness, was considered the height of beauty. Blond hair was especially prized, and women would often sit for hours on their rooftops wearing large straw hats with a hole cut from the center. They would extend their hair over the top, having applied

Figure 5.1 Lo Scheggia (Giovanni di Ser Giovanni Guidi), *Adimari Wedding Cassone*, c.1450, Accademia, Florence. The painting represents the wedding festivities of two elite Florentine families, the Adimari and Martelli

104 *Hearth and Home*

various chemicals to bleach it until it ideally achieved the golden color of Botticelli's *Venus*. Aside from physical characteristics, however, the absolute requirement, without which marriage would not take place, was that the girl's honor was impeccable. The slightest hint of a dalliance, any indication of loose morals, would ruin a girl's chances of marriage. Families that could afford it would often have girls raised in a convent to safeguard their virtue. The girls of these wealthy families were then married off as soon as they came of age, usually at around fifteen or sixteen. Men married later than women, usually in their mid-thirties. Far from being expected to be a virgin at marriage, the man not only had sexual experience, but often had already fathered one or more illegitimate children who sometimes lived in his household.

Once the suitability of the family had been established, practical financial matters were considered. First of all was the matter of the girl's dowry. Though the money technically belonged to the woman, as long as her husband was alive, he had control over it and could use it or invest it as he saw fit. During the Quattrocento, dowries among the elite grew to astronomical sums. In the 1430s it cost around 1,000 florins for a magnate to marry his daughter; by the 1460s the amount had doubled. To address the problem of dowry inflation, beginning in 1425 Florentines instituted a dowry investment fund called the *Monte delle doti*. When a daughter was born, parents could invest money in a municipally funded account that accumulated interest. If the girl died before reaching marriage age, the money was lost, but if she survived, she could count on a substantial dowry.

Other financial questions might include: Would this match open up business possibilities for the families involved? If a clan wanted to expand its business ventures, for instance, in France, and the bride's family already had established offices in Paris, this could smooth the way for entry into a new market, bringing potentially huge returns. If the family of the groom was short on cash, but was well-connected with the ruling elite, boasting many priors and other city officers in their ranks, they could be very useful in promoting the long-term interests of the bride's family. Who you knew—access to power—was a bankable commodity in Renaissance Italy.

Of lesser concern was the compatibility of the couple themselves. The two might be given several opportunities to meet under very controlled and strictly supervised conditions so they could get to know each other, but once the engagement was under way, the outcome was a foregone conclusion. A series of formal meetings took place involving handshakes, kisses exchanged between the representatives of the two clans, and preliminary agreements. These formalities culminated with the signing of the marriage contract before a notary, and the couple exchanging vows as specified by the church. Though practices varied by region, a visit to the church itself was often not involved. The wedding festivities included the bride's public entrance into her husband's home, and once their union was consummated, the couple was officially married.

Governing the household: The woman's realm

We can try to imagine what life must have been like for these sheltered teenage brides, who, once they were married, were suddenly thrust into a new life, in unfamiliar surroundings, with new duties and responsibilities. In Leon Battista Alberti's fictional dialogue *I libri della famiglia* (translated and published in English as *The Family in Renaissance Florence*), a husband describes his bride's orientation to her new home:

> After a few days, when my wife had settled down in my home, and she suffered less from missing her mother, I took her by the hand and went with her through the whole house, showing her everything. I taught her that the grains are kept up above, while below there is the cellar for wine and wood. I showed her where everything necessary for the table is kept, so that she saw every household item, learning both where it was located, and what purpose it served. Then we returned to my chamber, and locking the door shut I showed her all the valuables—the silver, tapestries, garments, jewels.

Girls were raised from an early age to be obedient, first to their parents, and then to their husbands. Subservience and submission was the message from the pulpit, and it is echoed by Alberti, who writes: "she had learned to obey her father and mother and they had ordered her to obey me, thus she was prepared to do anything that I commanded." Yet, women exercised a large amount of authority within the household. In addition to supervising a staff of servants, seeing to the preparation of meals, sewing, and spinning, one of a woman's most important responsibilities was educating her small children. This crucial role is emphasized in the 1415 marriage manual *De re uxoria* by Venetian humanist Francesco Barbaro (1390–1454). As it was the mother who taught her children the ABCs, the Florentine humanist Matteo Palmieri (1406–1475) in his *De vita civile* (*On Civic Life*) recommends that to make learning fun the mother should form letters out of "fruits, candies and other childish foods."

A widow and her choices: Alessandra Strozzi

> Don't be surprised that Alfonso is so advanced for his age, as I am teaching him to read. I tell you if you saw him, he'd seem even more advanced than I've said. I swear, you don't need to tell him anything more than once for him to understand it. One evening I whispered in his ear: "Daddy is in Naples." I didn't need to say anything else, and when he was asked about it, he said "Dada in Napi." He is that way with everything he does, which is a sign that he has a good memory.

This is how Alessandra Macinghi (1408–1471), the widow of Matteo Strozzi, brags about her two-year-old grandson in one of her letters. It was important

106   *Hearth and Home*

for women to know how to write not only so they could educate children, but so they could stay in touch with male family members who were exiled or traveling abroad on business. After she was widowed, Alessandra wrote dozens of letters to her exiled sons. Her writing reveals much about women's activities in the household, as well as the woman herself.

For twenty-three years Alessandra Strozzi wrote letters to her sons, keeping them informed of the latest events in Florence and explaining to them how she was taking care of family business. When it was time for the young men to think of marriage, Alessandra evaluated many prospective Florentine brides for them, carefully describing each girl's qualities. About one, Alessandra writes: "she has good skin ... a long face, not the most delicate features, but not rustic, and it seemed to me from her manner of walking and her look that she is not slow." She described yet another as having "a complexion not of the fairest, but not dark ... she is bright and knows how to sing and dance ... her father was one of the nice youths of Florence and has a gentle manner. He adores this girl and one imagines that he has raised her with good manners."

Her letters give us an intimate glimpse into the daily life of a Florentine matron of the very highest social class. She is a shrewd manager of the family's resources, making crucial financial decisions, such as taking out life insurance in the event of her married daughter's death in childbirth, an all too common occurrence. Maternal mortality was high, as indicated by the 1427 Florentine Catasto records: "Out of every 69 women who gave birth, one died from puerperal complications. About one-fifth of the deaths of married women in Florence seem to have been associated with childbearing."[6]

Alessandra is tough, determined and proud, fighting for decades to improve the clan's fortunes and hold her family together, though we also see her break down, when, after sending her youngest son away to join his brothers in exile, she expresses her grief at the news of the twenty-three-year-old Matteo's sudden death from malaria. Death was a regular part of daily life; the untimely loss not just of a child or parent, but of a spouse was all too frequent. Given the difference in age between husbands and wives, it was natural that many women, even with the high percentage of deaths in childbirth, would outlive their husbands. Widowhood for poor women usually meant complete destitution; a cloth-worker's widow, who during his life had barely been able to take care of her family, would be reduced to begging on the streets to find enough food to keep herself and her children from dying of starvation. If her deceased husband had been a craftsman belonging to a guild, the widow might be able to receive support from that organization.

A well-to-do widow like Alessandra had several options: she could remain in her deceased husband's home with his family, re-marry, or return to her

6 Herlihy and Klapisch-Zuber, 1985, p. 277.

family's home. Although her dowry was returned to her on the death of her husband and legally a widow was free to choose, many psychological and social factors made the decision complicated and often wrenching. If she decided to re-marry, the children from her former marriage automatically belonged to their father's family and she, along with her dowry, would be separated from them. If, on the other hand, she decided to stay with her children and in-laws, she might be looking forward to a long lonely life as an unwanted dependent in the home. If she returned to her parents' house she could be resented as a burden or subjected to relentless pressure to re-marry so that the clan might capitalize once again on the benefits that would accrue along with a successful match. Living on her own was rarely an option because of the disgrace that was associated with a single woman living in an unsupervised, and, hence, it was assumed, licentious manner.

The nun in her cloister: Protected or imprisoned?

Yet another option for widows who could afford it, was to join a convent. Convents were not just places for quiet devotion where a woman intent on dedicating her life to God could pray and meditate. Convents often served the social purpose of caring for and educating young girls before marriage, as well as providing a respectable place for women to live out their lives when no suitable arrangement could be found for them in the outside world. Some women welcomed the companionship and quiet pleasures of a convent. In addition to the practical tasks such as caring for the sick, gardening, embroidering, preparing foods and pharmaceuticals, nuns also engaged in recreational activities such as singing and acting in sacred dramas. Many convents put a strong emphasis on learning; nuns could devote themselves to the study of Latin authors, reading, copying, and illuminating manuscripts.

The life was not for everyone, however, and once this path was chosen, there was no turning back for a cloistered nun. The cloister (from the Latin *claustrum* meaning "an enclosed place") is the inner courtyard of the convent, the part most removed from the outside world, and claustration meant that once a nun took her vows, for the rest of her life she would never be permitted to leave its walls. If she was allowed to see visitors it was only from the other side of a barred window in the convent parlatory or parlor (speaking room). Some convents could be relatively comfortable, with daughters of noble families, who were called choir nuns, waited upon by servants known as *converse* (singular: *conversa*), women of humble origins who had taken religious vows. Other convents were more austere. Some orders imposed very strict rules of silence and obedience, and nuns were often constrained to accept ascetic living conditions, enduring cold and hunger. The sisters lived in very close quarters with one another, and personality conflicts could burst into conflagrations of antagonism that smoldered over the years. It could be a difficult enough lifestyle if a young

108   *Hearth and Home*

woman felt a deep religious vocation, but for a girl who was forced against her will to become a nun (forced monachization) it was a tragedy. Parents could often barely afford to pay the dowry for one daughter, so from the moment of their births, the other daughters were marked out for the convent, where the dowry required to become a bride of Christ cost a fraction of that for a secular marriage.

Working women: Domestic servants and wet nurses

Few options were available for women outside of marriage or the convent. Unlike parts of northern Europe, where women were entrepreneurs, sometimes running businesses or artisan's workshops, in general, in Italian cities, women's employment opportunities were limited. A woman could work at home preparing or spinning wool, or sewing, and of course she could help her husband in the shop; but for the most part Italian women were excluded from membership in the major guilds. The most common employment for a single woman of the non-patrician classes was as a domestic servant. Girls, often from the country, when still very young would come to work for a family—carrying water from the well, sweeping, and emptying buckets of slops—and in exchange they were fed and clothed and, when they came of age (the age for marriage was higher for the laboring classes), were provided with a dowry so that they could marry.

The most highly paid domestic servants were wet nurses. The custom among the elite in much of Italy was for women not to breastfeed their infants themselves, but to hire a nursing mother, called a wet nurse, to nourish their babies for them, often in a village in the country. There were a number of reasons for this practice, one was the belief that if a mother had sex while lactating, her milk would harm the baby, and husbands were unwilling to endure the enforced abstinence that this would have entailed. Another reason was that while lactating, the body produces hormones, similar to those during pregnancy, that act as a kind of natural contraception. Patrician clans were concerned that their women produce as many offspring as possible so as to provide a male heir. To offset the high infant mortality, women were encouraged to have as many babies as they could, and it was not unusual for a woman to undergo as many as fifteen to twenty pregnancies in her lifetime.

It is unclear how women felt about handing their infants over to other women to nurse. It appears that, as a part of a general repugnance for all things rustic, many fashionable women considered it peasant-like to breast-feed, while others, inspired by the many visual images of Mary holding the baby Jesus to her breast (*Madonna lactans*), may have preferred to nurse their infants themselves. In any case, a woman had little say in the matter; the father chose the wet nurse for the child, and soon after birth the baby was generally removed from the home and taken to live in the country with the surrogate. If they survived infancy, at around two years old the child would be brought back into the household to be raised by their mother.

Social outcasts: Prostitutes, outsiders, and slaves

There were other women who found themselves on the margins of society—because of sexual misconduct, lack of kin, or accident of birth. Single women were often driven into crime and prostitution as a result of being seduced or raped. Certainly, the custom of men not marrying until their thirties meant that men were looking for sexual encounters outside of marriage. Alarmed by the number of sex crimes, some cities opened public brothels—Venice in 1360, Florence in 1403, Siena in 1421—in an attempt to accommodate men's sexual energies. Inevitably, many men looked for satisfaction closer to home, seducing domestic servants. Although the taboo against premarital sex was not as rigid for women lower down the social ladder, a maid could lose her position if she became pregnant. From that point, her social options were limited. Without a dowry, marriage was nearly impossible, and after being dishonored it was not easy to find another position as a servant. Many women then found themselves on the street and were forced to turn to prostitution or other illegal activities to earn a living. Country girls or foreign women similarly ended up as prostitutes, lured to cities by unscrupulous men intending to exploit them.

Many households also included enslaved women who did domestic work, and not infrequently they became pregnant by a male member of the family. These women were usually brought from parts of eastern Europe, hence the word *schiavo* or slave, from "Slav." It was not uncommon for a man to keep a slave openly as his mistress; indeed, Alessandra Strozzi mentions her son's lover, the slave Marina, in a number of letters to him. In the family's Catasto report, a Florentine man would often list as members of the household not only his wife and legitimate children, but also a slave and illegitimate children he has had with her.

Although illegitimate children were sometimes raised by their fathers in their homes, many others were abandoned on the streets. So serious did the problem become that foundling homes were created all over Italy. The most famous was the Ospedale degli Innocenti in Florence, which featured a little window where a mother could leave her infant anonymously. After ringing the bell, the woman could slip away and the staff would bring the child inside to care for it. Up to 50% of children left in Renaissance foundling homes died; those that survived needed to be provided for.[7] Thus guilds and confraternities arranged for boys to be taught trades and organized dowry funds for girls to help set them up in respectable marriages.

Images of women in Renaissance art

Much in the same way as the lives of country people and laborers tend to disappear from the historical record, it is often hard to find traces of poor

---

7 Mortality rates for orphans would be even higher in institutions several centuries later: during the eighteenth century in Paris, London, and Petersburg mortality rates reached 90%.

110 *Hearth and Home*

widows, prostitutes, servants, slaves, and artisans' wives. Although we are fortunate to have writings by patrician women such as Alessandra Strozzi, how can we know more about women's lives from the entire spectrum of society? Scholars of women's history draw upon sources that include criminal records, tax reports, and household inventories drawn up at death. Often, however, we are left wanting to have a closer look at the women themselves. We can get some intimate glimpses of women through art of the period. For instance, if you look closely at Domenico Ghirlandaio's *Birth of John the Baptist* (1486–90 Tornabuoni Chapel, Figure 5.2), you will see St. Elizabeth, who has just given birth, sitting up in bed welcoming neighbors who have come to congratulate her. The visitors, female members of the wealthy Tornabuoni family, stand on the right-hand side, while in the foreground, in the center-left of the fresco sits the *balia* or wet nurse. She breastfeeds the infant while turning her healthy, fresh-faced gaze toward the newcomers. Next to her is another servant, with arms outstretched ready to tend to the baby after he has finished nursing. In the background, surprisingly central, but almost imperceptible, is the silent figure of a serving girl who brings a tray of refreshments to the new mother. Another birth scene—a tragic one—is represented in the bas-relief of the *Death of Francesca Pitti Tornabuoni* (attrib. to Verrocchio or Francesco Ferrucci, Florence, Bargello). The young mother, clearly exhausted from labor, lies in bed disheveled, her nightgown

Figure 5.2 Domenico Ghirlandaio, *Birth of John the Baptist*, 1486–90, Tornabuoni Chapel, Church of Santa Maria Novella, Florence

Hearth and Home 111

falling from her wasted shoulder. She breathes her last breath as female family members grieve, and at the foot of the bed a wet nurse sits cradling the swaddled infant in her arms.

Though many portraits of upper-class women were painted on the occasion of their marriage, fewer paintings portray women from humble stations in life. Instead of having starring roles, they make appearances as extras, in paintings such as Ghirlandaio's *Visitation* (1486–90 Tornabuoni Chapel, Santa Maria Novella, Florence), in which on the left-hand side, ascending the stairs, is a serving woman carrying a heavy load in a basket on her head (on the cover of this book); or in Giotto's *Life of Joachim: The Annunciation to St Anne* (Scrovegni Chapel, Padua), in which Anne reverently kneels and listens to the angel's message, while on the porch just outside, a peasant woman imperturbably sits, spinning her thread. In his *Distribution of Alms and the Death of Ananias* (1426–27 Brancacci Chapel, Santa Maria del Carmine, Florence, Figure 3.4), Masaccio depicts a group of beggars and a poorly dressed woman with an intense expression of concern on her face; on one arm she balances her toddler, who is wearing nothing but a short shift, his bottom bare. Even rarer are sightings of enslaved women. If you look closely, however, at Filippo Lippi's *Birth of St. Stephen* (1452–65 Duomo, Prato), you will see in the background, standing mutely behind the bed, a dark-skinned woman in a turban, and in Ambrogio and Pietro Lorenzetti's *Martyrdom of the Franciscans in Tana* (c.1320 Friary of San Francesco, Siena) two girls with Tartar features who cringe in fear in the right-hand corner; most likely domestic slaves served as the models for these figures.

As for the fate of foundlings, in a fresco painted for the wall of a hospital in Siena, *The Rearing and Marriage of Female Foundlings in Siena* (1441–42 Ospedale di Santa Maria della Scala, Siena), Domenico di Bartolo (1400–1447) provides a vivid narrative of the lives of these children. On the left, babies are being cared for; a plump wet nurse sits nursing an infant, as a toddler affectionately hangs over her shoulder grabbing her free breast. On the right-hand side of the fresco, grown female orphans are getting married. We see a groom placing a ring on the finger of a suitably humble and modestly attired girl who has benefited from the charity of the institution. The Roman painter Antoniazzo Romano (c.1452–1512) in his *Annunciation* (1485 Santa Maria sopra Minerva, Rome) depicts the Virgin Mary herself bending forward toward little kneeling foundling girls and handing them sacks of money for their dowries.

And finally, even in depictions of the sacred, we can see a reflection of real women's lives. There was not always a sharp dividing line between the sacred and the everyday, as we have witnessed with the "living saints." Artists drew their inspiration from the women around them, as in Piero della Francesca's *Madonna del Parto* (*Madonna of Childbirth* c.1460, Monterchi, Figure 5.3). In this painting, a heavily pregnant Mary stands before us, leaning backward slightly on her heels, with one hand resting on her hip, the very picture of the

Figure 5.3 Piero della Francesca, *Madonna del Parto, c.* 1460, Museo della Madonna del Parto, Monterchi

weary, uncomfortable late-term pregnant woman. With the other hand she parts her gown, which looks as if it were splitting like an overripe fruit, her body ready for childbirth. We are brought back to the sacred context of the image by her solemn and vaguely melancholy gaze as Mary reflects on the momentous events that have already been set in motion within her womb. Similarly, the many depictions of the scene of the *Annunciation* when the Angel Gabriel appears to Mary, announcing that she has been chosen by God to bear His son, reveal aspects of real women's lives. Mary is depicted as little more than a girl, barely out of childhood, with facial expressions and body language that register a range of emotions, from startled or frightened to resigned and accepting. Yet the seriousness of this moment, the lightning-fast shift from childhood to womanhood, was an emotion familiar to the child brides of the Renaissance. Furthermore, very frequently during this period, Mary is represented with a book in her hand, the Angel having interrupted her quiet reading time, yet another indication of the growing literacy of Italian women during the period. More often than not, the room that Mary is reading in is a bedroom, not a *studiolo* (study), as a man would have; a woman at this time had no "room of her own."

Considerations: A Renaissance for men, but the Dark Ages for women?

This chapter opened with an exploration of the deep current of religious feeling that ran throughout Renaissance Italian society. Deep faith managed to coexist with sentiments of anticlericalism and the increasingly secular values introduced by humanists during the same period. As we examine the era more closely, we can see it is full of such contradictions. There is also an incongruity in an age that emphasizes creative expression for the individual, and fosters self-fashioning, but rarely for women. All the works of art described in this chapter were created by men; their representations of women, even the most sensitive and expressive, can be considered as examples of the "male gaze." Women artists, excluded from guilds and workshops, were few; only rarely during the fourteenth and fifteenth centuries were women allowed to express themselves in paint or other media.

During the Italian Renaissance, a period of extreme cultural vitality, tradition shackled women's lives. Girls of the upper classes were kept under lock and key to protect their honor. They were either married off very young as pawns in their families' business strategies or put away in convents where they would not be a drain on the family fortunes. Women lower down on the social ladder paradoxically may have had more freedoms, but they also had no safety net to keep them from plunging into poverty and prostitution if they were unmarried and fell upon hard times. Even when women were widowed and came into possession of their dowries, they were often still constrained to act against their own will. Local conditions did vary by region—historian Samuel Kline Cohn has suggested that Florence "may well have been one of the worst places to have been born a woman in the Italian Renaissance"—yet there is no doubt that the period in general did not witness a golden age for women's rights. Rather than improve during the Renaissance, women's lives actually seemed to worsen; indeed, that is what Joan Kelly claimed in her 1977 essay provocatively titled: "Did Women Have a Renaissance?"

On the other hand, women could command impressive authority during this period; the ideal of sanctity in many ways was a female model during the Renaissance, and Italians revered holy women living among them. Not only did people admire the examples of famous saints, such as Catherine of Siena, but throughout Italian cities female tertiaries, garbed in their simple robes, everywhere tended the sick and the dying. The respect afforded to these nurturing laywomen was also extended to wives and mothers who took care of their families. Within the household realm women were gaining new self-respect, as preachers such as Bernardino of Siena asserted that their work

114   *Hearth and Home*

within the family was worthy in the sight of God. Women such as Alessandra Strozzi, who was the pillar of her family, earned the respect of all around her as she held her family together through her long years of widowhood and her sons' exile.

Women had no role in the political sphere and had yet to openly challenge the patriarchal structure of Italian society. They did have an advantage over women in other parts of Europe, however, and that was literacy. As we shall see in later chapters, Italian women would take up the pen to criticize a system that kept them in an inferior position to men. The dramatic political changes that affected Italy by the end of the fifteenth century affected women as well. Yet another incongruity was that as republican governments gave way to rule by princes or signori, and eventually regional autonomy disappeared, the more freedoms women would gain, expressing themselves as poets, playwrights, painters, and patrons of the arts.

Sourcebook

Catherine of Siena, *Letter to Gregory XI*
Raymond of Capua, *St. Catherine of Siena's Mystic Marriage*
Francesco Barbaro, *On Wifely Duties*
St. Bernardino of Siena, *Vernacular Sermons*
Sandra Pierozzi, *Catasto Tax Report*
Gregorio Dati, *Diary*
Alessandra Macinghi Strozzi, *Letter to Filippo Strozzi*

Further reading

Brown, Peter. *The Cult of the Saints: Its Rise and Function in Latin Christianity*, University of Chicago Press, 1981.
Brucker, Gene. *Giovanni and Lusanna: Love and Marriage in Renaissance Florence*, University of California Press, 1985.
DePrano, Maria. *Art Patronage, Family, and Gender in Renaissance Florence: The Tornabuoni*, Cambridge University Press, 2018.
Herlihy, David and Christiane Klapisch-Zuber. *Tuscans and Their Families: A Study of the Florentine Catasto of 1427*, Yale University Press, 1985.
Johnson, Geraldine A. and Sara F. Matthews Grieco (eds.). *Picturing Women in Renaissance and Baroque Italy*, Cambridge University Press, 1997.
King, Margaret. *Women of the Renaissance*, University of Chicago Press, 1991.
Klapisch-Zuber, Christiane. *Women, Family, and Ritual in Renaissance Italy*, University of Chicago Press, 1985.
Strocchia, Sharon. *Nuns and Nunneries in Renaissance Florence*, Johns Hopkins, 2009.
Tinagli, Paola. *Women in Italian Renaissance Art*, Manchester University Press, 1997.
Verdon, Timothy and John Henderson. *Christianity and the Renaissance: Image and Imagination in the Quattrocento*, Syracuse University Press, 1990.
Zarri, Gabriella. "Living Saints: A Typology of Female Sanctity in the Early Sixteenth-Century," in *Women and Religion in Medieval and Renaissance Italy*, ed. Daniel Bornstein and Roberto Rusconi, University of Chicago Press, 1996.

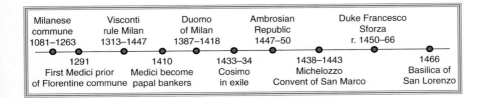

6 Lords of the Renaissance
The Medici, Visconti, and Sforza Dynasties through 1466

In our change-loving Italy, where nothing stands firm, and where no ancient dynasty exists, a servant can easily become a king.
                                    Aenea Silvio Piccolomini, Pius II

In my dominions I am pope, emperor, and lord, and no one, not even God, can do anything in my lands unless I permit it.
                                    Bernabò Visconti to Archbishop of Milan

Most Italians during the Renaissance—women, men, mothers, merchants, and saints—lived not in republican city-states, but in cities and regions ruled by the forceful figure of the signore. Strong-man, bully, despot, tyrant—these are some of the terms used to describe the signori who ruled most of the Italian city-states by the fifteenth century. Some were petty local thugs, others were powerful, sophisticated lords; some ruled minuscule states, others vast territories. By this period the model of the republican commune had given way in most of the peninsula to that of the signorial regime. The word signore, which means "sir" or "lord," is a form of respectful address that can also be used to refer to God, as *il Signore* (the Lord). As indicated by the quotation from Bernabò Visconti, signore of Milan, among these temporal lords there were some who considered their powers to be equal to, or even greater than, those of the Lord Himself.

DOI: 10.4324/9781003270362-6

116 *Lords of the Renaissance*

From commune to signoria

By the end of the fourteenth century, most of the city-states of Italy had gone over to rule by signori. With the notable exceptions of the large republics that held on to their system of government long after the others had given way—Florence until 1532, Siena until 1555, and Venice until 1797—and the cities of Lucca, Genoa, and Pisa that fitfully wavered between the two systems of government, all of the central and northern Italian city-states had given up their autonomy for good by this time.[1] Like a tidal wave rolling across northern and central Italy, the power of the despots seemed irresistible, as one by one, the self-governing republics gave way (Maps 6.1, 6.2). How exactly did one man or one family take over and dominate a city government and, in some cases, establish respected, long-lasting dynasties? Who were these men, where did they come from, and what means did they use to seize and maintain power? And perhaps the most important question of all: Why did this happen? How could citizens of any independent self-governing commune cede control of their community to one man and his heirs?

Dissatisfaction within the communes

Though many lords overthrew city governments using violent force, it should not be assumed that people were always resistant to the new signore. Citizens often had serious grievances with their communal government, predisposing them to accept change in the form of autocratic one-man rule. Life in a Renaissance republic was far from the democratic idyll imagined by some nineteenth- and twentieth-century historians. Despite claims of broad representation in these communes, money and influence counted more than general consensus in city governments. Even though elaborate systems of controlling and auditing government officials were in place, corruption was rampant. Somehow the wealthy, influential members of society managed to evade taxation, military service, and harsh punishment by the law. The intricate bureaucratic organization the communes required was often run by incompetent, inefficient clerks. The constant turnover of officeholders, meant to protect the city against any one faction taking control, often only guaranteed inexperienced leadership; by the time an official actually learned how to carry out his job, his term was up. Over time, disillusioned citizens came to resent the high level of participation required of them to keep their communes running. They tended to shirk their civic duties, reluctantly sitting on municipal committees or serving in the city militia—indeed most cities had ceased expecting it, and by this time city governments hired *condottieri* rather than their own citizens to fight their battles for them.

---

1 There is one autonomous Italian city-state that exists to this day: the tiny Republic of San Marino, located in an inaccessible hilly region to the southwest of Rimini, occupies a 24-square-mile territory.

Lords of the Renaissance 117

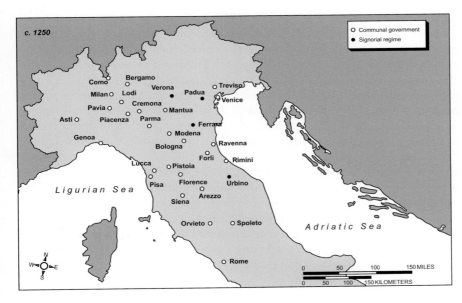

Map 6.1 Communes and signories in Italy c.1250

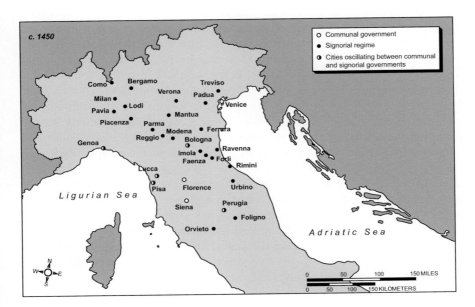

Map 6.2 Communes and signories in Italy c.1450

118   *Lords of the Renaissance*

Most of all, people were tired of the constant fighting; the rabid violence in the communes of Italy, described by Dante, had not lessened a century later. Violence between rival political factions was only part of the problem. In general, there was a lack of adequate law enforcement in the communes and violent crime of all kinds was widespread. Domestic violence, rape, assault and battery, crimes of passion, street fights, as well as banditry, highway robbery, and murder by paid assassins were common. Many of these crimes went unpunished by the legal system, as witnesses were easily corrupted or intimidated. In any case, justice was considered a private matter, and in most cases the offended family would take the law into their own hands. Private acts of vengeance could blossom into full-fledged vendettas that led to a proliferation of violence. Although laws existed on the books, as Dante wrote: "The laws are there but who enforces them?" So, when a strong leader came forward who promised to bring a regime of law and order, citizens were often drawn to him. People felt that since the ideals of full and equal representation in city government were unattainable, they had little to lose by being governed by a single man; loss of liberty seemed a small thing to exchange for the prospect of peace.

Life under the signore

Peace, of course, was not generally what people got when they accepted the rule of a signore. A leader might emerge who was capable of temporarily quelling the violence, but the ousted party would often return a number of years later only to overthrow the signore. Either a new signore from the opposition party would come forward to take his place or the citizens would attempt to re-establish the commune. In the words of historian Trevor Dean, politics in northern Italy resembled a "permanent revolution," as cities were continually overthrowing one political regime for another. If anything, this constant regime change increased the violence, rather than lessening it. It is true that the transition to signorial government was sometimes smooth and almost imperceptible. In responding to a crisis, a respected community leader, serving repeated terms as *podestà* or *capitano del popolo*, would in some cases assume extraordinary powers. Afterward he remained in office, keeping those same powers and was tacitly recognized as signore. However, in the majority of cases the signori organized violent coups to seize control of the government.

Once in control, the lord did indeed use force of arms; rather than being exclusively employed in keeping the peace, he would surround himself with bodyguards and hired assassins to protect himself and eliminate the opposition. People would watch helplessly as he ransacked the treasury amassed by the commune, exploited its lands, subverted its laws, and almost always increased taxes beyond all measure. The rule of signori was all too often marked by extreme cruelty and ruthless tactics designed to keep the populace subdued; the general attitude of the signore was that of a nobleman's arrogant sense of superiority and entitlement.

Many of the signori emerged from the class of nobles once created by the emperor—the Malatesta in Rimini, Carrara in Padua, the Riario in the Romagna, della Rovere in Genoa, Este of Ferrara, Gonzaga of Mantua, and Montefeltro of Urbino. Although leaders could also rise from the *popolo*—the della Scala in Verona, the Scotti in Piacenza, Pepoli, Castracani, Boccanegra in Genoa—he could be a Guelf or a Ghibelline, a merchant or a landowner. Indeed, many signori relied heavily on their power base in the *contado* and counted on the peasants who tilled their land to support them in their take-over of the town. Though individual circumstances varied, the important thing was that the aspiring signore had strong factional support and military clout. However, this last aspect has frequently been misunderstood. Often the signori have been represented as former *condottieri*, who, like the generals of some banana republics, seized control of power through force of arms. Few *condottieri*, however, ever rose to become signori; the notable exceptions were Francesco Sforza (see later in this chapter) and the Montefeltro of Urbino (Chapter 12). However, to maintain power, the signori often had to give their allegiance to other, more powerful despots, and in serving them militarily, they became de facto *condottieri*.

And this was the important point—maintaining power. It was relatively easy to topple a small city government already weakened by dissension; but once the signore took control, how could he guarantee that he, and possibly his heirs, would keep that position? All the signori, from the smallest to the greatest, faced the problem of establishing the legitimacy of their right to rule. Monarchs often claimed divine right to rule—barons in France and England boasted pedigrees that went back many generations—but what could a local upstart boss claim? Vicariates, which gave a local lord the right to rule without succession, could be had from the pope or the emperor (usu-ally for a steep price), but more was needed than being appointed imperial or papal vicar to assure continuity of a dynasty. Here we will examine the rise of three of the most important Italian Renaissance dynasties, the Visconti and Sforza of Milan and the Medici in Florence (Chapters 11 and 12 focus on the smaller courts, those of Ferrara, Mantua, and Urbino), with special attention to how, through a combination of crafty calculations, underhanded tactics, overt violence, inspired statesmanship, occasional good governance, and profuse patronage of the arts, they ensured that their fame would endure for generations.

Milan: In the middle of it all

Milan, the city that would become the home of the powerful Visconti and Sforza dynasties, had formerly been a prosperous colony of the Roman Empire. The Romans called it Mediolanum, meaning "in the middle of the plain." Dominating the wide, fertile plain watered by the River Po, the city was a rich prize, both for its agricultural bounty and for its strategic con-trol of the northwestern portion of the peninsula through the Alpine passes

120 *Lords of the Renaissance*

linking Italy with northern Europe (Map 8.2). From a colony, Milan became incorporated into the empire, and in 293 CE the Emperor Diocletian chose it as the site for the capital of the entire Western empire. For a time, Milan, not Rome, was the *caput mundi*. The city thrived and its bishop, Ambrose of Milan (St. Ambrose *c.*339–397 CE), became one of the most important individuals in the West, exercising enormous influence over the emperor and dictating religious doctrine. After the waves of invasions that toppled the Roman Empire, in 569 CE Milan was conquered by the German tribe of Longobards (meaning "Longbeards"). These Lombards, as they came to be known, settled there, hence the name "Lombardy" for the region (Map 7.1). The Lombards ruled from nearby Pavia, controlling much of the Italian Peninsula until the eighth century, when Charlemagne brought Milan and most of northern Italy under his control.

Milan was in the forefront of the Italian cities that blossomed during the medieval Commercial Revolution. The Milanese commune, founded in 1081, played a central role in the Lombard League, which took arms against the emperor and defeated him at the Battle of Legnano. By the year 1300, with over 100,000 inhabitants, Milan was one of the five largest cities in Europe, its trade network booming. Like other communes, however, Milan suffered from factionalism. In particular, the *popolo* never managed to subdue the violent antagonisms of the local nobility, which crystallized around two powerful clans, the Visconti and della Torre, who vied for control of the city government throughout the Duecento (thirteenth century). In a bid for broader public support, the della Torre aligned themselves with the *popolo*. In 1263 Filippo della Torre declared himself "perpetual lord of the *popolo* of Milan." It was a shrewd strategy, but the della Torre were outmaneuvered by the cunning Visconti.

The Visconti: The clan of vipers

The Visconti family chose a coat of arms depicting a man being swallowed by a viper; they claimed that one of their crusader ancestors had adopted this heraldic device from a defeated infidel and that the individual consumed was a Moor, not a Christian. Whatever its origins, the image was an apt one for a clan noted for its bloodthirsty, single-minded pursuit of political hegemony, eventually swallowing up city after city on the Lombard plain. Ottone Visconti (1207–1295) gained the upper hand over the della Torre, using his connections with the pope to have himself appointed Archbishop of Milan in 1262. Ottone also had the shrewdness to have his nephew Matteo (1250–1322) appointed *capitano del popolo* in 1287. Thus the family enjoyed both spiritual and temporal powers, benefiting from ties to both the nobility and the *popolo*. The Visconti continually grew stronger; in 1313 Matteo was declared signore, and his descendants would maintain dominance over Milan for the next 135 years. They succeeded not only by demonstrating tenacity and iron will but also through spending on civic projects and by promoting

Lords of the Renaissance 121

an image of themselves as cultural patrons. Azzone Visconti (1302–1339) funded lavish public works—including paving streets; widening piazzas; improving sewers; and constructing bridges, buildings, churches, and towers. Azzone had a palace built across from the cathedral that beautified and ennobled the city, while also proclaiming the magnificence of the Visconti clan. He hired the Pisan Giovanni di Balduccio (active 1317–1349) to create many sculptures and Giotto to paint frescoes in the palace. (The only portion of the palace that remains today is the tower of San Gottardo.) Giovanni Visconti (1290–1354), like Ottone, was both signore and Archbishop of Milan. It was Giovanni who persuaded Petrarch to work for the Visconti, as their ambassador at foreign courts, to project a sophisticated, enlightened image for the family.

After Giovanni Visconti, his nephews Matteo II (*c.*1319–1355), Bernabò (1319–1385), and Galeazzo II (1320–1378) ruled Milan. After Matteo's death, the two brothers divided the territory, warring constantly with the

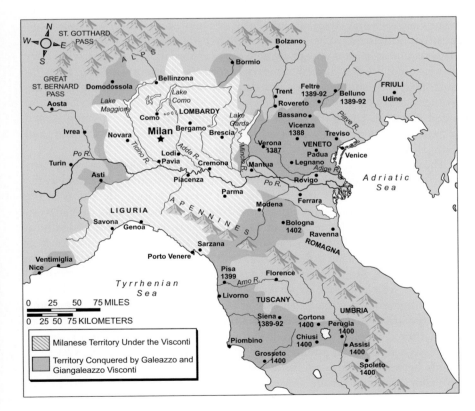

Map 6.3 Milanese territory under the Visconti

122   *Lords of the Renaissance*

states of Genoa, Mantua, Modena, Ferrara, and Bologna. Their incursion on the Papal States antagonized the pope, who in 1373 sent orders of excommunication against the two brothers. Bernabò, in his rage, had the papal emissaries arrested and allegedly would not release them until they ate the bull of excommunication. Galeazzo conquered the city of Pavia, where he built a castle and established a splendid court. He also founded the University of Pavia in 1361. Life at Bernabò's court centered on hunting and aristocratic amusements; the palace was full of baying hunting dogs, jugglers, and musicians. Living a dissolute life, Bernabò boasted of having fathered thirty illegitimate children; to enhance the prestige of the Visconti he arranged marriages for many of his children, both legitimate and illegitimate, with European nobility. After the death of his brother Galeazzo, Bernabò gained sole command of Milan and the surrounding territories, increasing taxes and giving full reign to his despotic tendencies.

Giangaleazzo Visconti: A prince among tyrants?

In the midst of waging war, and occupied with tending his mastiffs and mistresses, Bernabò it seems paid little attention to his brother Galeazzo's cultured, bookish son Giangaleazzo (1347–1402). Bernabò sensed no threat to his regime in his young nephew who kept to himself in Pavia, and who, after his wife died, docilely agreed to marry Bernabò's daughter Caterina. Bernabò must have been stunned when one day in 1385 his quiet son-in-law, having arranged a country outing, arrived with 500 armed men, ambushed, and seized Bernabò; Giangaleazzo at the same time had his cousins imprisoned or exiled. His uncle died, it is said by poison, before the year was out, and Giangaleazzo declared himself the sole ruler of Milan.

Though his ruthless rise to power was typical, Giangaleazzo was in many ways different from other signori. As part of the strategy to ennoble the dynasty, Giangaleazzo's first marriage had been to Isabelle de Valois of the royal house of France. Having acquired from her the County of Vertus in Champagne, the young signore of Milan afterward chivalrously styled himself in Italian as *Il Conte di Virtù* (the Count of Virtue). With its overtones of manly valor and excellence (see Chapter 10 on Machiavelli's use of the term in *The Prince*), the name in many ways fit him well. Despite the criminal manner by which he came to power, Giangaleazzo created an image of himself as an enlightened despot. Especially in the early years of his rule, the Count of Virtue attempted to establish a tradition of good government in Milan. He instituted a policy of fair taxation, reformed the law code, and began an impressive program of public works, notably building a navigable system of canals between Milan and Pavia that, by providing irrigation through the Po valley, facilitated trade as well as agriculture. He also organized an efficient postal service and monitored public health by expanding and rigorously enforcing quarantines instituted by Bernabò. Through such measures, the

Milanese enjoyed unprecedented well-being, and the city's wealth came to rival that of Venice.

Not only did Milan prosper economically under Giangaleazzo—architecture, painting, sculpture, and humanist studies also thrived under his patronage. In 1385, soon after coming to power, he gave approval for the building of a new cathedral and was himself a major donor. That building, the immense Duomo of Milan, is the most impressive example of Late Gothic style in Italy, conveying a message of the strength and permanence of the Visconti. Likewise meant to promote the grandeur of the family, not only in this world, but into the next, was Giangaleazzo's construction of the vast monastery complex of the Certosa, or "Charterhouse," of Pavia in 1395. The monks who spent their lives in the monastery in devotion also prayed for the souls of departed Visconti, whose earthly remains lay in tombs in the splendid mausoleum. A learned man, Giangaleazzo supported the University of Pavia, endowing a chair for the Greek teacher Chrysoloras in 1400; and was patron to humanists such as Antonio Loschi, Pier Paolo Vergerio the elder, Uberto Decembrio, and Gasparino Barzizza. He also commissioned many manuscripts, including the precious *Visconti Book of Hours* with illuminations by Giovannino de' Grassi (*c*.1350–1398), the *capomaestro* (chief master builder) of his Duomo (Figure 6.1).

Having successfully petitioned the emperor for the title (at a cost of 100,000 florins) in 1395, Giangaleazzo was proclaimed the first Duke of Milan, and later of all Lombardy, becoming the first ruler with a ducal title in northern Italy. He pursued a vigorous policy of expansion of his territory, not only in Lombardy, but throughout northern and central Italy, reaching into the Veneto, Piedmont, the Romagna, and eventually Tuscany (Map 6.3). Some territories, like Pisa, he bought (for 200,000 florins), others he conquered by force of arms. In 1400 he took possession of Perugia, Grosseto, Cortona, Chiusi, Spoleto, Assisi, and Siena; the following year both Lucca and Bologna fell to the Duke of Milan. The proud Florentines trembled as, in the summer of 1402, they waited for Giangaleazzo to attack Florence.

Florence was saved by a stroke of fortune when Giangaleazzo died suddenly of a fever in September 1402, and his forces dispersed. Giangaleazzo's oldest son Gianmaria (1388–1412) was only thirteen when his father died, leaving him the ducal title. During the power struggle that took place before the boy came of age, much of the territory his father had conquered was lost, and the Milanese state weakened. Gianmaria himself grew up to be a sadistic tyrant who was assassinated by his nobles ten years later. Gianmaria's brother Filippo Maria Visconti (1392–1447) who succeeded him as Duke of Milan, managed to win back the Lombard territories that had belonged to his father's empire through his own political astuteness and the use of forceful *condottieri*. As documented in the biography written by Pier Candido Decembrio (1399–1477), a humanist employed at his court, Filippo Maria tended to extreme cruelty like his brother, and suffered constant fear of assassination.

124 *Lords of the Renaissance*

Figure 6.1 Giovannino de' Grassi, *Visconti Book of Hours*, Psalm 118:11 with portrait of Giangaleazzo Visconti, c.1389, BNCF Banco Rari 397

An intermission between dynasties: The Ambrosian Republic 1447–50

When Duke Filippo Maria died in 1447 without an heir, there was a struggle for the control of Milan. Because of the Visconti strategy of marrying into foreign nobility, France had claims on the Milanese duchy (through Valentina Visconti); the king of Naples and the German emperor each had his own justifications as well to why he should take possession of the wealthy territory. However, surprisingly, the group that came forward to claim the city was that of the Milanese citizens themselves. As news of the Duke's death spread, violence broke out in the city, and on August 14, the people gathered at the Palazzo del Commune and declared the Milanese commune revived, calling itself the Ambrosian Republic. It was not simple to re-establish the commune after over a hundred years of signorial rule; the size and infrastructure of the city had greatly changed. Moreover, the inhabitants of the *contado*, who had paid high taxes to the Visconti lords, were unwilling to submit to the new Milanese government. Further complicating matters, Milan was at war with Venice, which had already taken the cities of Pavia, Lodi, and Piacenza from Milan. Representatives of the Ambrosian Republic petitioned her sister republic for peace, but Venice, aware of the weakness of the Milanese, refused.

Francesco Sforza: From soldier of fortune to statesman

At this desperate point, the Ambrosian Republic turned to the most powerful and effective *condottiero* of the day, Francesco Sforza (1401–1466), for military help. One of seven illegitimate sons of a mercenary soldier, Sforza from an early age made his living by force of arms. He had been employed alternately by the Duke of Milan and by the Duke's enemies—the papacy, Florence, and Venice. Duke Filippo Maria Visconti, in his day, had recognized Sforza's value as a military commander, but needed to do something to assure his loyalty to Milan. To entice the mercenary soldier to fight for him, the Duke gave Sforza his illegitimate daughter Bianca Maria (1425–1468) in marriage, with the cities of Cremona and Pontremoli as part of the dowry. This move bought Sforza's allegiance—only up to a point—as the city fathers of Milan were to learn. The Ambrosian Republic engaged Sforza as captain on the condition that he would return all re-conquered territories to Milan, except Brescia, which he could keep. As one by one cities fell to Sforza, the Milanese alternately rejoiced and panicked. The citizens of the Ambrosian Republic increasingly became aware that though they had a contract with Sforza, he had the military power and, if he wished, could turn on them and take Milan itself. And that is in effect what happened, when in 1449, after a string of victories, Sforza laid siege to Milan. By March 1450 the starving, debilitated population opened its gates to Sforza as the *capitano del popolo* and Duke of Milan.

Though he had been a wily self-serving soldier of fortune—surviving attempted assassinations, changing sides with few scruples, and finally ruthlessly starving the city of Milan into submission—Francesco Sforza turned out to be an enlightened and just ruler. On assuming power, he immediately saw to it that the population, which had been reduced to eating dogs and rats, was provided with adequate food, and he was unusually moderate in punishing his political enemies in the city. He pledged himself to the economic initiatives of reforming taxation, fixing the price of salt, and recognizing the former duke's debts. He also agreed not to billet troops in the city; to reside at least eight months of each year in Milan; to appoint officials from among a list compiled by the Milanese; and to pass the ducal title only to sons born of his wife, a descendant of the Visconti.

Like Giangaleazzo Visconti, Francesco Sforza dedicated himself to major urban planning and architectural projects. He built the dramatic Castello Sforzesco, founded the city's major hospital, and completed an ambitious irrigation project (the Naviglio Martesana). Sforza's court became a cultured center for artists and humanists who praised their patron, raising his status in the eyes of Europe. From an upstart soldier of fortune, Sforza transformed himself into a patron of the arts, a prince. But even more significantly, Francesco formed alliances with other Italian states, which created an exceptional period of peace and stability in the peninsula. The most important alliance was the one he created with Milan's former sworn enemy, Florence, and it was founded on a common understanding with the head of another family that had recently risen to the heights of power—the Medici.

The Medici: Where did they come from?

Though in the sixteenth century the Medici would claim an exalted genealogy stretching back to a knight in the service of Charlemagne—the equivalent of an American family claiming to have its roots among the passengers of the Mayflower—the origins of the family were more recent, like most of the Florentine elite who had driven the older, established magnate families from power (see Chapter 1 "Tensions between magnates and *popolo*"). The Medici (pronounced "MED-ee-chi" with the stress on the first syllable) have come to be synonymous with the Italian Renaissance itself, their coat of arms with the famous Medici balls emblazoned on buildings and monuments throughout Florence and all over Tuscany. However, the meaning of this symbol on their family crest is of uncertain origin. Some scholars have suggested that, because the Italian word *medici* means "physicians," the balls represent pills, as coats of arms often represent the source of a clan's fame or livelihood. However, there is no evidence that any of the early Medici ever worked in the medical profession. Others claim that the balls represent *bisanti*, a weight of measure used in Byzantium. Whatever the derivation, their partisans would enthusiastically embrace the symbol, chanting "*Palle, palle!*" in public demonstrations in support of the Medici.[2]

The first members of the Medici clan appear in the historical record in the thirteenth century. The family had its origins in the country region just north of Florence known as the Mugello; the first time a Medici served as prior of the Florentine commune was in 1291. Known for their violence,

---

2 *Palle* means "balls," with precisely the same slang meaning in Italian as in English, and identical connations of manly courage and daring. Indeed, Medici supporters were often referred to as the *palleschi* or "balls party."

Lords of the Renaissance 127

members of the clan often ran afoul of the law. Between 1343 and 1360 five Medici were sentenced to death (none were executed); this did not prevent them from serving nineteen times in the Signoria (office of the priors and the standardbearer) during those years. However, the house was somewhat in decline when in 1373 Foligno di Conte de' Medici wrote wistfully in his memoirs: "Such was our greatness that there used to be a saying: 'You are like one of the Medici,' and everyone feared us." A number of Medici had supported the ill-fated 1378 Ciompi Rebellion, causing the family to fall out of favor with the conservative regime that followed. During the 1390s several Medici were convicted of conspiracy, and this time one was executed. By 1400, when they were accused of involvement with yet another plot, the whole clan was officially disqualified from serving in the government, except for Vieri di Cambio de' Medici and his brothers, Francesco and Giovanni di Bicci.

Giovanni di Bicci lays the foundations of the Medici banking fortune

Giovanni di Bicci de' Medici got his start in business working as an apprentice in Rome at the bank of his distant cousin Vieri di Cambio de' Medici (1323–1395), whose nickname was "Cambiozzo" or "Big Change." Florentine bankers had been lending money to popes for a long time; the Alberti family, for instance, turned an especially good profit while the papacy was at Avignon. Technically, the business the Medici and other bankers were involved in was not known as lending money at interest, a sin according to church doctrine (usury.) Instead, they were money changers; Giovanni di Bicci was elected prior of that guild in 1402, 1408, and 1411. A money changer would provide local currency for an individual who had credit with one of his agents in a foreign country. The so-called bill of exchange would come due in a predetermined amount of time, with a commission added, and the banker made lucrative adjustments by exploiting currency fluctuations. Vast amounts of money from merchants in all of Europe passed through the Medici banks this way.

The Medici fortune, in particular, was tied to the papacy; enormous quantities of cash flowed into the pope's coffers, and those handling his finances made profits on all the transactions. After Vieri retired in 1393, Giovanni di Bicci opened his own bank in Rome, where he established an especially close friendship with the influential prelate Baldassare Cossa (*c.*1370–1419). After he became Pope John XXIII—later to be declared antipope—in 1410, Cossa granted Giovanni di Bicci the title of *depositarius camerae apostolice*, making him papal banker. Giovanni was involved in the cloth business as well, but those profits were dwarfed by the vast sums he acquired through banking. The bond between the founder of the Medici fortune and the antipope is forever celebrated in a magnificent funeral monument to Cossa in the Baptistry in Florence, created by Donatello and Michelozzo (di Bartolomeo 1396–1472).

128 *Lords of the Renaissance*

Cosimo de' Medici: A moneychanger's son becomes father of his country

Giovanni di Bicci's son Cosimo (also known as Cosimo il Vecchio or "the Elder" to distinguish him from Grand Duke Cosimo I de' Medici, Chapter 13) took over the family business when his father retired in 1420. Having spent his youth working in banking, Cosimo was a shrewd businessman, and under his direction the Medici banking empire expanded throughout Europe. In addition to the branches in Rome, Florence, and Venice founded by his father, Cosimo added many others and established a vast network across Europe of resident agents who worked for the Medici bank (Map 6.4). Cosimo achieved this, in large part, by maintaining the family's close ties to the papacy, befriending popes Eugenius IV, Nicholas V, and Pius II; over half of Medici banking profits came from Rome. When Cosimo assumed control of the Medici business, the family was the third richest in Florence; by the time of his death, it would be the wealthiest in all of Europe, and Cosimo would be honored with the title *pater patriae*—father of his country. Used during the time of the ancient Roman Republic, the term implies that citizens are bound as they would be to a father to obey and honor the civic hero. The Florentine government edict passed after his death praised Cosimo for conferring "upon the republic innumerable benefits in times of both war and peace … aiding and augmenting it with his concern for its greatest profit and glory … governing it with every care and concern and diligence as a *paterfamilias*."[3]

How the proud Florentines, or at least a significant number of them, came to regard Cosimo as their leader and father-figure is a complex tale involving his savvy manipulation of public image; diligent maintenance of a close network of friends and business associates; and the wise use of the family's vast wealth in a variety of ways that were perceived to contribute to the civic good.

"Be careful not to draw attention to yourself"

This was the advice that Giovanni di Bicci on his deathbed had given Cosimo. Although a man so fabulously wealthy cannot help but attract attention, the sense of his father's words was, "Don't be flashy and try not to stand out above others." The Medici had participated in politics over the course of the past century, serving as officeholders for the commune as well as being active in their guild. After the 1382 suppression of the more broadly representative government initiated by the Ciompi Rebellion, the government of Florence was ever more tightly controlled by a handful of rich and powerful families. Despite going through the outward motions of voting and reaching public consensus in the commune, in reality, these powerful leaders increasingly made decisions and deals behind closed doors. The elite clans were

3 Dale Kent 376.

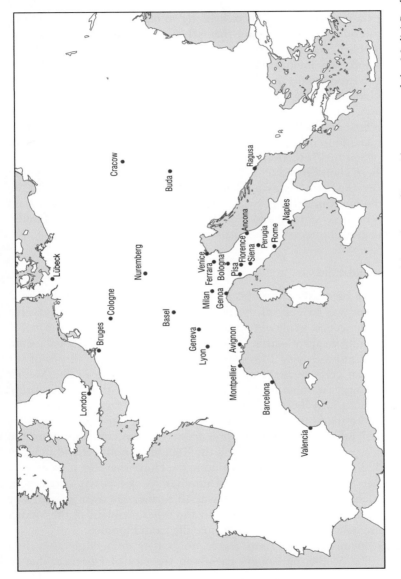

Map 6.4 Cosimo the Elder's banking empire. Locations of branches and/or resident agents of the Medici Bank at its greatest extent under Cosimo

130 *Lords of the Renaissance*

constantly forming alliances with one another, on the watch for any family that tried to seize too much power, in the hopes that one of theirs would become signore of Florence.

Florence had flirted with the idea of a signorial government on a number of occasions, always in moments of crisis. In the 1320s, after a crushing military defeat against Pisa (in which 2,000 Florentine citizens, not mercenaries, died), when threatened by the overwhelming military force of the signore of Lucca, Florentines decided to put themselves under the protection of the Neapolitan noble Charles of Calabria. Again in 1342 during a period of dire financial turmoil, they invited Walter of Brienne, a French knight, to govern their city. Both experiments in rule by a signore were disastrous; the one was dissolute and incompetent, the other corrupt and repressive. Fortunately for the Florentines, these regimes were short-lived: Charles died after nineteen months in office, and Walter of Brienne was ousted in an armed rebellion after a year. The Florentines had learned their lesson and would not have a lord. Thus, when in 1386, after amassing wealth and increasing their influence, the Alberti clan showed off at a public festivity, their knights splendidly dressed and everywhere displaying their coat of arms, rather than that of the commune, the punishment was swift. The other families accused the Alberti of trying to become signori and exiled the leaders of the Alberti family, including the grandfather of Leon Battista.

1433: Arrest and exile

In order not to be crushed like the Alberti, Cosimo had to keep his head down. The idea was to control the political situation as much as possible from behind the scenes, while outwardly presenting the image of a normal—albeit fantastically wealthy—citizen. Cosimo managed this delicate balancing act effectively until the early 1430s when Florence was in the throes of yet another financial crisis brought on by war, again with Lucca. The Medici had been lending vast sums to the commune to conduct this war; refusing the money would have been unpatriotic, and besides, there was considerable profit to be made from the interest on the loans. Gradually Cosimo's role as moneylender had crossed the line, from a citizen contributing to the war effort to a powerful figure dictating the Republic's political and military policy. In 1433 enemies of the Medici among the Florentine elite took action. On September 5, Cosimo was arrested on charges of bribery, corruption, and having deliberately prolonged the war to further his own gains. After they were imprisoned for a month, Cosimo and other members of the Medici family were sentenced not to death, but to exile from Florence.

Cosimo's enemies would soon regret not killing him while they had the chance. The Medici had many friends in the city of Florence, due to Cosimo's genius for creating enduring personal networks. The technical term anthropologists, sociologists, and political scientists use to describe this skill is "clientelism"; however, the word has a cold ring to it that barely describes the many close bonds Cosimo created. When a neighbor needed a loan to pay his daughter's dowry, a business acquaintance wanted help getting his brother-in-law a job as a city official, the butcher wanted his tax assessment lowered, a widow needed someone to put in a good word in Rome to help her son be appointed priest to a local parish, they all knew they could expect help from Cosimo. Cosimo's role has been viewed as similar to that of a "godfather," a kind of mob boss. Indeed, Cosimo's way of operating was that of a local political boss, only that he was vastly wealthier than others, and his influence, through the Medici banks, spread beyond the immediate Florentine neighborhood to all of Europe. From his exile in Venice, where he was warmly received because of his many business associations, Cosimo was able to put into play a vast network of political connections to advocate for his return to Florence. The Venetian Republic wrote to the Florentine Republic on his behalf, as did the pope.

Cosimo's triumphal 1434 return

> After this, nothing was denied to Cosimo. He controlled all decisions concerning war and peace and matters of law; he was considered not so much a citizen as the lord of the city.
>
> Pope Pius II, *Commentaries*

Through pressure exerted by the many supporters of the Medici faction, especially by Pope Eugenius IV, in October 1434, almost exactly a year after being exiled, Cosimo triumphantly re-entered Florence, accompanied by supporters whose numbers included thousands of armed peasants from the family's native Mugello region. Immediately all members of the anti-Medici faction were exiled from Florence; 500 individuals, the largest number for more than a century, were forced to leave. Many of these people were from the oldest elite families in the city. Crushing taxes were imposed on those adversaries who remained, with the Medici, graciously offering loans from their bank, profiting.

Cosimo managed to control Florentine government through manipulating the lists of those who were eligible to hold public offices. After his return to Florence, Cosimo saw to it that certain adjustments were made to the political system so there would be no more unpleasant surprises for his faction in the future. Potential candidates for city government had always been reviewed in a *scrutinio* or scrutiny, by election officials who were called *accoppiatori*, and the names of eligible individuals written on slips of paper placed in a pouch to be drawn at random (sortition). From this point on, the *accoppiatori* were permanent functionaries appointed by the Medici; whenever names were drawn, only members of the Medici faction appeared. So transparent was the veil of democracy over these maneuvers that by 1439 no eyebrows were raised when Cosimo's name turned up as the city's standardbearer of justice, just in time to head the delegation welcoming the pope and the Byzantine

132   Lords of the Renaissance

emperor to the Council of Florence. So effectively did Cosimo establish the symbiotic relationship of his family with the state that Medici hegemony within the context of the Republic lasted until 1494.

1454: Peace breaks out in Italy

Throughout the first half of the fifteenth century, the entire peninsula existed in a state of more or less constant warfare. The century opened with Milanese territorial expansion, which had caused Florence to seek alliances with Rome and Naples. No sooner had the Milanese threat temporarily dissolved with Giangaleazzo's untimely death, than Florence backed the pope in his war against the Kingdom of Naples in 1409. From 1424 to 1433 the Florentines were involved in a long and costly war against the Milanese, this time with Venice as their ally. In 1439 war once again broke out between Florence and Milan; hostilities temporarily ended with the Florentine victory at Anghiari in 1440. Then the death of Filippo Maria Visconti in 1447 threatened to desta-bilize the tenuous balance of power on the peninsula. As we have seen, Venice was closing in on the Ambrosian Republic; to the rest of Italy it looked as if the powerful Venetians might conquer all of northern Italy. When Francesco took control of Milan and turned to attack Venice, it was Medici money that helped pay his troops.

Sforza, in his capacity as *condottiero*, had worked for all the important powers in the peninsula—Milan, Rome, Venice, Naples, Florence—at one time or another. It was when he was serving Florence briefly in 1435 that he most probably met Cosimo de' Medici for the first time. The two men seem to have hit it off. Italy's most powerful soldier and her most powerful banker developed what would be a close friendship and lasting alliance. Over the course of the next twenty-five-odd years Cosimo kept up his ties with Sforza. The Medici lent vast sums of money to the Duke of Milan, amounts so great that there was no expectation of repayment. What were Cosimo's motives in providing him with so much money? Cosimo's interest in funding Sforza's career was not merely a generous gesture of friendship. By helping Sforza establish a stable state in Lombardy he achieved a balance of power between Milan and Venice, while guaranteeing that Milan and Florence would remain at peace. Peace, after all, is good for business.

In 1453 Constantinople fell to the Turks, weakening Venice's position in the Mediterranean and inclining the Venetians to come to terms with Milan, signing the Peace of Lodi in 1454. At this point, all five major powers of Italy, feeling menaced by the aggressive Turks in the east, signed a historic twenty-five-year peace treaty, the *Lega Italica*, the Italian League, in 1455. Though it took considerable cooperation to reach this agreement, the keystone of the treaty was the bond established years before between the soldier of fortune and the Florentine money changer. The agreement brokered by these two would usher in an unprecedented nearly forty years of peace on the Italian Peninsula.

Cosimo de' Medici: Patron of art, music, and learning

In addition to his knack for amassing vast amounts of wealth and skill at manipulating a complex and contentious political system, Cosimo was a cultured man who had a deep and abiding love of literature, history, music, and art. Trained as a merchant and money changer, Cosimo was largely self-educated; through personal contact with the great intellects and artistic innovators of the day he learned to appreciate the revival of the classical world that was exploding around him in Florence. He was friend and patron to humanist scholars Leonardo Bruni, Ambrogio Traversari, Niccolò Niccoli, and Poggio Bracciolini, financing many of the discoveries of ancient manuscripts undertaken by Niccoli and Poggio. On his death, Niccoli left Cosimo his substantial humanist library, which Cosimo eventually incorporated into his magnificent collection when he founded the library at San Marco. These rare, exquisite manuscripts can be seen today at the Laurentian Library (Biblioteca Medicea Laurenziana) in Florence, many of them with the heavy chains that once bound them to lecterns still attached.

Cosimo was also an enthusiastic patron of music, as were other members of the Medici family (see Chapter 9 on Lorenzo's patronage of music). When the Florentine Cathedral with its newly completed cupola was consecrated on March 25, 1436, Cosimo who had returned from exile barely eighteen months earlier, was a prominent participant in the festivities, alongside his good friend Pope Eugenius IV. The pope had commissioned the Franco-Flemish composer Guillaume Du Fay (1397–1474) to write the motet *Nuper rosarum flores* for the occasion. It was composed in the complex polyphonic style that was the rage among connoisseurs, and when the pope appointed Cosimo to found a school of cathedral singers, Cosimo sent agents to the Low Countries in search of singers who were expert in this avant-garde style and had them brought to Florence.

Medici projects, public and private

The most visible of Cosimo's contributions to Florentine culture are his architectural commissions, to this day stunning testaments to what enormous wealth, coupled with civic pride and artistic genius can achieve. One of the oldest churches in the city, dedicated in 393 CE by St. Ambrose, the Basilica of San Lorenzo was enlarged and restored during the Quattrocento. Designed by Brunelleschi and directed by citizens living in the neighborhood along with Giovanni di Bicci, it was eventually completed in 1466 by Michelozzo and Antonio Manetti (1423–1497). This was carried out under the patronage of Cosimo, who funded the project with the cooperation of his friends. The Medici coat of arms is prominently displayed throughout the central area of the church and in the Medici Chapel; the coats of arms of Medici associates are scattered in the other chapels. The large church with its elegant nave, its classical pillars in grey *pietra serena* stone set against candid

134   *Lords of the Renaissance*

white stucco, simultaneously links the Medici, who lived nearby, not only with one of the earliest Christian monuments in the city, but with the most recent Renaissance innovations in architecture.

The house that Cosimo had built for his family, in the neighborhood of San Lorenzo, is an architectural reflection of Cosimo's public persona, at once understated and grand. The Palazzo Medici was begun in 1446 and completed in 1460, probably under the architect Michelozzo. It occupies a large piece of land close to the basilica, the family's garden facing it. Unlike other buildings in Florence, such as the Palazzo Rucellai, which incorporated pre-existing structures into the design, Cosimo had buildings that stood on the site razed to the ground before beginning work, having subtly or not-so-subtly influenced neighbors to sell their real estate. Thus, even before a stone was laid, the large, gaping worksite already proclaimed the force of Medici influence in the city. Unlike the Palazzo Rucellai with Alberti's elegant paraphrasing of classical motifs, the Medici home presents an imposing face to the world, with its rough-hewn stone façade, impressive in its sheer bulk. Moreover, the detail of the double-arched windows on the upper floors escaped no one, echoing as they do the windows of the Palazzo Vecchio, and thus underscoring the inextricable links binding city government to the Medici.

If the house was forbidding and fortress-like on the exterior, its interior garden and central courtyard surrounded by graceful porticos were charming, each containing a masterpiece by Donatello—the bronze *David* (Bargello, Florence), and *Judith and Holofernes* (Palazzo Vecchio, Florence). Visiting dignitaries such as popes, cardinals, foreign royalty, or close business associates lucky enough to be admitted beyond the antechambers into the family's home were awed by the splendor of the art. Here any pretension at being ordinary citizens fell away, and the Medici revealed the full glory of their wealth and discriminating taste. Room after room was filled with works commissioned from the finest artists of the day, including Fra Angelico, Fra Filippo Lippi, Domenico Veneziano, Paolo Uccello, and Benozzo Gozzoli.

Though other artworks have been spirited away to be displayed in museums and much of the building is used for municipal government offices, Gozzoli's (*c.*1420–1497) dazzling fresco in the family's private chapel can still be seen in the palace today. Covering three walls of the chapel, the subject of the painting is *The Journey of the Magi*, a magnificent depiction of the procession of the Three Kings on their way to Bethlehem to bring gifts to the Christ child (Figure 6.2). Despite the fictive Biblical scene, the painting is full of references to the Medici family's personal history. The landscape suggests the family's country home in the Mugello, and the exotic participants in the Council of Florence for which the Medici acted as hosts are represented. Among the many individuals making up the scene, there are portraits of Cosimo, his children and grandchildren, relatives, friends, business associates, and retainers.

Figure 6.2 Benozzo Gozzoli, *Journey of the Magi*, detail, 1459–60, Palazzo Medici-Riccardi, Florence. Cosimo is seated on the brown mule; his son Piero is on the white horse to his left. In the foreground on Cosimo's right side are his two principal allies: Galeazzo Maria Sforza on the white horse and Sigismondo Malatesta, lord of Rimini on the brown horse. Between the two allies, in the row above them, wearing a bright red cap and with his face turned three-quarters is the ten-year-old Lorenzo the Magnificent

Cosimo's gift to the Convent of San Marco

Cosimo, like many of the wealthy of his day, identified personally with the Magi, the only New Testament figures who make a positive statement about riches. Worried that it would be easier for a camel to go through the eye of a needle than for the wealthy to enter Heaven, Renaissance patrons could take comfort in the thought that like the Three Wise Men they could also serve God by offering up precious things to the church. The Medici participated in the elaborate public processions held by the Confraternity of the Magi (*Compagnia de' Magi*) on the Feast of Epiphany each year, and this is reflected in Gozzoli's *Journey of the Magi* in the Palazzo Medici. Cosimo had another fresco painted by Gozzoli on the theme in his private room in the Convent of San Marco in Florence, as part of Cosimo's rebuilding of the complex, which included the dormitories and library begun by the architect Michelozzo in

136   *Lords of the Renaissance*

1437, and the church the following year. The headquarters for the Confraternity of the Magi, San Marco became ever more identified with Medici largesse, and served as a spiritual refuge for its patron. Cosimo's contemporary, the Florentine bookseller, Vespasiano da Bisticci (1421–1498) included a biography of his client and friend in his *Lives of Illustrious Men*, in which he describes how Cosimo decided to fund the project because he was driven by guilt over ill-gotten gains, hinting that like Enrico Scrovegni a century earlier, Cosimo de' Medici was not above a little "spiritual money laundering."

Considerations: Was the Renaissance a cultural byproduct of the signori?

In his obsession with establishing legitimacy to rule and marking his territory—whether princeling, political boss, or *pater patriae*—the Renaissance lord was a creator of great art. Nowadays we like to think of art in terms of the creative act of the individual artist; however, patronage of the arts is a powerful opportunity for self-expression. Many of the people footing the bill for works of art in the Renaissance were tyrants anxious to promote a glorious self-image. Some of the most sublime paintings, sculptures, and soaring cathedrals were paid for and often conceived of by these men. Once it had been frowned upon for rich citizens to indulge in ostentatious display; there were sumptuary laws to restrict the wearing of fine clothing and excessive manifestation of wealth of any kind was condemned as a sign of pride—the worst of the Seven Deadly Sins. Now ostentation, or as it was called "magnificence," was in. Humanists came up with a justification for opulent spending; it was an idea that came from Aristotle, who the humanists liked to cite:

> The magnificent man is an artist in expenditure: he can discern what is suitable, and spend great sums with good taste ... his motive in such expenditure will be the nobility of the action ... he will spend gladly and lavishly, since nice calculation is shabby; and he will think how he can carry out his project most nobly and splendidly.

Before, the ruling classes had struggled to project for themselves an image of Christian humility and held back from opulence in their manner of dressing, dining, and dancing. The wealthy had refrained from excessive spending on paintings, sculptures, and architecture, but now they threw off all restraint. Both Francesco Sforza's son Ludovico, and Cosimo's son Piero and grandson Lorenzo, known as "the Magnificent," would likewise achieve fame as patrons of poets, philosophers, painters, and sculptors.

Great art was just one of the by-products of the rule of signori in Renaissance Italy. In most of the Western world today we tend to believe that if people are left free to choose, they will always prefer a form of self-government over one-man rule. Close study of the gradual transformation of

Lords of the Renaissance   137

Italian communes into *signorie* during the Renaissance challenges that belief. Not everything about living in a self-governing commune was positive, neither was everything about living under a signore negative. There were a wide range of Renaissance signorial regimes, from petty provincial courts to large principalities whose leaders were players on the European stage. Some of these signori were mere despots, controlling their subjects through fear and intimidation. Others were enlightened rulers whose civic works earned the appreciation, even love, of the citizens. Most signori openly proclaimed their sovereignty, proud of the power they wielded, even though they came by it through violent criminal behavior. Cosimo de' Medici did not rule openly; he shrewdly manipulated the city's politics to become signore in all but name, and earned himself the title *pater patriae*.

This age was receptive to new men and new ideas; daring *condottieri* and enterprising bankers not only could attain immense power to rule but sometimes ruled very well. Francesco Sforza and Cosimo de' Medici were innovative rulers with new ideas about statesmanship that were more in tune with the changing world of Italian diplomacy. That traditional enemies such as Milan and Florence, joined by the other major Italian states, for once could reach an agreement in the interests of a larger, shared political goal is a harbinger of a future state system. The modern *raison d'état* (reason of state), by means of which leaders determine policy guided not by ideology or blind adherence to tradition, but based on a critical analysis of mutual advantage is a notion understood by all today, was being pioneered at this time. A generation after Francesco and Cosimo, Niccolò Machiavelli would be the first to shock the world by elevating that policy to a science. Italy during the Renaissance was a kind of laboratory of political experimentation, in which ideas of democracy, oligarchy, and autocracy were constantly being tested, fine-tuned, and then accepted or rejected. In Chapter 7 we will consider yet another form of government—monarchy—which grew and developed under a very different set of cultural circumstances in the Italian south.

Sourcebook

Antonio Loschi, *Invective Against the Florentines*
Pier Candido Decembrio, *Life of Filippo Maria Visconti*
Niccolò de' Carisisimi da Parma, *Letter to Francesco Sforza*
Fra Angelico, *Annunciation*, Convent of San Marco, Florence
Vespasiano da Bisticci, *Lives of Illustrious Men*

Further reading

Black, Jane. *Absolutism in Renaissance Milan: Plenitude of Power under the Visconti and the Sforza, 1329–1535*, Oxford University Press, 2009.
Bueno de Mesquita, Daniel Meredith. *Giangaleazzo Visconti: Duke of Milan (1351–1402)*, Cambridge University Press, 1941.

138 *Lords of the Renaissance*

Gamberini, Andrea, ed. *A Companion to Late Medieval and Early Modern Milan: The Distinctive Features of an Italian State*, Brill, 2015.

Goldthwaite, Richard. *The Economy of Renaissance Florence*, Johns Hopkins University Press, 2009.

Jones, Philip. *The Italian City-State: From Commune to Signoria*, Oxford University Press, 1997.

Kent, Dale. *Cosimo de' Medici and the Florentine Renaissance: The Patron's Oeuvre*, Yale University Press, 2000.

Lubkin, Gregory. *A Renaissance Court: Milan under Galeazzo Maria Sforza*, University of California Press, 1994.

Welch, Evelyn S. *Art and Authority in Renaissance Milan*, Yale University Press, 1995.

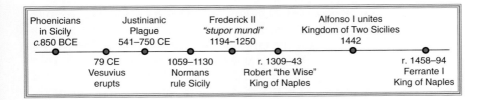

7 The *Mezzogiorno*
The "Other Renaissance" in Naples and Sicily

> We sailed hence, always in much distress, till we came to the land of the lawless and inhuman Cyclopes. Now the Cyclopes neither plant nor plough, but trust in providence, and live on such wheat, barley, and grapes as grow wild without any kind of tillage, and their wild grapes yield them wine as the sun and the rain may grow them.
>
> Homer, *Odyssey* Book IX

Land of myth and midday sun

The regions of Italy south of Rome were as different as day and night from the central and northern regions that we have looked at until now. In fact, Italians have come to call these lands the *mezzogiorno* (mid-day), distinguishing them from the rest of the peninsula by the blazing southern sun that warms their soil. Despite the sunshine, something sinister lurked in the ancient Greek legends about the south. Parthenope, the siren who attempted to lure Odysseus and his men to their deaths, dwelt in the Bay of Naples. Persephone, daughter of Demeter the goddess of grain, was abducted by Hades and carried into the underworld at Lake Pergusa in the center of the island of Sicily. The monsters Scylla and Charybdis were said to inhabit the Strait of Messina, the narrow, treacherous waterway between Sicily and mainland Italy. In the passage earlier, the poet Homer in the eighth century BCE tells of the island of Sicily, home to the vicious Cyclops Polyphemus, who was blinded by the Greek hero Odysseus.

DOI: 10.4324/9781003270362-7

140   *The* Mezzogiorno

Apart from his description of its fearsome one-eyed inhabitants, however, Homer paints a vivid picture of a land so fertile that food and wine seem to grow by themselves under the blazing southern sun. Ancient Mediterranean peoples prized these lands for the rich volcanic soil and hillsides perfect for growing grapes and olives; offshore, the waters were plentiful with fish. Even before the Greeks arrived, as early as 800 BCE, the Phoenicians had landed in Sicily (the name derives from the "Sicels," a people who were among the island's earliest inhabitants) and settled along the coasts, where they harvested massive quantities of tuna. It was the Greeks, however, who made a lasting impact on the island they called "Trinacria" (meaning "three-sided" island). They settled there beginning around 750 BCE and incorporated it into *Magna Graecia* (greater Greece). The settlers brought more than trade: the temples and theaters at Selinunte, Segesta, Agrigento, and Siracusa (Syracuse) are eloquent memorials to the vibrant ancient Greek culture on the island. The philosopher Empedocles (*c.*490–430 BCE) was born in the city of Agrigento, the rhetorician Gorgias (*c.*485–380 BCE) in Lentini, and the mathematician Archimedes (287–212 BCE) in Siracusa. Despite its remoteness from the Attic Peninsula, Sicily was not spared from the conflicts that raged there. Rivalries between Greek city-states brought violence to the island when in 415 BCE during the Peloponnesian War the Athenians sent a huge fleet there to do battle against Sparta and its allies. This was not to be the last time that distant powers battled in Sicily. Because of its strategic location, Sicily was destined to be the stage upon which the imperial ambitions of many nations were played out.

Sicily: Bread-basket and lumber yard for Rome

Sicily was not only a storehouse of provisions to us, but was also an old and well-filled treasury left us by our ancestors; for, supplying us with hides, with tunics, and with corn, it clothed, armed, and fed our most numerous armies, without any expense at all to us.

Cicero, *Second Oration against Verres*

After Greek power declined, the Romans looked to Sicily as the strategic point from which they could command undisputed control of the Mediterranean, which they called *Mare nostrum* (our sea). Rome went to war with Carthage in North Africa to gain possession of this valuable territory. The First Punic War (264–241 BCE) was fought on the island of Sicily itself. In particular those Sicilian cities that sided with the Carthaginians suffered after the Romans won in the Second Punic War (218–202 BCE); thereafter Sicily became a Roman province. Whereas the Greeks had clustered their cities around seaports clinging to the coast, the better to fish and trade, powerful Roman citizens also founded enormous plantations known as latifundia (singular latifundium from *latus* "wide" and *fundus* "farm") in the rugged heartland of the island. The remains of the main building on one of these estates in central Sicily, the Villa Casale, built during the fourth century BCE, gives an idea of the way wealthy Romans spent their leisure time in Sicily. In its many guest rooms and baths, elaborate mosaic-tiled floors represent scenes of hunting, sports, and feasting. These Romans made great fortunes by exploiting the natural resources of the island, harvesting lumber and growing wheat, but the ecological consequences were devastating. The dense forests of Sicily were chopped down to build the ships of the Roman navy, and deforestation led to soil erosion. Meanwhile Sicily's rich arable land was depleted by the production of grain crops to the exclusion of all others.

Campania felix: Naples and surroundings under the Roman Empire

Like Sicily, the region of Campania was once heavily colonized by the ancient Greeks. Its center was the city of Naples, or Neapolis as it was originally called. Later the region came under the control of the Romans, who carpeted the inland areas with vast latifundia. The coastal areas, on the other hand, became favorite holiday resorts for prosperous Romans, who nicknamed the region *Campania felix* (happy countryside) for its pleasant climate, stunning views from cliffs overlooking the sea, and lush surroundings. Mount Vesuvius, a live volcano that periodically shoots off natural fireworks, looms picturesquely over the Bay of Naples. The Romans harnessed the steam, which was caused by underground volcanic activity, into thermal baths, creating fashionable spas in the region around Naples. Adding to its appeal was the "Greekness" of the region. Like wealthy Americans at the turn of the twentieth century who yearned to acquire European sophistication, ancient Romans had a special affinity for everything Greek. The Greek language was still spoken throughout Campania, and the culture of *Magna Graecia* was very much alive here. Roman emperors especially favored this area—Augustus had villas in Sorrento and Baia, Tiberius in Capri; Sulla, Julius Caesar, and Nero all vacationed here. However, "Happy Campania" also had its dark side. Southern Italy, with its many volcanoes (Sicily's Mount Etna, also spelled "Aetna," being one of the most active), has always been a seismically active area, and continues to experience frequent earthquakes today. Disaster struck in the form of an earthquake in 62 CE, followed by an eruption of Vesuvius in the year 79. The region was devastated; the cities of Pompeii and Herculaneum, along with their inhabitants, were completely buried under lava, rubble, and ash.

Fifth- to ninth-century invasions: Vandals, Goths, Byzantines, Arabs

More destructive than volcanic eruptions was the long-term chaos brought on by the fall of Rome. Like the rest of Italy, the *mezzogiorno* suffered during the death throes of the Western Roman Empire, as waves of Germanic tribes overran the peninsula. Not only the mainland was affected; the tribe of Vandals swept into Sicily from North Africa, taking control of the island

142 *The* Mezzogiorno

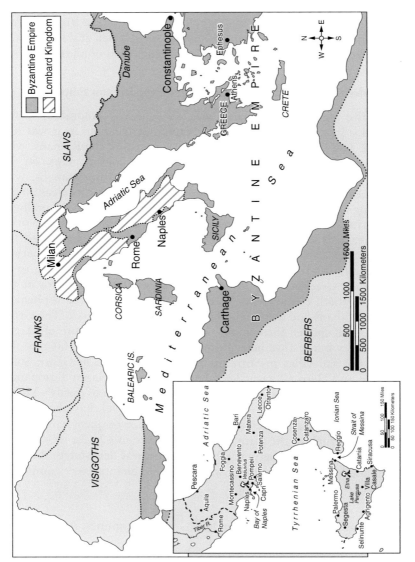

Map 7.1 Southern Italy and the Mediterranean *c*.600 CE

The Mezzogiorno   143

under Gaiseric in 468 CE. Next Sicily passed into the hands of the Goth Theodoric, until the Emperor Justinian (*c.*482–565) stepped in. Ruler of the Eastern Empire at Constantinople, by this time known as the Byzantine Empire, Justinian was determined to remove first the Vandals, then the Goths, from all the territories of the former Roman Empire. Though the peoples living in the south sided with the Greeks, the Gothic Wars (535–54) were devastating to them, as was the plague that broke out in 541 (the Justinianic Plague). War, hunger, and disease took a heavy toll on the population and economy of the once thriving southern cities. Yet another consequence of this conflict was that by concentrating so much effort on ejecting the Vandals and Goths, Justinian unintentionally opened the way for the Lombards to invade. In 568 they descended from the ancient Roman province of Pannonia (modern Hungary), eventually taking much of the Italian Peninsula from the region in the north, which will come to be called Lombardy (Chapter 6) to as far south as Salerno (Map 7.1).

The south emerges as an economic powerhouse and cultural melting pot

A land to which the dove lent its collar and the peacock dressed in its brightly-colored cloak.

Ibn Hamdìs, "Sicily"

On the mainland, the cities of southern Italy began to recover in the seventh century. By the ninth century the ports of Naples, Bari, and Amalfi resounded with the voices of Greeks, Turks, Jews, Arabs, Slavs, and Lombards. The region developed a reputation for learning as well. Throughout the previous centuries of chaos, its monasteries located on remote hilltops had preserved valuable ancient texts, meticulously copied and studied by generations of monks. The most famous of these monasteries, Montecassino, founded in 529 by St. Benedict (480–547) was destroyed by Lombards in 577 and by Saracens in 883; yet, time and again it was rebuilt and its learning passed on.[1] The monks and other learned men skilled in Latin, Greek, Hebrew, and Arabic were able to assemble some of the finest scholarship of the day, especially in the fields of philosophy and medicine. As a result, Europe's premier medical school was founded in Salerno during the ninth century.

Meanwhile in 827 Muslims invaded Sicily, largely driving out the Greeks, and by the end of the century had taken the entire island. Mostly Arabs from North Africa, these conquerors dominated Sicily for nearly 200 years. Although they had invaded the country using violent force, once they came to power, Muslim governors of Sicily were for the most part wise and tolerant. Christians and Jews were allowed to practice their religions, so long as they

---

1 Having survived various barbarian attacks, the Abbey was demolished by Allied bombs in three hours on February 15, 1944. Once again it was rebuilt.

144 *The* Mezzogiorno

made no efforts to convert followers of Muhammad. Unlike the Byzantines who had drained the economy by imposing high taxes on Sicilian subjects, the Arabs stimulated the economy by building canals for irrigation networks and cultivated not only wheat, but also rice, melons, dates, bananas, almonds, pistachios, citrus fruits, and sugarcane, carrying snow down from Mount Etna to make frozen desserts in summertime. They also introduced cotton, silk, and hemp production; increased tuna fishing; as well as mining of sulfur, lead, and silver. Under Arab rule trade links were expanded to other Muslim countries, from the Iberian Peninsula (present-day Spain and Portugal) to Egypt. Not only did Sicily enjoy an economic boom under its new rulers, but Arab music, poetry, and scholarship flourished. The poet Ibn Hamdìs, who died in Mallorca in 1133, was born in Siracusa. After being driven out of Sicily by the next wave of conquerors, he wrote the following poignant verses of longing for the land he left behind:

> The memory stirs sorrow in my soul, when I recall Sicily,
> Site of youthful follies, once enlivened by the flower of the noblest minds.
> If I have been driven out of Paradise, how is it that I can tell of it?
> If it were not for the bitterness of my tears,
> I would think them streams flowing from Heaven.

Norman domination of the south 1059–1130

> After it pleased the Almighty King who controls both seasons and kingdoms that the land of Apulia, long possessed by the Greeks, should no longer be occupied by them, the people of the Normans, distinguished by their fierce knights, should enter, expel the Greeks, and rule Italy … So when they returned to their homeland, the Normans immediately started to encourage their people to accompany them to Italy. They told of the fertility of Apulia and of the lazy nature of the people who lived there … they convinced many to go; some because they owned little or nothing, others because they wanted to increase the great fortunes they already possessed. All of them lusted for gain.
>
> William of Apulia, Deeds of Robert Guiscard

Into this cultural mix of southern Italy stepped yet another group: the Normans. These warlike adventurers, whose name derives from "northmen" or "norsemen," were descendants of Vikings who had settled originally in northern France; the name of the region of Normandy derives from them. Normans first arrived in southern Italy as mercenary soldiers helping Christians fight Muslims or fight each other. Word spread to Normandy of the opportunities that this rich land offered to enterprising knights, and the northerners flocked to Italy. The passage cited earlier is by a contemporary chronicler, William of Apulia, from his work celebrating the victories of the

Norman Robert Guiscard (de Hauteville, *c.*1015–1085). By 1054 the Roman Church had split from the Greek Church (Great Schism), so the pope was grateful to have the Normans rid the peninsula not only of Muslims but also of Byzantines. So successful was Robert, that in 1059 the pope made him Duke of Calabria and Apulia, regions roughly corresponding to the toe and the heel of the boot of Italy, which had formerly belonged to the Byzantine Empire. In 1061, along with his younger brother, Robert invaded Sicily, and thirty years later he had driven the Muslims out. The Normans joined the southern regions of the peninsula with Sicily to form the Kingdom of Sicily in 1130.

The Norman rulers, perhaps surprisingly, accepted many elements of Arab life and were able to rule this diverse population effectively. The Normans brought with them their version of feudalism, which meshed with the centuries-old system of latifundia established by the ancient Romans, producing a highly organized centralized government. As a result of all these factors, Sicily prospered under the Normans, producing exquisite art and architecture, which blended Gothic, Byzantine, and Muslim elements (Figure 7.1). The Jewish traveler Benjamin of Tudela (1130–1173), who had probably seen more of the world than any other man of his age, and was not easily impressed, described Palermo, the capital of Sicily, in glowing terms as a lovely and sophisticated cultural melting pot.

Figure 7.1 The Cappella Palatina, 1129–43, Norman Palace, Palermo

146 *The* Mezzogiorno

Frederick II (1194–1250): An emperor who was the wonder of the world

In barely a century, the Normans conquered almost all of Italy south of Rome; yet the line of the Norman kings of Sicily died out, and their power passed into other hands. Because a Norman princess was married to a member of the Germanic Hohenstaufen dynasty, the crown of Sicily as well as that of the Holy Roman Emperor went to a descendent of that dynasty. One of the most extraordinary rulers of his, or any, time, Frederick II Hohenstaufen (1194–1250) was called *stupor mundi* (wonder of the world) during his lifetime. Born of a Norman mother and a German-speaking father, the Emperor Frederick spoke six languages—Latin, Greek, Sicilian, German, French, and Arabic—a combination that could only have emerged from the diverse cultural climate of southern Italy in this period. The emperor had an insatiable desire for knowledge, and he brought to his court scholars from many disciplines, including Leonardo Fibonacci (1170–1250), who promoted the use of Arabic numerals in Europe. He commissioned translations from Greek, Arabic, and Hebrew into Latin from experts such as the alchemist and astrologer Michael Scot (d. 1236), who translated Aristotle's works on nature and animals. Frederick's intellectual interests extended to the law, and in 1224, he founded the University of Naples, specializing in legal studies; in 1231 he instituted a uniform legal code, the Constitutions of Melfi. Building upon the centralized administration established by his Norman predecessors, Frederick governed Sicily efficiently through a well-organized bureaucracy.

Like the humanist notaries in the north, Frederick's bureaucrats were not simple pen pushers, but educated, literary men. Frederick, himself a poet, encouraged the literary efforts of his employees, and under his patronage the Sicilian School (*c.*1230–50) of poetry flourished. This courtly verse, inspired by the troubadour tradition from Provence and later translated from Sicilian into Tuscan, was widely read, most notably by Dante. The poets Stefano Protonotaro, Cielo d'Alcamo, Guido delle Colonne, Rinaldo d'Aquino, Pier della Vigna, and Giacomo da Lentini were all functionaries at Frederick's court. Lentini is credited with inventing the sonnet form, which Petrarch later elevated to such heights.

Frederick did not limit himself to Christian poets and scholars; he had no special attachment to any one religious faith or cultural outlook. He had the writings of the Jewish philosopher Maimonides (1135–1204) translated so he could read them and corresponded with Muslim philosopher Ibn Sab'in (1217–1268). A great patron of the arts, Frederick surrounded himself with Muslim craftsmen, artists, and musicians. It is believed that the lute, precursor to the guitar, developed in Europe from the Moorish stringed instrument, the oud, largely due to musicians in his retinue, as he made royal journeys across the Alps.

Though the emperor's open-minded, tolerant attitude was an asset in ruling his diverse subjects in southern Italy, it brought him into conflict with the church. This was the age of crusades, and before bestowing the imperial title, Pope Innocent III had extracted a promise from Frederick to lead Christians in driving the infidel from the Holy Land. After many years of delay and excuses, Frederick finally left for Jerusalem on Crusade in 1228, but not before Pope Gregory IX (r.1227–41) excommunicated him. Despite excommunication—he was excommunicated three times during his lifetime—Frederick carried out a successful mission, crowning himself king of Jerusalem in 1229. Rather than adopting the traditional crusading technique of indiscriminate violence, Frederick made the innovative move of negotiating with the Sultan of Egypt for the return of Jerusalem, only further enraging the pope by his friendly relations with Muslims.

The popes had even more serious underlying motives for attacking Frederick than merely his heterodox world view. At his coronation, in addition to the promise to carry out a crusade, Frederick agreed to Innocent's demand that he renounce the crown of Sicily once he became Holy Roman Emperor. In their struggle for control over the Italian Peninsula, the last thing the popes wanted was to be encircled by imperial power to the north as well as the south of Rome. However, after becoming emperor Frederick not only refused to give up the Kingdom of Sicily but also waged wars to conquer territories within the Papal States. Finally, in 1245 Pope Innocent IV (r.1243–54) declared Frederick a heretic and called for a holy war against him. After Frederick's death in 1250, the crown of Sicily was contested, and the pope, concerned to keep the possession of the south of Italy out of German hands, offered the title to a Frenchman, Charles of Anjou, Count of Provence (1226–1285).

The Sicilian Vespers

> In the month of April, in the year one thousand two hundred eighty-two, on Tuesday, during Easter, Lord Palmieri Abate and Lord Alaimo de' Lentini and Lord Gualtieri di Caltagirone and all the other barons of Sicily were all agreed, and had come to Palermo to make a rebellion. Thus, on that day, when it is the custom to hold festivities outside the city of Palermo in a place called Sancto Spirito, a Frenchman took hold of a woman touching her with his hands indecently, as they were used to doing. The woman then screamed and the men of Palermo came running and began to fight. Then the barons came and joined in, and then all the men cried out: "Death to the French!"
>
> Thirteenth-century anonymous chronicler, *Lu Rebellamentu di Sicilia*

The rule of the foreigner Charles of Anjou did not sit well with the Sicilians. Though born of a Germanic father, Frederick had grown up in the south of Italy and reigned largely from there. Charles of Anjou, on the other hand, rarely appeared in Sicily, and his French governors were unpopular. Charles was constantly raising taxes for his military and crusading projects as well as demanding that his Sicilian subjects serve in his armies. When, in Palermo

148   *The* Mezzogiorno

on March 30, 1282, during the early evening hour of Vespers service, a French soldier offended a Sicilian woman, it was as if a lighted match had been dropped onto a pile of dry leaves. Crying "Death to the French!" the inhabitants of Palermo began slaughtering French soldiers, and eventually the whole island rose up in the rebellion known as the "Sicilian Vespers," in which thousands of Frenchmen and Angevin sympathizers died.

Obviously, beyond the offence to the woman's honor, there were much deeper underlying motives that sparked the Sicilian rebellion. Though the population of the island had once been predominantly Muslim, over the years of Norman and then Hohenstaufen rule, Arabs gradually left, and merchants and farmers from the Italian mainland took their place. This gradual "Latinization" of the island had not only cultural and linguistic, but also political consequences. It has been suggested as one of the factors that may have led to the Sicilian Vespers, that former citizens of northern Italian communes now settled in Sicily bristled at being subjected to "taxation without representation." In the wake of the rebellion, a delegation of Sicilians went to Rome and appealed for papal approval of a loose federation of their self-governing, independent cities. When the pope refused, defending Charles of Anjou, the Sicilians turned to the king of Aragon for protection. Peter III of Aragon ("the Great" 1239–1285) was married to Constance Hohenstaufen, granddaughter of Frederick II, and thus had legitimate claims to rule Sicily. On August 30, 1282, exactly five months after the rebellion, Peter arrived in Sicily, and a week later in Palermo he was named king of Sicily.

Aragon and Anjou fight over the Two Sicilies 1282–1442

Thus began what historian David Abulafia has termed a "200 years' war" between the Spanish house of Aragon and the French house of Anjou over possession of the *mezzogiorno*. The Strait of Messina that had once been a nexus of trade now became a point of armed conflict dividing the two realms. The economic and cultural impact of this division on both Sicily and Naples was dramatic. Sicily became isolated from the peninsula except for the presence of Genoese and Florentine merchants shipping Sicilian grain, the island's most important export. The production of other goods—silk, cotton, and minerals—began to fall off as increasingly powerful Spanish barons squeezed their estates for all the grain they could produce. Meantime, the rulers of Naples missed the large income from Sicilian grain that had once poured into their coffers. Continual warfare drained the resources of both kingdoms. Moreover, the cultural climate in both Sicily and Naples began to change during this period. Southern Italy, which before had been a kind of melting pot of Mediterranean cultures, now began to identify exclusively with European culture and to persecute outsiders. Most Muslims remaining in southern Italy had been forced into slavery, and the once-flourishing Jewish communities began to fade as Jews were either compelled to convert or expelled.

The Mezzogiorno   149

Though both Sicily and Naples were the losers from this split, Naples came out better. During these two chaotic centuries in the south, there was a brief cultural flowering in Naples. As Sicily became ever more isolated, a colonial outpost under Spanish rule, with no university and little contact with the developments in humanism and the arts blossoming on the Italian Peninsula, Naples began to look northward and became a thriving cultural center during the fourteenth century under the Angevin King Robert "the Wise" (1277–1343). The patron of Giotto, Boccaccio, and Petrarch, Robert was widely regarded as one of the most cultivated men of his day.

Robert became known as "the Wise" not only for his learning but because of his ability to make judicious political alliances during turbulent times. To keep his kingdom afloat, maintain a glittering court, and patronize arts and letters, he developed close relations with Florentine bankers. These bankers loaned the king enormous sums of money, and in exchange, Robert gave them the lucrative task of collecting taxes and customs duties. Florentine merchants also profited from the arrangement with Naples; some were entrusted with shipping grain, while Florentine cloth manufacturers were granted favored status in selling their fabrics in Naples. The vibrant trade and cultural exchange that characterized Robert's rule between 1309 and 1343 gave the *Regno di Napoli* (Kingdom of Naples) a reputation during this period as a prosperous and cosmopolitan center.

Shortly after Robert's reign, however, the Florentine banks crashed, the Black Death struck, and a series of unexceptional Angevin kings and queens did nothing to improve the situation in the Regno. The Aragonese kings in Sicily, meanwhile, were increasingly unable to control powerful barons who dominated vast stretches of the island. Then suddenly in 1410 the line of Aragon ruling Sicily died out, and Aragonese nobles gathered to choose a successor. They picked a Castilian, Ferdinand of Antequera (1380–1416) to rule as king of Aragon, as well as king of Sicily. No longer was the king of Sicily a monarch who governed, however ineffectively, from the island itself, but now "king of Sicily" became a title added to that of the increasingly powerful realm of Aragon (Ferdinand's grandson married Isabella of Castile, creating the powerhouse of Spain in 1469; see Chapter 12). Though Sicily would henceforth become a territory ruled by viceroys of a distant king, it retained its strategic importance in its proximity to the Italian mainland, and became a base for the man who would unite both Sicily and Naples into one of the most powerful of Renaissance Italian states.

The Two Sicilies reunited under Alfonso of Aragon, 1442

When Ferdinand died in 1416, his son Alfonso ("the Magnanimous" 1396–1458) inherited the kingdoms of Aragon and Sicily; yet from the beginning he had his eyes on a much wider Mediterranean realm, embracing the islands of Sardinia, Corsica, the Kingdom of Naples, and indeed all of Italy. After the deaths of the king and queen of Naples in 1435, Alfonso made his move

150   *The* Mezzogiorno

to take Naples, but was captured by the Genoese in a battle off the coast of Campania. The Genoese were supporters of the Angevins; however, they also owed allegiance to the Duke of Milan, so they turned their prisoner over to Filippo Maria Visconti, who took a liking to Alfonso. Moreover, Visconti recognized the strategic importance of an ally in Italy against both the pope and the French; thus the Duke of Milan agreed that Alfonso would dominate the entire *mezzogiorno* and Visconti eventually take over all of northern Italy. (When Filippo Maria died, Alfonso claimed that as part of this agreement the Duke had left Milan to him; see Chapter 6.) Visconti supported Alfonso despite protests from the Genoese and more important from the papacy, both supporters of Anjou. For seven years Alfonso continued to wage war in southern Italy and in 1442 finally succeeded in taking Naples itself.

Alfonso ousted the Angevins, whose court spoke French, and replaced the court with Catalan and Castilian speakers. Though he staffed the royal household mostly with Spaniards, Alfonso chose Italians for almost every other administrative and military post. His sensitivity to maintaining local traditions was a major factor that contributed to the success of Alfonso's regime. This policy was not prompted by purely "magnanimous" motives, however. Because Neapolitan barons had grown so powerful during the many years of discord between Anjou and Aragon, Alfonso was forced to make many concessions to local warlike nobles in order to hold his throne and to ensure the succession of his illegitimate son Ferrante. In exchange for their support, Alfonso agreed to let the barons continue holding the legal right to complete political and judicial authority in their own lands and to exempt them from paying the hearth tax.

When he consolidated Naples and Sicily, Alfonso also streamlined the bureaucracy and raised revenues by taxing heads of livestock, particularly the many sheep that grazed in Sicily. He ejected most of the Florentine merchants and bankers who had profited during the Anjou years. Their place was swiftly taken by vigorous and wealthy Catalan entrepreneurs (Catalonia is the region along the northeastern coast of modern-day Spain). Furthermore, recognizing their economic importance, Alfonso also permitted Jews once more to do business in Naples. Unusual among Italian rulers of his day, Alfonso used his plentiful economic resources to assemble and maintain a standing army, which further strengthened his kingdom.

Alfonso's power was constrained, however, not only by the powerful barons but by the papacy, which continued to claim lordship of all the *mezzogiorno*. Because tradition held that the lands south of Rome belonged to the papacy, the king of Naples only held the land in fief and was obliged to pay a yearly tribute of money as well as a symbolic white horse to his feudal lord, the pope. In addition, the pope could demand troops from the king and require him to participate in costly crusades. Alfonso's relationship with Pope Eugenius IV (r.1431–47) was crucial for them both. Whereas his predecessor Martin V (r.1417–31) opposed the Aragonese claim, supporting the house of Anjou, Eugenius made a treaty with Alfonso in 1443. He recognized

The *Mezzogiorno* 151

Alfonso's right to rule Naples in exchange for military protection. The pope, who had been in exile for nearly ten years, opposed by Roman barons, and fighting off the claims of the antipope Felix V and the Council of Basel, needed Alfonso's assistance so he could return to Rome. He also granted Alfonso an exemption from paying the monetary tribute, although Alfonso chivalrously continued sending the white horse each year to Rome.

Ferrante I: The "bastard" who brought stability to Naples

When Alfonso died in 1458, he left Aragon, Sardinia, and Sicily to his brother Juan, while his bastard son Ferrante (1423–1494) inherited the Kingdom of Naples. From the outset, Ferrante's right to rule was challenged. The fact that his kingdom was now divided weakened his position, as did his illegitimate birth. Although the two previous popes had accepted his position as heir to Alfonso's throne, Ferrante's claim to rule was insecure. When a former Spanish employee Alonso de Borja or Borgia, as the name is better known in Italian, was elected pope in 1455, it seemed as if the crown of Naples was entirely assured. But Calixtus III (r. 1455–58) refused to recognize Ferrante as king of Naples, supporting the claims of the house of Anjou instead. Pope Pius II, who succeeded him, was an old friend of Alfonso; he not only recognized Ferrante as king in a treaty he signed in 1458 as soon as he became pope, he also reinstated Alfonso's exemption from all but the tribute of the white horse. When Paul II (r. 1464–71) was elected as pope and Ferrante sent only the horse, the pope sent it back, demanding the money owed him instead; for the next seven years the king of Naples and the pope were constantly on the verge of war.

Nor did Ferrante's troubles end with the papacy; he found the Neapolitan barons more difficult to manage than his father had. The barons, many of whom sided with the Angevins, led two major rebellions against Ferrante; he survived at least one assassination attempt, defending himself at sword point. Ferrante developed a reputation for cruelty, even sadism, as he became merciless in the suppression of his enemies. If not for the military and economic assistance provided by Francesco Sforza and Pius II, neither of whom wanted to see a strong French presence in Italy, Ferrante might have failed. Instead, in 1460 he successfully defeated the Angevins as they attempted to invade Italy.

Ferrante had an exceptionally long reign of thirty-six years, and under his rule the Kingdom of Naples prospered. Unlike his father, Ferrante did not have expansionist dreams of founding an empire and consequently did not wage many wars. Indeed, there were just nine years, from 1478 to 1487, that Ferrante was at war, and despite the hostilities of barons and popes, for the most part, his subjects enjoyed a period of tranquility and well-being. As we will see, Ferrante's foreign policy—his cautious dealings with the pope and wise allegiance with Lorenzo de' Medici (Chapters 9 and 10)—contributed to an interim of extraordinary peace in Italy. On the other hand, Ferrante had a more aggressive domestic program than his father, and much of the resistance

152   *The* Mezzogiorno

Ferrante encountered from the barons was the result of economic policies that tended to undercut their authority. Whereas his father had accepted broad compromises to secure their support, Ferrante antagonized the nobility by ending their monopolies, eliminating their tolls, and opening their pasture lands for grazing. In his desire to stimulate the kingdom's economy, Ferrante granted privileges to towns and supported printing, silk, and mining industries.

The Renaissance in Naples, 1443–94

Because of judicious economic policies and shrewd political maneuvering, Naples prospered under Alfonso I and his son Ferrante. Alfonso funded many public works projects in the city, enlarging the arsenal and building a customs house and a substantial breakwater in the port. He renovated aqueducts to improve the water supply, had engineers brought in to drain marshes that bred malaria, and repaired streets and sewers. In addition, Alfonso was a generous patron of the arts, music, literature, and learning, which flourished in Naples during the second half of the Quattrocento. He commissioned bronze medals inspired by imperial Rome, interwoven with chivalric themes, from Pisanello (Antonio Pisano *c.*1395–1455) and Cristoforo di Geremia (1410–1476). On these medals Alfonso is represented either in classical robes dressed like an ancient Roman emperor or in full battle array as a knight in shining armor. He had the entry for his palace of Castel Nuovo in Naples decorated with an immense triumphal marble arch like that of the Emperor Trajan. Alfonso clearly wanted himself portrayed as a wise, classical ruler as well as a powerful modern monarch on a par with the king of France. Though he was less well-known as a patron than his magnanimous father, Ferrante contributed to Alfonso's sculptural legacy. He had carvings on the arch completed, along with a magnificent set of bronze doors to the Castel Nuovo cast by Guglielmo Monaco.

The Aragonese kings of Naples were enthusiastic patrons of music; under their reigns, Naples became internationally famous as a center of musical excellence. Alfonso I brought many Spanish as well as Moorish musicians to Naples, especially string players. He was responsible for introducing instrumental accompaniments to choral singing in church, and attracted celebrated singers from all of Europe to his court. The complex polyphonic music that had begun to flourish during this time in Flanders (the area of Europe now known as Belgium, including parts of the Netherlands and northern France) was still new to Italy. Singers in church previously sang unaccompanied and in unison (monophonic music), as in Gregorian chant; Flemish composers introduced an intricate interweaving of voices and delicate harmonies. Toward the end of the fifteenth century, it was in palaces of the great signori and above all at the Neapolitan court that the irresistible new music first took hold in Italy. Ferrante had the Flemish singer and music theorist Johannes Tinctoris (*c.*1435–1511) brought to Naples, where the musician stayed for

The Mezzogiorno 153

twenty years, teaching music to Ferrante's children and writing musical treatises dedicated to the king. Ferrante also hosted the Franco-Flemish singer and composer Alexander Agricola (c.1445–1506) in Naples and offered him a high salary if he would remain. When the king of France wrote requesting that the renowned musician return to his court, love of music gave way to political necessity and Ferrante let Agricola go.

Alfonso I's tastes in painting tended toward Hispano-Flemish painters. The cities of the Low Countries (present-day Netherlands, Belgium, and Luxembourg) were lively commercial centers experiencing their own Renaissance during this period, and their art was becoming known in southern Europe as well. Flemish painting had exerted an influence on two painters that Alfonso brought with him to Naples from Spain, Jaime Jacomart (1413–1461) and Luis Dalmau (1428–1461). The works of both of these artists display the naturalism and attention to minute detail characteristic of the new Flemish art. Furthermore, the painters in Flanders and the Netherlands were painting in oil, while in Italy artists still primarily worked in tempera. The medium of oil produces an effect of rich, deeply saturated colors that made a striking impression on fifteenth-century viewers. Of all the emerging Flemish school, Alfonso preferred the paintings of Jan Van Eyck (c.1395–1441), which he enthusiastically collected. Alfonso also owned tapestries from Arras, the center of tapestry-making in northern France, and had a number of them woven based on designs of the Franco-Dutch painter Rogier van der Weyden (c.1400–1464). The native Neapolitan artist Niccolò Colantonio (c.1420–c.1460), a painter who picked up much of the style of Flemish painting, was one of Alfonso's favorites.

Ferrante's son Alfonso of Calabria (1448–1495) was an avid patron of architecture, although nothing remains of his magnificent villas of La Duchesca and Poggioreale, designed by Giuliano da Maiano, or of his planned Porta Reale triumphal gate for the city. One of Alfonso's best-known commissions is the *Lamentation* (Church of Sant'Anna dei Lombardi, Naples), by Modenese sculptor Guido Mazzoni (c.1445–1518). Each of the seven life-size, naturalistic terracotta figures grouped around the body of the dead Christ display their grief with dramatic gestures: Mary Magdalene plunges forward, her arms flung wide; the Virgin Mary crumples to the ground in despair, while kneeling near the feet of Christ one arm mutely gesturing, is Alfonso himself as Joseph of Arimathea, his face contorted in pain. The *Lamentation* is a fitting memorial to its patron, who ruled as King Alfonso II for only one year before being forced to abdicate by the invasion of the French in 1495 (Chapter 10). He died later that same year.

Antonello da Messina's paintings: Meticulous realism and haunting mystery

Born in Messina, in Sicily, Antonello da Messina (Antonio di Antonio c.1430–1479) was one of the most innovative painters of the Renaissance;

he incorporated techniques from Flemish painting and influences from his native Sicily to create a vivid, new style. Little is known with certainty about his life, except that he spent his years of apprenticeship in Naples, probably with the painter Colantonio; there he was exposed to the stunningly realistic style and intense colors of the northern European painters favored at the court of Alfonso. Antonello may have studied with Flemish masters as well, though there is no documentary proof of this. Nevertheless, the paintings of Jan Van Eyck, Petrus Christus, and Rogier van der Weyden had particularly strong influences on the young Sicilian artist, as is demonstrated in his atmospheric *St. Jerome in His Study* (National Gallery, London), painted around 1470. The subject of this painting was a favorite among humanists;

Figure 7.2 Antonello da Messina, *Virgin Annunciate*, *c.* 1476, Museo Nazionale, Palermo

The *Mezzogiorno* 155

St. Jerome, who had translated the Bible into Latin was a kind of patron saint to scholars. The image of his study, charmingly cluttered with quills, inkwells, and many manuscripts, was a familiar subject, which Antonello has taken pains to represent punctiliously down to the tiniest details.

One of the first Italian painters to master oil technique, when Antonello traveled to Venice around 1475, he brought the new style with him, in turn influencing an entire school of Venetian Renaissance artists. Antonello traveled widely, yet he always returned to Sicily, and it was during one of his stays in Sicily that he painted his *Virgin Annunciate* (Museo Nazionale, Palermo, Figure 7.2). In this haunting work Mary sits behind a desk, with her book open, one hand lightly grasping her blue veil, the other just raised in a startled gesture. The viewer recognizes immediately from her garment and pose that this is the Virgin, who is listening as the angel Gabriel announces that she is to bear the son of God. The angel, however, is nowhere in sight. We are directly in front of Mary in the position of Gabriel, seeing the drama unfold in her eyes. Those eyes, knowing and melancholy, are unfocused, looking off to the side, while a gentle smile hovers around her lips. The light that illuminates her face is realistic—a beam of light that might fill a Dutch kitchen—but at the same time otherworldly, the light of revelation. The stark black backdrop serves to create drama and remove the figure from any temporal setting, giving it universal meaning. Altogether it is a stunning work displaying technical mastery of naturalistic effects while suffused with spirituality. Aside from being a work created by an individual master, Antonello, this painting also represents a pinnacle of southern culture, assimilating Italian and Flemish styles, while adding a subtle touch of Sicilian mystery.

Alfonso the Magnanimous and patronage of humanists

More than any other cultural contribution, it is his support of humanism for which Alfonso is remembered. Like his contemporaries Cosimo de' Medici and Francesco Sforza, to whom he is often compared, Alfonso was a cultured man who had a love of humanist learning. Vespasiano da Bisticci tells of how, while on military campaign, he would have works of the Roman historian Livy read to him and his commanders. However, like the Medici and the Sforza, Alfonso also shrewdly recognized the "propaganda" value of having humanists in his employ. He spent lavishly for their services, according to Bisticci, as much as 20,000 ducats a year. Humanists at Alfonso's court such as Antonio Beccadelli (1394–1471) became wealthy. Better known as *il Panormita* (the man from Palermo), the Sicilian humanist's task was not only to write works that would add luster to Alfonso's court, works such as *De dictis et factis Alphonsi regis Aragonum* (*On the Sayings and Deeds of King Alfonso*), but also to help assemble a splendid royal library and to attract renowned scholars to Naples. One of the celebrated humanists who came was the poet and Latinist Giovanni Pontano (1429–1503), and he remained

156 *The* Mezzogiorno

in Naples for eighteen years. Both he and Beccadelli were among the finest intellectuals of the day who gathered in the king's library; this group came to be known as the celebrated Accademia Pontaniana. Both the poet Jacopo Sannazaro (1458–1530) and Masuccio Salernitano (1410–75), writer of stories in the vernacular, received generous support from the king of Naples. Writers and visiting scholars such as George of Trebizond and Theodore Gaza were paid for translations made for Alfonso and were rewarded when they dedicated their books to him. Panormita and the others were also magnanimously paid for their efforts. Panormita started out with a salary of 450 ducats a year, which was later doubled. Along with the many other benefits he received, the scholar was able to buy himself a fine villa and other property, an unusual luxury for a man of letters at that time, when a humanist teacher in Venice earned 100–200 ducats a year, and a papal secretary could expect an annual salary of between 300 and 500 ducats.

Lorenzo Valla: Humanist scholar and freethinker

Some of the finest works of Renaissance scholarship were written by the humanist Lorenzo Valla (1407–1457) while he was employed as secretary to Alfonso. Valla, one of the most brilliant and original thinkers of his day, was born in Rome, the son of a lawyer from Piacenza. Having studied with such renowned humanists as Bruni, Barzizza, and Aurispa, in 1431 Valla took orders as a priest, but was unsuccessful in being appointed a post as apostolic secretary in Rome. Instead, he went to teach at the University of Pavia where he remained until 1433. Valla became fascinated with legal studies during this period and immersed himself in the study of canon law. At this time he also wrote a treatise *De voluptate* (*On Pleasure*), which was widely read and debated. In it, Valla argues against the Christian values of self-sacrifice and abnegation of physical pleasure; instead, he advocates Epicureanism, an ancient materialist philosophy that emphasized appreciation of life in the here and now. The church condemned these beliefs; indeed, Dante had placed Epicureans in the *Inferno* as heretics. As a result of his unorthodox views, Valla was fired from his post in Pavia, and for several years he wandered from one university to another teaching for brief periods at each.

   Therefore, when Alfonso offered him a highly paid job in 1435, Valla did not hesitate to accept. While employed by the king of Naples, for over a dozen years Valla produced some of the most important scholarly works of the Renaissance. Aside from writing an occasional work to glorify the Aragonese dynasty (*Gesta Ferdinandi Regis Aragonum*, 1445, never finished), Valla was given free rein to pursue his studies. He wrote philological treatises on Latin grammar, emphasizing the importance of precision and clarity of classical style (*Dialecticae diputationes* and *Elegantiae linguae latinae*). He also re-translated portions of the Bible based on his superior knowledge of the original Greek texts. It was not only his first-class scholarship that distinguished Valla; he had a skeptical frame of mind and he challenged beliefs that had been held for centuries. In his *Collatio novi testamenti* (*Annotations to the New Testament*), he writes: "none of the words of Christ have come down to us, for Christ spoke to us in Hebrew and never wrote anything down." In his *De libero arbitrio* (*On Free Will*), Valla systematically dismantles scholastic theology, and in *De professione religiosorum* he attacks the hypocrisy of the religious orders.

Both propaganda and pure humanist research dovetailed in Valla's greatest work, his *On the Forgery of the Alleged Donation of Constantine*, produced under Alfonso's patronage. This incendiary Renaissance treatise represents the apex of humanist historical–philological research while also promoting the king of Naples' political agenda. Written in 1440, Valla's *Discourse* debunks a document upon which the papacy for centuries had rested its claim not only to the Papal States in the *mezzogiorno*, but to all of Europe.

Understandably Valla's conclusions enraged the church, but his proof was irrefutable. Rather than being intimidated, he continued to challenge what he considered bogus claims including whether the Apostles themselves actually authored the Apostles' Creed. In 1444 Valla asserted that the work had been composed in the fourth century long after the Apostles were dead. This time he was called before the Inquisition, but he was defended by Alfonso who both admired Valla's intellectual bravery and appreciated the way the humanist had been able to weaken the pope's claims over the Kingdom of Naples. Most important, because of Alfonso's patronage and protection, Lorenzo Valla pioneered a field known as Christian or Evangelical humanism and opened the way for future scholars to analyze Biblical texts critically. One scholar who drew special inspiration from Valla's philological research was the Dutch humanist Desiderius Erasmus (1466–1536), whose writings on the Bible would be pivotal to the Protestant Reformation.

Considerations: Was the south backward or ahead of its time?

The history of the *mezzogiorno* was dramatically different from that of the rest of the Italian Peninsula. While in the north the many independent Italian city-states struggled with the choice between republican self-determination and rule by a signore, the vast, largely agrarian territories of southern Italy were ruled by a succession of foreign emperors and kings and languished under an antiquated feudal order. Yet it is too simple to jump to the conclusion that the south was backward or that it somehow "missed out" on the Renaissance, which was flourishing in central and northern Italy. Compared to the rich and varied cultural and ethnic tapestry of Sicily and Campania, areas such as Tuscany and Lombardy can seem homogeneous and almost provincial during the Middle Ages and early Renaissance. The south was a kind of cultural crossroads, a clearinghouse for ideas, languages, art, and music, which then circulated northward up the peninsula and throughout Europe.

The south perhaps had an earlier Renaissance than the rest of Italy. Renaissance secular learning and even the Italian language itself, it can be

158   *The* Mezzogiorno

argued, first emerged at the court of Frederick II, a generation before the birth of Dante. The languages of Latin and Greek that would be recovered by later humanist scholars were already flourishing in the *mezzogiorno*, where in a sense they had never entirely vanished. The widespread familiarity with Arabic and Hebrew writings that characterized the universal approach to scholarship in the south during this early period would not be equaled until several centuries later by Pico della Mirandola and certain Florentine Platonists (Chapter 9). Later, with the patronage first of Robert the Wise and then with Alfonso and his son Ferrante, the Kingdom of Naples, in particular, made lasting, significant contributions to Renaissance arts, music, and humanism. Under Aragonese rule, the importation of foreign talent especially from France and the Netherlands caused an effect of cross-pollination that enriched the Italian Renaissance, as the impact of foreign artists and musicians spread to other parts of the peninsula; and cutting-edge scholarship was funded by Alfonso, in part at least to further his political agenda. These innovations in polyphonic music, Flemish-inspired realism in art, and Christian humanism were the direct result of the tastes and political exigencies of the Aragonese monarchs.

Perhaps, however, rather than emphasizing its differences, the similarities between north and south should be noted. Were the monarchies in the south so very different from the signories in the north? Kings such as Alfonso, though they sometimes seem to prefigure European enlightened monarchs of the seventeenth and eighteenth centuries, had nowhere near the absolute power of the French King Louis XIV or Frederick the Great of Prussia. The kings of Naples were never entirely secure on their thrones, both Anjou and Aragon weakened by the claims of the other. The power of the kings was circumscribed by that of the local barons, whose control was deeply entrenched. In a traditional feudal order, nobles owed subservience to the king, as in France and England, yet in Sicily and Naples there was no such clear-cut hierarchy. Italian historian Benedetto Croce characterized the prevailing system in the south as a "perversion and corruption" of the traditional feudal order, the result of which was "utter anarchy." Just like the signori to the north, the kings of Naples felt a need to make a magnificent display of artistic and cultural patronage to legitimize their rule. And this strategy worked. Combined with shrewd statesmanship, compromise with local traditions, and the powerful backing of the Kingdom of Aragon, by the mid-fifteenth century the Kingdom of Naples was among the most powerful players in Italy.

Many histories of Renaissance Italy leave out the *mezzogiorno* entirely. This is due in part to the fact that we have less historical documentation about the south; the destruction wreaked by Allied bombs on Montecassino during World War II were matched by the Nazi firebombing of the Neapolitan State Archives stored in Nola. Precious, irreplaceable archives from this period were destroyed, making it impossible to reconstruct with certainty much of its past. Neither the sometimes sketchy historical documentation nor the

The *Mezzogiorno* 159

exotic "otherness" of the south justifies its traditional neglect by historians, however. Furthermore, because of the crucial role the Kingdom of Naples played in the catastrophic events that overtook the Italian Peninsula at the end of the fifteenth century, no coherent history of Renaissance Italy can exclude the *mezzogiorno*. Similarly, no comprehensive history of modern Italy, with all its many contradictions, organized crime, and corruption, can ignore the complex combination of historical events that over centuries shaped the south.

Sourcebook

Benjamin of Tudela, *Book of Travels*
Giacomo da Lentini, *Sonnets*
Pere Joan, Pietro da Milano, et al. *Triumphal Arch of King Alfonso of Aragon*
Raffaele Lippo Brandolini, *On Music and Poetry*
Lorenzo Valla, *On the Forgery of the Alleged Donation of Constantine*

Further reading

Abulafia, David. *Frederick II: A Medieval Emperor*, Penguin, 1988.
Atlas, Allan W. *Music at the Aragonese court of Naples*, Cambridge University Press, 1985.
Bentley, Jerry H. *Politics and Culture in Renaissance Naples*, Princeton University Press, 2014.
Cilento, Adele and Alessandro Vanoli. *Arabs and Normans in Sicily and the South of Italy*, Riverside Book Co., 2007.
Hersey, George. *Alfonso II and the Artistic Renewal of Naples 1485–1495*, Yale University Press, 1969.
Metcalfe, Alex. *The Muslims of Medieval Italy*, Edinburgh University Press, 2009.
Ryder, Alan. *Alfonso the Magnanimous: King of Aragon, Naples, and Sicily, 1396–1458*, Oxford University Press, 1990.
Tronzo, William, ed. *Intellectual Life at the Court of Frederick II Hohenstaufen*, National Gallery of Art, 1994.

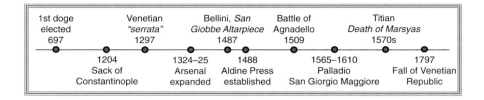

8 *La Serenissima*
When Venice Ruled the Seas

> Virgin citie of Venice, the Queene of the Christian World, that Diamond set in the ring of the Adriatique gulf, and the most resplendent mirrour of Europe.
>
> English traveler Thomas Coryat, 1611

Approached from the open sea, the city of Venice appears suddenly, rising out of the mists—a city of solid brick and marble floating on water. In the Renaissance, to a traveler who was accustomed to the fortified cities and towns of Europe surrounded by massive stone walls, Venice, wide open, with dazzling light glinting off the water on all sides, must have seemed like a vision of Paradise. The closer the traveler gets, the more hectic the activity: enormous merchant galleys crowd the port, with small fishing boats darting in and out. Once the Grand Canal appears, the wide waterway that snakes its way like the letter S through the city, the water itself is hardly visible, so dense is the boat traffic. Narrow, stately gondolas glide past, adeptly maneuvered by gondoliers by means of long poles, missing one another by a hair. One after another regal palazzi decorated with Gothic tracery, which look like confections made of spun sugar, rise up on both sides of the canal.

Once they step off the boat, the visitor's senses are assaulted on all sides. Voices of stevedores, peddlers, and whores assault the ears, all offering their services in a babel of languages. Fishmongers and spice merchants thrust their odorous wares under the nose as bearded, turbaned Turks; Black Africans in caftans; Jews wearing skullcaps; Greeks; Germans; Dalmatians; Dutchmen; Circassians all jostle one another on the narrow banks. The clanging of a bell announces the end of the working day, and the several thousand men who toil in Venice's shipyards, grimy and exhausted, come pouring onto the

DOI: 10.4324/9781003270362-8

La Serenissima   161

streets and bridges, adding their shouted greetings and insults to the din. Taverns fill, brawls break out, mothers send their children into the night to find their fathers and bring them home. The stranger who ventures out after dark will almost certainly lose their way, following narrow passageways that lead inevitably to the wrong bridge, the wrong canal, or dead-end into a reeking, shadowy alley pregnant with menace.

This is Venice, a city born of the sea. Just as Sicily's destiny was shaped by the Mediterranean, so too Venice was formed by its relationship with the sea. As we have seen, Italy's geography—a narrow peninsula, poised in the center of the Mediterranean—was crucial to its rise to pre-eminence in the Middle Ages and the Renaissance. During this time there were three seagoing Italian republics whose navies, merchants, and pirates dominated the region: Genoa, Pisa, and Venice. Of these three, Venice attained the greatest splendor, wealth, and enduring political power; the city known as La Serenissima (her most serene highness) was the recognized queen of the Mediterranean. By the fifteenth century, the Venetian Republic was one of the most feared and respected powers in the world. The extraordinary wealth of her merchants, political acumen of her ruling class, attractions of her courtesans, strength of her navy, skill of her artists and craftsmen, and sheer physical beauty of the city were legendary everywhere in the known world. How the Republic of Venice attained this greatness is as amazing and unlikely as the physical foundations of the city itself—a city built on water—yet this most improbable of cities, a fairy-tale realm that arose out of the marshes of the northern Adriatic, became the most enduring of Western political entities, lasting for more than 1,000 years.

"You live like sea birds, your homes scattered over the water"

The history of this most glorious of cities began inauspiciously in the swampy marshes near the place where the Po River empties into the Adriatic Sea. Unlike the other maritime republics of Genoa and Pisa, and the Italian cities we have looked at thus far—Naples, Milan, Florence, and Rome—Venice was a "new" city. The Roman region of Venetia (named after the local people, the "Veneti" in Illyrian) and Istria had the mainland city of Aquileia as its capital (Map 8.1). The soggy islands upon which the city of Venice would one day be built had never been inhabited during ancient times, when the only sounds to be heard in the Lagoon were the occasional splashing of fishermen's oars and the squawking of seabirds overhead. Everything changed though with the end of the Roman Empire. As the northern tribes poured down over the Alps in the early fifth century and ravaged Aquileia, Padua, and other cities in the northeastern area of the peninsula, inhabitants took refuge by boat to the archipelago and built makeshift huts among the watery reeds. The strategy worked, for the Goths, who came from landlocked country and were unused to the sea, avoided this area. What had seemed a temporary refuge, however, developed into increasingly permanent settlements as wave after wave of invaders swept

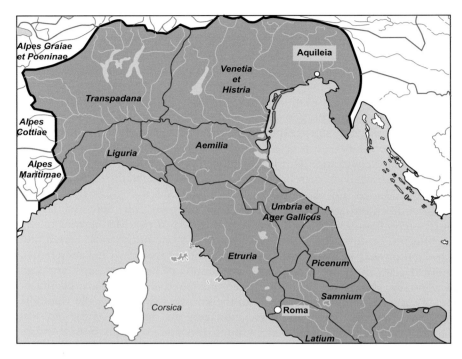

Map 8.1 Ancient Roman regions of northern and central Italy

over the land. Sometime in the fifth century the settlers of the hundred or so islands of the archipelago formed a loose confederation for their mutual protection.[1] The Lombard invasion in 568 CE brought the largest influx of refugees; by 639 the church on the island of Torcello was dedicated, marking the presence of a permanent community in the area now known as Venice.

Documentation for the earliest years of the Venetian settlements is sketchy; the description of the Sicilian scholar Cassiodorus (*c*.490–*c*.583), who went there in 523, is the earliest account we have of Venice:

> You live like sea birds, your homes scattered over the water, like the Cyclades islands. There, not upon solid earth, but on watery plains with great patience have they fearlessly built, out of flexible reeds bound together, a fragile rampart against the wildness of the sea. These inhabitants have

---

1 Venetian histories traditionally dated 25 March, 421, at noon, as the legendary founding of the Church of San Giacomo di Rialto, and hence the city of Venice, but this date appears to be fanciful.

one great source of wealth: the plentiful fish that allows all to live equally, with no differences of rich and poor. All eat the same food, live in the same kind of dwellings, unaware of the affliction of envy to which other people are constantly subject.

The Venetians' battle for survival

From the earliest times, Venetians put the collective good above individual interests, which was not merely a political stance but a question of survival.

Figure 8.1 Vittore Carpaccio *Hunting on the Lagoon*, c.1490–95, Getty Museum, Los Angeles. Although painted nearly a millennium later, this painting gives an idea of the rough and ready lives of the first settlers in Venice

164 La Serenissima

They needed to cooperate to dominate their natural environment. Though Cassiodorus portrayed the inhabitants of this island paradise as living "free as birds," the challenges Venetians had to overcome to survive in this watery world were many. Protected by the sea from outsiders, their most challenging and constant combat was not as much with humans, as with nature. Food, in the form of fish, was plentiful, but there was the problem of maintaining a supply of freshwater to drink, despite their ingenious methods of collecting rainwater in cisterns. Ironically, the Venetians who lived surrounded by water were always short of that precious resource. Though their early habitations were made of poles and twigs, bound with reeds, as their community grew, buildings became more substantial. To support the heavy foundations, long poles had to be sunk deep into the muddy substratum beneath the islands; eventually millions of poles were sunk this way in order to hold up the city of Venice. Aside from fish and sea fowl, their other foods, and most important, grain, had to be acquired through trade with towns and villages on the *terraferma* (solid ground), the term Venetians use for the areas on the surrounding mainland. In the earliest days Venetians traded primarily fish and salt harvested from the sea to acquire what they needed to live. Nearby forests along the coasts of the northern Adriatic provided a plentiful source of wood for shipbuilding.

The lagoon dwellers had access to other resources as well. The Emperor Justinian had conquered the nearby city of Ravenna in 540, making it the capital of the Byzantine Empire in Italy. For 200 years Venice was a province of the Byzantine Empire and part of a strip of territory along the eastern coast of Italy that, along with a portion of the south, owed allegiance to Constantinople. Because of their ties to the Byzantine Empire, the Venetians had access to luxury goods from the East: silk, cotton, incense, and spices that were in high demand throughout Europe. During the eighth through tenth centuries, Venetian merchants sailing in their flat-bottomed barges were a common sight on the Po and other rivers of northern Italy. They traded their exotic wares not only for grain and agricultural produce from the fertile Po Valley, but sent their goods to northern Europe as well (Map 8.2). At key places along waterways and at cities such as Ferrara, Verona, Milan, and Pavia, Italian merchandise was shipped over the Alpine passes to be traded at fairs in Champagne, France. Merchants from all of Europe converged at these fairs, particularly anxious to acquire the luxury goods that came from the faraway Orient. In exchange, fabrics from Flanders and metals mined in Germany, particularly silver, began arriving in large quantities in Venice. From the earliest days, international trade was not just an activity involving a few; it was crucial to the livelihood of all Venetians. The mercantile way of life was a necessity without which survival in this soggy outpost of the Byzantine Empire would have been impossible.

La Serenissima 165

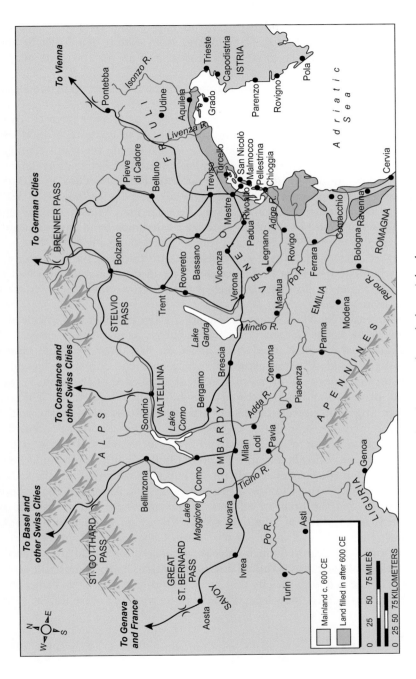

Map 8.2 The early settlement of Venice and trade routes through the mainland

166 La Serenissima

Inventing a Venetian identity: The city of St. Mark takes wing 810–1000

I was born a Venetian and I live in this happy homeland, defended by the prayers and protection of St. Mark, from whom that Most Serene Republic recognizes its greatness, victories, and all the fortunate events that have befallen her.

Gabrielle Fiamma, fifteenth-century Venetian cleric

After ensuring Venetian independence through a decisive victory over the Frankish fleet,[2] the city we know today began to coalesce around the island known as Rivo Alto (high shore) or Rialto during the ninth century. Previously this muddy island had been scarcely inhabited, but its more defensible, central position made it ideal as the nucleus of the city. Thus, in 810 the center was relocated to the Rialto; ten years later the Doge's Palace (Palazzo Ducale) was built there. Then in 828 some Venetian merchants returned from a voyage to Egypt and brought not only their usual merchandise of silks and spices but also the body of St. Mark (one of the four Evangelists) they had stolen from Alexandria. These enterprising tomb raiders gave the precious relic to the doge (the ruler of Venice, see later in this chapter) who had it placed on display in his chapel, which was later consecrated as St. Mark's Basilica (San Marco).

The arrival of St. Mark's remains signaled a key moment in Venice's history. Every medieval Christian city had a patron saint, usually associated with a miracle the saint worked there, and some part or parts of that saint's body usually resided in the cathedral where the relic conferred blessings on the citizens. More than a mere mascot, the presence of the saint, it was believed, protected and guided the city, providing divine assistance. The city gained prestige and power if the saint was very important, as there was a recognized hierarchy among relics, the closer to Christ, the more potent the object. Because Christ was believed to have resurrected, and Mary at her death to have ascended bodily into Heaven, obviously no church could hold their bodies, but the next most valuable holy bodies were those of the saints who had known Christ: the Apostles and Evangelists. Among its many holy relics, Rome had the body of St. Peter; Constantinople had thousands of relics, including the arm of John the Baptist. When Venice acquired St. Mark, it implicitly declared itself on a par with both Rome and Constantinople.

Additionally, it acquired much more than a sacred force field and valuable symbol of power—it also acquired a founding myth. Every saint had a story that was connected with the city that he or she protected, so now Venice, the "new city," invented a "new legend" to go along with its holy relic. The story

---

2 In 810 after subduing several coastal towns, Charlemagne's son Pepin (King of Italy r.781–810) launched an attack on Venice. The battle lasted six months, ending with heavy casualties for the Franks; Pepin himself died several weeks later.

La Serenissima   167

was that during the first century CE, after Mark had been preaching in nearby Aquileia, he was returning by boat on the Adriatic when a storm forced him to look for a safe harbor. He took shelter overnight in the Venetian Lagoon on the site where St. Mark's Basilica would one day stand. Here an angel appeared to Mark announcing: *"Pax tibi Marce evangelista meus"* (peace be with you Mark, my Evangelist). The Venetians, who had invented the entire episode, explained the words as meaning "Rest here, Mark," the angel announcing to Mark that his final resting place would one day be on this spot in Venice. The fictional association with the saint contributed in no small part to what has been called the "myth of Venice," an image of a city blessed with supernatural internal tranquility and impervious to outside attacks.

Before the Venetians acquired Saint Mark, the patron saint of Venice had been the fourth-century Greek warrior-saint Theodore. Now Theodore reminded Venetians of their origins as a province of the Byzantine Empire, and they moved Theodore and the bones of Saints George and even Nicholas, patron saint of mariners, out of the way for their more powerful "Latin" saint, Mark, whose symbol was the winged lion. Representations of lions with wings that spread like sails began to appear everywhere on Venetian buildings, sculptures, paintings, and flags—a fierce new image for the proudly independent state. Though a large part of the Venetian identity was shaped originally by the Byzantines, when during the Middle Ages Venice took for its cultural model the refined East, rather than the crude, untutored West, now as they were coming into their own, the people of Venice readily embraced this new symbol of their identity, neither Eastern nor completely Western, but fiercely Venetian.

From the "Venetian Gulf" to "Beyond-the-Sea", 1000–1204

Long after the Byzantines lost control of their possessions on the Italian Peninsula in 751, and even after the schism between the Greek and Roman churches in 1054, Venice maintained a close connection with Byzantium.[3] Like members in the British Commonwealth, whose commercial interests and cultural affinities keep them tied to their former colonial rulers, Venice found it advantageous to remain close to the Byzantines. There was also another reason to maintain the connection—to have an ally against the Normans. While the pope was thrilled to see Robert Guiscard taking control of the south away from the Greeks and the Muslims in the mid-eleventh century, Venetians were wary of these seafaring "Northmen" who threatened their control of the Adriatic Sea. Venetian domination of that body of water had become so complete that by 1154 the Sicilian Arab cartographer Al-Sharif

---

3 To this day, like Greek Orthodox cities, Venice has as the leader of its church a patriarch rather than a bishop. Though the Venetian patriarch is answerable to the pope in Rome, Venice still retains that distinctly eastern privilege.

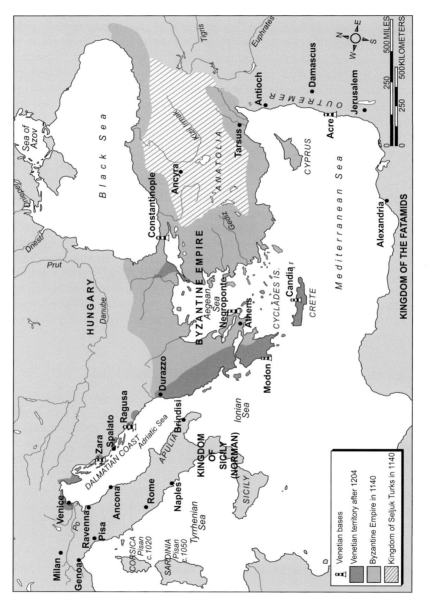

Map 8.3 Venice and the Eastern Mediterranean 1140–1204

Al-Idrisi (*c*.1100–1166) on one of his maps had labeled the Adriatic simply the "Venetian Gulf." When in the 1080s Robert Guiscard began to attack Byzantine trading posts, the Venetians feared that the Normans might block their access in and out of the Adriatic, cutting Venice off from Constantinople. Rome allied with Guiscard in this conflict, but the Venetians took the side of the Byzantines against the Normans, neither the first nor the last time that Venice defiantly opposed the papacy. In return for coming to the Greek emperor's aid in naval battles, the Venetians, who already enjoyed privileged trading status, in 1082 were granted lands and full rights to trade. Not only did they receive important ports, Venetian merchants were permitted unrestricted trade in all of the eastern Mediterranean, without having to pay taxes or customs duties.

Thus, Venice began to expand its mercantile interests well beyond the Adriatic, but what really boosted the city's fortunes were the Crusades. In 1095 in a stirring speech in Clermont, France, Pope Urban II had called upon European nobles to liberate the Holy Land of the infidel and save their Christian "friends," the Greeks, from the attacks of the Muslim Turks. Thousands of zealous crusaders from all of Europe set out for Jerusalem, concerned less for the plight of the faraway Byzantines than for the wealth to be acquired in the fabled lands of *Outremer* ("beyond the sea," the Medieval name for the regions of present-day Israel and Syria). With access to eastern trade routes, this was a place where fortunes could be made and Europeans saw this market as theirs for the taking. The Venetians, however, were initially reluctant to participate, not only as it would mean an alliance with the Normans, but because diplomatic relations between Byzantium and Venice had broken down. The Greek emperor, angered at Venice's rapaciousness, had retracted the former trade privileges granted them, making the Venetians decidedly less willing to come to his assistance. And finally, although profit was to be made in this endeavor—many ships would be needed to transport the crusaders to *Outremer*—the Venetians hesitated to antagonize Muslim countries, thereby endangering their trade relations. Their rivals, the Pisans, instead profited immensely from the First Crusade. Venice, thereafter, was never slow to offer its services.

The Fourth Crusade, in particular, stands out as a turning point when the Venetians used all their mercantile instincts, cunning, and naval force to establish themselves as the dominant power in the eastern Mediterranean. The crusaders contracted for passage to the Holy Land with Doge Enrico Dandolo (r.1192–1205), who cut a tough bargain, receiving 85,000 silver marks in advance for providing armed galleys as well as transport for thousands of crusaders. When it came time to embark, only a fraction of the number of crusaders appeared and a large sum was still owed to the Venetians. Dandolo still agreed to transport the crusaders, but on the condition that they fight a few battles for Venice on their way to Jerusalem. The crusaders had no choice but to comply. The first stop was the port city of Zara, positioned on the southern portion of the Dalmatian coast and a pivotal strategic point between the Adriatic and Ionian seas. Venice had long attempted to dominate this port, which had repeatedly rebelled. Needless to

170 La Serenissima

say, with the immense forces they now had at their disposal, the Venetians brought Zara to its knees.

Thereafter, instead of heading directly to Jerusalem, several leaders of the crusade saw the opportunity for great enrichment nearer at hand. Taking the side of a pretender to the Byzantine throne, the crusaders decided to attack Constantinople. They did this with the assistance of Doge Dandolo, who had accompanied this crusade. Though well into his eighties and blind, Dandolo led the charge when, on April 12, 1204, the attackers broke through the city's defenses. The crusaders surged through the gates, for three days indulging in an orgy of massacre, rape, and pillage in this Christian city. The plunder was valued at hundreds of thousands of silver marks, and Venice's part in the booty can be seen in the rich decorations of the Basilica of San Marco, including the *Triumphal Quadriga*, the four bronze horses of classical antiquity that prance at its entrance. Moreover, through the government of Byzantium set up by the victors, Venice gained control of all the trading privileges of the empire. From this point there was no stopping the Venetians; dominance of the eastern Mediterranean was theirs (Map 8.3).

The Venetian commune comes of age, 1032–1297

During the same years in which Venice was growing as a commercial and naval power beyond the Adriatic and expanding into the eastern Mediterranean, she was undergoing changes in political structure at home. Since 697, when they were formally a part of the Byzantine Empire, the Venetians had been gathering in a general assembly known as the *Arengo* to elect one of their own to represent them. The man they chose was called the doge, a term in Venetian dialect from the Latin *dux* ("leader", from which both "duke" in English and duce in modern Italian are also derived). Though elected by consensus, during the early centuries of Venetian history, doges were often bold, willful men who thought of themselves as princes and handed power down through their sons, attempting to create hereditary dynasties. Though many observers, from Cassiodorus on, portrayed Venetians as governing themselves in a kind of rough-and-ready democracy, for its first 100 years Venice was in fact a dukedom, governed by a single lord.

The shift toward communal government that was taking place throughout northern Italian cities in the late eleventh and early twelfth centuries also occurred in Venice, although with some significant differences. Venice's successes overseas could not have continued if there had been unrest at home, and indeed the transition to communal government in Venice was relatively swift and peaceful. There was little turmoil, compared to other Italian cities that needed to oust feudal barons or placate powerful bishops to establish themselves. One of the characteristics of the Venetian polis from its earliest times was that, as a "new" city, Venice had no native landed nobility; indeed, there was no "land" at all, no feudal lords to whom homage was owed. Because the Venetians were independent from both pope and emperor, their city was not divided by Guelf and Ghibelline antagonisms. In Venice the structure of the commune was not an abrupt and dramatic change from the past; rather it was superimposed over the existing political structure, and adjustments were gradually eased in.

This is not to say that there was no violence involved in the change. Sparked by the nepotism and monarchic pretensions of doges from the Orseolo family, unrest broke out in Venice during the first decades of the eleventh century. General dissatisfaction arose with the way the position of doge had begun to belong to a smaller group of families, whose names came up for election time and again. In 1032 Domenico Flabanico, a wealthy silk merchant, was elected doge, though no one in his family had ever held the office. Flabanico opposed hereditary rule, and once he became doge, he himself introduced some of the first measures to limit the doge's powers. As the Venetian state had been expanding, the doge increasingly needed advisors to help him rule, but now councilors and judges were elected by the *Arengo* to advise, control, and supervise the city's top official.

Though the commune could elect councilors, it was not always easy to get doges to follow their advice. In 1172 Doge Vitale II Michiel led the Venetian fleet to disastrous defeat, ignoring all his councilors' advice, and after a meeting in the *Arengo*, the doge was killed in the streets by angry citizens. To ensure that future doges would not similarly overstep their powers, a written agreement called a *promissione* was introduced around this time. The solemn oath of office, in which the doge promised to follow specific guidelines of behavior, was essentially a contract with the people of Venice and St. Mark.

The Great Council: Keystone of the Venetian Republic

In his *promissione*, the doge specifically vowed to serve the judgment of the Council of the *Sapienti* (the wise men)—the legislative branch of government introduced in 1143. The members of the council were first elected from among the *Arengo*. But this unwieldy assembly, composed of all eligible Venetian citizens, was increasingly phased out in favor of a communal government run by a cluster of elected committees. The numbers of members and names of the councils and committees changed over time—the Council of *Sapienti* was replaced by the Council of Forty and then by the Senate—but the terms of office were invariably short, ensuring turnover so that no one family or interest group dominate the others for long. Moreover, the large body of the *Arengo* could easily be swayed by factions, so an electoral commission was established, culminating in election reform in 1268. The *Arengo*, whose main function had been to elect the doge, was now officially replaced by the Great Council, composed of 300–400 men. This is the elaborate system they devised for nominating the doge, which was intended to weed out factional influence:

Members of Great Council drew lots, selecting 30 men
   the 30 drew lots to reduce their number to 9;

172   La Serenissima

those 9 named 40 "electors";
"electors" drew lots to reduce number to 12;
those 12 named 25;
the 25 drew lots to reduce their number to 9;
the 9 named 45;
the 45 drew lots to reduce their number to 11;
the 11 named 41 who nominated the doge.

Thus, by shuffling and re-shuffling the electors, it was hoped that no single faction could stack the deck in their own favor.

Similarly extreme measures to avoid influence peddling were employed in Florence and other communes, and in many respects the structure of Venetian government resembles that of other Italian republics. The tendency to rule by committee, elaborate checks and balances between executive and legislative, and an overall concern for reducing factionalism was common to all communes; however, the differences are significant. By examining the unique system devised by the Venetians, we can come closer to understanding a characteristic Venetian frame of mind and gain a clue to the secret of the longevity of the Venetian Republic.

The "aristocratic commune" closes ranks: The 1297 *serrata*

One element that, unlike other communes, never made its way into Venetian government was the *popolo*. Trade guilds never had the clout in city government that they did in other Italian cities. Though guilds existed in Venice, they were never as powerful as those, for instance, in Florence; the goldsmiths, tailors, physicians, and other small craftsmen and professionals who formed the Venetian guilds had relatively little power. Venice's ruling elite of merchant–aristocrats held the reins of government tightly, and by 1260, laws were passed limiting guild activity. Just ten years earlier the *popolo* had taken control of the commune in Florence—Venice was taking no chances.

Likewise, toward the end of the thirteenth century the Great Council had become the main legislative body, the most powerful organ of government, and had reached around 500 individuals. Venetian elites asked themselves how great should the Great Council be; how many members could be added before it began to lose its effectiveness? More significantly, who should qualify for membership? If too many "new" men were allowed to join, how long before serene Venice would be troubled by discord as the newcomers attempted to unseat the old guard?

Venice now did something at odds with its image as a republic of egalitarian marsh-dwellers. The Great Council, under the leadership of Doge Pietro Gradenigo (r.1289–1311), passed legislation that restricted membership to noble citizens only. The council doubled in number, naming 1,000 men eligible to hold office, and then they shut the gates behind them. This event, known as the *serrata* (closing), meant that for the next 500 years only

La Serenissima   173

a group of designated aristocrats ruled Venice. In 1315 the names of over 200 noble families were recorded in the so-called Golden Book and only descendants of those families were allowed to belong to the Great Council and hold office. Though many of the Italian republics such as Florence were actually oligarchies controlled by a small network of powerful families, this was something very different. Enough families were drawn into the circle of government that it enhanced the city's stability. Rather than fostering animosity by excluding less powerful elite families from a tight oligarchy, Venice with its broader official ruling class actually diffused tensions. Moreover, the number of families did not remain absolutely static; new families and foreigners were occasionally allowed to buy their way into the Great Council and the number of its members more than doubled, reaching 2,000 by the fifteenth century.

The Council of Ten: The vigilant lion

Another characteristic of Venetian government was its heavy emphasis on secrecy and national security. No other Renaissance state had a better organized or more feared central intelligence agency than Venice's Council of Ten. Despite all the safeguards against factionalism built into the Venetian political system, in 1310 a conspiracy of the Tiepolo and Querini families (who opposed Gradenigo's reform of the Great Council) caused Venetians to create a council whose task was to seek out conspiracies and suppress rebellion. When in 1354 Doge Marino Falier conspired to overthrow the Great Council, the Council of Ten discovered the plot, the seventy-year-old Doge was beheaded, and his co-conspirators hung. Thereafter the Council of Ten became a permanent part of the government structure, employing a substantial spy network. They were assisted by hundreds of citizen informers who could anonymously drop a denunciation into a carved stone structure like a mailbox, the *bocca di leone* (lion's mouth). Other cities had their similar systems for reporting crimes; Florence, for instance, had its *tamburro* (drum). Any Florentine could secretly drop a note reporting the misdeeds of another Florentine; a favorite was denouncing a neighbor who had evaded paying taxes. Venetians dropped accusations of a variety of crimes into the lion's mouth, but their government was especially concerned with crimes against the state. The council investigated accusations through an efficient network of secret police. Even if a criminal fled Venice, he could never feel entirely safe; even decades later, assassins working for the Ten were known to track down and kill enemies of the state. The agents of the council had a reputation: they always got their man.

The Doge of Venice: Prince or *primus inter pares*?

The most enduring and distinctive element of Venetian government was the figure of the doge. The doge had similarities with other types of rulers; for

Figure 8.2 Giovanni Bellini, *Portrait of Doge Leonardo Loredan*, *c.*1501, National Gallery, London. As was traditional, Bellini portrayed the doge wearing his sumptuous state robes and the *corno ducale* (dogal cap)

instance, like the pope, the doge was appointed for life. As with the men elected to the papacy, doges were usually quite old when they took office. Renaissance Venice is often referred to as a gerontocracy (government ruled by the aged); the average age for doges when they were elected was seventy-two. This was partly because Venetians, like many eastern societies especially, valued the wisdom and experience of older people and the continuity they represented for the state; the highest levels of most government positions tended to be held by Venetians of well beyond middle age. The authority of the doge was enhanced by his ceremonial attire and public appearances; he participated in numerous religious and civic rites and processions wearing long flowing robes and distinctive headgear. He lived in the Doge's Palace where he was waited on with elaborate protocol and surrounded by splendor fit for an eastern potentate. Though the Venetians accorded their doge many of the trappings of royalty, they never again permitted the doge to behave like a hereditary monarch. The other reason that they chose doges of advanced age was that Venetians were concerned that no one man or one family dominate their government for too long.

With the advent of the commune, Venetians did not choose to do away with the office of doge. They needed a chief executive, but as there was no strong, organized *popolo*, a *capitano del popolo* was not called for. Because Venetians always fiercely resisted outside influence, they never embraced the concept of an outsider serving as a *podestà*. They had found their own ways to reduce internal factional dissent and did not feel the need to hire a short-term administrator to run their government. Instead, proud of their traditions, Venetians would continue to select one of their own, *primus inter pares* (first among equals) as doge, to hold the executive office in their republic. As a symbol of the state, the elderly doge in his regal garb set a dignified tone for the Venetian mercantile republic and impressed foreigners. A *promissione* from 1462 that specifies that the doge must have an ermine cape to be worn at least ten times a year underlines the importance of his magnificent attire. His presence at the head of the many ceremonial processions in the city lent a sacral quality to civic festivals. However, the doge was not just a figurehead; as the only elected official who held an extended term of office, he endured as various councilors came and went. Among the doges were many forceful men, whose experience was respected and whose leadership the Great Council relied upon.

"Lords of the Sea"

> Merchandise flows through this noble city like water through fountains.
> Martin da Canal, *Les Estoires de Venice, c.*1275

After 1300, following the example of their rivals the Genoese, who had been sailing these waters since the 1270s, the Venetians ventured into the English Channel and the North Sea, sailing to England and Flanders. And inspired by their countryman Marco Polo, who had recently returned from the court of Khublai Khan, Venetians began to travel farther east. Venice had become one of the world's largest emporia as goods such as perfume, pearls, dyes, sugar, spices, tapestries, furs, carpets, porcelains, and precious metals, as well as slaves poured into the city. Venetian trading activities were now so vast, stretching from Beirut to Bruges, that shipbuilding needed to be stepped up to meet the demand (Map 8.4).

The place where all these ships were produced was the largest industry in all of Europe—Venice's state-owned Arsenal (*arsenale* from the Arab term for workshop or factory). Contemporaries were awed not only by the scale of the

176 La Serenissima

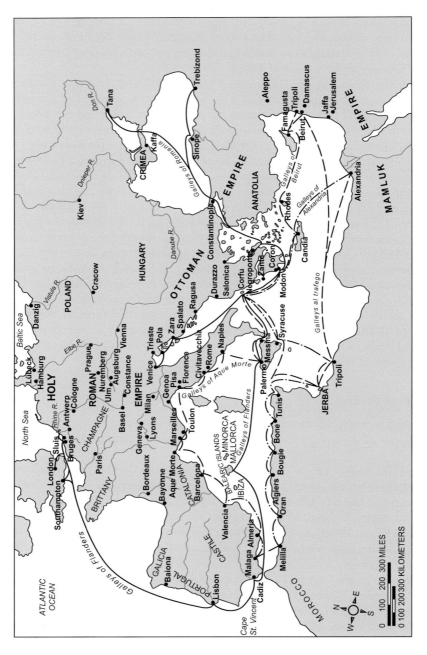

Map 8.4 Venetian merchant fleets in the fifteenth century

Arsenal, but by its efficiency—standardized measurements, interchangeable parts, and assembly-line production were in use here centuries before Henry Ford—and by the ceaseless activity. The Arsenal was founded in 1104 and was in full swing two centuries later when Dante visited it, making such an impression on the exiled Florentine that in the *Inferno* he compares devils' feverish activity to Arsenal workers caulking the hulls of ships with boiling pitch (*Inferno* XXI, 6–15). During the poet's lifetime, the Arsenal's production rose to meet increasing demand and its size doubled between 1303 and 1325.

At its height during the fifteenth century, there were 3,300 ships in their fleet, and in 1570 when the Turks threatened their colony in Cyprus, the Venetians were able to step-up production and built 100 ships in around 60 days. The Venetian government built both merchant galleys and warships, as the interests of the state and trade were inseparably linked. Because merchant galleys carried huge quantities of valuable merchandise, they usually traveled in convoys accompanied by warships, but they also needed to be able to defend themselves and were thus designed to be able to be converted swiftly into warships when needed. The versatility of the republic's fleet, along with their superior ships and well-trained crews, made Venice the most powerful force in the Mediterranean. The Venetians, it seemed, were unstoppable, and when in 1380 they crushed the Genoese in the War of Chioggia they eliminated the competition. In the words of Pope Pius II: "from that time Venetians were the lords of the sea."

Expansion of the Venetian Empire into the *terraferma*

Venetians, whose mercantile interests for centuries had drawn them across the seas ranging from Asia Minor to the shores of Albion in search of profit and glory, were suddenly in the Quattrocento forced to pay close attention to the affairs on the Italian mainland. By this time there were fewer and fewer independent Italian city-states; power on the peninsula was concentrated around larger geographical areas. We have seen in Chapter 6 how Giangaleazzo Visconti initiated a policy of aggressively expanding the territory of the Duchy of Milan until it covered much of the Po Valley. Although Visconti did not succeed in conquering all of northern Italy, he came dangerously close, and the Venetians were worried that the Milanese could cut off their access to the trade routes across the Alps and perhaps eventually attack the city of Venice herself.

The Venetian Republic began now to wage war on the Italian mainland in order to gain territory in northeastern Italy. Having already taken possession of Treviso in 1389, one by one the cities of the *terraferma* fell to Venice. In 1404–05 the forces of the Republic took the nearby cities of Vicenza, Verona, and Padua; in the 1420s they added Friuli to the north and Brescia and Bergamo to the west. Venice, like the other cities of Italy, now had its own *contado*, an agricultural hinterland to exploit, and by 1420 it established a colonial government, the *Savi di Terra Ferma* to administer the territory.

178 La Serenissima

Many Venetians disapproved of this turn to the mainland. The greatness of Venice was to many its buccaneer spirit, and abandoning the sea was a betrayal of the city's destiny. Regardless, Venetian nobles began to invest in land on the *terraferma*. Being landlords was becoming a more appealing way to make a living, more secure than overseas trade. Always a risky endeavor, trade with the Levant became even more so after 1453, when the Ottoman Turks conquered Constantinople. Venetian fleets, from that point on, were engaged in constant naval battles with the Turks, and business endeavors on dry land looked like a safer bet.

Daily life in Renaissance Venice

By the fourteenth century Venice was one of the largest cities in Europe. Its 120,000 inhabitants lived in densely packed neighborhoods, which were crisscrossed by canals and connected by many wooden bridges. It was a vibrant city, but overcrowded and not an easy place to live in. There was a constant influx of new residents from the *terraferma* in need of housing, and in order to accommodate the growing population, more and more of the Lagoon was filled in. Thus, canals were created that were unaffected by the tides; in these stagnant areas garbage and human waste poisoned the air and bred disease. When epidemics broke out here, they were especially deadly: it has been estimated that the Black Death of 1348 killed around three-fifths of the population. As word of new outbreaks spread, people fled in terror, but they always returned. Despite the dangers, immigrants were constantly drawn to this city as a place of opportunity, and by 1500 the population of Venice returned to around 120,000. Over the course of the sixteenth century, the population would swell to 190,000, only to be devastated again by two more epidemics in 1575 and 1630.

Strangely, however, Venetians, who lived cheek by jowl with one another and who were constantly squeezed to make room for foreigners and immigrants from the mainland, tended to be peaceful. There was plenty of crime, of course; Venice had its share of pickpockets, thieves, conmen, pimps, and murderers, but there were surprisingly few workers' riots or popular uprisings such as that of the Ciompi in Florence. Why were Venetians so placid? In a population of over 100,000, never more than 2,500 were allowed a vote in government. What prevented the other 98–99% from overturning the status quo?

To answer this question we must examine the various groups that composed Venetian society to see what roles they played in the functioning of their city and how they viewed themselves as a part of the civic whole. Beneath the self-appointed Venetian aristocratic ruling class was a distinct and respected citizen class known as *cittadini originarii* (original citizens). These citizens, who could prove their families' residence in the city going back for several generations, held the many administrative offices required in Venice's ever-expanding bureaucracy. Lawyers, notaries, and clerks in the Venetian Chancery were mostly original citizens; in a sense they ran the city government on a steady basis, unlike the rotating officeholders drawn from the aristocratic Great Council. Citizenship was also open to newcomers who established a certain period of residency and married a Venetian. If an individual practiced an "honorable" trade, that is, if he was not a manual laborer and paid taxes, he could apply for legal citizenship status. Moreover, the Venetian government encouraged newcomers to apply for citizenship, thereby increasing the city's revenues. With citizenship, a naturalized merchant could trade with full privileges accorded to Venetians and pay favorable shipping and customs rates. In the early modern world of strict social hierarchies, paradoxically Venice, despite its rigidly designated aristocratic class, offered unique opportunities for social mobility.

Beneath the citizen class were the commoners known as the *popolo minuto* (little people). This was the largest group, including artisans, dock workers, shipbuilders, ropemakers, glassblowers, silk workers, gondoliers, fishermen, and notably the skilled craftsmen and laborers who were employed in the shipbuilding industry. At its height over 16,000 workers were employed in the Arsenal. Although Dante's hellish description conjures up dark images, the reality was not so bleak; the shipbuilders, *arsenalotti*, as they were called, were respected workers, and the most skilled especially were well paid; all were provided with plentiful rations of wine. Though Venice had no police force, the *arsenalotti* acted as a kind of honor guard for the doge and served as a fire brigade in emergencies. In the words of historian Frederic Lane, the Arsenal workers "were not 'factory hands.' They differed in spirit and in discipline, for they were master craftsmen and naval reservists."

The Venetian government concerned itself with protecting the city's most lucrative and prestigious products, in particular, its glassmaking industry. The glassworkers on the island of Murano in the Lagoon (they were relocated there when glass furnaces were banned from Venice in 1291 as a fire hazard) were world famous for their craft. From the molten silica in those furnaces, glassblowers spun out creations of elfin delicacy—goblets, candlesticks, flasks in blazing crimson or filmy milkglass, and sparkling incised crystal mirrors. Murano was also a center for producing lenses for spectacles and hour glasses for measuring time, both of which required technical expertise and precision. Like the workers in the Arsenal, Murano glassblowers were accorded special privileges. Permitted to wear swords, master glassmakers were accorded honors and even allowed to marry Venetian noblewomen. They were forbidden, however, on pain of death to leave the Venetian Republic, for fear that they would practice their craft elsewhere and reveal their glassmaking secrets. The production of other luxury goods—among them lace, leather, and in particular silk—was similarly controlled and protected. It has been calculated that by the end of the fifteenth century as many as 3,000 men and women worked in the Venetian silk industry. The fabrics they produced were of a quality so fine, that rather than exclusively importing eastern silks, these silks were now exported to the Levant. Like

180   La Serenissima

the glassmakers, these workers were also given privileges and incentives to ply their trades in Venice.

Though it would be an over-simplification to claim that the privileges awarded to specialized workers such as the *arsenalotti* or the Murano glassmakers were enough to placate them, it is true that workers in these trades were conscious that they were contributing a resource that was valuable to the state and they were proud of their status. Nevertheless, without decent work conditions and sufficient pay, it is unlikely that glassblowers would have been satisfied by being permitted to strut around wearing swords, and even less likely that the Venetian government would have granted unhappy workers the right to wear them. There was no need for a police force to suppress workers' riots, indeed the trusted Arsenal workers themselves served as a kind of police. Venetian authorities were careful to guarantee this trust by always maintaining an adequate source of grain; food riots, which were frequent in medieval and early modern Europe, were a rarity in *La Serenissima*.

Festivals, *scuole*, and *venezianità*

Recognition of the specialness of the work these individuals performed contributed to their sense of *venezianità*, their "Venetian-ness"; however, other factors also contributed to Venetians' feeling of belonging. The many festivals staged by the city delighted the public, but they went well beyond keeping the public well fed and entertained. More than mere "bread and circus," civic celebrations helped fuel Venetians' pride and reaffirmed their belief in the divinely ordained superiority of their city. Take, for instance, the celebration of the *Sensa*. Every year the anniversary of the founding of Venice was celebrated in the spring, when the doge set out on a ceremonial barge called the Bucintoro, surrounded by boats carrying members of the aristocracy and the representatives of the clergy in all their finery, as the population looked on, cheering. When his barge left the Lagoon and reached the open Adriatic, the doge cast a golden ring into the water, ceremonially wedding the sea. Every year since about 1000 CE this ceremony was repeated, renewing Venice's sacred union with the sea. This ritual, which joins a Christian holiday of the Feast of the Ascension (the fortieth day after Easter Sunday, when Christ is said to have ascended into heaven) with something like a pagan fertility celebration, further fueled the Venetians' self-fashioned myth of the city's divine predestination.

A prominent role in these civic celebrations was played by the *scuole*, a Venetian term for lay confraternities. The *scuole* were an essential part of Venetian life, and it has been estimated that there were around 300 by the year 1500. Although Pius II once referred to the Venetians as living in a "godless republic without a soul, fearless even of the fires of Hell," religion played an important part in Venetian civic identity. Next to the numerous churches in Venice, which proliferated despite limited space, the most visible

La Serenissima   181

aspect of religious life in the city were the *scuole*, divided into the *scuole grandi* and the *scuole piccole*, the large and small confraternities.

There were six *scuole grandi*, so-called because they numbered between 500 and 600 members each; these were religious confraternities that subsidized many religious celebrations as well as institutions such as hospitals and charities. Members would gather in the large, impressive headquarters of the *scuola* to engage in devotional activities, such as penitential flagellation and group prayer. A distinctive characteristic of the *scuole grandi* was that membership was open to all, from nobles to commoners. Officials were elected and could come from any social class; however, the leader had to be from the *cittadino* (citizen) class; aristocrats were prohibited from leading a *scuola*. The egalitarian nature of these fraternal organizations diffused class tensions, further contributing to the social stability of Venice.

The more numerous *scuole piccole* were, on the other hand, limited to participation by members of specific professions. Like the confraternity, the *scuola* had a spiritual function, as members would gather to pray together, and they collected dues that paid for activities such as participation in civic festivals and charitable projects. A *scuola* connected to a trade guild was like a small community with frequent town hall meetings in which members gathered to discuss and vote on measures that affected their common interests. For the individuals who belonged to the *scuola*, the cradle-to-grave social services the association provided were crucial. A member could expect help paying for his daughter's dowry, financial assistance if he fell ill, or needed emergency assistance, and finally, when the time came, he was given burial services. Though Venetian guilds did not have much political power, they provided their members with the security of a miniature welfare state, which went a long way to compensating for their exclusion from participation in government.

Early modern cities had various pressure valves for defusing social tensions; these were pronounced in Venice, where carnival season, which lasted from the day after Christmas until the first day of Lent, included fireworks, street theater, and games. The *arsenalotti* climbed on top of one another to make human pyramids, delighting onlookers; gondoliers held canal races; and neighborhood clubs fought ritualized battles on bridges, in which the victorious side was the one that knocked the opposing group off the bridge.

And let us not forget, among the public spectacles perhaps most likely to guarantee social stability was public administration of justice. Venetian law was inexorable, punishing criminals, whether noble or commoner. Indeed, an aristocrat who committed a capital offense would be executed in a particularly public manner, his head severed, and his body strung between the two pillars beside the Doge's Palace for everyone to see. Clearly the Venetian justice system had flaws; however, the law was generally more even-handed than in most other places at the time. In Venice, there was a sense that there was "justice for all," and that everyone had equal recourse to the law.

Humanism, printing, the sciences

It was members of the literate *cittadini* class who codified the laws of the Republic and transcribed the letters of the Venetian Chancery in Latin. Like their Florentine counterparts, they were educated in the liberal arts and reveled in the new humanist learning. Unlike Florence, however, the humanist intelligentsia in Venice was separate from the ruling class; the Venetian merchant–patricians did not at first embrace humanism. They had been bred not only to study the abacus, so they could take care of business, but also to command at sea. An essential part of young Venetian aristocrats' education was traditionally practical service aboard Venetian galleys—this, rather than memorizing speeches by Cicero, was their finishing school to prepare them for government.

Nevertheless, humanism began to take root among noble Venetians. Guarino Guarini of Verona (1374–1460) went to Constantinople, where he studied ancient Greek with Chrysolorus, and came back to teach the children of Venetian patricians for a time before setting up his school in Ferrara. Humanist Gasparino Barzizza (1360–1431) likewise taught for a time in Venice before relocating to Padua. Around the time Venetian nobles began to relinquish some of their overseas interests, turning to the mainland of Italy for profit, they also began to be exposed to the currents of Renaissance ideas that were circulating in the rest of the peninsula; the career one of Guarino's renowned pupils, Francesco Barbaro embodies this trend.

Though humanism was slow to take off in Venice, it was in full swing by the second half of the fifteenth century when the printing press was introduced there in 1469. The Venetian entrepreneurial spirit caught hold of this machine invented by Johannes Gutenberg in Germany around 1450, and before long Venice became the leader in the printing industry in all of Europe. The most renowned of all early modern printers is Aldo Manuzio (Aldus Manutius *c.*1450–1515). An accomplished humanist scholar, Manuzio set up a press in 1488, turning out numerous fine editions of classical texts, as well as Renaissance Italian works, printed not in Venetian, but in Florentine dialect. Moreover, ironically the one man responsible for forever enshrining the language of Petrarch as the official Italian tongue was a Venetian, the nobleman Pietro Bembo (1470–1547, Chapter 12). The so-called Aldine Press printed works in Latin and Greek, and also sheet music. One of the many innovations introduced by Manuzio was italic type, which we still use today. The distinctive symbol of this Venetian press, appropriately an anchor entwined with a dolphin, was printed on the front page of thousands of humanist texts that circulated throughout Europe.

If humanism was late in developing in Venice, scientific studies were not. The University of Padua, which was officially absorbed into the Venetian state in the early Quattrocento, had, alongside the literary component of the liberal arts curriculum, a reputation for excellence in what we today define as the sciences. Even before taking Padua, however, Venice was known

La Serenissima   183

throughout the peninsula for its highly skilled physicians and pharmacists. Furthermore, it was also only natural, with mariners' study of the stars for navigation, that Venetians had an interest in the astronomical sciences, as well as cartography. The world map created in the mid-fifteenth century by the Venetian cartographer Fra Mauro, a Camaldolese monk, is considered a landmark in the history of mapmaking for its attention to detail and attempt to bring together a vast array of ancient and medieval sources. Technology and engineering also figured importantly in Venice with its emphasis on precision in shipbuilding. Galileo, indeed, was to combine the theoretical and the technical in the research he conducted while employed by the Venetian government at the University of Padua, where he did some of his finest work. It was there that he designed his telescope, which he presented to the doge (Chapter 15).

Venetian painting of the early Renaissance: Bellini and Carpaccio

Renaissance Venice always presents an unusual combination of innovation and tradition, and nowhere is this more evident than in the visual arts. Venetian painting was undergoing striking changes in the fifteenth century. As Venice turned toward the mainland, painting especially began to show the influence of Renaissance developments elsewhere on the peninsula, while still retaining very distinct characteristics of its own. The social, geographical, historical, and political circumstances that set Venice apart from the rest of the peninsula affected every aspect of Venetian culture, and most strikingly its art. The play of light off of the Lagoon, the types of materials used in the damp climate, the taste for rich mosaic texture, the nature of patronage, and an ineffable quality of *venezianità* all shaped Venetian Renaissance art, distinguishing it from works that were created in other parts of Italy during the same period. Two quattrocento painters who represent the early Renaissance style of Venetian art stand out: Giovanni Bellini (*c*.1431–1516) and Vittore Carpaccio (*c*.1460–1526).

Giovanni Bellini came from a family of artists: his father Iacopo (*c*.1400–1470), brother Gentile (*c*.1429–1507), and his brother-in-law Andrea Mantegna (1431–1506, Chapter 12) were renowned painters. But it was Giovanni with his embrace of oil techniques; warm, luminous use of color; realistic style; and innovative subjects who most brilliantly defined a distinctive Venetian style in painting. During his long and extraordinarily productive career, Giovanni Bellini created portraits (Figure 8.2) and devotional paintings for private Venetian patrons, altarpieces for churches and *scuole*, as well as a series of historical paintings for the Doge's Palace (lost in a fire in 1577). The subject of Madonna and Child was one that Bellini painted again and again, either on small panels representing the two, or as monumental works with the pair surrounded by saints as depicted on his *Frari, San Zaccaria*, and *San Giobbe Altarpieces*. This latter painting was commissioned by the Scuola di San Giobbe, the confraternity named after

184   La Serenissima

the biblical character Job. The *scuola* sponsored a hospital, and the painting, which represents both the figure of Job, who had suffered many afflictions, and St. Sebastian, patron saint of plague victims, attests to the confraternity's focus on healing. In these paintings Bellini has represented a vaulted ceiling with a Byzantine mosaic like that of St. Mark's, whose shimmering tiles recede back from the viewer in perfect Renaissance perspective. It is often said that in Venetian Renaissance painting, as contrasted with the Florentine school, color predominates over form, and indeed each of these paintings, at the center of which is the rich blue of the Virgin's cloak, is suffused by warm, golden light that lends the work a gentle, meditative mood. The realistic features on the saints' faces and attention to minute details of the leather binding of a book, the light glinting off a porphyry bowl, and the heavy embroidery on bishop's robe all show the influence of the northern schools of art. The richly expressive use of oil Bellini had picked up from Antonello da Messina (Chapter 7). Bellini was one of the first in Venice to fully exploit oil paint, which was to become the medium of choice for Venetian painters. The watery city with its damp climate did not favor fresco painting: tempera colors faded with time as the stucco on the wall decayed. Bellini also pioneered landscape painting, which became a uniquely Venetian genre, ironically for a city without land. Using the same play of light and color as in his altarpieces, Bellini infuses natural scenes with emotional intensity. In his paintings *The Agony in the Garden* and *St. Francis in Ecstasy*, the natural surroundings convey a reflective, spiritual mood.

Vittore Carpaccio (*c.*1460–1526) is most known for the "eyewitness" style of painting, which concentrates on landscape; his work displays a completely different side of Venetian painting, in many ways unrelated to Bellini. Carpaccio did most of his work for the *scuole*, and he represented biblical or legendary Christian scenes set in places resembling Venice. Carpaccio delighted in depicting scenes set in his vibrant, crowded city, such as *Miracle at the Rialto* (*c.*1494 also called *Healing of the Possessed Man* or *Healing of the Madman*, Galleria dell'Accademia, Venice). His paintings, *Two Venetian Ladies on a Terrace* (*c.*1495 Museo Correr, Venice) and *Hunting on the Lagoon* (*c.*1495 Getty Museum, Los Angeles, Figure 8.1), which were once part of the same panel, depict other moments of daily life in his city. Though many of the scenes are crowded, Carpaccio portrays an idealized image of his city, a place where tranquility, harmony, and light reign.

Serenity expressed in the structure of buildings and political theory

This serene, harmonious image had to wait another generation until being given an architectural form. Unlike their innovative counterparts in painting, Venetian architects in the Quattrocento continued to proclaim their link to the past in the golden onion domes of the Basilica of San Marco, the rounded Romanesque arches, the Flamboyant Gothic style displayed on its palazzi, and the fortress-like crenellations on the Arsenal. A distinctive Venetian Renaissance style of architecture did not develop until Sansovino (Jacopo Tatti 1486–1570), a Florentine sculptor arrived in Venice in 1527. In 1529 Sansovino was appointed chief architect of San Marco, and he remained in Venice for the rest of his life designing many classically inspired buildings that changed the face of the city. He introduced the Renaissance style of architecture to Venice, but adapted it to blend harmoniously with surrounding buildings. Three of his buildings in particular—the Zecca (or Mint 1536), the Loggetta (1537–1545, Figure 8.3), and the Marciana Library (1537–1560)—pull together the disparate buildings around Piazza San Marco, unifying Venice's civic and religious center. The Marciana, with its delicate stone tracery and elegant classical statues reaching skyward, harmonizes with the Gothic elements of the Doge's Palace across the square, while at the same time updating it with the latest contemporary Renaissance aesthetic. It would be a younger contemporary of Sansovino, however, whose buildings in Venice and the Veneto region, constructed during the second half of the sixteenth century, epitomize Renaissance ideals in architecture—Palladio (Chapter 14).

Figure 8.3 Jacopo Sansovino, detail of Loggetta 1537–1545, Marciana Library 1537–1560 on left, the Campanile behind it, Piazza San Marco, Venice

186 La Serenissima

Likewise, the harmony and unity of the Venetian Republic was celebrated in political theory; the most eloquent contemporary description of the structure of Venetian government was written by Venetian humanist Gasparo Contarini (1483–1542). Contarini authored many books on philosophy and theology, but his most well-known and influential work is *The Commonwealth and Government of Venice* (*De magistratibus et republica Venetorum*), which describes the republic's "mixed constitution." It was published in Latin in 1543 and translated the year after into Italian and French. In 1599 it was translated by Englishman Lewis Lewkenor, a contemporary of Shakespeare.

Considerations: The myth and countermyth of Venice

Both Contarini's idealized portrayal of Venetian harmony and the doge's ritual marriage to the sea are elements of the "myth of Venice." The historian Edward Muir has written that creating this myth was "an act of communal genius" on the part of the Venetians. The myth itself is complex. It involves of course the supernatural assistance of divine forces protecting the city— how else to explain its miraculous protection from invaders—but it also had to do with civic virtues. The myth was already at work in Cassiodorus's description of Venetians, in which he painted an image of a community bound together by common virtuous and democratic purpose. The Venetians liked to portray themselves as extraordinarily harmonious, their serene city not only impervious from outside attack, but free of internal dissent. In this island paradise, the inhabitants ruled themselves; free from the yoke of a tyrant, they were a beacon of liberty to the rest of the world.

Like all myths, this one had elements of truth. Though the Venetians never had a system of rule that approached a democracy, they nevertheless did develop into a republic governed by a group of their own citizens. Though they never lived in complete unity, in general they did put the common good over individual concerns in ways that other societies did not. And even if their own citizens, from the doge down, were subjected to many restrictions on their personal freedom, the city as a whole enjoyed complete liberty from outside invasion for over 1,000 years.

This myth was so powerful that it also bred a countermyth, the other side of the coin of this supernaturally peaceful city. Just as often as it was praised for its unusually stable political system, so too Venice was criticized for maintaining that stability at the cost of the personal freedoms of its citizens. Rumors of the secret activities of the Council of Ten spread and magnified until the Ten seemed like the KGB. Venice was presented, in this view, as a repressive police state, which kept its citizens under control through intimidation and torture. Moreover, this countermyth suggested that Venetians had won their position and wealth because of their craftiness and that they were untrustworthy. From the time of Charlemagne, who distrusted the Venetians, outsiders considered them wily. Their early association with Byzantium seemingly tinged the Venetians with qualities of "oriental" treachery. In their narratives, crusaders often portrayed them as sinister and underhanded. Rather than a beacon of liberty, to the inhabitants of the *terraferma* whose cities were conquered by Venice, she was "the city of 3,000 tyrants."

Nevertheless, the Venetian Republic has inspired many other republics over the centuries. Lewkenor's readers in Great Britain during the seventeenth century considered its "mixed government" as a model for their parliamentary monarchy. And among the Founding Fathers, William Penn wanted to include Venice's secret balloting system in the U.S. Constitution. Indeed, if imitation is the greatest form of flattery, we will see in Chapter 9 how the Florentines paid the Venetians the highest tribute of all by imitating their Great Council in the late fifteenth century following the advice of Girolamo Savonarola.

Sourcebook

Enrico Dandolo, *Promissione*
Marco Polo, *Description of the World*
Geoffrey of Villehardouin, *Chronicle of the Fourth Crusade*
William Wey, *Description of the Funeral and Election of a Doge*
Francesco Barbaro, *On Wifely Duties*
Gasparo Contarini, *The Commonwealth and Government of Venice*

Further reading

Brown, Patricia Fortini. *Private Lives in Renaissance Venice: Art, Architecture, and the Family*, Yale University Press, 2004.
Chambers, David. *Venice: A Documentary History 1450–1630*, Blackwell, 1992.
Crouzet-Pavan, Elizabeth. *Venice Triumphant: The Horizons of a Myth*, Johns Hopkins Press, 1999.
Horodowich, Elizabeth. *A Brief History of Venice: A New History of the City and its People*, Robinson, 2009.
Humfrey, Peter. *Painting in Renaissance Venice*, Yale University Press, 1995.
Lane, Frederic C. *Venice: A Maritime Republic*, Johns Hopkins, 1973.
Muir, Edward. *Civic Ritual in Renaissance Venice*, Princeton University Press, 1981.

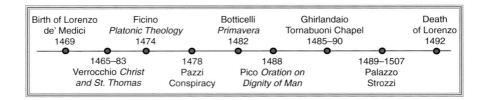

9 Magnificent Florence
Life under Lorenzo de' Medici

> I am not the signore of Florence, just a citizen with a certain authority
> Letter of Lorenzo de' Medici, 1481

The false modesty of these words fooled no one. By the time he wrote this, Lorenzo de' Medici, better known as Lorenzo il Magnifico, "the Magnificent" (1449–1492), had made himself de facto ruler of Florence and one of the most powerful men in Italy. Through his shrewd manipulation, the government of Florence had become a republic in name alone, a puppet theater in which the Medici pulled all the strings. By controlling domestic dissension and guiding foreign policy, however, Lorenzo also enabled the city to enjoy a period of unprecedented stability and prosperity. Florence under Lorenzo the Magnificent experienced a period of cultural flowering; this period is often singled out as a golden age, similar to that of Periclean Athens in the sixth century BCE.

The restlessness of the Florentine elites 1464–69

As his father lay dying in 1469, the twenty-year-old Lorenzo worried that anti-Medicean forces would oust his family from power. His father, Piero the Gouty (1416–1469), assumed power on the death of Cosimo in 1464, but did not govern Florence as expertly as Lorenzo's grandfather had. Aside from being unhealthy—he died from the inherited family malady that gave him his nickname—Piero did not take care of the Medici clients in Cosimo's style. To shore up the family's finances, he called in debts, alienating many former supporters. This weakening of support and the death of Francesco

DOI: 10.4324/9781003270362-9

Sforza, the Medici's strongest ally, gave the family's adversaries the opportunity they had been waiting for, and in 1466 the disgruntled elites rebelled. Luca Pitti, Agnolo Acciaiuoli, and Niccolò Soderini planned a coup to unseat the Medici. These members of leading Florentine families obviously wanted to see an end to the Medici monopoly on political power and a return to an oligarchy, led by members of their own class. Yet they also voiced idealistic republican values, desiring a return to traditional government with freely elected officials and broader representation. Alessandra Strozzi's son-in-law Marco Parenti, in his private *ricordi*, sums up the sentiments of much of the Florentine elite during the years following 1464:

> When I began writing these memoirs, at the time of the death of Cosimo de' Medici, we believed that in the future we would be able to write about the affairs of a free city and of men who would become better citizens, tired of the servitude of times past.

The coup failed and republican liberties were once again suppressed, but hostilities simmered. Would the many independent-minded, proud families in this city of factions continue to accept the Medici as their overlords? As the oldest male descendant of Cosimo, his grandson Lorenzo was suddenly in charge, while the web of connections his grandfather had labored to construct seemed to be unraveling. The future of the Medici now rested entirely on the shoulders of this one young man.

Lorenzo takes control 1469–77

Lorenzo at the age of twenty thus found himself at the helm of the Florentine state. Young by today's standards, Lorenzo had to grow up fast in a world in which the average life expectancy was not greater than forty; indeed, his father had died at age fifty-three and he himself would die at forty-three. Though men holding public office in Florence were usually much older, Lorenzo had the maturity to assume this position as ruler, having been groomed his whole life to one day govern the city. As a boy he had been involved in receiving ambassadors and other important visitors, and at the age of sixteen he was sent on his first diplomatic mission to Milan. He participated in city government from an early age, sitting on committees and taking part in public ceremonies. By twenty, Lorenzo was also a husband; earlier that same year he had married Clarice Orsini (1453–1487) from the powerful Roman baronial family. Whereas his father and grandfather had married into Florentine families in the manner of private citizens, Lorenzo's alliance was arranged in order to strengthen Medici ties with Rome. Like that of a young prince, Lorenzo's marriage was an affair of state, and indeed Medici marriages from this point on would be strategic alliances made with political goals in mind.

As soon as he took command, Lorenzo realized that the anti-Medici faction was gaining in strength and at the slightest hint of weakness his family could

190   *Magnificent Florence*

be toppled from power. Anticipating unrest at the transfer of power, even before his father had died, Lorenzo wrote to the Duke of Milan, Galeazzo Maria Sforza, and asked him to continue giving his "protection and support." Within days the Duke wrote back, promising troops should Lorenzo need them. Lorenzo also followed the Milanese ambassador's advice to eliminate the participation of opposing factions from city government. By 1470 Lorenzo had tightened his control over the *accoppiatori*, who determined eligibility for candidates for public office, by filling the Cento (council of one hundred) with forty handpicked Medici supporters. Yet it was impossible to suppress the Florentines entirely; their tradition of self-government was too strong. Moreover, even an individual vastly wealthier than Lorenzo—whose fortune was meanwhile diminishing—could not have bought the votes of all the Florentine oligarchs, and those who were left out inevitably felt resentful. One of the problems with running a government based on favoritism shown to special groups is that it automatically creates disaffected outsiders, who are always ready to overthrow the regime.

The homey clientelism once practiced by Cosimo was becoming ever more difficult to pull off, especially as Lorenzo tried to exercise complete control over the outlying provinces under Florentine dominion. Under Lorenzo, Florence pursued an expansionist policy throughout Tuscany and beyond. When in 1471 the community of Volterra, about fifty miles southwest of Florence, resisted his will, Lorenzo responded with brutal force. Alum, a chemical used for fixing dyes in woolen cloth, had been discovered near Volterra, and a Florentine company claimed the right to mine it. Formally an autonomous commune, now under Florentine control, Volterra opposed the company, a number of whose owners were Medici supporters. In reprisal for a Volterran crowd's murder of two members of the Medici faction in February 1472, Lorenzo hired the *condottiero* Federico da Montefeltro, duke of Urbino to attack the city. After negotiating a surrender, Federico's forces entered the city, massacring and plundering for twelve hours. The sack of Volterra was a horrible miscalculation; although Lorenzo achieved his short-term goal of subjugating the rebellious city and impressed Florentines with his display of force, in the end it appeared like the act of a tyrant and won him more enemies. This was not the kind of mistake Lorenzo would repeat; in the future, his actions would be less rash and his diplomacy would show a mature command of power.

"Brigades" of poets and jousts for love

The Volterran episode demonstrates how the young Lorenzo was in the process of learning how to wield his authority; he needed to find a way to govern wisely in treacherous times. Lorenzo's intelligence and extraordinary gift for politics led him to find new and creative solutions to political dilemmas from then on. Even if he had wanted to abdicate his role as de facto ruler of Florence, he could not have, so great now were the Medici. With the

Figure 9.1 Sandro Botticelli, *Portrait of Young Man with the Medal of Cosimo de' Medici*, c.1475, Uffizi. The youth, who has never been identified, holds a medal of Lorenzo's grandfather close to his heart to demonstrate his allegiance to the family

family name came a unique celebrity, and members of the Medici clan lived constantly in the public eye. The intense, witty Lorenzo and his handsome younger brother Giuliano (1453–1478) led glamorous lives, participating in public jousts, throwing parties for their friends at their country villas; they were truly the golden youths of Florence.

192 *Magnificent Florence*

Both Lorenzo and Giuliano received exquisite education in Latin and Greek from the most learned humanists of the day. Lorenzo, in particular, excelled in literature; over the course of his life he wrote hundreds of pages of Latin and vernacular prose and especially poetry. Though he showed almost no interest in the family banking business, which suffered as a result, Lorenzo was passionate about two things: politics and poetry. The young Lorenzo gathered about him a group of learned literary men, known as his *brigata*, a playful use of the term for "brigade" or "company." This group was mixed, a combination of rich, privileged Florentine youths as well as gifted literary men of lesser means from Florence and elsewhere, all united by a love for the arts and learning. The painter Sandro Botticelli, who was himself a member of Lorenzo's inner circle, represents one such supporter of the family in his *Portrait of Young Man with the Medal of Cosimo de' Medici* (Figure 9.1). They met at Medici country villas for hunting and boisterous picnics where they improvised ribald verse, dance parties where the poets would compete in praising ladies in Petrarchan-style love lyrics, or discussions of the philosophy of Plato by firelight, which lasted into the early hours of the morning.

Marsilio Ficino and Florentine Platonism

Though it may seem odd to imagine young men spending much of their free time discussing philosophy, Lorenzo and his circle were entranced with the ideas of Plato (429–347 BCE). The ancient Greek philosopher's writings had only recently been rediscovered in the West and had spawned a new branch of humanist thought known as Florentine Platonism, an offshoot of Neoplatonism.[1] The Florentine school of thought originated around the time of the Council of Florence in 1439, when many learned Greek scholars came to Florence and taught there. While he was hosting the Byzantine delegation in his home on the Via Larga, Cosimo de' Medici, too, became interested in Greek learning and came into possession of a number of precious books in Greek. He also arranged for John Argyropoulos (1415–1487) to come and teach at the Florentine Studio (university) and funded a chair in Greek. Later when he discovered the brilliant intellectual abilities of his physician's son, who was a student of Argyropoulos, Cosimo hired him as tutor for his grandsons, Lorenzo and Giuliano. He also gave the young man, who had studied Greek, a valuable manuscript containing works of Plato to translate for him.

This young scholar was Marsilio Ficino (1433–1499); he was the first to produce a translation of all the existing writings of Plato into Latin, and

---

1 There had been various philosophical reinterpretations of Plato's thought dating from the time of late antiquity. These reinterpretations are known as Neoplatonism (new Platonism). To distinguish it from earlier schools of Neoplatonic thought, the terms Florentine Platonism or Renaissance Neoplatonism are often employed.

Magnificent Florence 193

through his scholarship introduced all of Europe to the works of the ancient Greek philosopher in a fresh, complete edition. Cosimo also gave Ficino a villa outside Florence in which to live, where in 1462 Ficino founded the Platonic Academy. It was named after the original Academy where Plato taught, located in the garden, or grove of Academus (an ancient Greek hero) on the outskirts of Athens. Not a formal institution, but more of a private club open by invitation only, the Academy was where the finest minds in Florence gathered to discuss philosophy. Members included Leon Battista Alberti, humanist scholar Cristoforo Landino (1424–1498), the poet Angelo Poliziano (see later in this chapter), philosopher Giovanni Pico della Mirandola (see later in this chapter), as well as Lorenzo and Giuliano de' Medici. The humanist theologians John Colet (1467–1519) and Jacques Lefèvre d'Etaples (c.1455–1536) came from as far away as London and Paris, respectively, to join in the discussion of these newly rediscovered ideas.

What were these ideas, and what made them so exciting to fifteenth-century scholars? Plato had tried to explain why it is that humans strive for perfection and beauty while existing in an imperfect and often ugly reality. He believed that before birth each person's soul was part of the perfect realm of the universe, and that after entering into earthly life, an individual can only imperfectly remember the divine order. Being surrounded by imperfect things in this world, our sensory perceptions do not reflect the truth. To attain pure knowledge and to discover the truth outside sensory reality, Renaissance Neoplatonists explored various forms of mystical experiences, including astrology, Kabbalah, and a variety of magical practices. They were open to ideas from various religions and philosophies and believed that all of these ideas possessed some elements of truth. Ficino and the Florentine Platonists were, however, decidedly Christian; Ficino himself became a priest. Moreover, they were able to reconcile many of the ancient Greek philosopher's ideas with Christian doctrine. Plato believed the human soul to be immortal, and that it is always straining and yearning to return to the divine. According to Plato, the soul could return to its perfect state through love for another human soul—so-called platonic love. Christian Neoplatonists adapted this concept to mean that the soul could return to God through love of Jesus Christ. In 1474 Ficino published *Platonic Theology*, a work that had an enormous impact in reconciling Platonic concepts with Christian doctrine. Furthermore, in *The Republic*, Plato had introduced the concept that the ideal ruler would be a philosopher–king, an individual who had been trained in a strict philosophical education and raised to govern. Ficino dedicated *Platonic Theology* to Lorenzo, not only expressing his gratitude for Medici economic support but also praising his benefactor and former student in the following terms:

Our Plato would have been pleased that I show my respect to you in this way, since you have accomplished what he most desired from men long

194   *Magnificent Florence*

ago: you have joined the study of philosophy with the exercise of the loftiest public authority.

No longer merely a leading citizen, nor a despotic signore, Lorenzo was undoubtedly pleased to see himself praised as no less than a philosopher–king.

Vernacular magnificence: Lorenzo and literature

No one was more aware of this "loftiest public authority," than Lorenzo himself, yet he found plenty of time to devote to other occupations, including having numerous love affairs and writing erotic poetry. Did Lorenzo himself see any contradiction in a serious head of state writing verse that could be considered frivolous? In his *Commentary on My Sonnets*, Lorenzo defends his writing of love lyrics:

> To those who would criticize me for writing about things unworthy of such effort, dealing with amorous passion and so forth, especially as I have many indispensable obligations to take care of … . I believe love is not only praiseworthy, but almost essential, the truest argument in favor of the greatness and nobility of the human soul and above all what impels men to worthy and excellent deeds.

With these words Lorenzo reveals how deeply he assimilated the Platonic belief that love in its highest form can ennoble the soul. And he always maintained that his intense love for Lucrezia Donati, a married patrician woman, was entirely platonic.

Luigi Pulci's *Il Morgante*

Yet alongside the refined, there was an earthy side to Lorenzo's personality that can be seen in his patronage of the poet Luigi Pulci. A member of the *brigata*, Luigi Pulci (1432–1484) was older than Lorenzo and most other members of the group, but he had the most vivid imagination and madcap personality of all. Born of an elite family that had fallen on hard times, Luigi and his brothers Bernardo and Luca were all gifted in letters and, to supplement their meager incomes, they needed wealthy patrons to support their writing. Luigi began to frequent the Medici household in the early 1460s; his effervescent personality and quick wit soon made him a favorite of the Medici. Recognizing his poetic invention, Lorenzo's mother Lucrezia Tornabuoni (1427–1482), herself an author (see later in this chapter), asked Pulci to write a poem based on the life of Charlemagne. The book Pulci wrote, *Il Morgante*, was the first in a series of chivalric epic poems famous in Italian literature, which eventually included works by Boiardo, Ariosto, and Tasso (Chapters 12, 15).

Tales from romances had been sung by French minstrels during the thirteenth and fourteenth centuries when they accompanied pilgrims into Italy. Translated into Italian dialects, the adventures of Charlemagne's knight Roland, in particular, were very popular by the fifteenth century in Italian cities. In public piazzas crowds gathered to listen, as street singers, storytellers, and puppetry troops recounted heroic battles with giants and demons, encounters with sorceresses who cast magical spells, tales of thwarted love, and flight on winged horses. Pulci worked with a number of Tuscan versions of these legends, embroidering freely as he went along to create a rollicking story featuring Orlando's (from Roland in French) sidekick the good-natured giant Morgante, the naughty mini-giant Margutte, and the demon Astarotte. Charlemagne, the supposed reason for writing the whole work, is lost from sight as the reader is carried away by Pulci's wild imaginative fancy.

Angelo Poliziano's *Stanzas for Giuliano de' Medici*

Another poet who worked for Lorenzo de' Medici, but possessing an entirely different temperament and artistic style, was Angelo Poliziano (in English sometimes "Politian," 1454–1494). While steeped in classical learning, Poliziano shared with Lorenzo a deep appreciation for the spoken language of Tuscany. In 1476 he had helped Lorenzo compile an anthology of Tuscan verse to send to the Aragonese court in Naples. This anthology celebrated two centuries of Florentine poets, beginning with Dante and including works by Lorenzo himself.

In addition to his writings in Latin, the humanist Poliziano was a master stylist in the Tuscan vernacular, in which he composed many short poems as well as two longer works, the *Stanzas Begun for the Tournament of the Magnificent Giuliano de' Medici* (1478) and the play *The Fable of Orpheus* (1480). *Stanzas for Giuliano* commemorates a tournament held in 1475 and won by Lorenzo's brother Giuliano. No one was surprised that a Medici won this joust; Lorenzo had won a similar event in 1469 and these public spectacles sponsored by the ruling family were intended to promote their image. However, unlike Lorenzo, who by all accounts was rather ugly, Giuliano was dashing and had a warm, outgoing nature that made him a favorite with the public. Poliziano's poem praises the young man, as well as the woman he loves, the celebrated beauty Simonetta Cattaneo, wife of patrician Marco Vespucci:

> A sweet serenity flashes from her eyes, where Cupid hides his torch; the air becomes agreeable all around her, wherever she turns those amorous eyes. Her face is sweetly painted with privet and roses, full of heavenly joy; every breeze is silent before her divine speech, and every tiny bird sings out in its own tongue.

Simonetta, sadly, died the year after the tournament, but here in these verses she breathes and moves gracefully, embodying the freshness of spring itself.

The Renaissance on the streets: Popular entertainments and festivals

The tournaments held by the Medici are but one example of the public festivities the citizens of Florence enjoyed during this period. It is sometimes suggested that only a small portion of Florentine society, the elite, experienced the art and culture of the Renaissance, but this is not entirely true. Though the public at large obviously did not participate in refined evenings of music or poetry in the salon of the Medici Palace, or listen to Ficino's discussions of Plato, they were nevertheless exposed to many recent cultural developments in their everyday lives. Not only were paintings and sculptures commissioned for churches or civic buildings on view for everyone, but it was impossible to ignore the buildings in the new Renaissance style springing up everywhere (see later in this chapter). In addition, at public displays such as Giuliano's tournament, the Medici commissioned banners and standards to be painted by artists such as Botticelli and Verrocchio. The priors of Florence even had images of men who were imprisoned for bankruptcy or hanged traitors painted on the façade of the Bargello (prison) or sometimes on that of the Palazzo della Signoria (city hall), and the people could admire the excellent art—regardless of its gruesome subject matter—of artists of no less stature than Botticelli and Andrea del Castagno (c.1419–1457). Because of such paintings, the latter earned the nickname *Andrea degli Impiccati* (Andrea of the Hanged Men).

There was of course public humanist oratory that citizens would listen to on civic occasions, and there were also numerous opportunities for hearing poetry. *Sacre rappresentazioni* (sacred dramas in verse) were performed on holy days such as the Annunciation (March 25); the Feasts of the Ascension and Pentecost following Easter; and the Feast of John the Baptist, patron saint of Florence (June 24). Some of these dramas were performed on streets or piazzas; some in churches; and others in convents, acted by nuns. Confraternities vied with one another in producing these spectacles with elaborate stage effects: children dressed as angels were lowered from the rafters of churches by machinery; a martyr's hands cut off, only to miraculously reappear; angels and saints materialized in front of spectators' dazzled eyes. Characters representing Roman emperors, biblical heroes, and demons wore elaborate costumes, and the drama was enhanced with musical interludes. The authors were often poets of note, for instance: Feo Belcari (1410–1484) and Castellano Castellani (1461–1519); Lorenzo de' Medici himself also composed one of these dramas: *Saints John and Paul*. Luigi Pulci's brother Bernardo Pulci (1438–1488) wrote *Barlaam and Josephat* and his wife Antonia Tanini Pulci (1452–1501) wrote a number of plays, of which *St. Guglielma* appears to have been the most popular. Compared with the English, French and other northern European mystery plays, the Florentine sacred dramas employed a greater unity of action; they were shorter, and rather than featuring allegorical figures, emphasized human drama. When the Virgin Mary intercedes with Jesus on behalf of a sinner, she does so as a mother, wheedling and cajoling her son. The secondary characters—soldiers, peasants, priests, and doctors—were dressed in contemporary clothing, encouraging the audience to identify with the drama onstage. Even greater naturalistic effects were achieved by so-called *frottole*, vaudeville-like scenes that were inserted in between the serious action, often while scenery was being changed. In these scenes two nuns might appear, griping that their costumes were not as fancy as the others; a child perched on his father's shoulders might complain about not having a good enough view of the action; or a group of drunken good-for-nothings might start hurling profanities at one another.

Italian Renaissance theater had its roots in these public spectacles; indeed, Poliziano's *Fable of Orpheus* was modeled on the form of a *sacra rappresentazione*. Here we see a crucial element in the dynamism of the Florentine Renaissance: the highly permeable boundaries between high and low culture. Today we draw sharp distinctions between street theater and drama that is enacted on a stage viewed by a paying audience, as well as between vulgar songs sung by drunken party goers and refined art songs performed at recitals. While he recognized differences in tone and style, Lorenzo himself wrote both exalted love poetry and bawdy carnival songs. During the festivals of Carnival, the season preceding Lent, and *Calendimaggio*, which began on April 30, celebrating the arrival of spring, the men and women of Florence swarmed into the streets, singing and dancing without restraint. Lorenzo's carnival songs, typical of those popular at the time, featured such unsubtle lyrics as, "Ladies, we are young bakers, very masterful in our art and we have big loaves to put in your ovens." Like Pulci, who borrowed from street singers to create his epic poem on the hero Orlando, Lorenzo wrote many songs. The most well known, his *Song of Bacchus*, begins:

> How beautiful is youth
> That forever flees!
> Let him who would be joyous, be so:
> For there is no certainty of tomorrow.

And indeed, although Lorenzo could not have known it at the time, the whirlwind of parties, jousts, and love affairs of the two young Medici was about to be brought to an abrupt halt. Poliziano's *Stanzas* were to remain unfinished and Pulci's *Morgante*, which was published in 1478, was overshadowed by an act of violence that shook Florence to its foundations and triggered a chain reaction of potentially devastating consequences.

Lorenzo and Pope Sixtus IV collide

A violent attack on the Medici family that threatened Florence's security was set off by Lorenzo's conflict with Pope Sixtus IV (Francesco della Rovere 1414–1484) over a territory in the Romagna. When he heard that Duke

198 *Magnificent Florence*

Galeazzo Maria Sforza of Milan had offered to sell the semi-autonomous town of Imola to Lorenzo for 40,000 ducats, the pope was furious. Sixtus, who took papal nepotism[2] to all-time heights, doling out lucrative church appointments and command of towns in the Papal States to his relatives, had his heart set on giving Imola to his nephew Girolamo Riario. Lorenzo had agreed to the Milanese offer, considering Imola a valuable strategic defense to the northeast of Tuscany and an additional source of tax revenue; but before he could purchase it, Sixtus convinced Galeazzo Maria to sell it to him instead. The pope then turned to Lorenzo, as the head of the Medici bank, to lend him the money. Suddenly, Lorenzo was caught in a difficult situation: if he lent money to Sixtus he would be acting against Florence's best interests, a traitor to his city; if he refused, he would risk losing the pope's business. He responded to the papal request by saying he did not have the money, meanwhile asking the prominent Florentine banking family of the Pazzi not to lend it to Sixtus either.

The Pazzi family not only lent Sixtus the money, but informed him of Lorenzo's request. Sixtus retaliated by depriving the Medici of their favored position as papal bankers and then started appointing archbishops in Tuscany who were unfavorable to the Medici. In 1473 he named his nephew Pietro Riario archbishop of Florence. When Riario died the next year, Sixtus wanted to replace him with the anti-Medicean Francesco Salviati, first cousin to Jacopo de' Pazzi. Understanding the pope's intention to undermine Medici control by patronizing rival families, Lorenzo opposed Salviati and forced in his own brother-in-law Rinaldo Orsini instead. When soon afterward Sixtus appointed Salviati archbishop of Pisa, Lorenzo succeeded in keeping Salviati out for three years. Though Lorenzo eventually gave in on this issue, hostilities had been declared; and the simmering resentments of the powerful Pazzi and Riario clans would soon come to a full boil. The leaders of these families, along with the pope and the archbishop of Pisa, began in 1475 to plot the downfall of the Medici. Furthermore, both the Duke of Urbino, who had carried out Lorenzo's massacre in Volterra, and King Ferrante of Naples backed the plot, seeing an opportunity to wrest control from the Medici. Initially, Jacopo de' Pazzi, the family's leader, was reluctant; however, when in 1476 Lorenzo had the inheritance laws altered in such a way as to damage the Pazzi's interests, the outraged Jacopo joined the conspiracy and became its spearhead in Florence.

The Pazzi Conspiracy: Murder in the cathedral

After a number of aborted plots, the conspirators, led by the Pazzi, planned to assassinate both Lorenzo and Giuliano at a banquet arranged at one of the

---

2 The word "nepotism" derives from the Italian *nipote* meaning nephew and refers to the practice of popes awarding favors to their nephews and other relations.

Medici villas outside Florence on April 19, 1478. When the younger brother fell ill and did not attend the lunch, the conspirators had to alter the plan once again. If both Lorenzo and Giuliano were not struck down simultaneously, Medici supporters would rally around the surviving brother and foil the plot. Becoming desperate that their plans might be discovered before they could act, the conspirators decided to strike on April 26, while the two brothers attended Sunday High Mass in the Duomo. Committing murder in such a sacred place struck terror in the heart of the hired assassin, who at the last minute refused to participate. Instead, to carry out the deed, the plotters enlisted two priests, one of whom was from Volterra and seethed with hatred for Lorenzo. At a pre-arranged sign, the assassins struck and instantly stabbed Giuliano to death, while Lorenzo, wounded, took refuge in the sacristy. Archbishop Salviati, intending to seize control of city government, went to city hall, the Palazzo della Signoria, while Jacopo de' Pazzi had gathered a company of mercenaries in the piazza below shouting "People and Liberty!" in an attempt to rally Florentines to overthrow the Medici dictators. News spread that Lorenzo was alive, and the people did not rise up to support Pazzi. The standardbearer of justice in the Palazzo, sensing the danger, had called guards who trapped Salviati inside. Within hours the archbishop of Pisa and the leaders of the failed coup were killed, and their bodies were hung from the upper windows of the Palazzo della Signoria. There is a sketch in one of the notebooks of the young Leonardo da Vinci, who was present in Florence at the time, depicting the body of the conspirator Bernardo Baroncelli dangling there. The other conspirators were hunted down, with over fifty men killed that day; eventually more than eighty were executed for their involvement in the plot against the Medici.

Florence at war with the pope

Though he had survived the attempted assassination, Lorenzo now found himself in an open conflict with the pope, who, with the support of King Ferrante of Naples, declared war on Florence. On June 1, Sixtus excommunicated Lorenzo for the murder of the archbishop and insisted that the Florentines turn him over to justice. When the city refused, on June 22, the pope placed all the citizens of Florence under an interdict.[3] Ferrante sent troops, which swiftly occupied towns in the Florentine *contado* within miles of the city walls. Lorenzo meanwhile sought help from Venice and Milan, but the Venetians were at war with the Turks, and Milan was unstable, as Galeazzo Maria Sforza had just been assassinated. With no one else to turn to, Lorenzo made a bold move and secretly left for Naples on December 5,

---

3 An interdict is a punishment officially issued by the pope. When a town and its inhabitants are placed under interdict, priests are forbidden to hold Mass and perform the other Sacraments there.

200 *Magnificent Florence*

1479, to negotiate personally with Ferrante. Though Lorenzo had received assurances beforehand that he would be safe in Naples, it was nonetheless a risky undertaking. His city was at present surrounded by troops sent by his host, and even if his personal safety was guaranteed in Naples, his absence from Florence could lead to dangerous advancement of anti-Medicean factions there. During his stay in Naples, Lorenzo had to draw upon all his charm, wit, and statesmanship to convince the king of Naples to make peace. Florence's allies, Milan and Venice, were upset at Lorenzo's overtures to Ferrante, while the pope in turn was angered by Ferrante's dealings with his Medici enemy. Lorenzo wrote to his allies explaining his motives in this visit, and meanwhile hinted with Ferrante at how he might use his influence in France on the Neapolitan ruler's behalf. Finally, after two and a half months, Lorenzo left with no deal negotiated, although soon afterward Ferrante, worried by a possible French invasion to reinstate the house of Anjou in Naples, and under attack by the Ottoman Turks, signed the treaty. The Turks had invaded southern Italy, and Sixtus, desiring to present a united Christian front against them, agreed to the treaty; he removed troops from Tuscany and lifted the interdict from Florence. When Lorenzo returned to Florence in March of 1480 he received a hero's welcome.

Lorenzo as "boss of the shop"

Lorenzo emerged from this political crisis as the triumphant leader of the Florentine people, and he made sure after his return to tighten Medici control over government to prevent future uprisings. He introduced a new council, the Seventy, which became the most important legislative council, and packed it with Medici supporters, who became, in effect, senators for life. No individual had ever commanded Florence to such an extent, and around this time he began to be referred to as *maestro della bottega* (boss of the shop), indicating the absolute authority he had attained as power broker in the Republic. He clamped down on civil liberties, instituting martial law and forbidding many public gatherings, including performances of *sacre rappresentazioni*. After his brother's murder, Lorenzo no longer walked the streets of Florence in a carefree manner as Cosimo had once done; all the members of the first family of Florence became much more circumspect in their public appearances. Nevertheless, the Medici presence was felt everywhere. Little of importance happened in Florence in which Lorenzo was not either directly or indirectly involved. He not only handpicked officials to serve in government, but also served on numerous public works committees (*opere*), belonged to a number of confraternities, and arranged marriages for members of elite families.

He also acted as a kind of broker in the arts, promoting his favorites and recommending artists to foreign courts. In a gesture of rapprochement with his former enemy, Lorenzo arranged for the finest Florentine artists to decorate the walls of the chapel of Pope Sixtus IV, the so-called Sistine Chapel.

Through his personal patronage of painters, sculptors, architects, musicians, poets, and philosophers, Lorenzo set the model that was emulated by his contemporaries. His vast collections of medals, gems, and classical statuettes, not to mention classical manuscripts, were the envy of Florentine patricians. Lorenzo played several musical instruments and followed in his father and grandfather's footsteps as a patron of music, employing the services of Florentine organ virtuoso Antonio Squarcialupi (1416–1480). Lorenzo also had talented musicians brought from Ferrara, Naples, and Flanders to perform in Florence, notably the Netherlandish singer and composer, Heinrich Isaac (c.1450–1517). Isaac married a Florentine woman, and remained in Florence where he wrote and performed not only sacred music but also secular motets and madrigals. Lorenzo's favorite architect was Giuliano da Sangallo (c.1440–1491), who worked on a number of buildings for the Medici, most notably the country villa at Poggio a Caiano begun in 1485. Lorenzo had the intention to undertake not only architectural projects but also urban planning, and had he not died so early, undoubtedly, he would have built even more.

Money and art in Renaissance Florence

> I find that from 1434 through 1471 my family has expended enormous amounts of money … the sum is an incredible 663,775 florins spent on charity, buildings, and taxes, as well as other expenses. I do not, however, regret this, although some would say it would have been better to keep a part of that aside in one's purse, I believe it casts a brilliant light on our state, and it seems to me well spent, and for that I am very pleased.
>
> Lorenzo De' Medici, *Libro di ricordanze*

It takes money to produce art. Who paid for all the art in fifteenth-century Florence? It is often mistakenly assumed that nearly all the achievements of quattrocento Florence were the direct result of Medici patronage and that Lorenzo "The Magnificent" was in some way singlehandedly responsible for the Renaissance itself. Lorenzo's title "il Magnifico" is deceptive; it was an honorific commonly used in the Quattrocento as a sign of respect and did not refer exclusively to expenditures of princely largesse. The Medici were lavish in spending on civic projects, particularly Cosimo the Elder, as his grandson noted in the previous passage from his memoirs. However, no single family, no matter how rich or powerful, could have been responsible for all the cultural developments in Florence during this period. And, indeed, during the last third of the fifteenth century, Medici spending decreased; the number of major art commissions that can be traced directly to Lorenzo is relatively small, especially compared with those of his father and grandfather.

Florence during the latter half of the Quattrocento experienced an explosion of artistic creativity, funded by magnificent private expenditures. In 1427, 100 men, comprising 1% of the population, owned roughly a quarter

202   *Magnificent Florence*

of the wealth of the city of Florence. The division between the wealthy and the laboring classes was wide, with 1,649 Florentines possessing at least 1,000 florins, or approximately fifteen times the yearly salary of a well-paid artisan. As the century progressed that divide widened, as did that between the merely wealthy and the fabulously wealthy. Moreover, there was a shift, around the middle of the century, in the way the rich spent their money. Partly in emulation of the Medici, and partly to compensate their loss of political autonomy after 1434, Florentine elites began to express themselves through conspicuous consumption of luxury goods and artistic patronage. Shorn of its overtones of sinfulness and excess, spending was now in fashion (see Chapter 6 on magnificence). This increased demand for luxury goods stimulated production, encouraging competition among craftsmen. The well-organized workshops of goldsmiths, wood carvers, painters, and masons mobilized to meet the demand.

Competition and innovation in the arts

The artistic workshops of quattrocento Florence vibrated with feverish activity and competitive spirit. Painters, sculptors, and goldsmiths all closely scrutinized one another's work, each striving to outdo the other, eager to assimilate new styles and techniques. Sometimes changes in artistic style can be traced to a single event, for instance when the *Adoration of the Shepherds* (1470s, Uffizi) by Flemish painter Hugo van der Goes (1440–1482) appeared in Florence in 1483. This large panel painting, which had been commissioned by Medici agent Tommaso Portinari while he was working in Flanders, was placed above the altar at the Church of Sant' Egidio, where it created a sensation. The so-called *Portinari Altarpiece* impressed Florentine painters with its naturalistic representation of rocks and plants, the expressive depiction of faces and hands, its overall meditative mood, and especially its rich colors achieved through the medium of oils, rather than tempera. Filippino Lippi's (1458–1504) early oil painting *The Apparition of the Virgin to St. Bernard* (1486, Badia Fiorentina), with its craggy mountain setting and saturated colors, shows how closely the Florentine artist had studied the northern work and mastered its lessons. Moreover, in his *Nativity and Adoration of the Shepherds* (1485, Sassetti Chapel, Santa Trinita), painter Domenico Ghirlandaio directly imitated the group of three shepherds in the Flemish painting. This is merely one example of how the dynamic process of innovation in the arts functioned during the Renaissance.

Competition thrived not just between workshops, but within them as well; each apprentice, as he mixed paints, prepared plaster for frescoes, or stoked the fire for casting bronze, dreamed of creating masterpieces that would win him fame. Success would mean he could open his own shop, marry and have children, and become a leader in his guild, honored with the title of "maestro." As the young apprentice gained in skill, he would gradually be trusted with minor parts of the master's commissions to work

Magnificent Florence 203

on—an angel, a background landscape, draperies, or animals—leaving to the master the important figures and facial features. The hothouse environment of the workshop could lead to violent antagonisms, but could also create close bonds between pupil and master, like those between son and father. Thus, for example, Sandro Botticelli (Sandro Filipepi 1445–1510), worked as an assistant to Fra Filippo Lippi (1406–1469) for several years while Lippi was painting the frescoes in the Cathedral of Santo Stefano in Prato in the years 1452–65. Looking at Botticelli's *Judith's Return to Bethulia* (*c.*1472, Uffizi) there is a distinct echo of the figure of Salome from Lippi's *Feast of Herod* in Prato. The artistic affinity between the two is visible in the gossamer fabrics, graceful movement, and vigorous treatment of line. Moreover, art historian Giorgio Vasari (Chapter 13) wrote of the great affection with which Lippi treated his pupils. When Filippo died, Botticelli, who had meanwhile opened his own shop, also took charge of the career of the master's son Filippino Lippi (1457–1504), who in turn learned from him.

The realism of Pollaiuolo and Verrocchio

Not only were surrogate artistic families common in workshops, but actual artistic dynasties were created, as father passed to son or son-in-law the techniques of the family trade. Sometimes it is indeed difficult to discern which member of the family has created a work, or part of a work that bears a particular surname, as for instance Antonio del Pollaiuolo (1432–1498) and his brother Piero (1441–1496) worked side by side. Antonio trained first as a goldsmith—it was common in the Renaissance for artists to be skilled in a variety of fields as greater versatility meant more work—and his modeling of the bodies in his paintings reveals his sculptural expertise with anatomy. Antonio's small bronze group of *Hercules and Antaeus* (1470s, Museo del Bargello, Florence) shows mastery not only of every muscle and tendon of the human form, but also a startling ability to convey a sense of movement. Because, according to mythology, Antaeus's mother was Earth, each time he fell she gave him strength; so to defeat him, Hercules needed to keep his enemy from contact with the ground. This statue represents Hercules, every fiber tensed, lifting the struggling Antaeus, whose legs flail in the air, head thrown back in agony, while with his fingers he tries to push away from his assailant. The Pollaiuolo workshop also produced engravings, notably Antonio's highly influential *Battle of the Nude Men* (1470–75). The print, which circulated widely, depicts a variety of naked figures in active poses with detailed anatomical accuracy.

A contemporary of the Pollaiuolo brothers who was equally well known as a painter and sculptor was Andrea del Verrocchio (Andrea di Michele Cioni 1435–1488). In his painting, *The Baptism of Christ* (1476, Uffizi), Verrocchio, like Pollaiuolo, demonstrates a masterful command of anatomy; both Christ and John the Baptist's musculature are well delineated. The quality of the whole painting is at once enhanced and undermined, however, by the presence of the exquisitely sensitive figure of the blond angel painted by an apprentice in Verrocchio's workshop, the young Leonardo da Vinci, one pupil who far surpassed his master. It is as a sculptor, however, that Verrocchio is primarily remembered. His bronze group, *Christ and St. Thomas* (1465–1483, Orsanmichele, Florence; Figure 9.2), represents the moment when Christ invites "doubting Thomas" to touch the wound in his side to verify the truth of the Resurrection. Commissioned by the Mercanzia commercial tribunal, it is an appropriate scriptural scene of judgment based

Figure 9.2 Andrea del Verrocchio, *Christ and St. Thomas*, 1465–83, Orsanmichele, Florence. This is the original, which is now located inside the building; the figures in the niche outside are reproductions

on examination of evidence. Thomas, who has one foot poised slightly outside the frame of the sculptural niche, swivels his upper body toward Christ, who delicately opens his robe exposing the puncture in his side, raising his other hand in a graceful blessing. The apostle clutches his robe with one hand, while with the other still close to his body, he tentatively stretches his fingers toward the gaping wound. The taut stillness between the two figures creates powerful dramatic urgency.

The idealism of Botticelli

An artist who took off in a strikingly different direction from the vigorous realism of Pollaiuolo and Verrocchio was Sandro Botticelli. Strongly influenced by the ideas circulating among Lorenzo's humanist friends, the painter's works often directly represented ideas or images suggested in their writings, such as Angelo Poliziano's description of the myth of how the goddess of love was born from the sea. In his painting *The Birth of Venus* (1484–86, Uffizi), Botticelli not only closely follows the poet's description, but also portrays Venus in the pose common to classical Roman statuary known as the *Venus pudica* ("modest Venus"). The artist captures the gracefulness of ancient sculpture, but does not attempt to depict actual physical reality; a real woman would topple over if standing in Venus's position in this painting. Rather than having volume and mass, the figures float across the surface of the painting, as if in a dream. Venus's skin, instead of a lifelike coloration, gives off an iridescent pinkish glow like the mother-of-pearl from which she has emerged. In this painting, the artist does not attempt to naturalistically portray the beauty of an actual woman, but rather the philosophical concept of ideal beauty as embraced by Florentine Platonists.

Depicting the here and now: Ghirlandaio

One of the most sought-after quattrocento Florentine painters was Domenico Ghirlandaio (Domenico Bigordi 1449–1494). His workshop, which he ran with his brother Davide (1452–1525) and their brother-in-law Bastiano Mainardi (1466–1513), was constantly busy with commissions, both large and small. Small jobs might include a painted wedding chest (*cassone*), a painted platter to celebrate a birth (*desco da parto*), or a portrait; the biggest commissions were altarpieces and immense fresco cycles painted on the walls of chapels in the churches of Florence. All these works, especially the paintings in churches, were intended to perpetuate the name of the individual or lineage. The most powerful Florentine families owned private chapels in the city's various churches, and they closely guarded the privileges and responsibilities that ownership entailed. In addition to paying for having masses said there, the family was responsible for the upkeep and

206 *Magnificent Florence*

decoration of their chapel. Leaving behind a fine work of art in a sacred building gained one fame in this world, and was believed could help in the next, as well.

Artists would often include portraits of the patron, as we have seen, for instance, with Giotto's depiction of Enrico Scrovegni and Masaccio's of Lenzi in the *Trinity*, further adding to the patron's status. Ghirlandaio specialized in vivid portraits of his clients; he was a master at representing in vibrant color the people and scenes of daily life of Florence in his day. In his frescoes in the Sassetti Chapel (1483–1486) in the Church of Santa Trinita, Ghirlandaio painted scenes from the life of St. Francis, the patron saint of the banker Francesco Sassetti, who had commissioned the work. In the uppermost fresco, *The Confirmation of the Rule*, the artist placed Francis kneeling before Pope Honorius III, an event that had occurred in Rome over two centuries before; in the background Florence's Piazza della Signoria is clearly visible and in the foreground are recognizable contemporary Florentines. To the right stand a solemn Sassetti and his son, accompanied by Sassetti's benefactor Lorenzo de' Medici, with his long black hair and characteristically flat nose, while before them, climbing a set of stairs, is Angelo Poliziano, leading Lorenzo's sons and nephew, his pupils. In the lower fresco, *St. Francis's Resurrection of the Boy*, Ghirlandaio includes portraits of Sassetti's daughters and their husbands, with the actual piazza, and the Church of Santa Trinita in the background. Florentines delighted in seeing themselves and their world represented this way and saw no incongruity in being placed alongside miraculous or holy events from the past. The detail and realism of Ghirlandio's paintings is such that modern historians can reconstruct much of the clothing, interior decoration, and social life of quattrocento Florence by studying them (Figure 5.2).

Building for posterity

> There are two principal things men do in this world: one is procreating, the other is building.
>
> Giovanni Rucellai (1403–1481)

In addition to commissioning portraits, altarpieces, and decorations in private chapels, there were other ways Florentines could leave their mark on the city and be remembered to posterity. As suggested by Giovanni Rucellai's comment in his private notebook, just as having children continued the family line, building was a way to leave something to posterity. Like Rucellai, many of the elite in Florence in the later Quattrocento looked to architecture not only as a way of expressing their status and taste, but also as a permanent memory of their family. Florence experienced a building boom during the second half of the fifteenth century when many large private palazzi were

Figure 9.3 Giuliano da Sangallo and others, Palazzo Strozzi, 1489–1507, Florence

constructed, inspired by both the Palazzo Medici (1446–60, Chapter 6) and the Palazzo Rucellai (1446–51, Chapter 4). Among these were the Palazzo Antinori (1461–69), Palazzo Pitti (begun 1460s, Chapter 12), Palazzo Pazzi (1462–72), and Palazzo Gondi (1490).

The most impressive of these private residences was Palazzo Strozzi (1489–1507), the building commissioned by banker Filippo Strozzi (1428–1491), the son of Alessandra Macinghi Strozzi (Chapter 5). Strozzi had been exiled along with the other male members of his family for their opposition to Cosimo de' Medici. In Naples, Filippo made an immense fortune, and once he was allowed to return to Florence, he wanted to express the sense

208 *Magnificent Florence*

of achievement and triumph of his family, with the hope that, in his words, "the building will perpetually serve as an abode for great, noble men of status." So enormous was the scale of the plans for his building that Filippo Strozzi was concerned that he might anger the Medici by overshadowing their palazzo. Strozzi had smaller plans drawn up to show Lorenzo, who rejected them as too modest; the banker was then able to confidently launch the impressive project he had dreamed of. Among the architects, masons, and stonecutters who worked on the palazzo were Giuliano da Sangallo and Cronaca (Simone del Pollaiuolo 1457–1508), as well Benedetto da Maiano (*c.*1442–1497) and his brother Giuliano (1432–1490). Despite the number of craftsmen involved over the course of the almost twenty years it took to complete, the finished construction is a monumental structure with an appearance of absolute regularity and classical balance. Behind the rusticated stone façade, the building encloses a spacious, airy courtyard. Whereas patrician homes in the previous century were built over a shop, making use of the valuable ground floor space as storerooms for merchandise, the quattrocento Florentine residence, represented in its highest form in the Palazzo Strozzi, celebrates a refined, leisured lifestyle (Figure 9.3). Surrounded by graceful classical arches, the visitor's gaze is led upward to the semi-enclosed loggias of the family's private living quarters, opening above to a wide view of the sky, perhaps the greatest luxury of all in the dense urban environment of Renaissance Florence.

The spiritual mood in late quattrocento Florence

All the spending on building and art, the hectic festivity, lavish banquets, brocaded garments, and jewels only partly masked a spiritual malaise that was growing in Florence in the late Quattrocento. Many Florentines were repelled by the excess and turned to spirituality instead. This spiritual quest took two distinct forms: one was a devout Christianity, embodied in the writings of Lorenzo's mother Lucrezia Tornabuoni. In one of her sacred *canzoni* (songs), she writes of Adam and Eve banished from Paradise:

> They lost not garments woven of fine wool or silk,
> Nor jewels from the Orient, nor great treasures.
> Neither castles, cities, nor empires did they lose.
> What they lost was delight; and excluded from the heavenly choir,
> They found themselves in great pain and trouble.

In the final decades of the Quattrocento, increasing numbers of Florentine men and women turned away from pursuit of material things and returned to an older, more austere lifestyle, seeking solace in traditional Christian practices. Others sought answers from arcane forms of mysticism suggested by Neoplatonism and in locating universal truths in religious traditions outside Christianity.

Giovanni Pico della Mirandola's philosophical quest

Both tendencies are evident in the life of the humanist and philosopher Giovanni Pico della Mirandola (1463–1494). Pico wanted to organize a conference in Rome in which he intended to create a synthesis of all knowledge. He had written a work, *The 900 Theses*, in which he attempted to reconcile Christianity with works of Plato, Arabic scholars, the Jewish Kabbalah, and the ancient Persian religion Zoroastrianism to arrive at a universal truth. The conference was blocked, and Pico's heterodox views were condemned by the pope. While continuing to pursue his studies in Neoplatonism, Pico eventually reconciled with the church, and went on to become an ardent supporter of the reforming Dominican friar, Girolamo Savonarola. Pico's was one of the most influential voices in convincing Lorenzo de' Medici to invite Savonarola to Florence (Chapter 10). Today his most famous writing is the *Oration on the Dignity of Man*, which Pico intended as a preface to the Roman conference that never took place. It has become one of the most influential works of Renaissance thought, an expression of a tireless quest for knowledge and a celebration of the limitless potential of the human spirit that characterized the age.

Considerations: Golden Ages

Did Florence during the era of Lorenzo the Magnificent truly experience a "golden age"? Contemporaries seemed to have thought so. Marsilio Ficino wrote: "If we are to call any age golden, it must be our age which has produced such a wealth of golden intellects … and all this in Florence." The idea of consciously recreating an ideal age was in the mind certainly of Lorenzo himself when he rode into a joust in 1469 carrying a banner with the motto *Le tems revient*, "the times return" in Old French. Not content with merely reviving the classical world, however, Florentines saw their own as equally worthy. No longer standing "on the shoulders of giants," Renaissance Italians perceived themselves as standing on their own feet, equal to, and sometimes surpassing, the achievements of the ancients. Poliziano admired and imitated ancient authors, yet aware of his own originality, he also wrote: "Someone tells me: 'You do not express yourself as Cicero did.' And so what if I do not? I am not Cicero. I express myself." This is the spirit of freedom and self-invention celebrated by Pico in his *Oration*. This same spirit can be seen in the efforts of Florentine bankers to commemorate themselves as patrons of art and architecture. These wealthy Florentine patrons—called *mecenati* in Italian, after the wealthy ancient Roman Gaius Cilnius Maecenas (70–8 BCE)—were engaged in a kind of "self-fashioning," as well. By modeling themselves on the famous patron from antiquity who used his wealth to support the finest poets in Augustan Rome, these Renaissance Maecenases were making a statement, which raised their social status. Moreover, expressing artistic taste

210 *Magnificent Florence*

and civic spirit brought honor and glory not only to the individual, but to the entire clan.

Certainly, we must keep in mind that many of the intellectuals and artists who proclaimed this golden age were in the pay of Lorenzo, their "philosopher–king," and much of their cultural production functioned as Medici propaganda. Nonetheless, it was a unique moment that Florence experienced; cultural innovations were expressed in many forms, in Neoplatonic images in poetry and painting, through celebration of the human spirit in writing, and the human form in the visual arts. And these new cultural ideas were not just the property of so-called high culture that occasionally trickled down into popular culture. It was a society with highly permeable barriers between "high" and "low" culture, and irrepressible vernacular traditions were just as liable to percolate upward, infusing humanist poetry with expressiveness and vitality. This willingness on the part of the cultural elite to absorb influences from diverse sources extended for many to an open-mindedness about other religions and philosophical systems, a spirit of experimentation, and an understanding of other cultures that prefigures the Enlightenment in many ways.

Finally, golden ages are often defined after the fact, by what follows: imperial Rome glitters all the more brightly because of the darkness cast over it by the Gothic invasions. Lorenzo's legacy can be endlessly debated, but one thing is certain: after his death nothing would ever be the same again. The peninsula was about to be plunged into a time of troubles that would soon cause many Italians to look back at Laurentian Florence as a truly magnificent moment in history.

Sourcebook

Lorenzo de' Medici, *Letter to Bianca Maria and Galeazzo Maria Sforza*
Marsilio Ficino, *On Love*
Angelo Poliziano, *Stanzas for Giuliano de' Medici*
Antonia Tanini Pulci, *St. Guglielma*; *St. Theodora*
Melozzo da Forlì, *Sixtus IV Appoints the Papal Librarian*
Bertoldo di Giovanni, *Medal Commemorating the Pazzi Conspiracy*
Angelo Poliziano, *Commentary on the Pazzi Conspiracy*
Sandro Botticelli, *The Birth of Venus*
Giovanni Pico della Mirandola, *Oration on the Dignity of Man*

Further reading

Dempsey, Charles. *The Portrayal of Love: Botticelli's "Primavera" and Humanist Culture at the Time of Lorenzo the Magnificent*, Princeton University Press, 1992.
Goldthwaite, Richard. *The Building of Renaissance Florence*, Johns Hopkins University Press, 1982.
Hook, Judith. *Lorenzo de' Medici: An Historical Biography*, Hamish Hamilton, 1984.

Kent, F.W. *Lorenzo de' Medici and the Art of Magnificence*, Johns Hopkins University Press, 2004.

Lightbown, Ronald. *Sandro Botticelli: Life and Work*. Complete Catalogue, 2 vols, Paul Elek, 1978.

Martines, Lauro. *April Blood: Florence and the Plot Against the Medici*, Jonathan Cape, 2003.

Partridge, Lauren. *Art of Renaissance Florence 1400–1600*, University of California Press, 2009.

Wind, Edgar. *Pagan Mysteries in the Renaissance*, Yale University Press, 1958.

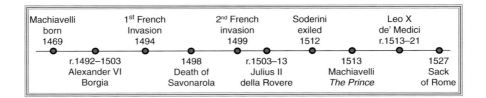

10 The Beginning of the Calamities of Italy

The year 1494 was a most unhappy year for Italy, and in truth was the beginning of our years of misery, because it opened a door to innumerable horrible calamities, of which, due to a variety of circumstances, it can be said that a large part of the world participated.

Francesco Guicciardini, The History of Italy

A prince ought to guard against making alliances with someone more powerful than himself in order to attack others, unless forced by necessity, as I have said. If he wins, he will become the prisoner of the other and princes ought to avoid being at the mercy of others.

Niccolò Machiavelli, The Prince

Barely two years after Lorenzo de' Medici's death in 1492, all hell broke loose in Italy. In 1494 the calamities known as the "Italian Wars" began, and they would last until 1559 (Map 10.1). Foreign soldiers, barking orders in French, German, Spanish—it became hard to keep track of the languages—surged across the peninsula. The soldiers trampled vineyards, slaughtered cattle, violated women, pillaged art, and defiled churches. The stench of death hung in the air as the stunned Italian people asked themselves: "How did this happen?" Political mistakes motivated by greed, fear, and short-sighted policies, combined with accidents of chance, together triggered a chain reaction of disasters of such overwhelming proportions that the greatest minds in Renaissance Italy were in shock. Francesco Guicciardini and Niccolò

DOI: 10.4324/9781003270362-10

The Beginning of the Calamities of Italy 213

Machiavelli were two contemporary thinkers, heirs of humanist culture, who grappled with this problem: Guicciardini in his *History of Italy* and Machiavelli in *The Prince*. The two not only lived through and observed the debacle as it unfolded, but were politicians who actively participated in the course of events, working at the highest levels of government throughout the crises. In this chapter we will explore the events that led Machiavelli to pioneer the field of political science and develop his startling new theories, which revolutionized the way we look at our world.

The Italian League unravels

When in April, 1492, Lorenzo de' Medici died ... it was most untimely for the rest of Italy ... because he had been the means of moderating, acting as a kind of brake to restrain the disagreements and suspicions that often arose for a variety of reasons between Ferdinando [king of Naples] and Lodovico Sforza, princes of almost equal ambition and power.

It began with Lorenzo's death, according to Guicciardini. Through this unlucky chance, the diplomatic balancing act the Italian states had achieved over the past half-century, however precarious, suddenly collapsed. For years Lorenzo had managed to maintain a tenuous alliance within the Italian League, holding at bay mutual suspicions and hostilities, particularly those between Naples and Milan. Lorenzo's son Piero (Piero di Lorenzo de' Medici 1472–1503), who inherited his father's position but not his wisdom, turned his back on Milan, while openly favoring Naples. This policy lit a fuse in Milan, where Lodovico Sforza "il Moro" (1452–1509) was anxious to maintain supremacy. Since the death of his brother Duke Galeazzo Maria in 1476, Lodovico had seized effective control from the rightful heir, his brother's seven-year-old son Giangaleazzo Maria Sforza (1469–1494). The young man, excluded from any authority in government since childhood, had however, been married very young to Isabella of Aragon (1470–1524), daughter of Alfonso II (1448–1495), king of Naples. Isabella was enraged by the marginalized position she and her husband occupied at the Milanese court and complained bitterly to her father. While he was alive, her grandfather King Ferrante managed to calm the situation, but when he, too, died in January 1494, relations between Naples and Milan worsened. After the young Giangaleazzo died suddenly in October the same year, probably poisoned on Lodovico's orders, matters came to a head.

Alienated from Florence, threatened by the rapacious Venetian Republic to the east, a hostile Naples to the south, and unconvinced by papal assurances, Lodovico turned to France for support. The young French King Charles VIII Valois (1470–1498) had claims on the crown of Naples through his Angevin ancestry and was enthusiastic about acquiring Naples, dreaming of launching

214 *The Beginning of the Calamities of Italy*

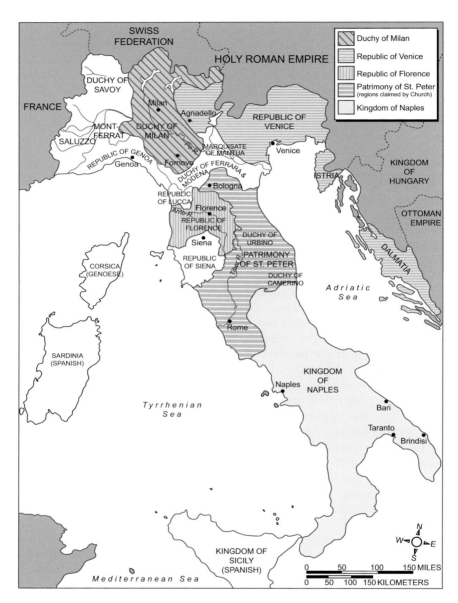

Map 10.1 Italian states in 1494

a crusade from that southern Italian base. Furthermore, the seemingly endless and financially draining Hundred Years' War had ended in 1453, and a newly reinvigorated France found herself with money and warlike nobles looking for an opportunity for conquest. Thus, in early fall of 1494, invited by Lodovico Sforza, the king of France, with 25,000 heavily armed troops prepared to cross the Alps through Milanese territory into Italy.

Rodrigo Borgia becomes Pope Alexander VI

By chance in 1492 a new pope had also entered the scene. When the corrupt, but relatively benign and ailing Pope Innocent VIII died in July 1492, the man elected to replace him was a powerful personality who reshaped the Renaissance papacy. A Spaniard, or more precisely a Catalan, Rodrigo Borgia (in Spanish "de Borja" 1431–1503), whose uncle was Pope Calixtus III, was marked out early for a glorious career in the church. After he had completed his studies in canon law in Bologna at twenty-five, Rodrigo became a cardinal. Capable and charming, the young man held a series of important posts, through which he learned the intrigues and politics of papal administration and forged important alliances. His uncle gave him dozens of lucrative benefices and bishoprics, and Borgia became very wealthy. A sensual man, Borgia was particularly susceptible to beautiful women, and over the course of his lifetime he fathered eight, perhaps nine, children. His unchaste way of life was not shocking in itself, for it was not uncommon during this period for churchmen to have liaisons with members of either sex; what was unusual was Borgia's openness in acknowledging his children and his shameless promotion of their careers.

Seemingly an unlikely candidate for the holiest position in the Catholic Church, Borgia was elected pope in August 1492 by a majority of the College of Cardinals, who recognized the need for a leader with practical political abilities over laudable, but less useful spiritual qualities during unusually uncertain times. As pope, Alexander VI swiftly applied those political skills, signing a treaty with Milan in April 1493. His next move, not unlike that of a secular prince making a dynastic match, was to marry his daughter Lucrezia Borgia (1480–1519) to a cousin of Lodovico Sforza in June of the same year. In July, Alexander likewise arranged a marriage for his son Jofrè (1482–1522) with a daughter of Alfonso II of Naples. However, none of Alexander's dynastic maneuverings could keep the French from entering Italy to take Naples. As long as he could, Alexander tried to appease both Milan and Naples, but eventually he was forced to choose. Charles VIII was coming and would pass through Rome. The pope could choose to flee or stay; if he stayed, he could either confront or welcome the French king.

By this point Alexander's way of life and imperious manner had made him numerous enemies among the noble Roman families and church leaders. To raise money and shift the favor of the church hierarchy in his direction, Alexander had created many new cardinals, most of them Spanish. This angered many in the College of Cardinals, the most prominent of whom was Cardinal Giuliano della Rovere (1443–1513). Della Rovere, who had lost to Alexander in the papal election, was also the nephew of Pope Sixtus IV della Rovere; Giuliano claimed Borgia had bought the papacy through bribery,

216   *The Beginning of the Calamities of Italy*

thus adding the charge of simony to the list of the pope's vices. The embittered cardinal left for France to add his support to the invasion and to stir up sentiment against Alexander. Though he knew that the Kingdom of Naples under the control of the powerful French monarchy could only further destabilize Italy and weaken the papacy, Alexander could not halt the advance of Charles' army. Unable to raise a sufficiently large force to defend Rome, and fearing the loss of his papacy, if not his life, Alexander now threw his support behind the French.

The French invasion of 1494

> They were bestial men: Swiss, Gascons, Normans, Bretons, Scots, speaking so many languages, not only did we fail to understand them, they could not understand each other.
>
> Bartolomeo Cerretani, (1475–1524), *Storia Fiorentina*

In September 1494, Charles VIII entered Italy. The majority of the French troops, their numbers augmented with companies of foreign mercenaries—Swiss, Dalmatian, Scots, and others—came by land, crossing the Alps, while others came by sea, bringing heavy artillery with them. The diplomat and memoirist Philippe de Commynes (1447–1511), who accompanied Charles VIII, describes the effect that the sight of the French weapons had on the Italians:

> Aboard that galleass [an immense sailing ship] was the heavy artillery and large weaponry, for she was a powerful ship, and sailed so near the shore that the enemy was nearly undone, since never had such a thing been seen, and it was a new thing in Italy.

As they marched down the peninsula, the French troops encountered barely any military resistance; where they did, they committed brutal massacres. Horrified at the way Charles' troops were ravishing the country, in March, the pope, the Republic of Venice, and the Duke of Milan formed an ad hoc alliance with Charles' adversaries, the king of Spain and the German emperor, to combat the French. This alliance, known as the League of Venice, could have been the basis for a more lasting diplomatic understanding between the Italian states if Florence had joined. Florentine politics, however, had taken a course that led the Republic away from the interests of the rest of the peninsula, causing it to side with France during this conflict.

Piero di Lorenzo de' Medici, unlike his father, was no statesman. When he assumed power and especially after he began to demonstrate his poor judgment, many Florentines once again looked for an opportunity to overthrow Medici rule. In 1494 many in Tuscany looked forward to the arrival of the French who would rid them of Piero. When French troops reached

Tuscany, Piero di Lorenzo, in imitation of his father's successful visit to Naples in 1479, went to Charles' camp to negotiate a peace. Rather than pulling off a diplomatic coup, however, Piero merely gave away Pisa and other Florentine strongholds to the French. When the Florentines heard what Piero had done, they were enraged that he had unilaterally made such a decision and expelled him and the rest of the Medici from Florence.

Afterward, the Florentine government sent its own chosen delegate to negotiate with Charles. After terms were agreed upon, the king of France left Florence in late 1494. He then moved south, stopped in Rome, and pledged obedience to Pope Alexander; by February 1495 the French had taken Naples, and Charles had himself crowned king of Naples. Because there was little else for him to do there, and the supply lines for his troops were wearing thin, Charles left a garrison behind in Naples and made his way back to France. Northwest of Bologna the forces of the League attacked the French troops

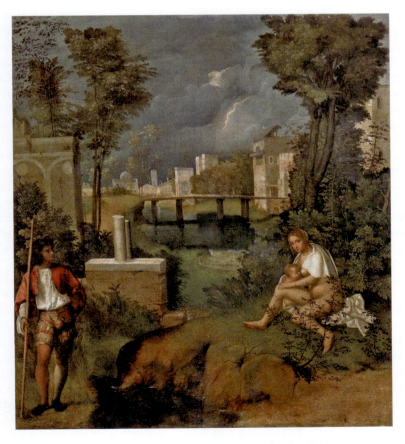

Figure 10.1 Giorgione, *The Tempest*, 1507–10, Accademia, Venice

in July at the Battle of Fornovo, driving them out of Italy. For the moment there was something that resembled peace on the Italian Peninsula, a kind of calm before an even greater storm. This mood is captured in *The Tempest* (Accademia, Venice; Figure 10.1) painted during the years 1507–10, by the Venetian artist Giorgione (Chapter 11).

Savonarola: The rise of the "little friar" from Ferrara

> As the French King and the revolution in the Florentine state were approaching ... I shouted from the pulpit so loudly that I almost became sick ...: "Oh Italy, because of your sins these adversities come to you! Oh Florence, because of your sins they come; oh clergy, this tempest has arisen because of you!"
>
> Savonarola, *Compendium of Revelations*

The delegate that the Florentines sent to parlay with the king of France was no ambassador or politician; he was not even a Florentine citizen, but an outsider, a Dominican friar named Girolamo Savonarola. Born in Ferrara in 1452, Savonarola came from a family of physicians, well-placed at the ducal court. A brilliant student, Savonarola received a degree from the University of Ferrara before devoting himself to religion. When he joined the Dominicans at the age of twenty-three, he was a serious young man naturally drawn to the austere observant branch of the order (Chapter 5). The young friar brought a passionate intensity to his study of theology, committing huge portions of the Bible and works of the Church Fathers to memory. Recognizing his academic excellence, the directors of the Dominican order sent Savonarola to teach at the Convent of San Marco in Florence in 1482. He remained in the city this first time for five years, occasionally preaching sermons, but they were complete failures. Savonarola was a rather small man, very pale, with piercing eyes, a large hooked nose, and bony hands. The Florentines, accustomed to the most polished preachers, who spoke in eloquent Tuscan dialect, their phrases ringing sonorously from the pulpit, were put off by this man's rough voice, his odd northern accent, and awkward gestures.

No one would have expected this same preacher to capture the hearts and minds of the Florentine public as he did, when he returned in 1490 at the request of Lorenzo the Magnificent. Now nearly forty years old, Savonarola was a respected theologian, and he had become a powerful, confident speaker. He was elected prior of San Marco, and as the leader of the institution founded by Cosimo, he had frequent contact with the Medici. Indeed, when Lorenzo lay dying, it was Savonarola who administered the Last Rites. As prior of San Marco, Savonarola also had high public visibility, delivering fiery sermons to packed audiences. What some exalted as a golden age and exuberant flowering of the arts, Savonarola condemned as decadent. He accused Florentines of being obsessed with the accumulation of wealth and beautiful worldly objects; he warned them to repent their

The Beginning of the Calamities of Italy 219

immoral ways or an angry God would soon send a scourge, a penitential whip, in punishment.

In September 1494 he preached a series of sermons on *The Book of Genesis* in the Duomo, which was packed to capacity. His sermon on the Flood, in particular, struck home. Delivered soon after it became known that the French army had invaded Italy, Florentines were terrified by his vivid description of the Biblical deluge. Giovanni Pico della Mirandola, who was present at that sermon, admitted that the vision was so chilling that it made his hair stand on end. The friar's predictions seemed to be coming true when the French appeared, and many Florentines accepted Savonarola as a prophet. The success of his negotiations with Charles—Savonarola met with the king on four occasions—resulted in the French leaving Florence untouched. This seemed nothing less than miraculous to a frightened populace, the majority of whom were by now devoted followers.

The "New Jerusalem": The Florentine Republic renewed

Safe from the French, and without the Medici—with Piero gone, after sixty years, the Medici regime was overthrown—Florentines were uncertain which way to turn and what kind of government to establish. Moreover, regime change, as everyone was aware, is always risky. The frightening possibilities of overzealous revolutionaries exacting violent revenge on the one hand, the resurgence of Medici partisans carrying out bloody reprisals on the other, loomed over Florence. The citizens of Florence looked to their preacher for guidance. The Flood had passed, explained Savonarola, and the Ark, Florence, survived; he preached peace and reconciliation between rival factions. He spoke of renewing the Republic and building a moral, just society so that Florence would become the City of God, a "New Jerusalem."

The friar was an anti-Medicean and staunch republican, and told Florentines in his sermons that they should reorganize their constitution in imitation of the Venetian model, with its Great Council (Chapter 8). Many among the Florentine elite wanted a return to a tightly controlled oligarchy, but the *popolo* now had a voice from the pulpit urging them to seize control. For unlike the large but closed circle of aristocrats that ruled Venice, an even larger segment of Florentine society, the *popolo*, was demanding to be included in the new government. The agreement reached shortly before Christmas 1494, after much debate, was for a Great Council composed of nearly half of the male population aged thirty or older, one of the most broadly representative governments that Europe had ever seen.

Weepers, angry men, and ugly companions

Though Florentines succeeded in establishing a revolutionary new republican constitution, the result was not joyous harmony among its citizens. Already riven by class divisions, Florence was now further splintered by conflict over

220 *The Beginning of the Calamities of Italy*

spiritual issues. Savonarola's fanatical supporters, who became known as *piagnoni* (weepers), came from all walks of life and all levels of society, and included prominent Florentine humanist intellectuals and artists. Marsilio Ficino and Pico della Mirandola were early supporters of Savonarola; painters Filippino Lippi and Botticelli also turned to him. Savonarola offered a model of a deep inner religious devotion that many felt was lacking in Renaissance society, and he tried to institute many social reforms. He criticized Florentines for their hypocritical morals and opulent, worldly manners. Inspired by his sermons, youths from confraternities wandered the streets of Florence, stripping women of jewels and luxurious garments. The anti-materialistic fervor of the populace overflowed in the famous "bonfires of the vanities," in which sumptuous garments, musical instruments, and works of art were publicly burned. Savonarola also tried to crack down on sodomy and attempted to have those accused of homosexual acts put to death.

Not everyone was enthusiastic about these reforms. The Florentines who opposed Savonarola's religious, social, or political agenda were known as the *arrabiati* (angry men). More violent in their opposition, gangs of youths appeared who opposed the *piagnoni*, taunting them and getting into street fights. These were called the *compagnacci* (bad or ugly companions); they disrupted Savonarola's sermons and created unrest in the city. Largely hidden from view was the party of Mediceans, the *palleschi*, who did not engage in open dissent, but were watching and waiting for the opportunity to restore the family to power.

The fiery end of Savonarola

Fearing greatly for himself and believing that the new Signoria might harm him ... Savonarola began by preaching scenes of great terrors ... Because I was there, I shall briefly relate some of these matters ... he seeks to alienate everyone from the Supreme Pontiff and, turning toward him and his attacks, says of the pope what could be said of the wickedest person imaginable.

Niccolò Machiavelli, *Letter to Riccardo Becchi*, March 9, 1498

Savonarola did not limit his criticism to secular behavior; a major focus of his program was reforming the clergy. He reserved his harshest criticism for Pope Alexander VI, who retaliated by suspending the friar from preaching in October 1495 on suspicion of heresy; when Savonarola's attacks resumed and intensified, the pope excommunicated him in June 1497 and threatened to place his Florentine followers under interdict as well. Disobeying the pope's orders, at Christmas Savonarola said Mass, and in early 1498 he began preaching again. The tide of public opinion was turning against the friar by this point; there had been grain shortages, famine, and resurgence of the plague in the "New Jerusalem." Moreover, Savonarola's continued support of the French was controversial as a new French invasion loomed. Perhaps the most powerful element undermining Savonarola's position, however,

The Beginning of the Calamities of Italy 221

was the pope's threat to institute sanctions against Florentine merchants and bankers.

By late March 1498 events came to a boiling point. Savonarola's undoing began when one of the Franciscans, the Dominicans' arch-rivals, publicly accused the prior of San Marco of being a fraud. A Franciscan preacher from his pulpit hurled a challenge to Savonarola—let him prove his divine inspiration by undergoing a trial by fire with him. When one of Savonarola's Dominican friars accepted, Florentines were swept up in the drama. His supporters were expecting a miracle, while his enemies were looking forward to seeing the friar burn. Savonarola hesitated to participate personally in the ordeal and sent a delegated friar. On April 7, the day fixed for the fire, the Dominicans and Franciscans kept the crowd waiting for hours in the Piazza della Signoria while they argued over rules. Suddenly, with crashes of thunder and lightning, rain poured down, drenching the stage. Cheated of its spectacle, the angry mob began rioting and surged toward San Marco. The violence escalated, as on the way, they murdered several prominent Savonarolan supporters. To "protect" him, the Signoria had Savonarola taken into custody. Headed by the recently elected anti-Savonarolan standardbearer of justice, the Signoria held the friar for questioning, which included torture, a standard interrogatory procedure at the time. After Savonarola confessed that his prophecies had not come from God, on May 23, he and two other friars were publicly hanged and burned.

Among the thousands of Florentines who witnessed this spectacle, jostled by the throng and observing attentively, was in all likelihood the twenty-seven-year-old Niccolò Machiavelli. He, too, must have watched as the once-powerful friar was dragged through the streets reviled and must have listened to the cheering as the air filled with the acrid smell of burning flesh. Savonarola had relied on the goodwill of the people to raise him up, and now it was the people who brought him down. This was a lesson that would not be lost on the future author of *The Prince*, who would ridicule "unarmed prophets," who either unable or unwilling to use force to back their words, are easily destroyed.

Louis XII and the French Invasion of 1499

By chance, in 1498 King Charles VIII, while playing tennis, hit his head against a door frame and died. It happened that Charles had no male heir, and so he was succeeded by his cousin Louis the duke of Orléans, who became King Louis XII of France (1462–1515). Louis' grandmother was Valentina Visconti (Chapter 6), which gave the new French king a justifiable claim to the Duchy of Milan. No sooner was he crowned than Louis began to plan to seize Milan. After having participated so recently with the other Italian powers in ejecting the French, Lodovico Sforza did not believe the Italians would permit the French to enter the peninsula once again. The Duke of Milan presided over one of the wealthiest, most glittering courts in Europe,

Figure 10.2 Luca Signorelli, *Rule of the Antichrist*, detail, 1499–1504, Chapel of San Brizio, Duomo, Orvieto. The violence of the times is reflected in the apocalyptic mood in some art created during this period, notably Botticelli's *Mystical Nativity* (*c*.1500, National Gallery, London), in which Botticelli includes prophecies from the Revelation of St. John, while here Signorelli depicts himself and fellow painter Fra Angelico standing beside a heap of corpses. The figure dressed in black on the far left is Signorelli's self-portrait and beside him, also in black, is the painter Fra Angelico

and with the finest military engineers working for him (Chapter 11), he felt confident. But Venice, looking to gain territory in Lombardy, backed Louis.

At this point, Alexander, seeing that a French presence in Italy was inevitable, abandoned both Milan and Naples and hastened to ally himself with Louis as well. Moreover, the French king needed papal support to divorce his wife and marry the widowed queen of Charles VIII as he wanted, so he was anxious to establish good relations with the pope. Alexander let it be known that his son Cesare (1475–1507), who had been pursuing an ecclesiastical career, no longer felt the vocation for a religious life. No sooner had Cesare resigned his cardinalate than the king of France gave him the noble title Duke of Valence, and in Italy Cesare became known as Duke Valentino. The ambitious Cesare, twenty-three years old, now headed to France on a diplomatic mission. Duke Valentino brought with him the document approving the king's new marriage (a papal dispensation) and other papal favors, bartering them

The Beginning of the Calamities of Italy 223

for a noble bride for himself, Charlotte d'Albret, sister of the king of Navarre. In addition, Cesare promised to help the French attack Milan and reconquer Naples, if Louis would supply him with troops to fight in the Romagna. They struck a deal, and in September 1499 French troops once again invaded Italy, this time taking Milan. Within a month the French had possession of Lombardy, and Lodovico Sforza was driven into exile. Lodovico returned briefly in an attempt to retake Milan the next year, but was captured by the French and imprisoned; he died in captivity in France in 1508.

The meteoric career of Cesare Borgia

Once he had assisted the king of France in taking Milan, Cesare Borgia's plan was to oust the rulers of the cities in the Romagna, the northeastern region of the Papal States, and to carve out a state of his own there. These semi-autonomous cities were governed by papal vicars who were in theory obedient to the pope, but in recent years these cities had become more independent. Furthermore, troubled by their restiveness, as well as the possibility of Venetian expansion in the area, Alexander wished to have his son bring the region under his control—papal policy and advancement of the Borgia family neatly coinciding.

The year 1500 opened with the bells clanging in Rome to celebrate the papal Jubilee. Thus, as his father was greeting pilgrims and handing out indulgences, Cesare set off on his conquest of the Romagna. First were the cities of Imola and Forlì, ruled by Caterina Sforza (1463–1509). Imola fell almost immediately; Forlì, under the command of Caterina herself, held out for three weeks. Caterina was a powerful woman; in 1488 when rebellious subjects had taken her children hostage threatening to murder them, she had stood at the top of her battlements, raised her skirts, and cried "Go ahead and kill them, I still have the mold here for making more!" Cesare captured Forlì, and Caterina Sforza was taken prisoner. By 1501 he had also taken Fano, Pesaro, Rimini, Cesena, and Faenza, assuming the title Duke of Romagna. He then turned to Tuscany in May 1501; terrifying the Florentines when he came to within miles of their city walls. Borgia demanded that Florentines give him a *condotta* (military contract), essentially paying him to leave Florentine territory unharmed. When they refused, he seized the Tuscan coastal fort of Piombino and added the title "Lord of Piombino" to his many others. Meanwhile Cesare's forces, under the command of hired *condottieri*, captured town after town in Tuscany, effectively surrounding Florence. Alarmed, the Republic called on the French king to halt him.

Cesare was at this point called south by Louis. The French and Spanish kings had come to an agreement over southern Italy. Ferdinand II of Spain, who through his Aragon inheritance had a claim over the Kingdom of Naples, and Louis XII amicably divided the Kingdom between them in November

224 *The Beginning of the Calamities of Italy*

1500 at the Treaty of Granada. All that remained was to oust King Federigo of Naples (Ferrante's second son, 1452–1504). Cooperating with the French and Spanish, Alexander excommunicated Federigo on trumped up charges of heresy, thereby justifying the removal of a legitimate king from his papal fief. French troops were assembled in Rome, preparing their attack on Naples, and the only stronghold standing in the way was Capua. Cesare's intervention was decisive; his brutal strike there was all that was needed for the French to take Naples. Here is the account given by Alexander VI's Master of Ceremonies Johann Burchard:

> Late that night [July 26, 1501], the Pope received news of the capture of Capua by Duke Valentino .... It was a citizen of Capua, a certain Fabrizio, who let the troops in. He was soon murdered by them, and afterwards around 3,000 foot soldiers and 200 knights, as well as citizens, priests, monks, and nuns were killed, even in churches and convents. Women and girls were dragged out of hiding, raped, and treated most cruelly. The total number of dead has been estimated at around 6,000.

This brief description summarizes Cesare's highly effective methods: cunning, trickery, terror, and unbridled violence. Even by the standards of his day his techniques as a military commander and politician were shocking. In 1502 he captured Urbino, tricking his faithful ally Guidobaldo da Montefeltro (Chapter 12) and forcing him to flee. Contemporaries were awed by his ruthless style and commanding personality. The Florentine envoy sent to meet with him wrote the following report:

> This signore is a man of splendor and magnificence, and in fighting is so spirited that he treats the greatest enterprise as if it were a small thing. In his search for glory and in order to gain a state for himself he never rests, scorning fatigue and peril. Before it is even known that he has left one place, he has settled himself in another. He is well-loved by his soldiers, and he has gathered the best in Italy. All these things make him victorious and formidable, along with perpetual good fortune.

That envoy was Niccolò Machiavelli; the impression left by Cesare would later strongly influence the theories he expressed in *The Prince*. After taking Camerino, also through treachery, word came to Cesare of a conspiracy against him organized by his captains. After taking the town of Sinigaglia (or Senigallia), Cesare arranged to rendezvous with his *condottieri* captains. Machiavelli was with him on December 31, 1502 as the Duke greeted his hired warriors outside the city gates; the Florentine was watching as they rode off to banquet together, but no one would ever see those captains alive again. By the summer of 1503 Cesare was at the zenith of his career, on his way to establishing a hereditary principality controlling a large swath of central Italy. There seemed to be no stopping him.

The Beginning of the Calamities of Italy 225

Then by chance on August 12, 1503, both Alexander and Cesare fell sick. Although it was rumored that they were poisoned, the two most likely caught a malarial fever that was blazing its way through Rome that summer. That same week Alexander died, while Cesare hovered between life and death. The cardinals met to elect a new pope in September, but their choice, the eighty-year-old Pope Pius III Piccolomini, died three weeks later. Weakened physically by illness and politically by the death of his father, Cesare could not prevent the election of his family's arch-enemy, Giuliano della Rovere, as Pope Julius II on November 1, 1503. Julius had Cesare imprisoned for a time, and then he was allowed to leave for Naples, where he was recaptured and sent as captive to Spain. Having escaped from prison to fight for his brother-in-law, the king of Navarre, Cesare Borgia died in battle in 1507.

Julius II the "terrible" pope takes on Venice

Not only did the new pope eliminate the threat of Cesare Borgia, he also took on and defeated Venice. The seemingly invincible Venetians, widely admired for their system of government and their ability to withstand the storms that raged in the Italian Peninsula, created about them an aura of wisdom and infallibility. The myth of *La Serenissima* caused even the Venetians themselves to believe they could commit no political mistakes. In actuality, Venice's foreign policy had not been that wise. In exchange for their cooperation with the French in the invasion in 1494, Venice had received the wealthy city of Cremona, but little else. Their aggressive expansion on the *terraferma* was making many enemies, both among the local nobles whom they dispossessed and the lords of neighboring principalities who felt entitled to those territories. The French king wanted all the cities that formerly belonged to Milan, including Cremona; the German emperor wanted Trieste and other border cities that Venice had taken. The king of Spain, having recently taken the Kingdom of Naples, wanted Venetian-held ports in Apulia. The lords of Mantua and Ferrara both longed for more territory to the north within the Venetian *terraferma*. When Alexander VI died, the Venetians swept in and seized many of the states of the Romagna formerly occupied by Cesare. Enraged, Pope Julius resolved to regain these strongholds, which had belonged to the Papal States.

Julius II was, in Francesco Guicciardini's words, "a spirited and resolute prince, but impetuous and given to oversized schemes." Between the years 1506 and 1507 Julius waged battles to win back the territories in the Romagna (Map 10.2). He was known to put on battle armor and personally lead forces in the field. The sight of a pope wielding a sword amazed even the Italians, who were used to worldly pontiffs, and they called him *il papa terribile* (the terrible or awe-inspiring pope; see Chapter 11 on Michelangelo and *terribilità*). In December 1508, the pope organized a coalition known as the League of Cambrai and aligned practically all the powers of Europe against Venice. In the spring of 1509, the pope excommunicated Venice and

226 *The Beginning of the Calamities of Italy*

Map 10.2 Expansion of the Papal States in the sixteenth century

then launched an offensive against the Venetians, crushing them with foreign troops at the Battle of Agnadello on May 14, 1509. The Republic lost all her mainland territory, and her soldiers were forced, as long ago, to flee the "barbarians," seeking refuge within the shelter of the Lagoon. The panicked citizenry prepared for a siege, while donating vast amounts of gold and

The Beginning of the Calamities of Italy   227

silver to pay the army of mercenaries. In this way, the Venetians raised nearly 200,000 ducats. Padua was recovered, and the city saved from attack, but it was a sobering experience. For years they had been losing battles against the Turks, the once-invincible Venetian sea-power dwindling, but the Venetians had felt themselves to be safe from the disasters that befell the rest of the peninsula. They had to admit that *la Serenissima*, too, was now a casualty of the calamities of Italy.

The Holy League: A brief alliance born of mutual enmity

In the quickly changing political climate of these years, however, the Venetian Republic soon found itself realigned with the papacy. In 1510, intent on driving the French out of Italy, Julius II began to organize an alliance known as the Holy League, among Rome, Venice, the Holy Roman Empire, the Swiss Federation, and Spain. The Spanish had been gaining an ever-stronger foothold on the peninsula since dividing the Kingdom of Naples with the French in 1500 (Treaty of Granada). The Spanish succeeded in taking the entire Kingdom of Naples from the French by January 1504. A Spanish army with their Swiss allies then expelled the French troops from Milan in May 1512. One crucial state that did not join the alliance, however, was Florence.

The Florentine Republic under Soderini gives way to Medici rule in 1512

Once again, Florence's allegiance to the French kept the Republic from making common cause with the other Italian states. This time, however, the antagonism created with the pope was to prove fatal to the Republic. After much discord during the years 1498–1502, the Florentines adopted yet another element from the Venetian government to add to their constitution. In 1502 Florentines decided to strengthen the executive branch by electing a standardbearer of justice who, like the doge of Venice, would serve for life and lend stability to the Republic. They chose a prominent statesman, Piero Soderini (1450–1522) to serve as lifetime standardbearer. A member of the elite, yet also sympathetic to many Savonarolan reforms, Soderini never sided exclusively with any one party. He introduced many profitable financial measures and popular tax reforms; the city's increased revenue led to a period of renewed prosperity for Florence.

Soderini had at one time served as Florentine Ambassador to France, and under his guidance, ties between Florence and the French king became even closer. Throughout these years Florence had been waging war to win back Pisa, agreeing to give Louis an immense sum of money in exchange for military support. Eventually after a merciless siege, the Florentines triumphantly seized Pisa in 1509; the triumph, however, would be brief. When in 1512 the French were driven out of Italy for a second time, Pope Julius turned his anger on Florence for having supported France. He demanded that Florence join the League, siding with the papacy and Spain.

228   The Beginning of the Calamities of Italy

Soderini's government was in a dilemma; even if the Florentines had not felt loyal to the French, the pope was supporting the Medici, and an alliance with Julius would endanger the autonomy of the Republic. The head of the Medici family was no longer Piero di Lorenzo, who had died in an accident in 1503, but his brother, Giovanni de' Medici (1475–1521), the younger son of Lorenzo the Magnificent. Lorenzo had been intent on expanding Medici influence in Rome, and with an eye on a potential Medici papacy, he spent enormous sums of money—many said public funds—to have Giovanni made a cardinal at the age of sixteen. Now thirty-seven, Giovanni was an extremely influential figure in Rome and was indispensable to Julius, whom he would, indeed, succeed as pope the following year. Thus, forced to choose between the Medici and France, Florence backed France. The Spanish sent troops against Florence; they attacked nearby Prato, slaughtering its citizens, and plundering the town. Overwhelmed and surrounded by enemies, Florence capitulated, and Soderini fled into exile on September 1, 1512. Two weeks later the Medici were back in control of Florence.

Niccolò Machiavelli out of work

Niccolò Macchiavelli's political career was one of the casualties of the regime change. Well-versed in literature and the classics, bright and well-spoken, it was only natural that as a young man Macchiavelli had risen, working for the Florentine Republic. In 1498, only five days after Savonarola's execution, Machiavelli was named Second Chancellor of the Republic; later that year he became Secretary to the Council of Ten of War. For the next fourteen years he served the Florentine Republic as a secretary and diplomat. Throughout the tumultuous events from 1498 to 1512, Machiavelli was in the thick of the action; he traveled back and forth on embassies to meet with key figures such as Caterina Sforza, the king of France, the German emperor, and Cesare Borgia. The dispatches that he wrote describing these encounters provide vivid and incisive portraits of these individuals, as well as lucid analysis of the political situation. A valuable insider in the Soderini government, when he insisted that an army of mercenaries would never win the war against Pisa, Machiavelli was entrusted with training a citizen militia in 1506.

When the Medici returned to Florence, former members of the Soderini administration were rounded up, held for questioning, and either imprisoned or exiled. Machiavelli was arrested under suspicion of conspiracy against the Medici, imprisoned and tortured. Though he was eventually acquitted of charges and released, his former high profile with the Soderini government made Machiavelli unemployable now. After a lifetime in public service engaged in high-level politics, the former diplomat moved to his family's small farm seven miles outside of Florence, where he found himself batting away horseflies and shaking clods of earth from his muddied boots. Furthermore, Machiavelli was now poor. Although the Machiavelli name was an old and highly respected one in Florence, the family had lost its wealth by 1469 when Niccolò was born.

The Beginning of the Calamities of Italy 229

Deprived of his government salary and with a wife and children to support—he would have six—Machiavelli was anxiously seeking a patron.

The Prince: A mirror for the Medici?

> I spoke to Filippo about this little work of mine ... I am driven by necessity to give it [to Giuliano], for here I am using up my resources; I cannot remain this way much longer or I will be despised for my poverty. Thus, I desire that these Medici lords begin to make use of me, even if they would begin by having me roll a stone.
>
> Machiavelli, *Letter to Francesco Vettori*, December 10, 1513

It was under these circumstances that Machiavelli began writing *The Prince* in 1513. Machiavelli dedicated his "little book" first to Giuliano di Lorenzo de' Medici (1479–1516), installed as leader of Florence by his brother Giovanni, who had become Pope Leo X. When Giuliano died, Machiavelli re-dedicated the book to Giuliano's nephew, Lorenzo di Piero de' Medici (1492–1519), who succeeded Giuliano. There was nothing unusual about the fact that Machiavelli would write a handbook on politics and send it to the ruler of Florence. This kind of book was known as a "mirror of princes," and it was customary for scholars to compose such works for a new monarch. The author of the advice book, usually a humanist, would select examples from antiquity to guide a new prince, while lavishing praise on him, in hopes of a rich financial reward.

The form of Machiavelli's work was thus thoroughly conventional, as was the author's immediate intention, inasmuch as *The Prince* was meant to function as a sort of job application. In almost every other way, however, Machiavelli's short political treatise broke new ground. First, it was written in Italian, not Latin, giving it a more immediate, powerful punch. However, the most dramatically new aspect of *The Prince* is its content. Machiavelli laid the groundwork for modern political thought by doing something no one had done before—describing the political world as it actually functions. Mocking the humanist tradition of advising a ruler to be good, trustworthy, and compassionate, Machiavelli proposes to describe things as they are:

> I suspect, writing as I do, that I will be considered presumptuous to discuss this material in a manner so divergent from the rules given by others. But as it is my intention to write something useful for one who understands such things, I felt it more practical to go directly to the real truth, rather than the way it is imagined to be. Many have written of imaginary republics and principalities that they have never seen, nor existed in the real world; however, because there is such a separation between how one lives and how one ought to live, he who abandons the way things are really done to behave as one ought to behave will learn how to destroy himself rather than how to survive.

230   *The Beginning of the Calamities of Italy*

Further breaking with tradition, in addition to providing examples from antiquity, Machiavelli demonstrates the truth of his arguments using many contemporary figures and events. These recent examples help drive home his point, but they also underline how Machiavelli placed contemporary Italian achievements on a par with antiquity. To show two ways in which a new, rather than hereditary, prince can take over a state, he uses Francesco Sforza and Cesare Borgia as examples. He explains that Sforza had exceptional military and political skills that enabled him to seize power. On the other hand, Borgia had luck on his side, and he acquired his state through his father's influence.

When *virtù* is not necessarily virtuous and *fortuna* is not always fortunate

> Concerning becoming a prince through either *virtù* or *fortuna*, I would like to add two examples from our times: Francesco Sforza and Cesare Borgia. Francesco, through use of proper means and his great *virtù*, from being a private citizen, became Duke of Milan … Cesare Borgia, commonly known as Duke Valentino, on the other hand, gained his state through the *fortuna* of his father.

In this passage Machiavelli elaborates on two of his great themes: the forces of *virtù* and *fortuna* that shape men's lives. There is no precise English translation for the Italian word *virtù* (pronounced veer-TWO) in the sense that Machiavelli uses it. The word comes from the Latin *virtus*, the root of which is *vir* (man), as in the word "virile." The most essential personal quality of a successful prince, according to Machiavelli, *virtù* carries overtones of the manly courage, self-discipline, and military prowess of the ancient Romans, but he also added daring components of his own. When he advises the prince to "know how to act like a beast," like a fierce lion and a cunning fox, the Florentine is recommending violence and subterfuge as skills needed by a prince. These traits were not considered part of the manly "virtues" of ancient Rome; Cicero wrote that "fraud is a trait of the cunning fox, force is a quality of the lion; both are wholly unworthy of man, but fraud is more to be despised." Machiavelli's prince does not despise it.

Though *virtù* is crucial for success, Machiavelli concedes that *virtù* is useless unless an individual is not also helped along by *fortuna*. *Fortuna* is easily translated as "fortune"; written with a capital F, Fortuna was a goddess in antiquity, who was believed to control human destiny. From the earliest Christian times, Fortuna continued to be represented as a woman turning the wheel of fate, upon which a king, poised on top, will be cast down, a beggar raised up. Dante, in Book VII of the *Inferno*, includes an extended digression on the allegorical figure of Fortuna. In Machiavelli's time, Florentine merchants understood only too well how a man could be ruined by a stroke of bad luck; an enterprising merchant could lose all his merchandise in a shipwreck at sea, thus Giovanni Rucellai's family symbol was a ship with full sails, that he had Leon Battista Alberti emblazon on the façade of the Church of Santa Maria Novella (Figure 4.2). In a particularly lyrical passage of *The Prince*, Machiavelli refers to fortune as an impetuous, unpredictable river, and in a brutal image, as a woman who must be beaten and dominated.

Machiavelli demonstrates how both *virtù* and *fortuna* functioned in the career of Cesare Borgia, about whom he says, "I know of no better precepts to give a new prince than those derived from his [Borgia's] actions." For though Cesare came to power through the intervention of *fortuna*, it was through his own *virtù*—the clever and ruthless application of violent force—that he conquered the territories in the Romagna. Machiavelli warns against the "bad use of compassion," explaining that "Cesare Borgia was considered to be cruel, nevertheless that same cruelty brought order to the Romagna, unified it, establishing peace and loyalty." That Cesare ultimately failed, writes Machiavelli, "was not his fault, but due to an extraordinary and extreme malice of fortune." Fortune's wheel turned when sudden illness struck both Alexander and Cesare. Otherwise, "the Duke had such ferocity and *virtù* ... that had he been healthy, he could have withstood every difficulty."

Questions of morality and religion in *The Prince*

"Yes, but ...," the reader of *The Prince* is left thinking. Despite Machiavelli's compelling arguments, it is hard to see Cesare Borgia as anything but a violent, underhanded, self-serving despot. It is good to create order, but does it justify slaughter? The "bad use of compassion"—what is that? How can compassion ever be a bad thing? Even if this Italian word *virtù* does not exactly mean "virtue," how can being sneaky ever be considered a positive quality? These are just a few of the troubling questions raised by *The Prince* that have led many to define the message of the book reductively—and unjustly—with the phrase "the end justifies the means." In this way the author's name, turned into the adjective "Machiavellian," has been used to describe every wicked, unscrupulous politician from the Elizabethan age through the totalitarian regimes of the twentieth century down to our own times. Ironically, these are questions that Machiavelli himself was never forced to answer because his "little book" went largely unnoticed in his lifetime. Whether the Medici rulers, to whom it was dedicated, gave it more than a passing glance we will never know. We can, however, attempt to answer some of the questions concerning *The Prince* by looking more closely at the text itself, taking into consideration the historical circumstances in which Machiavelli wrote it; what we know of his life; and Machiavelli's other writings, particularly his *Discourses on Livy*.

One of the most frequent charges against *The Prince* is that it is an amoral or irreligious book, advocating evil or "unchristian" behavior. Machiavelli never actually advocates cruelty, deception, or violence, per se; the prince,

232 *The Beginning of the Calamities of Italy*

he writes, "should not deviate from what is good, but know how to do evil when necessary." Violent intervention in a crisis can prevent greater loss of life, as in the example he provides from Florentine history during his lifetime. During 1501–02 Machiavelli was present when the Republic's refusal to intervene ended in a factional bloodbath in the Tuscan town of Pistoia. "Cesare Borgia was actually more compassionate than the Florentine people," writes the former envoy, "who in order to avoid being called cruel, permitted Pistoia to destroy itself." Here he emphasizes that the decision whether to use harsh measures must be weighed rationally, because unclear thinking, as much as intentional cruelty, can lead to increased human suffering.

Machiavelli is a compelling writer, and he is famous for short soundbites, which are often taken out of context and misunderstood. For instance, his phrase "it is much better to be feared than to be loved," is often taken to mean that a ruler should oppress and terrify his people in order to keep them under his control. In fact, immediately after this statement, and in a number of places in *The Prince*, Machiavelli warns that the ruler should never make himself hated. Senseless cruelty only undermines the power of the prince, whose "best fortress is not to be hated by the people."

Similarly, Machiavelli writes that the prince

> should *appear* [emphasis added] to be a man of compassion, faith, humanity, integrity, and religion. And nothing is more necessary than to seem to possess this last quality, because men generally judge by their eyes, not their hands; though all will see you, few will be close enough to touch and experience what you do.

But appearances aside, the prince should be able to "act against faith, against charity, against humanity, and against religion," when necessary. This passage is, of course, an injunction for the prince to be flexible, as the author writes: "to be able to turn, depending on what way the wind of fortune is blowing." The passage is often interpreted to mean that religion is useful merely as a means of fooling the people, that a veil of piety should be used to cloak evil deeds. Though we will never know exactly what Machiavelli's deepest inner beliefs were—whether he believed in God is open to debate— what he is advocating is no more than that a prince should behave as one of the most successful princes of his time: Pope Alexander VI Borgia. For in this passage, he gives Alexander as a prime example of a "pious" prince, "who never did or thought of anything other than deceiving men." Here Machiavelli adds his voice to the many others in his day who were critical of the church, a chorus that the followers of Martin Luther would soon bring to a thunderous climax.

Machiavelli went even further: he blamed the church for all of Italy's calamities. In 1515 he wrote in his *Discourses on the First Decade of Titus Livius* that,

> Through the evil example of the papal court our country has lost all devotion and all religion ... we Italians owe this to the church and its priests, that we have become wicked and irreligious. And we owe them an even greater debt for having been the cause of our ruin, for the church has kept our country divided.

Indeed, in this quotation, the supposedly cynical Florentine laments his country's loss of moral values.

Does Machiavelli advocate tyranny?

The Prince has often been seen as an argument in favor of dictatorship as the ideal form of government, but this is not exactly what Machiavelli was trying to promote. Machiavelli dedicated his entire career to the Florentine Republic, and watched as Soderini, unwilling to employ "tyrannical" measures, let the city fall back into the clutches of the Medici. At this pivotal moment in his country's history, this intelligent, experienced observer of international politics recognized that, unless unified, the Italian states would be unable to prevent foreign armies from crushing them. In the final chapter of *The Prince*, entitled *Exhortation to Seize Italy and Liberate Her from the Barbarians*, Machiavelli reveals his deeper motive behind writing this book, to issue a call for unification under a single Italian leader, as a response to the pressure of foreign invaders. Rather than an ideological stance in favor of tyranny, Machiavelli's position is motivated by desperate necessity.

The author's deep republican sympathies emerge clearly in the *Discourses*, where he compares both forms of government. While fully aware of the weaknesses and risks inherent in any form of democratic government, Machiavelli nevertheless writes that a populace that rules itself is "wiser and more constant than a prince." "Thus I conclude," writes Machiavelli:

> contrary to common opinion which says that the people, when they are princes, are changeable and ungrateful, affirming that they are just as full of sins as are particular princes ... a populace that commands and is well organized will be stable, prudent, grateful, and as much as, or even better than a prince, as wise as he may be esteemed. And on the other hand, a prince not bound by laws, will be ungrateful, inconstant, and more imprudent than a people.

Machiavelli never had a chance to put any of his political ideas to work again after 1513. The Medici and their supporters had no use for this former functionary of Soderini. They never trusted his repeated professions of devotion to the Medici, perhaps considering him something of a loose cannon. Machiavelli's dire warnings went unheeded and the author of *The Prince* died in June 1527, having lived just long enough to know that his worst predictions of barbaric invasions had come true.

234 *The Beginning of the Calamities of Italy*

Machiavelli lived out his final years on his farm, where he dedicated himself to writing—in addition to these two treatises, a treatise on the *Art of War*, two comedies, poems, and several historical works—and to contemplating the ever-deteriorating political scene, as a spectator, no longer an actor. Over the years he also wrote many letters to his friends, bubbling over with caustic humor and laser-beam insights. Did the intellectual, accustomed to the *vita activa* of politics, sending dispatches as he galloped from court to court, find peace in those last fourteen years of *vita contemplativa* passed in poverty and self-imposed exile among the vineyards and chickens? One would like to think so. This is how Machiavelli described how he spent his time during those years to his friend Francesco Vettori:

> When evening comes, I return to my house and go into my study; and on entering I take off my everyday clothes, full of mud and mire and put on my courtly, regal garments. Thus decently attired, I enter into the courts of the ancients, where graciously welcomed by them, I graze on that food that is mine alone, and for which I was born. There I am not ashamed to speak with them and to ask them for the reasons for their actions; and they, out of their humanity answer me; and for four hours at a time I do not feel boredom. Forgetting all troubles, I am not afraid of poverty; death does not terrify me.

Considerations: Fortuna, providence, or chance?

Machiavelli wrote *The Prince* at a crucial moment in Italian history. In this destabilized Italy, ingenious, skillful statecraft no longer worked; brute force was a more reliable tool. More precisely it was essential, for a ruler to survive, that he possess both intelligence and the ability to use force, when necessary. Likewise, Machiavelli insisted that societies be governed by laws, but law must be backed with force. The highly effective, well-ordered government of the rational Piero Soderini fell because he did not use extra-legal means to defend it. Because he was squeamish, Florentines suffered. A fine ethical sensibility is simply a luxury a ruler cannot afford. There is no more important consideration for a ruler than maintaining his state, and neither human laws nor divine laws should interfere with his plans.

The world was changing in other ways as well. There was suddenly no longer such a thing as "absolute authority": power equals authority in *The Prince*. Much had changed in the 200 years from the time Boniface VIII issued his bull *Unam Sanctam* to what historian J.G. Pocock has termed the "Machiavellian Moment." Boniface lived in a world in which there was no question that those who ruled—popes, bishops, and kings—did so by the will of God; their authority rested on a moral right to govern. Machiavelli, on the other hand, removes God and morality from the equation. Whereas before there was no questioning of a ruler's authority, by putting raw power centerstage, Machiavelli calls everything into question.

The Beginning of the Calamities of Italy 235

Though the existence of God was not yet being questioned as it would be during the Enlightenment, the extent of divine influence over human affairs was. Throughout the Middle Ages the figure of Fortuna was used to represent the element of chance in human events, but no one doubted that Divine Providence ultimately guided the course of our lives. In Chapter VII of the *Inferno* Dante asks: "Who is this Fortune?" and Virgil replies that Fortune is a "general minister and guide," ordained by God. Chance played a large part in the "calamities of Italy," and the many strokes of bad luck that afflicted Italy during his lifetime, according to Machiavelli, had nothing to do with God. He represents *fortuna* as a gushing river to be tamed, a wild wind that must be endured, and a woman to be mastered. Rather than the product of a wise, all-knowing god, the disasters that befall us are irrational and unpredictable; the individual who desires to be successful, rather than humbly submitting, should be bold, and in the words of Shakespeare, "take arms against a sea of troubles." In thus advocating the exercise of free will, Machiavelli is suggesting, like Pico della Mirandola, that individuals engage in self-fashioning, to shape themselves as they wish.

Directly opposed to this view, many saw the calamities of Italy as proof of God's intervention, punishing Italians for their sins. The depth and sincerity of religious feeling that existed in Italy at the time is evident from the success of Savonarola's preaching. By showing God's hand in everything on Earth and emphasizing prayer and penitence, he made contact with believers who yearned for a more direct, immediate spiritual experience beyond the formal rituals of the church. Savonarola tapped Italians' spiritual malaise, and at the same time, his criticism of the corrupt clergy sparked a hope for reform. These same longings were stirring in northern Europe, where the Protestant Reformation would take place, and indeed many of the writings of Savonarola would circulate through Europe as an inspiration to reformers.

The experiences of Italy at the end of the Quattrocento leave open a lot of questions for us as well. The figure of Savonarola remains controversial. Was he a figure of moral reform or a closed-minded bigot trying to turn the clock back to the Middle Ages; a radical political thinker wanting to institute democracy in Florence or a power-hungry demagogue; a prophet or a charlatan? Furthermore, one may or may not believe in Divine Providence, but what exactly is the role of chance in history? How much can human beings control their actions and the world around them? Overall, Machiavelli took a rather optimistic view. Though no one can overcome really bad fortune—even as coldly calculating an individual as Cesare Borgia was brought down—Machiavelli provides guidelines for survival. He studied the disasters around him and came up with a "scientific" explanation for events, foreshadowing the field we call political science. Just as the Black Death forced physicians to break away from Galenic and Aristotelian models and make use of empirical methods to explain medical phenomena, so too Machiavelli was compelled to observe the political realities around him. Empiricism would also characterize the startling discoveries of another inquiring Tuscan mind—Galileo.

236 *The Beginning of the Calamities of Italy*

Not everyone agreed with Machiavelli. His friend Guicciardini, for one, took a much more pessimistic view of history and criticized Machiavelli for expressing himself "too absolutely." Ultimately Guicciardini would come to see history as a series of random events, writing "neither fools nor wise men can in the end resist what must be." But then, there was worse to come; Guicciardini lived thirteen years longer than his friend Machiavelli, long enough to see events in Italy spin far out of control, beyond the abilities of the most capable politicians to master them.

Sourcebook

Girolamo Savonarola, *Sermon XIII on Haggai*
Sandro Botticelli, *The Calumny of Apelles*
Niccolò Machiavelli, *The Prince*
Niccolò Machiavelli, *Discourses on Livy*

Further reading

Dall'Aglio, Stefano. *Savonarola and Savonarolism*, Centre for Reformation and Renaissance Studies, 2010.
Gilbert, Felix. *Machiavelli and Guicciardini. Politics and History in Sixteenth-Century Florence*, Norton, 1965.
Machiavelli, Niccolò. *Machiavelli and His Friends: Their Personal Correspondence*, trans. and ed. James B. Atkinson and David Sices, Northern Illinois University Press, 1966.
Shaw, Christine and Michael Mallett. *The Italian Wars, 1494–1559: War, State and Society in Early Modern Europe*, 2nd edition, Routledge, 2019.
Skinner, Quentin. *Foundations of Modern Political Thought, Vol I: The Renaissance* Cambridge, 1978.
Weinstein, Donald. *Savonarola and Florence: Prophecy and Patriotism in the Renaissance*, Princeton University Press, 1970.

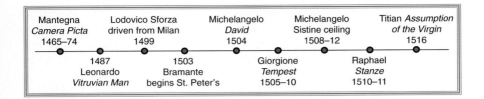

11 Paradoxes of the High Renaissance
Art in a Time of Turmoil

> It is an infinitely atrocious thing to take away the life of a man.
> In battle ... there is infinite discord; it is most bestial madness.
> — Leonardo da Vinci, *Notebook*

During the fourteen years of Machiavelli's forced retirement, from 1513 to 1527, the situation in Italy, which was already bleak, worsened dramatically. Ravaged by repeated invasions and battles, the land was desolated; a scorched-earth policy destroyed crops throughout the peninsula, resulting in widespread famine. There were more disasters to follow. A new disease, syphilis—known as the "French Disease," because many believed they contracted it from French soldiers, though it was also rumored to have come from the New World—began to spread throughout Italy. In addition to the newcomer, a familiar disease had returned—the plague. During the mid-1520s the undernourished Italian populace was especially susceptible, and between one-third and one-half of the population of Italian cities perished from the disease.

However, the turbulent years of marauding foreign armies, famine, and pestilence in the Italian peninsula, which began in 1494 and culminated in the horrific Sack of Rome in 1527, coincided exactly with the period of the greatest concentration of artistic innovation and creative genius in the Renaissance. Paradoxically, it was during the time that the Italian states were losing their political autonomy and economic clout that the period termed the "High Renaissance" in art reached its most perfect flowering. Italian painters, sculptors, and architects were creating works that, while inspired by the ancient Greek and Roman models, expressed a new,

DOI: 10.4324/9781003270362-11

self-confident style. How did these innovators, men of genius, not only survive the calamities but succeed in sustained production of works of artistic excellence? Many converged on Rome as the most stable, wealthy source of patronage on the peninsula; many wandered between the republics of Venice and Florence and the courts of signori throughout the peninsula, plying their trade.

Leonardo wrote a letter in search of employment at the court of Lodovico Sforza of Milan sometime around 1481–82, over ten years before the onset of the Italian Wars. In the letter, he offered his services primarily as a military engineer and only secondarily as a painter. Troubled times forced talented individuals to be versatile: just being a master of painting sometimes was not enough to land a job, even if one painted as well as Leonardo da Vinci. The very harshness of the times thus encouraged even greater artistic excellence and experimentation. Here we will examine the careers of only a few of the most extraordinary artists who flourished under the most extraordinary circumstances.

Leonardo: The pacifist artist who designed weapons for a prince

Leonardo got the job with Sforza. A refined man who despised violence, Leonardo nonetheless designed terrifying war machines for his patron. The artist was a man of contrasts. He was elegant, fastidious in his dress, and well-spoken; yet despite his courtly refinement, he had come from a humble, rustic background. Born in 1452 on a farm outside the tiny Tuscan village of Vinci, about thirty miles west of Florence, Leonardo was illegitimate, the son of Ser Piero da Vinci, a notary and a woman named Caterina, possibly a slave of Circassian origins. Leonardo did not receive a fine humanist education; he knew no Greek and little Latin. When as a boy he moved to Florence, the young Leonardo was to study a trade—art. After having served as an apprentice in Verrocchio's workshop (Chapter 9), the young artist's exceptional painting abilities were recognized, and he was admitted as a master in the painters' association, the Compagnia di San Luca at age twenty.

His earliest paintings from this period in Florence, in which he used the new medium of oils rather than tempera, were already stunningly innovative. In his *Portrait of Ginevra de' Benci* (*c*.1474–78, National Gallery of Art, Washington), Leonardo broke with the female portrait tradition, rotating his subject in a three-quarters pose toward the viewer. It was customary up until this time to represent the sitter stiffly in profile, distancing her from the viewer. In addition to being more natural and suggesting lifelike movement, the new three-quarters pose provided more nuance of facial expression. In those earlier Renaissance profile portraits, a woman's features were represented, as well as elaborate adornments that indicated her high social standing (Chapter 5), but her soul was absent. In Leonardo's portrait, Ginevra's nobility is not indicated by any outer decorations— her hair is drawn back and she is clothed as simply as possible with no jewels—but is evident through her quiet composure and meditative expression. Leonardo developed an extraordinarily subtle use of chiaroscuro, not just for modeling the figure in three dimensions, but to create dramatic effect, in which even the foliage participates. The juniper bush behind her (juniper in Italian is *ginepro*, thus a play on the woman's name), painted with a botanist's eye for detail, has light playing off its branches. Nature is never just a backdrop in Leonardo's paintings, but a protagonist in the drama. The dream-like hazy landscapes in the backgrounds of his paintings suggest a state of mind; the luminous waters, craggy peaks, and serene skies reflect the yearnings of the human spirit. Leonardo achieved this effect in his most famous portrait, arguably the most famous painting in the world, the *Mona Lisa* (also referred to as *La Gioconda*, *c*.1500–07 Louvre, Paris). Painted more than two decades after *Ginevra*, in the *Mona Lisa* the artist employed even subtler treatment of modeling, through his use of the technique of *sfumato*, a "smokiness" that blurs and softens the sharp contours between the forms. It is especially for this last quality, that Giorgio Vasari classes Leonardo among the High Renaissance artists of the next generation (Chapter 13). Though contemporary with Ghirlandaio, Botticelli, Perugino, and Filippino Lippi, rather than belonging to the quattrocento style of painting, Leonardo was literally "ahead of his time."

Leonardo stayed in Milan for seventeen years working for Lodovico Sforza. The wealthy and powerful lord of Milan supported the most accomplished artists, architects, and engineers in Italy. Together with his cultivated wife Beatrice d'Este (1475–1497), Duke Lodovico created one of the most glittering, magnificent courts in Europe. Aside from producing paintings for Sforza—including the portrait of the duke's mistress Cecilia Gallerani, often entitled *Lady with Ermine* (1490–91 Czartoryski Museum, Cracow), and the iconic *Last Supper* (1495–98 Santa Maria delle Grazie, Milan)—as resident genius for the duke and duchess, Leonardo designed costumes and scenery for court spectacles, devised hydraulic engineering systems, decorated interiors of the palace, worked on casting an ambitious bronze equestrian statue, and produced hundreds of detailed plans for war machines. Working for the Duke of Milan gave Leonardo the opportunity to explore an endless variety of scientific and artistic interests. Painting was only one of Leonardo's pursuits; his inquisitive mind led him to investigate the entire natural world. To accurately depict the human form, Leonardo sought first-hand knowledge of anatomy; he dissected corpses and made detailed drawings of the intricate workings of the human body. His notebooks—over 7,000 pages accumulated over a lifetime—are filled with these and similarly meticulous observations on every aspect of the natural world: botany, biology, mechanics, astronomy, hydraulics, aerodynamics, and optics. In his studies he anticipated many of the ideas of Copernicus, Galileo, and Newton. His many inventions in these notebooks, among them the armored tank, the parachute, the glider, and the diving suit, were so visionary that they would not be realized until hundreds of years later. It was during these years that he created his famous drawing of *Vitruvian Man* (*c*.1490 Accademia, Venice, Figure 11.1), which demonstrated the ideal proportions of man, based on the

240 Paradoxes of the High Renaissance

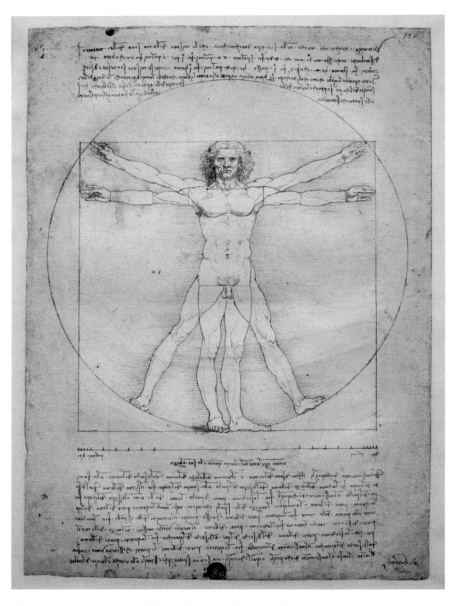

Figure 11.1 Leonardo da Vinci, *Vitruvian Man*, c.1490, Accademia, Venice

writings of Vitruvius. The ancient Roman author had advocated that to create good design the shapes used in architecture—squares, rectangles, circles—ought to have proportions based on the measurements of the human body. Leonardo's image, which was much studied and admired, represents a nude man with arms outstretched, inscribed within a circle and a square. However, beyond merely proving an axiom from ancient learning or demonstrating his mastery of human anatomy, Leonardo in this drawing affirms visually the message of humanists such as Pico della Mirandola, that humankind has a worthy and central place in the order of creation; man is literally the "measure of all things."

After Lodovico was driven out of Milan, in 1500 Leonardo was forced to look for employment elsewhere. He worked briefly for Cesare Borgia as a military engineer before returning to Florence. He moved from place to place in Italy after that, to Rome, Venice, and back to Milan. His wanderings came to an end at last in 1516, when Leonardo accepted a position as royal artist and engineer to the king of France. His only duties apparently were to converse with the king, sharing a lifetime's accumulated wisdom. Yet another paradox is that Leonardo, who defined himself as *omo sanza lettere* (a man with no Latin book learning), came to embody the highest of humanist ideals.

Mantua, Ferrara, Urbino: Small courts, big ambitions

> Master Leonardo, having learned that you are staying in Florence, we have begun to hope that the thing we so desired might come to pass—to have something by your hand.
>
> Isabella d'Este, *Letter to Leonardo da Vinci*, May 14, 1504

Isabella d'Este (1474–1539), the marchesa of Mantua, was desperate to possess a painting of Leonardo's. For years she wrote letters cajoling him, though she recognized the unlikelihood that an artist of Leonardo's stature would move to her court. The Marquisate of Mantua was a small state, and like the courts of Ferrara and Urbino it had limited means, compared to the large Italian states. Though great artists would occasionally pass through, the patronage these small courts offered could not permanently attract them away from Milan, Venice, Rome, and Florence, except in rare cases such as that of the painter Mantegna. This did not, however, stop their ambitious and cultivated rulers from creating exquisite court environments that vibrated with Renaissance artistic spirit.

Mantua: "The most beautiful chamber in the world" painted by Mantegna

Long before Isabella arrived there, Mantua was already established as a center of culture and art, during the time of her husband's grandfather, the *condottiero* Ludovico Gonzaga (1412–1478). Gonzaga commissioned Leon Battista Alberti to design the churches of San Sebastiano (1459) and Sant'Andrea (1470–76) and hired Andrea Mantegna (c. 1431–1506) as his court painter in 1457. The painter, who was related by marriage to the Venetian Bellini, was lured by a high salary and stayed in the Gonzagas' employ for the rest of his life. In addition to the many other works he produced, Mantegna immortalized Gonzaga and his family in the magnificent, frescoed *Camera degli sposi* (bridal chamber; also known as the *Camera picta* 1465–74 Palazzo Ducale, Mantua, Figure 11.2). Rather than merely a private space as the name might suggest, this so-called bridal chamber was the room where official guests, papal envoys, and foreign ambassadors were received. The images not only represent the Marchese surrounded by his family and the court conducting government business, but also feature a whimsical overhead fresco that represents a trompe-l'oeil (in French literally "fool the eye"—an illusionistic trick) opening in the ceiling, called an oculus. Through this imaginary hole the painter reveals tiny winged cupids against a sky with puffy clouds, while several smiling ladies peer down over a ledge. The Mantuan ambassador in Milan wrote in 1475: "Everyone here is talking and saying unanimously, those who have seen it, that it is the most beautiful chamber in the world."

Isabella d'Este's *studiolo* of her own

The Marchesa was a formidable woman who was married to Ludovico's grandson the *condottiero* Francesco II Gonzaga (1466–1519). She not only ruled in his stead when he was away fighting and while he was held captive, but also vigorously pursued the Gonzagas' program of artistic patronage. Unlike her sister Beatrice d'Este, who was married to the fabulously wealthy Duke of Milan, Isabella could not indulge in massive artistic projects; rather she focused on commissioning paintings and collecting precious antique objects for her *studiolo* (private study). The Renaissance *studiolo* was a kind of inner sanctum where humanists, usually men, would retreat for quiet study, surrounded by books and meaningful objects. One of the most sophisticated collectors of antiquities of her day, Isabella also commissioned small works on classical themes from contemporary artists. Her humanist tastes led the Marchesa to further her study of Latin, for which she hired her own tutor, the Neoplatonist Mario Equicola (*c*.1470–1525). Isabella's son, Federico II Gonzaga (1500–1540), when he ruled Mantua became an important patron of Correggio (Antonio Allegri 1489–1534), commissioning the *Loves of Jupiter*, some of the painter's finest works.

The dukes of Ferrara celebrated in poetry and music

Isabella d'Este was also an accomplished musician on several keyboard and stringed instruments and employed many northern European as well as

Figure 11.2 Andrea Mantegna, *Camera degli Sposi*, 1465–74, detail of Court Scene, Palazzo Ducale, Mantua. Seated in front are Ludovico III Gonzaga and his wife Barbara of Brandenburg; their younger children stand between the couple; two older sons and a daughter behind them; they are surrounded by courtiers, advisors, a nurse, and a female dwarf

Italian musicians. Both she and her sister Beatrice had been immersed in music during their childhoods at the court of Ferrara, where their father, Duke Ercole d'Este (1431–1505) was the most important Italian patron of music of his day. Next to the outsize role that the dukes of Ferrara would play as Renaissance literary patrons (see Chapter 12 on Boiardo and Ariosto; Chapter 14 on Tasso), the great cultural contribution of the Este court was music. Having spent fifteen years of his youth at the court of Alfonso of Naples, where he acquired a taste for the new polyphonic sounds, Duke Ercole attracted to his own court at Ferrara musical talents from all over Europe. It was, however, after Ercole's older half-brother Borso (1413–1471) received the title first of duke of the cities of Modena and Reggio (1451), and later that of Ferrara (1471) from the emperor, that the regal pretensions of the family grew. Borso was known for his patronage of artists and manuscript illuminators and for his restoration of the Palazzo Schifanoia, magnificently decorated with frescoes by Francesco del Cossa (*c*.1435–1477) and others. Ercole followed in his footsteps as a patron of the arts; he also laid out streets and funded architectural projects, but his first love was music.

244   *Paradoxes of the High Renaissance*

Private passion fueled the duke's need to display public magnificence, and Ercole strove to have the finest chapel choir in Europe. In this unfortunately he could not outdo Lodovico Sforza, as he complained to his wife Eleonora of Aragon in 1491: "I am not the Duke of Milan to be able to do things on such a grand scale, with such ample and magnificent provisions." Managing a small state was a tricky balancing act, one which required shrewdness and diplomacy, while exhibiting a façade of magnificence. In the words of Pius II, about Borso: "He wanted to appear to be magnificent and generous rather than actually be so." This was essentially the dilemma of all the lords of the small courts.

Urbino: The *condottiero's* refined court, library, and art collection

More remote than the courts of Ferrara and Mantua was Urbino, a small principality located in the rugged Apennines in the region of the Marche. This remote mountainous territory produced generations of *condottieri*, led by the powerful Montefeltro family. Federico da Montefeltro (1422–1482) was an invincible *condottiero*, who in addition to serving Lorenzo de' Medici (Chapter 9), was also employed by popes, kings of Naples, dukes of Milan, and the Republic of Venice, and commanded extraordinarily high fees. He used his earnings to make his court at Urbino one of the most sparkling centers of culture in Italy. In 1468 Federico began the construction of a palace, intending, in his words, "to make our city of Urbino a beautiful residence worthy of the rank and fame of our ancestors and our own status." The Palazzo Ducale he had built by architect Luciano Laurana (*c.*1420/25– 1479) is an imposing fortress as well as an elegant dwelling for a refined court, which reflects two distinct aspects of his personality. In addition to being a warrior, Federico was a humanist scholar who employed a full-time staff of scribes to copy Latin and Greek manuscripts, making his library one of the largest in Italy. The jewel of the Palace was the duke's *studiolo*, the walls of which were decorated with intricate wood intarsia (inlaid mosaic) by the workshop of Giuliano da Maiano (1432–1490), and hung with paintings of some of the finest artists of the day (Figure 11.3). Federico owned works by Italian artists Piero della Francesca, Sandro Botticelli, Paolo Uccello, Melozzo da Forlì, as well as Joos van Gent (active 1460–1475) from the Netherlands, and Pedro Berruguete (died *c.*1504) from Spain. Even with such sophisticated trappings, the dukes of Urbino could never be completely sure of their position, as Federico's son Guidobaldo discovered in 1502, when he lost the Duchy to Cesare Borgia. Despite their tenuous hold in the shifting political scene, however, these small northern Italian courts, through their competitive striving for cultural supremacy, managed to produce some of the leading trends in Renaissance art, music, and literature during the early sixteenth century.

Figure 11.3 Giuliano da Maiano, *Intarsia Representing Bookshelves, Lute, and Sword*, 1476, Palazzo Ducale, Urbino

The Venetian innovators: Painters in a watery city dream of idyllic pastures

Meanwhile as the small courts struggled to survive, the enemies of *La Serenissima* were bearing down on her, and the city was on the verge of losing her mainland possessions in 1509. Despite the shifting fortunes of the Republic, around the turn of the century, a uniquely vigorous Venetian High Renaissance style was emerging. Artists in Venice were experimenting with both new styles of painting and new genres. Until this point, Italian paintings were limited to relatively few genres. Religious art created for either

246   *Paradoxes of the High Renaissance*

public display or private devotion represented Biblical stories, Crucifixions, saints, and depictions of the Holy Family. The possibilities in secular art were limited mostly to representations of civic triumphs such as battles, scenes inspired by ancient mythology, and portraits of noteworthy individuals. However, painters in Venice such as Giorgione (Zorzi da Castelfranco *c*.1477–1510), created oil paintings that represented radically new subject matter. Here, artists were responding to the desires of a very particular set of clients: Venetian humanists fond of subtle allegorical images; wealthy patricians wanting sensuous representations of female beauty; and a Republic anxious to re-establish its glory through striking, monumental works of art. Furthermore, in great demand were paintings of idyllic landscapes. Of all the paradoxes in this period, the most surprising perhaps is that the one place in Italy where artists pioneered the painting of landscapes was in a city founded not on land, but on water.

The visual poetry of Giorgione

Venetian painters were beginning to explore the new genre of the landscape through idealized pictorial representations of the *terraferma*. The most famous of these early paintings is Giorgione's *The Tempest* (1505–10 Accademia, Venice, Figure 10.1). The artist represents three figures in a natural setting; across a body of water lies a city in the distance, above which a broad cerulean-blue sky is illuminated by a bolt of lightning. The man, fully clothed, stands to the left with a staff in hand, while the woman to the right seated amid the shrubs is nude, except for a cloth draped over her shoulders, and is nursing a baby. While evoking pastoral poetry that was coming into vogue at the time (see Chapter 12 on Sannazaro and Bembo), no explicit story is told in this painting. Painted around the time of Venice's defeat at Agnadello, the painting can be read as expressing a state of mind— the vulnerability of the individuals in the foreground with the lowering storm bearing down on the city, hinting at anxiety for the impending future; yet over the centuries the painting has resisted any absolute interpretation. Like a poem open to many readings, the beauty of the painting rests in its mystery.

This kind of *poesia* (visual poetry) was a brand-new concept in painting and one that was pursued by Giorgione's pupil Titian (Tiziano Vecellio *c*.1488–1576), whose works are also permeated with atmospheric mystery. Titian explored new genres of portrait painting, for instance, in his *Woman with a Mirror* (1514–15 Louvre, Paris). In this painting Titian represents a woman with her bodice unlaced, and billowing white blouse tumbling off one shoulder, while she gazes at her reflection in a pair of mirrors held by a male figure standing in the shadows behind her. The light falls fully on the creamy expanse of the woman's exposed skin. As the man's face is not clearly visible, the spectator in his imagination is free to participate in this intimate scene (see Chapter 5 on the male gaze). Traditionally, portraits had been painted of historical figures, prominent contemporaries, or private contemporary citizens, but they were always intended to be recognizable representations of individuals. In contrast to official portraits of highborn women, the identity of the woman in Titian's portrait is unknown; rather her idealized beauty and the desire that it inspires are the subjects of this painting. Indeed, many of the women modeling for portraits like this one, and even sacred paintings such as Titian's *Penitent Magdalene* (*c*.1533, Pitti Palace, Florence) may have been courtesans (Chapter 12); the physical beauty of the female form and womanly grace, rather than virtue or lineage, is what is celebrated over and over in these Venetian Renaissance female portraits.

Titian's bold colors, sensuality, triumphant images

As in the works of Venetian painters such as Bellini, the canvases of Giorgione and Titian are drenched with color, but these two artists explored the dramatic and expressive use of color and light as never before, through new techniques in applying oil paint (Figure 11.4). While Leonardo was smoothing his paints delicately on the canvas, in some cases blending the shades with his fingertips, Giorgione and Titian laid the paint on

Figure 11.4 Giorgione/Titian, *Sleeping Venus*, *c*.1510, Dresden. Probably begun by Giorgione and completed after his death by Titian, this painting combines two favorite genres favored by Venetian painters: landscape and the female nude. Note how the undulating curves of the woman's body are echoed in the soft, rolling hills in the background

248   *Paradoxes of the High Renaissance*

unevenly, in places building up thick, saturated areas of color—a style that became characteristic of Venetian Renaissance painting. While Giorgione's paintings were more dream-like, Titian, in his extraordinarily long and prolific career, experimented with bolder, more dramatic treatments, even of traditional subject matter. This drama is displayed in sacred works such as the immense and striking *Assumption of the Virgin* (1515–16 Santa Maria Gloriosa dei Frari, Venice), where the Madonna's body spirals upward to heaven, her blue dress and rose-colored robe swirling above the heads and outstretched arms of the startled Apostles. Equally striking are his secular works, such as his *Equestrian Portrait of Charles V* (1548 Museo del Prado, Madrid, Figure 12.2), in which the artist represents the calm determination on the emperor's face and the ominous cloudy sky enhancing the restrained energy in his ramrod-straight pose. In both cases, Titian's approach to composition and light is revolutionary (see Chapter 14 on the late works of Titian).

The explosive genius of Michelangelo: Extreme piety and extreme paganism

> Among all those artists, living and dead, he who wins the prize, transcending all others is Michelangelo Buonarroti; he reigns supreme not only in one art, but in all three [painting, sculpture, architecture]. He has triumphed not only over all those artists who have almost vanquished Nature herself, but without a shadow of a doubt he has surpassed the most celebrated ancients whose works are so praised ...
>
> Giorgio Vasari, *Lives of the Artists*, 1550

Michelangelo Buonarroti (1475–1564) changed not only the course of Western art, but the way we view the role and image of an artist. Born twenty-three years after Leonardo, Michelangelo grew up in Florence, and like his older fellow citizen, received only a limited formal education. His father, a man of high pretensions of nobility but of limited monetary resources, put the boy in a traditional school, setting him on the path for a respectable career. At the age of thirteen, with only a smattering of Latin and Greek, Michelangelo left school and entered the workshop of Ghirlandaio. Soon the boy's exceptional talent came to the attention of Lorenzo the Magnificent, who took the fifteen-year-old Michelangelo under his wing. For two years the young artist lived in the Palazzo Medici; during the day he studied art and carved in Lorenzo's sculpture garden across from San Marco, and in the evenings at dinner he listened to humanists discussing Florentine Platonism and reciting verse.

When Lorenzo died, Michelangelo returned to his father's home. A youth whose soul was stirred by beauty, Michelangelo was also troubled by spiritual conflict and was strongly influenced by the preaching of Savonarola. He told his biographer Ascanio Condivi that even fifty years later he "could

Paradoxes of the High Renaissance   249

still hear the sound of the Friar's voice in his mind." During his entire life Michelangelo expressed deep spiritual yearning for God, along with worship of the divine form of the human body. Paradoxically Michelangelo was a passionate Christian as well as a passionate pagan. Michelangelo spent the following years in Rome, where he studied classical statues and created two sculptures that vividly express the artist's dual nature: the *Bacchus* (1496–97 Bargello, Florence) and the *Pietà* (1499–1500 St. Peter's, Vatican, Rome). The first statue is a frankly sensual representation of the young god of wine, entirely nude and balanced in a tipsy contrapposto pose against a giggling little satyr, who is munching grapes. So perfectly did Michelangelo imitate ancient statuary that some contemporaries mistook the *Bacchus* for a work of classical antiquity. The other statue is one of the sculptor's most deeply moving sacred works. The subject is the *Pietà* (pronounced "pea-eh-TAH"; meaning both "piety" and "compassion"), which depicts the Virgin Mary with her dead son draped across her lap. Commissioned by a French cardinal, this statue's theme was common to northern art, but not yet familiar in Italy. In Michelangelo's hands the macabre scene takes on a transfigurative beauty; every tendon of Christ's nearly naked form lovingly carved and burnished to a high gloss. We feel the force of his mother's grief, not through any grimacing facial expression or overwrought gestures, but through her tender cradling of her adult son on her lap, which calls to mind the many depictions of Madonna and Child. Whereas many of those representations portrayed the Virgin as somber, viewing her baby with the premonition of his suffering to come, here her expression is composed. Recognizing the divine will that has at last been carried out, her body bent, she gestures eloquently with one hand, palm lightly held open toward heaven.

The *David*: Bold symbol of the Florentine Republic

The *Pietà* was an instant success, and the artist made sure that everyone would know who had created it by inscribing in Latin on the band across the Virgin's chest "Michelangelo Buonarroti the Florentine made this." Michelangelo's reputation was established, and on returning to his city in 1501, the proud twenty-five-year-old Florentine sculptor received a prestigious commission to make a statue out of an enormous block of marble to be placed atop the Duomo. Completed in 1504, the statue is a colossus seventeen feet high (nearly three times life size) of a nude youth, *David* (Accademia, Florence). Michelangelo portrays the Biblical hero poised with slingshot over his shoulder; his determination to overcome the giant Goliath is written not only on his face, but in every fiber of his taut body. In this sculpture it was not enough for Michelangelo, with his perfect grasp of musculature and assimilation of classical sculpture, to represent beauty of form; with the *David*, he portrays a human being standing alone, mustering all his potential against overwhelming odds. Because of the figure's nudity and

250 *Paradoxes of the High Renaissance*

absence of any characteristics that absolutely link him with a specific time or place, the sculpture can be viewed as an Everyman, prepared to fashion his own destiny.

By members of Soderini's government, this statue was read as a powerful tribute to the Florentine Republic, which was threatened by hostile outside political forces, as well as by the Medici faction from within. Like David taking on the giant Goliath, Florence defied tyranny, defending its republican traditions and maintaining its independence when most city-states had given in. It was immediately clear to the Florentines that this masterpiece was a symbol of such importance that it belonged not high atop the Duomo, but in clear view of all citizens. To decide where best to place the *David*, a committee was assembled, comprised of noted artists Filippino Lippi, Sandro Botticelli, Leonardo da Vinci, Piero di Cosimo, Giuliano and Antonio da Sangallo, along with city officials. The site they chose was directly to the left of the entrance to the Palazzo della Signoria, where a copy of the *David* remains to this day, gazing watchfully over his shoulder across the entrance to the seat of civic power. What was originally a religious symbol, by being placed in this location, became the most powerful visual symbol of civic humanism.

Recognizing the propagandistic impact of such art, the government commissioned frescoes to decorate the walls of the Salone dei Cinquecento (Hall of the 500), where Florence's Great Council convened. The artists chosen for the task were Leonardo, who began work on the *Battle of Anghiari* (1503–06), and Michelangelo on his *Battle of Cascina* (1504–06), in a spirit of fierce rivalry. The two battle scenes meant to inspire patriotism were revolutionary in their conception, as is evident from the artists' studies and from copies made at the time. The artists were drawn away from the Florentine project, at first it seemed temporarily; but tumultuous events prevented the works from ever being completed, and they were later painted over. Leonardo left for Milan, to return only briefly to Florence in 1508, and Michelangelo for Rome, where over the course of the next seven years, he carried out one of the most ambitious artistic projects ever undertaken, for one of the most ambitious patrons who ever lived.

Pope Julius II: A second Caesar

> To Julius II, Pontifex Optimus Maximus, who … beautified the city of Rome … by opening up and measuring out streets in accordance with the dignity of Empire.
>
> *Inscription on the Via Papale*, 1512

In 1505 Michelangelo was summoned to Rome by Pope Julius II. Despite the chaotic political situation in Italy, one city that through the first two decades of the sixteenth century was consistently stable and provided thriving patronage of the arts was Rome. We have seen how quattrocento popes

Paradoxes of the High Renaissance 251

Martin V, Eugenius IV, and Nicholas V began impressive projects of urban renewal and patronage of art and architecture. Pius II Piccolomini is often referred to as "the humanist pope," but he was really one of a succession of Renaissance popes obsessed with restoring, not only literature and learning, but the physical glory and grandeur of ancient Rome. Sixtus IV della Rovere (r.1471–84), the nemesis of Lorenzo the Magnificent, renovated the Senators' Palace on the Capitoline Hill and established a fine collection of classical art there. He constructed a new bridge, the Ponte Sisto, which revitalized an entire area of Rome, and rebuilt a hospital and churches. The many wealthy cardinals living in Rome also contributed through the building and restoration of palaces, churches, chapels, and monuments in the city. In little under a century, the bleak face of Rome that Martin V encountered in 1420 when he reentered the city had dramatically altered.

The appearance of Rome was to change even more drastically under Julius II, who of all the Renaissance popes, with perhaps the exception of Sixtus V Peretti (r.1585–90; Chapter 14), left the strongest mark on the city. In addition to his incessant military activity, Julius directed his impressive energies to the physical improvement of the Vatican and the city of Rome. Upon election as pope, each new pontiff had always chosen a name based upon his personal affinity with an individual who bore that name in the past—this is still done today—and it was no accident that Giuliano della Rovere selected the name "Julius." He encouraged association between himself and Julius Caesar, as is evident from the Latin inscription quoted previously. "Pontifex maximus" was a title given to Caesar, but it was also the Latin for "supreme pontiff"; della Rovere fashioned himself as a second Julius, another Caesar. An affinity with imperial Rome had led the popes to amass an impressive collection of ancient Roman statuary in the Vatican, including the *Laocoön*, the *Apollo Belvedere*, and the *Belvedere Torso* (first century BCE, Vatican Museums, Rome). These classical nudes with their thick rope-like muscles and expressive straining poses made an indelible impression on Michelangelo and other artists employed by Julius. The heroic depiction of nude bodies became a vigorous visual representation of Julius's warlike, aggressive papacy. Just as art was used to promote a republican image for Florence, Julius exploited its potential to project an imperial image for his papacy. It is amazing that a man with such oversized dreams managed to find three artists—Bramante, Michelangelo, and Raphael—who were able not only to match, but to anticipate and exceed his vision of an imperial papacy.

Bramante tears down St. Peter's

St. Peter: "Why have you ruined my temple in Rome ...?"

Bramante: "To lighten the Pope's moneybags a little, which were full to bursting."

A contemporary satire, 1517

252   Paradoxes of the High Renaissance

Before coming to Rome, the architect Donato Bramante (1444–1514), originally from Urbino, had worked as architect for the Duke of Milan. His buildings there included the churches of Santa Maria presso San Satiro and Santa Maria delle Grazie, the latter of which he probably collaborated on with Leonardo. Like Leonardo, Bramante was forced to leave Milan when the French ousted Sforza in 1499. Once in Rome, he found work building the Tempietto (*c.*1502–10), an exquisite round church modeled on an ancient temple of Hercules. Like Leonardo, Bramante was fascinated by Vitruvius's ratios, and the balanced proportions of the modest building exude an understated harmony and classical simplicity. Simplicity and modesty were not words used to describe the architect himself, however, nor was harmony the public response to his next project. Romans, who over the course of the past century had watched their city rise from the rubble, were outraged when they learned of the plan to reduce Rome's holiest site, the final resting place of St. Peter, to ruins. Julius had originally intended to carry out improvements and expansion on Old St. Peter's, which was begun by Nicholas V, as the fourth-century basilica was in need of structural repair. However, once he began, characteristically his plans became more magnificent. He envisioned a much larger, grander temple, so in one awesome stroke the pope, with Bramante's advice, decided to tear the venerable building down and to build a brand-new one in its place. As the words from a contemporary satire, quoted previously, indicate, there was a virulent public polemic about the architect, who was nicknamed "Bramante ruinante" (Bramante the ruining). The shock created by razing the second-most holy site in Christendom, desecrating sacred ground, and disturbing the bones of martyrs was matched in intensity only by outrage at the staggering price of the project. Julius and his supporters justified the cost by representing the project as a pious work, one that would renew and reinvigorate the church.

When the cornerstone for the new St. Peter's was laid on April 18, 1506, Julius II was sixty-two years old, and the scale of the project was such that it would not be completed in his or in any one pope or architect's lifetime. Eventually twelve architects worked on the project, directed by twenty-two popes, before it was brought to completion over a century later. Bramante's original plan, which was altered many times by subsequent architects, was based on Vitruvius. Bramante had laid out a design of circular apses fitted within squares forming a "Greek cross," an enormous cross with equal arms. Resting atop gigantic pillars was to be a dome like that of the Pantheon. The architect had applied from antiquity the concept of creating a well-proportioned design based on geometric relationships, albeit on an unparalleled scale, with a man at its center, for under the dome lie the remains of St. Peter. Peter in essence becomes "Vitruvian man," the human being inscribed in the center of two perfect geometric shapes. The first pope, Peter, the rock, upon whom Christ built his church, is thus placed literally at the center of the seat of Catholicism. Paradoxically, over the course of the century that it would take to complete this representation of Christendom united under one

Paradoxes of the High Renaissance   253

capacious dome, the Protestant Reformation would permanently shatter the possibility of such unity.

Michelangelo paints a "terrible" ceiling

> Arriving before the Pope, who was strolling with a staff in his hand, the Cardinal presented Michelangelo, saying that such men should be pardoned for their ignorance. The pope flew into a rage and smacked the Cardinal with the stick, saying: "You are the ignorant one!"
>
> Vasari, *The Life of Michelangelo*

One of the reasons Julius wanted to expand St. Peter's is that he wanted to have his own tomb placed within the basilica, so he sought out the most renowned sculptor of his day, Michelangelo, and commissioned him to create an immense three-story sepulcher. Excited by a project of this scale, Michelangelo enthusiastically set about quarrying choice marble blocks himself from the Tuscan mountainside of Pietrasanta. The dream soon turned into a nightmare for the sculptor, however, when papal funding was diverted to his hated rival Bramante's projects. Tempers ran high and Michelangelo stormed away from Rome. Julius, whose wicked temper was legendary, resented the artist's insubordination; yet so admired his work that, rather than having Michelangelo punished, Julius set him to work on a different, even more grandiose project—this one in the medium of paint. Risking the pope's wrath, Michelangelo protested that he was no painter, but there was no resisting Julius. Julius was known as *il papa terribile*, and he recognized that he had met an artist whose temperament matched his own; like Julius, Michelangelo possessed *terribilità*. This word, which translates literally as "terribleness" and denotes a larger than life capacity to inspire awe, would have been used to describe a tyrant, such as Cesare Borgia, or a monarch such as Frederick II, but never a mere artist. Until this point, artists were considered craftsmen, little more than servants, who were expected to carry out to the letter every specification dictated by the patron. Rather than the passive agent of the patron's will, we see with Michelangelo the first Western artist burning with his personal artistic vision; not only was this vision respected but he was allowed to give relatively free reign to its expression. Michelangelo wrote in a letter that

> Pope Julius did not want me to continue on the tomb, instead putting me to work on the Sistine ceiling, agreeing to pay me 3,000 ducats; the original plan was to paint the Twelve Apostles in the lunettes ... but then it seemed to me it would turn out a poor thing and I told the Pope ... so he gave me a new commission to do what I wanted and what would satisfy me.

What "would satisfy" Michelangelo turned out to be a vast Old Testament narrative, beginning with God's creation of the universe and involving a cast of hundreds of characters tumbling across the barn-like expanse of the Sistine ceiling, which is 133 feet long and 46 feet wide. Michelangelo later claimed that he carried out this enormous fresco entirely on his own, meaning to disassociate himself from the traditional workshop methods of painting, and proclaiming his creative independence. Though he must have sought learned advice and certainly did have assistants, in the short space of four years, from 1508 to 1512, Michelangelo with intense, ceaseless creative energy filled the space with images of unprecedented originality and power. Below the ceiling, the walls of the chapel are covered with frescoes by Botticelli, Ghirlandaio, and Perugino, which were commissioned by Sixtus IV (Chapter 9); but compared to the measured beauty of those images, the new work that explodes overhead unmoors the viewer from human history, raising the mind to cosmic thoughts of awe, or holy "terror."

Raphael in Rome: A painter of sweet-faced Madonnas creates majestic rooms for a pope

During these years the Vatican was a hectic construction zone, with workmen rushing past, dust swirling in the air from demolition, hammers banging, and scaffolding everywhere. For Julius, demolishing the old St. Peter's was not enough; he also looked to improving the living quarters in the Vatican. He had Bramante design the Cortile del Belvedere (begun in 1503 and completed in 1563) as a place where he could house his sculpture collection and entertain guests. This magnificent courtyard extension of the Vatican Palace, modeled on classical Roman villas, was a place where the pope could receive foreign dignitaries, hold tournaments, and preside over grandiose theatrical spectacles. Julius moved out of Alexander's apartments in the Vatican with their elegant frescoes by Pinturicchio (Bernardino di Betto c.1452–1513), which reminded him of his hated rival, and moved into the rooms once occupied by Cesare Borgia on the floor above.

In 1508, the same year Michelangelo began painting the Sistine ceiling, Julius called a young painter to Rome to work for him. A relation of Bramante, the young man from Urbino, Raffaello Santi (or Sanzio, 1483–1520), is known to us today as Raphael. The son of a painter and poet who worked for Federico da Montefeltro, Raphael grew up in a court environment surrounded by exquisite art. Displaying talent at an early age, the boy went to study with Perugino (Pietro Vannucci c.1445–1523) where he quickly assimilated the graceful poses, sun-drenched landscapes, saturated colors, and often Netherlandish-attention to detail that characterized his master's style. Around 1505 Raphael moved to Florence; there the young artist's sacred paintings and portraits came into high demand, in particular, his many images of the Madonna and Child. Always receptive to new influences, Raphael absorbed many elements from Leonardo's work, but infused his paintings with a freshness and joy all his own. Though his *Madonna of the Meadows* (Kunsthistorisches Museum, Vienna, 1506) shows the influence of the older artist in its pyramidical composition set against a hazy landscape, Raphael's painting is untroubled by mysterious psychological undertones, reveling instead in the harmony and sweetness of the moment. However, once summoned to Rome, Raphael's style was to undergo a dramatic transformation.

The *School of Athens*: Antiquity alive and energized

The turbulent creative activities of Michelangelo, Bramante, and all the combined talent assembled in Rome worked as a catalyst on the young Raphael. Hired to decorate the pope's *stanze* (rooms) with frescoes, Raphael began on the Stanza della Segnatura, which the pope used as his private library. Here Raphael represented, on each of the four walls, the main branches of knowledge—poetry, philosophy, law, theology—in his bright, harmonious style, but charged now with power and majesty. In his depiction of *Philosophy*, known as the *School of Athens* (1510–11), the artist represents a crowd of famous thinkers from ancient Greece in a setting of classically inspired barrel-vaulted arches like those Bramante designed for St. Peter's. Like St. Peter's, which was yet to be closed over with a dome, the imaginary classical arcade is wide open, revealing a tranquil sky. Although the overall impression is one of serenity, the painting is full of movement. The philosophers, mathematicians, astronomers, and others are clustered in vigorous groups, some drawing or writing; books or tablets balanced precariously against a knee; others engaged in discussions, gesticulating and debating; figures dash in and out. Not content to suggest merely implicitly the parallel between the golden age of Athens and the excited overwrought activity in High Renaissance Italy, Raphael has made the comparison explicit by including portraits of living artists in this work. The stately central figure of Plato, with his long white beard, is said to represent Leonardo, and the balding Euclid bending over in the right foreground, with compass in hand, Bramante. Raphael also included, apparently toward the end of the painting process, a portrait of Michelangelo as Heraclitus; he is the brooding unkempt figure sitting on the steps in the very front. Off to the far right, Raphael has also painted a self-portrait; under the curve of the arch, the young artist gazes directly at the viewer with an assured, dispassionate expression.

The banker's pleasure palace, talking statues, and risqué positions: The end of an era in Rome

Raphael continued to enjoy papal patronage under Julius's successor Pope Leo X, but his reputation had grown so great that he was not dependent solely on papal commissions for work. He was a favorite painter of the upper classes of Rome, who enjoyed a luxurious, pleasure-loving lifestyle. Raphael

256 *Paradoxes of the High Renaissance*

was in great demand to paint portraits of the mistresses of wealthy men and to decorate their villas. Of the private fortunes made in Rome during the boom years of Julius's papacy, the most fabulous was that of Sienese banker Agostino Chigi (1466–1520). Chigi started out as a "tax-farmer," making money off of revenues collected for the pope. He went on to pursue a monopoly of alum mines, among other enterprises, and eventually became one of the wealthiest men in Europe. The pleasure palace that Chigi had architect Baldassare Peruzzi (1481–1536) build for him along the banks of the Tiber, the Villa Farnesina (completed 1511), was decorated with frescoes on mythological and erotic themes by Peruzzi, Sodoma (Giovanni Antonio Bazzi 1477–1549), Sebastiano del Piombo (c. 1485–1547), as well as Raphael and his studio. Raphael's *Galatea* (1513) represents the sea nymph standing on a shell floating on the waves like Boticelli's *Venus*, but unlike Botticelli's serenely beautiful and immobile goddess, Galatea's half-naked body is twisted in a muscular yet seductive pose, as she is drawn through the water by a pair of speeding dolphins. All around her, the waters are roiled by semi-naked sea deities, struggling, clutching, and trumpeting on conch shells.

Raphael by this time employed many artists in his workshop, which guaranteed that his artistic style would spread. The new medium of print also assured the diffusion of images of his work. Some of the earliest printing presses in Italy were established in Rome as early as 1465, and the city had a vigorous print culture. Cultivated Roman humanists devoured newly printed editions of the classics as well as delightful lighter fare such as Latin pasquinades. These scathing humanist critiques on public figures and current events, written on sheets of paper, were attached, usually anonymously, to a bulky ancient Roman torso nicknamed Pasquino near the Piazza Navona. At the end of the year these witty and often scurrilous messages would be offered in print. Another popular use of the new medium was to reproduce works of art. Raphael had an agreement with Marcantonio Raimondi (1480–1534), a pioneer in engraving, who printed many reproductions of the master's drawings, in this way further spreading the artist's fame throughout Europe. Less welcome was the fame that came to Raimondi when he published the pornographic etchings known as *I modi* (the positions), from drawings by Raphael's pupil Giulio Romano (1499–1546) and was thrown into jail.

When in April 1520 Raphael died suddenly after a short illness at the age of 37, there was a public outpouring of grief in Rome. One humanist wrote in a letter to Isabella d'Este, "Here one speaks of nothing else but his death." The charming and talented young artist from Urbino who had become the toast of Rome was given a magnificent funeral and buried in the Pantheon. Over his tomb is a Latin inscription by humanist Pietro Bembo that reads: "Here lies the famous Raphael. While he lived, Nature feared she would be surpassed; and now that he is dead, she fears she herself will die."

Considerations: Terrible times and awesome art

The heady excitement of Renaissance Rome in 1520 was soon to end. In 1527 the feverish creative energy would be replaced by equally fevered destruction: the elegant villas would be looted, printing presses smashed, engravings destroyed. The names of Martin Luther and Emperor Charles V would be scratched into Raphael's Sala della Segnatura frescoes, and Spanish troops would file through the Sistine Chapel beneath Michelangelo's images of Creation. Though the bubble would burst, the year 1527 would not bring the Renaissance to a close. Paradoxically, it caused the artistic and cultural movement to spread beyond Rome. Artists such as Giulio Romano and Sebastiano del Piombo and writers like Pietro Aretino were forced to seek their fortunes outside of Rome, thus creating an effect of cultural cross-pollination throughout the peninsula and guaranteeing dissemination of Italian Renaissance innovations all over Europe. Furthermore, while Giorgione died in 1510, Bramante in 1514, Leonardo in 1519, and Raphael in 1520—these artists never lived to experience the after-effects of the Sack of Rome—both Michelangelo and Titian lived far into the sixteenth century, Michelangelo until 1564, and Titian until 1576. They continued to create and innovate, sharing their towering artistic legacies with a new generation of artists.

Adding to the paradox of the High Renaissance, as Italian states began to lose their political autonomy, artists were becoming in a sense autonomous. They cut loose from antique models, and, no longer satisfied simply imitating the ancients, they began imitating nature directly. Leonardo, whose name perhaps more than any other is associated with the Renaissance, imitated not the classics, but nature itself. Curiosity was a Renaissance trait, as was investigation into science, based on empirical observation and its exposition in the vernacular, as we will see in the discoveries of Galileo (Chapter 15). The Renaissance was also a time of sharp contrasts. Like the "*chiaro*" and "*scuro*," the light and dark on Leonardo's canvases, individuals had to exploit both good and evil to survive. For Leonardo this meant designing war machines; for Machiavelli it was giving advice to would-be tyrants. These same tyrants moreover, were men who, as Machiavelli wrote, "were suited to the nature of the times," and their very impulsiveness and dynamism made great art possible. Without Lodovico Sforza and Julius II, would Leonardo have found the leisure to pursue his research or Michelangelo and Raphael the scope to express their artistic visions? Furthermore, though not independent of patrons, artists were beginning to assert more control over their treatment of subject matter. The social status of the artist began to rise during this time, while simultaneously the artist's individual creative impulse was being recognized as never before. We will see in the writings of Giorgio Vasari, who pioneered the field of art history (Chapter 13), how modern concepts of individual inspiration and innovation were born during these troubled times.

Paradoxes of the High Renaissance

Sourcebook

Leonardo, *Annunciation*; *Sketch of Lily*
Leonardo, *Letter to Duke Lodovico Sforza*
Leonardo, *Portrait of Cecilia Gallerani*
Isabella d'Este, *Letter to Cecilia Gallerani*
Leonardo, *Portrait Sketch of Isabella d'Este*
Correggio, *Io and Jupiter*
Francesco del Cossa, *The Month of April*
Titian, *Penitent Magdalene*
Façade of Palazzo Vecchio, Florence
Raphael, *Portrait of Baldassarre Castiglione*
Belvedere Torso
Pasquino

Further reading

Clarke, Kenneth. *Leonardo*. rev. and introduced by Martin Kemp. Viking, 1988.
Cole, Alison. *Italian Renaissance Courts: Art, Pleasure and Power*, Laurence King, 2016.
Goffen, Rona. *Renaissance Rivals: Michelangelo, Leonardo, Raphael, Titian*, Yale University Press, 2002.
Jones, Roger and Nicholas Penny, *Raphael*, Yale University Press, 1983.
Rowland, Ingrid. *The Culture of the High Renaissance: Ancients and Moderns in Sixteenth-Century Rome*, Cambridge University, Press, 1998.
Stinger, Charles. *The Renaissance in Rome*, Indiana University Press, 1985.
Wallace, William E. *Michelangelo: The Artist, the Man, and His Times*, Cambridge University Press, 2010.

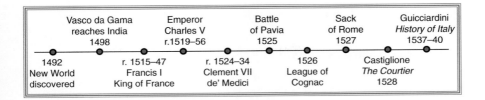

12 The 1527 Sack of Rome and Its Aftermath

> The affairs of Italy began to be disturbed with wars that were longer, greater, and more dangerous than those in the past, stirring the ambitions of two most powerful kings, filled with rivalry, hatred, and mutual suspicion, to exert the force of their power and rage in Italy.
>
> Francesco Guicciardini, *The History of Italy*, 1537–40

Enormous changes were taking place in the world. By the beginning of the sixteenth century, Italian states were no longer active players in the politics of Europe; rather, Italy was increasingly becoming the stage upon which the ambitions of Europe's two major powers played out their dramas. Two vigorous new monarchs had recently come to the throne: Francis I (1494–1547) and Charles V (1500–1558). The twenty-year-old Francis, descended from the Valois line of kings, inherited the French crown in 1515. Meanwhile, the next year the kingdom of Spain passed to sixteen-year-old Charles of Austria, a member of the Habsburg dynasty (also spelled "Hapsburg"), who soon after was elected Emperor Charles V in 1519. These two became locked in a duel over possession of the contested territory of Burgundy and dominance of the western Mediterranean. Aside from the riches that Italy had to offer, conquest of the Italian Peninsula was crucial to both France and Spain from a strategic perspective. If Charles could take central and northern Italy, he could link the Kingdom of Naples with the empire, effectively encircling France, something Francis wanted at all costs to prevent. From this point on, the destiny of Italy was to be decided by the outcome of the struggle between the Habsburg and Valois dynasties. Guicciardini recognizes as much in the passage quoted previously; however, there were deeper forces at play,

DOI: 10.4324/9781003270362-12

260 The 1527 Sack of Rome and Its Aftermath

of which he could hardly have been aware, that would permanently shift the balance of political and economic power away from Italy.

A New World and a new world order

> Marvelous were the voyages of the Spanish, begun in the year 1490 through the initiative of a Genoese, Christopher Colombus … and after him Amerigo Vespucci, followed by many others.
>
> Francesco Guicciardini, *The History of Italy*

Just six months before Lorenzo de' Medici died, in 1492 the Genoese navigator Cristoforo Colombo (Christopher Columbus, 1451–1506) set foot on a new continent, which came to be named after the Florentine explorer Amerigo Vespucci (1451–1512). A new era was opening in which Europe was broadening its horizons and looking westward—forward across the Atlantic rather than back toward the Mediterranean. Though Renaissance Italians took intense interest in the New World—they were foremost among the cartographers charting these new lands; naturalists studying their flora and fauna; and artists depicting its wonders (Chapters 14, 15)—the Italian states had no direct involvement in its exploration or colonization; both Italian navigators Columbus and Vespucci were funded by the Spanish and Portuguese crowns.

Within decades, vast wealth from the New World flooded into Spain. In 1474 the annual revenue had been 80,000 ducats; by 1504 the infusion of gold and silver pushed the figure to 2.3 million, surpassing 85 million by the last decade of the century. And while Europe was moving westward, Italy was losing control of the Mediterranean. The Turks, who had taken Constantinople in 1453, were exerting military and economic pressure in the eastern Mediterranean, putting an end to Venice's monopoly on trade in that region. A by-product of Turkish aggression was discovery of other routes to the East, bypassing the troubled Mediterranean entirely. In 1497–99, when the Portuguese explorer Vasco da Gama rounded the Cape of Good Hope and reached India, it meant that Italian merchants no longer had an edge as middlemen selling silks and spices from Asia. As Guicciardini commented, "the war against the Turks hurt the Venetians less than having the King of Portugal cut off their spice trade."

In 1492 Spain had only just had a military encounter of its own with the Islamic world and ejected the Arabs from the Iberian Peninsula in the final phase of the *Reconquista* (the "Reconquest"). Moreover, the Spanish state was a recent creation; formerly divided into the kingdoms of Castile and Aragon, it was unified as recently as 1469. While Italy's city-states had been consolidating their territories into ever-larger areas over the course of the past century, the same thing had been happening on a vast scale over

The 1527 Sack of Rome and Its Aftermath 261

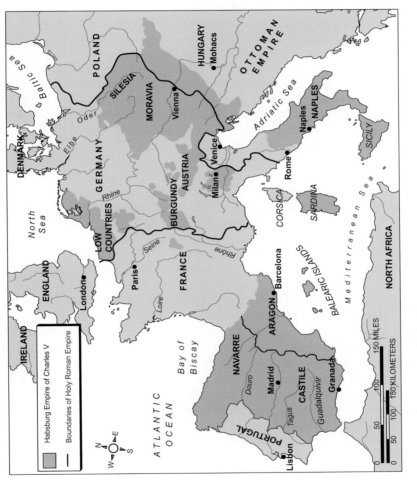

Map 12.1 The Empire of Charles V in Europe

much of Europe. By the end of the fifteenth century, France had also grown by absorbing the provinces of Burgundy and Brittany. The most populous country in Europe, France, in 1515, had a yearly income of 6 million ducats, its land was fertile, and its power was expanding. The Habsburgs, who had held the title of emperor since 1452, expanded their territory to include the Low Countries (present-day Holland and Belgium); so that suddenly, with Charles V in possession of all this, as well as Spain and the lands of the New World, the Spanish Empire, extending from Vienna to Peru, was set to become the largest, wealthiest empire the world had ever seen (Map 12.1).

What chance did a divided, war-torn Italy have against two such powerful nation-states as France and Spain? Though the French were defeated in 1513 and the Sforza restored to power in Milan, two years later when Francis I came to the throne, the French, allied with Venice, again invaded. Sweeping in with an army of 40,000, at the Battle of Marignano in 1515, the French destroyed papal forces (Swiss mercenary troops), regained Milan, and with it control of northern Italy. Pope Julius II's advantage over Venice was lost. And that was not all the papacy would lose.

The profligate papacy of Leo X 1513–21

> Julius II: "What's happened to St. Peter's and all my cash?"
> Leo X: "On my soul, I thought to see 200 popes go by before it went."
> Julius II: "I know I left much gold and silver there unspent."
> Leo X: "It's all gone, the wind has carried it away in a flash."
>
> *Anonymous pasquinade*, 16th century

The younger son of Lorenzo the Magnificent, Giovanni de' Medici was elected Pope Leo X in 1513, inheriting large and prosperous territories of the Papal States from his predecessor Julius II. Leo proceeded to squander the financial resources through his lavish spending on the arts and maintaining a splendid court. Leo allegedly said, "Let us enjoy the papacy, as God has given it to us." He kept a menagerie with exotic animals, including for a time a white Indian elephant named Hanno. Leo was a singer and lutenist, as well as a patron of the arts, theater, and music, like his father. And like Lorenzo, he had studied both Greek and Latin, was interested in humanistic pursuits and curious about the wider world. The cultural atmosphere in Rome during Leo's papacy was vibrant and cosmopolitan, including the presence at the papal court of the Muslim scholar al-Hassan al-Wazzan (*c*.1486–*c*.1537) who, to honor his patron, took the name Giovanni Leone de' Medici (also known as Leo Africanus).

Though perhaps not much interested in the spiritual aspects of the papacy—Giovanni de' Medici became pope without ever having been ordained a priest—Leo was obsessed, like Popes Alexander and Julius before him, with protecting the possessions of the Papal States in the Romagna. He purchased the cities of Modena and Reggio from the emperor, and in 1515 he promised to give them back to the Este family. He never returned these two cities, however, thereby creating permanent hostilities between the Duke of Ferrara and the papacy. He regained Parma and Piacenza by abandoning Milan, and the Sforza, to the French. From 1516 to 1517 Leo waged a costly war to oust Julius II's nephew Francesco Maria della Rovere from Urbino, to install his own nephew Lorenzo di Piero de' Medici as lord there. In advancing the short-term interests of the papacy and his Medici relatives, Leo alienated important allies within Italy and endangered the security of the Italian Peninsula.

Figure 12.1 Raphael, *Portrait of Pope Leo X with Cardinals Giulio de' Medici and Luigi de' Rossi*, 1517–18, Uffizi. Giulio de' Medici, the figure on the far left, would become Pope Clement VII

264 *The 1527 Sack of Rome and Its Aftermath*

Realizing belatedly that it was in the best interests of the stability of the peninsula to have Milan ruled by a strong, autonomous Duke, in 1521 Leo allied with the Emperor Charles V to drive the French out of Milan and appointed the exiled Francesco II Sforza to the throne. Shifting support back and forth between the king of France and the emperor, playing them off against one another, was only a temporary means of survival, though. This wily, short-sighted strategy worked only as long as the two monarchs were evenly balanced, but soon the balance tipped dramatically in the favor of the emperor. Leo, who died in December 1521, did not live long enough to see the disastrous consequences of his policies.

Francesco Guicciardini's career as papal governor in the Romagna

Judging by his harsh criticism of Leo's policies, one would hardly know that one Florentine who benefitted greatly from his papacy was Francesco Guicciardini himself, whom Leo appointed governor of Modena in 1516, Reggio in 1517, and Parma in 1521. Later, when he was brought low by *fortuna*, Guicciardini looked back and described himself during this period:

> Certainly if you had seen Messer Francesco in the Romagna … with his house full of tapestries, silver, servants, all the province competing for his attention … his unbounded authority, his great domain and government, the pomp of his court, he would have seemed to you the equal of any duke.

Born in Florence in 1483 into a patrician family of Medici supporters—his godfather was Marsilio Ficino—Francesco Guicciardini received an excellent education and earned his degree in civil law in 1505. In 1511 he was sent by Soderini's government as ambassador to Ferdinand of Spain, and spent two years at the Spanish court. When the Florentine Republic fell in 1512 and the Medici returned to power, unlike his friend Machiavelli, Guicciardini not only found a job, but acquired fame and riches. He worked first for Leo X and then for another Medici pope, Clement VII, who in 1524 gave Guicciardini the governorship of all the Romagna, except Bologna. It was here in the Romagna, ravaged by numerous battles and divided by factionalism and violence, that Guiccardini was able to observe first-hand the negative effects of decades of papal intervention, as he tried to pacify the region. In January 1526, however, he was forced to leave his post because he was urgently summoned to Rome by Pope Clement VII.

The tragically indecisive Pope Clement VII

A papacy made of many features:
Of considerations and of speeches,
Of "yet"s, "then"s, "but"s, "if"s, and "um"s,
Of so many words and no outcomes.

Francesco Berni (1497–1535) *Poem on Clement VII*

When Leo died in 1521 his place was taken by Pope Adrian VI, a Dutchman, who died only eighteen months after his election. In November 1523 the College of Cardinals elected a new pope, yet another Medici, Giulio di Giuliano de' Medici (1478–1534), who became Pope Clement VII. The son of Lorenzo the Magnificent's assassinated brother Giuliano, Giulio was born a month after his father's death. Having worked for years as his cousin Leo X's right-hand man—literally portrayed as such in the portrait by Raphael (Figure 12.1)—Clement VII was an intelligent, experienced administrator. Like many intelligent people, however, Clement liked to think things out thoroughly before making a decision. Unfortunately, the crisis was escalating very swiftly by the time he became pope, and there was very little time for considered decision making.

Clement's first year as pope was not yet over when the French again invaded at the end of 1524. The Spanish held much of the territory in Lombardy, and Clement, alarmed by the increasing strength of the Spanish in Italy and angered by the emperor's arrogant manner, decided to support the French. After a number of clashes between French and Spanish troops, in February 1525, at the Battle of Pavia the French forces, led into battle by Francis himself, were crushed, and the French king was taken prisoner. The humiliation of the French was total, and Charles V had become overnight the most powerful man in Europe (Figure 12.2).

On the brink of disaster, 1526

> I believe that no matter what, we will have war in Italy, and soon. Thus, the Italians must have France with them and if they cannot, they must decide what steps to take. It seems to me that in this case there are two alternatives: either surrender to whomever comes, greeting him with money, or truly to arm and defend ourselves as best we can. In my opinion buying ourselves off will not help. Money is not enough; if it were, I would say let us stop here and think of nothing else. But it will not be enough, for either I am completely blind, or they will take first our money, then our lives.
>
> Machiavelli, *Letter to Guicciardini*, March 15, 1526

In January 1526 Pope Clement VII sent for Francesco Guicciardini. The pope was undecided at this crucial juncture whether to back the emperor or the French king. Guicciardini fatally added his voice to those urging the pope to side with France. Fear of Spanish force and personal enmity for Charles outweighed in Clement's mind the practical consideration that France had been soundly defeated and its king held captive in Spain. In May 1526 the League of Cognac, an alliance formed in defense of Italy, was agreed upon. Although it was said that both France and Spain were meant to be included, the intention of the League was to drive out the Spanish. Stung by this affront, Charles began expressing his anger toward the pope ever more openly, letting it be known that he intended to call a church council to unseat

266 *The 1527 Sack of Rome and Its Aftermath*

Clement. The parties who eventually joined the League were the Papacy; the Republics of Venice and Florence; the Duchy of Milan; and France (the French King had recently been released from Spanish prison after agreeing to huge concessions and leaving his two eldest sons as hostages). When news of the League began to spread throughout the peninsula, it generated enthusiasm and idealistic expectations that a strong, united Italy would liberate itself from the "barbarians."

It was thus with high hopes, intending to wrest Milan from imperial troops, that the forces of the League assembled in Lombardy in summer 1526. They were led by several commanders: Francesco Maria della Rovere—duke of Urbino, a celebrated *condottiero* who had fought for years for Venice—served as general for the Venetian forces, while Guicciardini was the lieutenant-general for the papal troops. Della Rovere, whose Duchy of Urbino had been seized by Pope Leo X, was, however, less than devoted to Leo's kinsman Pope Clement VII, and as a professional soldier of fortune he looked down on the pope's appointed commander, Guicciardini, whom he considered a civilian amateur. These forces were further supported by those of a respected and feared *condottiero*, Giovanni de' Medici (1498–1526), better known as Giovanni delle Bande Nere or Giovanni of the Black Bands. On the imperial side, the multi-national forces were composed of troops of Spaniards led by the Frenchman Charles III, duke of Bourbon (1490–1527), and regiments of German pikemen known as Landsknechts (sometimes written "lansquenets") led by Georg von Frundsberg (1473–1528). Frundsberg was a renowned military leader as well as a devoted follower of Martin Luther, who stirred his men to battle not only by promising them booty, but by inciting them with hatred of papists.

These individuals, then, were the main protagonists; but important roles were also played by Alfonso d'Este, Duke of Ferrara, and Federico II Gonzaga, Marquess of Mantua. These two rulers of small states in the Po Valley, which was close to the action, were anxious not to offend either side. Their allegiance to the papacy, never entirely reliable, weakened under imperial pressure. Gonzaga—who had been appointed captain-general for the pope, for which he received a large *condotta*—found excuses, when the time came, to avoid taking up arms. Behind the scenes Gonzaga supplied imperial troops with food, and Este provided them with valuable artillery.

Between Spaniards and Germans, the imperial side had amassed an enormous fighting force. However, these troops had not been paid for some time, and as a result, rather than an organized army, they became an angry rabble. Meanwhile, League commanders hesitated to attack, and precious time was lost throughout the summer. Though Giovanni de' Medici and his 4,000 infantrymen kept putting pressure on Frundsberg's forces, when Giovanni was struck by imperial artillery and died at the end of November 1526, the leaderless Black Bands were unable to hold off the enemy. It was

The 1527 Sack of Rome and Its Aftermath   267

only a question of time now until imperial troops began their march south toward Rome.

By March 1527, surrounded on all sides, with an immense army bearing down, and no aid from the French in sight, Clement abandoned the League and signed a truce with the Spanish, stipulating the payment of hundreds of thousands of ducats to send the foreign soldiers away. Despite the truce, in April, the troops were still advancing, their leaders unwilling, or unable, to stop them. Clement, realizing his mistake, rejoined the League on the 25th. Guicciardini and the duke of Urbino gave orders to turn their army back toward Rome, for imperial troops would very soon reach the Holy City. By April, the imperial forces reached nearly 35,000, among them Spaniards, Germans, and Italians, for this ragtag army along the way had swelled with deserters, bandits, as well as soldiers imprudently discharged by the pope; neither Bourbon nor Frundsberg could fully control them. Frundsberg had suffered a stroke trying to restrain their fury; even Charles V himself could not have stopped the hungry, ragged mob bent on the pillage and plunder of the glittering home of the papacy.

The Sack

Everyone is saying that Hell itself is a more beautiful sight to look at.
Letter from Rome, May 10, 1527

The attack began before dawn on May 6. Bourbon gave the signal, as supplies for feeding the enormous number of troops he had amassed would run out in a day or two. Knowing League reinforcements were on their way and would reach Rome any day, there was reason for haste. Besides, the ragged, underpaid, underfed troops could not be held back; they barely waited for the general to finish his address to them before they began storming the walls of Rome. Bourbon was apprehensive; though the imperial troops were strong numerically, they had very little artillery and lacked siege machinery. No one could say what the day's outcome would be.

For days Romans had been feverishly reinforcing their city's defenses. If they could hold out for just three days, the army of the League was close enough to come to their rescue, and Rome would be safe. Though he made the decision very late, Clement had called the Great Council of Rome with representatives of all the *rioni* (neighborhoods) to organize defense of the city. Renzo da Ceri (Lorenzo Anguillara or Orsini 1475–1536) was chosen as commander of the small number of troops available in Rome. Although there were only 4,000 foot soldiers, volunteers from each *rione* were pledged to turn up to form a citizen militia. The long circuit of walls that encircled the Eternal City was dilapidated, and stones placed there by Caesar's engineers needed shoring up. Knowing the weakness of this ancient, poorly maintained wall, and having too few men to defend its entire length, Renzo wanted to destroy the bridges across the Tiber. This way if the enemy got across the wall, they could be delayed from entering the central portion of Rome long enough for the reinforcements to arrive; but the Romans refused to destroy their bridges. When the militia was called, very few actually materialized and those who did were not the youngest and strongest. The more able-bodied had hired themselves out to protect private villas.

Romans trembled when they were awakened that morning by the ringing of the city's warning bells and the crackling of gunfire. Things did not go badly for the city in the first few hours; Charles of Bourbon was shot and killed almost at the beginning of the fighting, and the Romans were counting on the heavy guns at the Castel Sant'Angelo to hold off the attackers. The former Mausoleum of the Emperor Hadrian (built 139 CE), Sant'Angelo had been converted by successive popes into a heavily fortified castle, linked by a protected walkway to nearby St. Peter's Basilica. However, just as the attackers came within reach of its guns, a dense fog rolled in, rendering them useless. The imperial soldiers continued to attack the walls, some ripping at it with bare hands; toward evening, they broke through.

The pope's Swiss Guard, and those of the citizen militia who stayed, fought bravely against the flood of invaders, but the rest fled to protect their homes and families. The wealthy barricaded themselves in their palazzi; girls were shut away into convents, and the pope rushed to safety in the Castel Sant'Angelo. The scene that followed was one of unrelieved carnage. Even by the standards of the day, which dictated that a besieged city, once taken, could be legitimately subjected to the worst forms of brutality, the violence that was unleashed was of an unheard-of atrocity, as is clear from the many first-hand accounts of the Sack of Rome that have come down to us.

The orgy of violence was general among the imperial troops, but there was an added element of religious fury that fueled the German troops. During sieges, places of worship were traditionally spared, but nearly all the hundreds of churches and monasteries in Rome were pillaged. Greed for the fine objects competed in the minds of the Lutheran invaders with rage at the corruption that had engendered such an accumulation of wealth. Not only were churches and monasteries stripped of all precious gold and silverwork, fine fabrics, and art, the soldiers also defaced images of saints and desecrated altars and tombs. They pried open coffins to remove precious jewels from the bones of long-buried bishops and trampled venerated relics. The force of their fury was expended not only on bones of ancient martyrs and marble statues: breaking into convents, they violated nuns. Many nuns were dragged out of their seclusion and sold off in taverns to the highest bidders. Any member of the clergy encountered on the street or found cowering in a sacristy was brutally murdered. Hundreds were killed on the holiest site in Rome, the high altar in St. Peter's, and when the lust for slaughter abated, the great basilica itself was used as a stable for horses.

Figure 12.2 Titian, *Equestrian Portrait of Charles V*, 1548, Museo del Prado, Madrid

A traumatized Christendom takes stock

No reasonable person would deny that priests who deceive the people with false relics to make money, who receive the Holy Sacrament while in mortal sin have erred greatly, or that those who greedily try to accumulate gains, using illegal means, acting contrary to the commands of Christ and to human laws and are very bad men. But I cannot imagine, as you do, that these instances of wrong-doing prove that the spoliation of relics, whether true or false, the massacre of clergy, the robbing of altars, profaning of sacred objects, and ruining churches was justifed … nor can I lift from my soul the continual affliction I feel in imagining their pain, anxiety, amazement, agitation, tears, sighs, and longing for death.

Letter of Papal Nuncio, July 1528

In the aftermath of the Sack, a shocked and divided Christendom tried to make sense of what had happened. Emperor Charles V denied any responsibility for the event, saying that he had not been fully informed. Meanwhile, many claimed that Rome had been justly punished for her excesses, and those expressing this opinion were not exclusively Lutherans. The emperor's secretary, Alfonso de Valdés, in late 1527 had written: "Every single horror of the Sack is a precise, necessary, and providential punishment for each of the iniquities that soiled Rome." The outrage felt in Rome at such an assertion is given eloquent expression in the words of the papal nuncio (diplomatic representative of the pope) to the Spanish court, quoted above.

That papal nuncio was Baldassarre Castiglione (1478–1529). Destined to be one of the most influential writers of the Renaissance, Castiglione was born near Mantua, of a noble family related to the Gonzagas. The well-born young man, educated in Greek and Latin, found a place first in Milan at the court of Ludovico Sforza, then in Mantua, working for Francesco II Gonzaga (1466–1519), and most famously at the court of Guidobaldo da Montefeltro in Urbino. Working for these lords, Castiglione not only made use of his skills as a man of letters, composing official correspondence, speeches, and other documents, but also served as a diplomat and soldier. He was sent on official missions to the kings of England and France and fought in military campaigns alongside Julius II. In 1513 the duke of Urbino sent Castiglione to Rome as an ambassador, and it was at the court of Leo X that he made close friends with the intellectual and artistic elite of Rome. By this time, he was so highly regarded that Clement VII hired Castiglione to serve as papal nuncio to Spain; in 1525 he was received in Madrid by Charles V, with whom he established excellent relations. Castiglione did not live long after the celebrated exchange with Valdés; he died of a fever in 1529, causing the emperor reportedly to exclaim: "¡*Yo vos digo que es muerto uno de los mejores caballeros del mundo*!" (I tell you that one of the best gentlemen in the world has died!)

Baldassarre Castiglione's instant bestseller

> I do not wonder that you have described a perfect courtier, since you had only to hold up a mirror in front of yourself and describe your own qualities.
>
> Vittoria Colonna, *Letter to Castiglione*

In addition to being a diplomat, Castiglione was a writer. In *The Courtier*, the book that brought him international fame, the author sets out to express his "opinion of the form of courtiership most appropriate for a gentleman living at a princely court." Having himself been a courtier his entire life, as acknowledged by Roman noblewoman and poet Vittoria Colonna

The 1527 Sack of Rome and Its Aftermath   271

(*c.*1490–1547), Castiglione was the ideal person to write this treatise. Using the device of transcribing a series of conversations that he claims took place between gentlemen and ladies in the Palace of Urbino in March 1507, Castiglione distills his observations about court life. Castiglione's book was the product of a lifetime of practical experience; like the books of Machiavelli and Guicciardini, it was intended to be useful and instructive for others. The public responded to *The Courtier* immediately, and the book was an overnight success. It is impossible to exaggerate the work's impact, not only in Italy, but all over Europe when it appeared. Translated into five languages, *The Courtier* was printed in over 115 editions by 1600. In 1582 a Spanish inquisitor in Peru fretted over censoring a copy; in 1586 a Florentine merchant found a copy in a match-seller's house in India, and in 1701 a plantation owner in Virginia owned a copy.

Advice manuals became very popular during the early years of printing and circulated widely. This book, in particular, written by an elegant Italian court gentleman, contained a variety of information valued by contemporaries. Castiglione provides much advice on etiquette—how to dress: "it seems to me that the most agreeable color is black, and if not black, then at least something fairly dark," and how to behave: "always be diffident and reserved rather than forward." There is an entire section devoted to jokes, which could be memorized and repeated by the reader eager to make an impression as a sophisticated wit. The author lists accomplishments of singing, dancing, reciting poetry, and sports that the courtier should master, but he adds that to carry them off it is essential that the courtier make them look easy. For this, the most important quality is a word Castiglione coined in Italian, *sprezzatura* (pronounced "spreh-tsah-TWO-rah"). The word, difficult to translate, means something like "nonchalance" or "acting cool." "Who doesn't laugh," writes Castiglione, "when our page Pierpaulo dances in that way of his, with those little leaps and with his legs stretched on tiptoe, keeping his head rigid as if made of wood, looking as if he were carefully counting every step?" Although dancing is complicated, involving precise counting and skillful coordination, the courtier must feign carelessness, making it appear to be the simplest thing in the world. The courtier must apply this principle to his every activity, exercising caution, however, not to exaggerate the carelessness, or he will cross over into the realm of affectation. To appear affected or mannered is just as bad as being awkward and overexerted, warns Castiglione. In all his actions the courtier ought to be guided by a sense of *grazia* (grace). Grace is an ineffable quality of good taste inspired by nature; the author advises the would-be courtier to speak "with a simplicity and candor that makes it seem as if Nature herself were speaking, touching the heart, almost intoxicating in its sweetness." Castiglione's characterization of grace as seductive and affecting in its seemingly artless simplicity could just as well be a description of the Italian High Renaissance aesthetic embodied in the paintings by his friend Raphael. This image of elegance, civility, and sophistication promoted by Castiglione ensured that Italian Renaissance culture would be the model emulated by generations to come.

Contradictions and tensions within *The Courtier*

> The liberty we enjoyed was accompanied by the utmost restraint.
> *The Courtier*, Book 1, Description of the Court of Urbino

The Courtier is more than an advice manual; it is a complex and multi-layered work written by a humanist. In it, Castiglione introduces lofty debates on how best to use the vernacular, expressed by his friend Pietro Bembo, whose *Prose della volgar lingua* (1525) enshrined the Tuscan dialect as standard Italian; elsewhere he takes up the contemporary polemic over which form of art is more noble, painting or sculpture, and he finishes the book with a rapturous description of platonic love. Underlying the entire book, however, runs a current of general malaise felt during the troubled times in which it was written. The book came out in 1528, the year after the Sack, and much had changed in the author's world during the time since he had begun writing. In Raphael's *Portrait of Baldassarre Castiglione* (c.1515, Louvre), a thoughtful, well-dressed scholar gazes at the viewer; the lower portion of his face is largely shrouded in a dark, bushy beard, making the expression of his mouth difficult to read, while melancholy lingers around his eyes. By 1527 this melancholy had intensified, as Castiglione admits in the preface, "as I re-read it [the draft of *The Courtier*] I experienced no little sorrow … realizing that most of those introduced in the conversations were dead." The world that he evokes, the elegant court of Urbino where the author had served from 1504 to 1516, no longer existed and perhaps never existed in the ideal form in which Castiglione represents it. Duke Guidobaldo da Montefeltro, unlike his father Federico, was a failure as a *condottiero* and ruler, having lost the duchy to Cesare Borgia in 1502. A sickly man who was unable to have children, the Duke adopted a nephew, Francesco Maria della Rovere, who succeeded him when he died in 1508. It was the Duke's cultivated wife Elisabetta Gonzaga (1471–1526) who in reality presided over this court. Indeed, in this book, with all its talk of serving a prince, the "prince"—Duke Guidobaldo—is entirely absent, having "retired to his bedroom," as the author informs us. This twice-exiled, literally impotent Duke is the hollow core at the center of the court of Urbino. Equally hollow in the light of recent foreign invasions was the chivalric ideal of the signori as represented by Castiglione. By this point, the image of noble *condottieri* leading small forces onto the battlefield, brightly colored pennants flying and territories changing hands after several dozen wounded, had been replaced by the realities of heavy artillery and devastating casualties. This book, which proposes to give practical advice for real courtiers, presents a world that is no longer real.

The Machiavellian courtier?

Yet, in his portrait of the court of Urbino, Castiglione is at once celebrating an ideal and recognizing the stark necessities of contemporary political reality. Though he portrays his courtiers and court ladies striving to perfect themselves within an impossibly utopian environment, he also proposes that these elegant dancing, singing, fencing courtiers provide an essential, practical service to the state. Like Machiavelli, Castiglione acknowledges that conditions are such in Italy that despotism has become a necessity. Under no illusions as to the character of most princes, he writes: "Signori, besides never hearing the truth, drunk with licentious freedom that comes with power and overindulgence in pleasure, become corrupt." The reason why courtiers must go to such lengths to become graceful and accomplished is to better serve the ruler and to improve him. It is

> the objective of the perfect courtier in acquiring these skills to earn the favor and mind of the prince he serves in order to always be able to tell him the truth ... turning him away from every evil purpose and encouraging him on the path of virtue.

Without this higher objective, Castiglione concedes that

> dancing, partying, singing, and joking would be frivolous and vain, for which a man ought to be criticized rather than praised. These frivolities belong among the entertainments of women and romances ... making the spirit effeminate, corrupting our youth through dissolute living, and it is in this way that the name of Italy is disgraced.

Gender-bending at court and the changing role of women

The preoccupation with appearing overly feminine, as well as defining the roles of men and women, is a central concern of Castiglione. Gender distinctions, the social and cultural, rather than biological ways of marking the differences between male and female, are often defined in terms of power. Since the male courtier is always submissive to the male prince, he is perceived as feminine, and gender roles are actually reversed when he is in service to a female ruler, as were the courtiers at Urbino. For this reason, Castiglione goes to great lengths to define the respective roles of men and women at court. The court lady's function is essentially decorative; Castiglione portrays her as less active and less vocal than her male counterpart. She must be beautiful, well dressed, and, like the courtier, well spoken, but she must not dominate the conversation. Her most important attribute is to set the proper moral tone. Castiglione has the court lady Emilia Pia say: "virtue is feminine and vice masculine." *Virtù* is a word used as frequently by Castiglione as it was by Machiavelli, but in a very different sense. The courtier does not strive for that

274 *The 1527 Sack of Rome and Its Aftermath*

masculine quality of daring and prowess; rather his energies must be tamed and subdued, his ambitions modified to fit the prince, and his sexual desire sublimated as platonic love.

Courtiers, court ladies, and courtesans

In *The Courtier* Castiglione enters into a long-standing debate about women's place in society—the so-called *querelle des femmes* (in French, literally the debate about women). It was first given eloquent expression in the Renaissance by author Christine de Pizan (or de Pisan 1364–1430) in her *Book of the City of Ladies* (1405). Born in Venice of Italian parents, and raised in France, Christine de Pizan challenged accepted views of gender roles in her many works, which were widely read at the French royal court. Courts, rather than republican city-states, gave more expression to women, primarily because alongside the monarch—and at times in his place—a female ruled. Courtly society was by its nature shaped by the civilizing influence of women. While attempting to circumscribe the role of women—Castiglione's ideal court lady is chaste, passive, and content to inspire the courtier—he also recognizes that

> no court no matter how great can have adornment or splendor or gaiety in it without ladies. No courtier is ever graceful, pleasant or bold, or moved to perform deeds of chivalry unless inspired by love and giving pleasure to women.

The reality of court life inevitably fell far short of Castiglione's ideal; neither courtiers nor court ladies were paragons of virtue. Both women and men at court often granted sexual favors in exchange for patronage. Courtiers with their elegant manners and effeminate dress were often accused of prostituting themselves to the signore. Even if there was no sexual relationship, the courtier could be considered to be figuratively prostituting himself, serving a wealthy patron with his charming manners and providing literary services. They had female competition, however, from courtesans. These women were actual prostitutes, but were distinguished from common streetwalkers by their education and refined manners. Around the beginning of the sixteenth century, these women, known as "honest courtesans," began to play an important role in Italian Renaissance culture. Rome and Venice were especially known for the large numbers of courtesans. In addition to providing sex, the courtesan entertained wealthy men by playing the lute, singing, and reciting poetry, often her own. The writer Pietro Aretino (1492–1556) employed his pen for a variety of patrons, including in Rome Agostino Chigi, Cardinal Giulio de' Medici, then in Mantua Federico Gonzaga and Giovanni delle Bande Nere. Eventually Aretino moved to the Venetian Republic where he wrote freelance, preferring it to life at court, where "the cruelty of harlots, the insolence of effeminate men" and every kind of vice ruled. Among the many works Aretino wrote were his satirical *Dialogues*, in which courtesans cynically discuss their trade. Aretino dismisses their artistic endeavors as merely a means to make their customers pay more, one courtesan saying:

> I took a fancy to strumming the lute, not because I had any desire to do so, but in order to show how I enjoyed the arts. These skills learned by whores are traps laid for fools … . Don't ever trust a whore who sings and reads music from a book.

Women's distinctive voice in literature

Male writers such as Aretino felt threatened that Italian women were beginning to enter men's terrain—the world of art, music, and above all letters—as never before and that their writings were being published, among them: Tullia d'Aragona (1510–1556), Gaspara Stampa (c.1525–1554), Moderata Fonte (Modesta da Pozzo 1555–1592), and Veronica Franco (1546–1591; Chapter 14). Though not all were courtesans, having one's private thoughts exposed for the public to read was considered a transgressive act for a woman; there was something indecent about those who had their works published. This stigma, however, did not stop nobly born writers such as Veronica Gambara (1485–1550) and Vittoria Colonna (1492–1547) from expressing themselves. Moreover, the social instability in Italy in this post-1527 world opened new opportunities for women's expression not only in literature, but in the visual arts as well (see Chapter 14 on Isabella Andreini and Artemisia Gentileschi; Chapter 15 on Sofonisba Anguissola, and Lavinia Fontana).

Ariosto and Sannazaro's escapist fantasies

The changing role of women is to some extent reflected by the many powerful female figures in Ludovico Ariosto's (1474–1533) rambling epic poem *Orlando furioso* (1515). Ariosto's masterpiece is an exuberant fantasy composed of intricate episode upon episode of magical incantations, flying horses, battles with Saracens, and indomitable warrior maidens clad in armor. This chivalric narrative, like *Orlando innamorato* (*Orlando in Love*) of Matteo Maria Boiardo (1441–1494) before, and *Gerusalemme liberata* (*Jerusalem Delivered*) of Torquato Tasso (Chapter 14) afterward, was written under the patronage of the dukes of Ferrara and was meant to exalt the ancient lineage of the Este clan. Despite its focus on a small, local dynasty, Ariosto's fanciful poem became enormously popular throughout Europe.

Another form of fantasy is evident in the works of another poet who was very popular during this period—Jacopo Sannazaro. Both his versified novel *Arcadia* (1504) and his posthumously published collection of poems *Rime* (1530), which represent an idyllic world of shepherds and shepherdesses frolicking in shady groves, were widely read. The escapist pastoral ideal

276   *The 1527 Sack of Rome and Its Aftermath*

developed by Sannazaro during these calamitous years became the dominant fantasy of the leisured classes of Europe through the time of Marie Antoinette and Jean-Jacques Rousseau. It is Castiglione, in the final pages of *The Courtier*, who sets the stage for this retreat into romantic dreaminess. There Pietro Bembo expounds an extended praise of platonic love, in which the lover sublimates physical desire to a higher, purer form of love, and only after "having become blind to earthly things," can the individual perceive true, heavenly beauty. Through the voice of Bembo, Castiglione exclaims:

> Here we will find the most happy end to our desires, the true repose from our labors, a sure remedy for our miseries, the healthiest medicine for our illnesses, and the safest harbor from the raging storms of this life's tempestuous sea.

Considerations: Accepting defeat with *grazia*

Up until this point, we have looked at the history of the Italian Peninsula without taking much notice of the rest of Europe; apart from the south, early Renaissance Italy was by and large immune from foreign intervention. From the end of the fifteenth century, however, it is impossible to study Italian history without considering the large nation-states of France and Spain. After 1527, Italy's autonomy was essentially over and remained so for more than three centuries. Italy did not regain her independence until the Risorgimento in the nineteenth century, when the country unified and rose up against foreign occupation. Many historians choose to end the story of the Renaissance at this point, motivated in part by a sense that the greatest impetus of creative energy was largely finished by the time Charles V subdued most of the peninsula. Except in Venice, the political experiment with self-rule, the glorious era of the Italian communes, was ending. However, the cultural vitality that had begun under the communal regimes had not exhausted itself just because the political situation had shifted. On the contrary, Italy's cultural supremacy became universally recognized during the sixteenth century, as the works of artists such as Michelangelo and Raphael, as well as books by Castiglione and Ariosto, spread throughout Europe.

It is easy to be swayed by emotional reactions in our judgments of history. The image of heroic citizens of small city-republics defending their liberty, like so many Davids battling Goliath, is more appealing than that of perfumed courtiers flattering princes and bowing to Spanish grandees. We may find the dissimulation, the artificiality of court life slightly repellent, viewing it as an emphasis on style over substance. Contemporary Italians sensed this as well; in *The Art of War* Machiavelli blamed the disasters of Italy largely on the cultured effeminacy of its leaders:

> Our Italian princes believed, before they had experienced the blows of the foreign wars, that it was enough for a prince in his study to know how to

The 1527 Sack of Rome and Its Aftermath   277

write a beautiful letter, displaying in his speech quickness of wit, to know how to weave deceptions, adorn himself with jewels, to sleep and eat with greater splendor than others ... from this were born the great horrors of 1494, the sudden flights and shocking losses, and thus three most powerful states in Italy were many times sacked and ruined.

Castiglione's approach in the end is very close to that of the much-maligned author of *The Prince*. Castiglione advises bending to necessity; the courtier ought to serve the prince and do whatever it takes to please, in order to ensure good, stable government. Machiavelli and Castiglione were not advocating resistance to the status quo, but trying to describe the changed realities of life in Italy as they saw it and to suggest wise means of responding to the new situation.

Guicciardini, as well, sought to respond to events and tried to make sense of the disasters that had occurred. Like other Renaissance humanists, Guicciardini was interested in human nature and in discovering the motivations for an individual's actions. His portraits of popes and princes in the *History of Italy* rival those of Leonardo and Raphael in their close attention to psychological detail. Like those artists, Guicciardini was also an observer, and like Machiavelli he took a scientific approach to assembling his information, using archival documents, and taking care to verify his facts. What ultimately makes Guicciardini's *History of Italy* such a ground-breaking work, the first modern work of history, is not only that he presents incisive psychological portraits of the political players of his time, or his attention to accuracy, but that he was able to envision how all the events in Italy fit into a larger whole. Whereas in the Middle Ages it was common to record events in the form of chronicles, in which one event followed another, listed chronologically with little if any analysis, Guicciardini was looking at a classical model, the *History of the Peloponnesian War* by the Greek historian Thucydides (*c*.460–395 BCE). Guicciardini tried to arrange his material to give it shape and make events more understandable. Just as humanists believed that the study of ancient history would help them understand their world, so too did Guicciardini believe that the study of recent events could teach—contemporaries, as well as future generations—lessons about the human condition. Possibly Guicciardini's most modern contribution in this work is the pessimistic vision of human history that emerges from the events he has witnessed. There is no rhyme or reason to the "calamities of Italy," no Divine Providence guiding human destiny; it is up to the individual to face events with dignity. Guicciardini wrote:

Some sages say that life is like a comedy, in which we ought to praise the actors, not paying attention to the roles they play, but to how well they play their parts. Since everyone must play the part assigned to him, that which belongs to him alone is the way he carries it out. Thus, the character

278   *The 1527 Sack of Rome and Its Aftermath*

we play in the world is given to us by Fortune, but the thing for which we are praised is the way we live, according to our station and fate.

Sourcebook

Christopher Columbus, *Letter to Luis de Santángel*
Amerigo Vespucci, *"Mundus novus" Letter*
Giovanni Leone Africano, *Cosmography of Africa*
Francesco Guicciardini, *The History of Italy*
Alberini, Buonaparte, Tebaldeo, Guicciardini, *Accounts of Sack of Rome*
Baldassarre Castiglione, *The Courtier*
Raphael, *Portrait of Castiglione*
Pietro Aretino, *Letter to Philip II*
Gaspara Stampa, *Sonnets*
Vittoria Colonna, *Sonnet*
Lodovico Ariosto, *Orlando Furioso*

Further reading

Arfaioli, Maurizio. *The Black Bands of Giovanni: Infantry and Diplomacy during the Italian Wars 1526–1528*, Pisa University Press, 2005.
Burke, Peter. *The Fortunes of the Courtier: The European Reception of Castiglione's Cortegiano*, Penn State, 1996.
Chastel, André. *The Sack of Rome*, trans. Beth Archer Princeton University Press, 1983.
Cox, Virginia. *Women's Writing in Italy 1400–1650*, Johns Hopkins University Press, 2008.
Hook, Judith. *The Sack of Rome 1527*, 2nd edition, Palgrave Macmillan, 2004.
Kolsky, Stephen. *Courts and Courtiers in Renaissance Northern Italy*, Ashgate, 2003.
Phillips, Mark. *Francesco Guicciardini: The Historian's Craft*, University of Toronto Press, 1977.

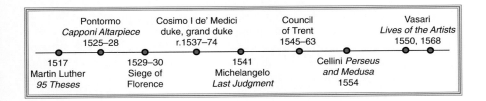

13 Reformations
Political, Religious, and Artistic Upheaval

> Thus the Pope remained in captivity, not even a single lance being broken to free from imprisonment one who had levied so many soldiers, spent infinite sums of money, and stirred almost the entire world into war.
>
> Francesco Guiccardini, *The History of Italy*

In June 1527 Clement VII remained shut within the walls of the Castel Sant'Angelo, essentially a prisoner, while imperial troops ravaged Rome. He signed an unconditional surrender and was forced to pay Charles V an immense ransom by melting down gold from the papal treasury. Clement was finally allowed to leave Rome in December 1527 when, disguised as a merchant, the pope fled to the town of Orvieto. Two years later Charles made his triumphal entry into Italy, and in 1530 was crowned Holy Roman Emperor by the pope, in a grand display of the monarch's absolute authority on the peninsula. So great was his power that Charles could have removed the pope, but rather than further destabilize Christendom, he preferred instead to assume the role of defender of the church and to manipulate the weak and ineffective Clement. No longer seeking alliances with the French, Clement was the emperor's man now, and Charles further assured the pope's loyalty by promoting Medici dynastic interests, especially as those interests coincided with the emperor's own. The south of Italy, known as the Kingdom of the Two Sicilies, belonged to Spain, which would also control the Duchy of Milan from 1536, after Duke Francesco II Sforza died without an heir. As king of Spain, Charles ruled these areas through viceroys, or governors. Charles did not feel the need to intervene militarily to crush the many small states in Italy, but was content to exercise indirect control over the Duchies

DOI: 10.4324/9781003270362-13

280 Reformations

of Ferrara and Mantua, as well as the Republics of Genoa and Lucca. Serene Venice maintained her independence through a delicate diplomatic balancing act—playing French interests off against Spanish and using her naval forces to support Charles's ventures against the Turks. Florence, however, situated in the center of the peninsula, with its long-standing connections to France and its militantly republican citizenry, posed a potential threat. A regime ruled by the Medici, under the supervision of garrisons of Spanish soldiers, would prove to be a more certain way of guaranteeing imperial control of Tuscany.

The Last Florentine Republic, 1527–30

Since the Medici takeover in 1512, a series of authoritarian Medici descendants had ruled the city, and Florentines were restive. By 1519 Lorenzo di Piero de' Medici, to whom Machiavelli dedicated *The Prince*, had died, and was replaced by Giulio de' Medici. Once Giulio left for Rome to become Pope Clement VII, he put the government of Florence into the hands of governors and foreign cardinals whom the people disliked. Florentines fondly remembered the decade of Soderini's government and resented being governed by appointees of an absentee Medici overlord. When on May 11, 1527, news of the Sack of Rome reached Florence, citizens seized the opportunity to throw off the Medici yoke, and Clement from his prison in Sant'Angelo could do nothing to stop them. This final incarnation of the Florentine Republic lasted only three years, but it was the city's most radical popular government since the Ciompi Revolt. The commune accused the Medici of having stolen from the city and then confiscated Medici property, imposing huge fines on family members. Despite their common cause against the Medici, however, the Florentines were, as always, divided into factions. The main divisions now were between patricians, men like Guicciardini who wanted the government run by a small class of educated, well-trained oligarchs, and the democratic faction, which desired broader representation and had strong Savonarolan tendencies. The patrician Niccolò Capponi, who was first elected standardbearer, was soon judged to be too conservative and was ousted in favor of a more populist leader, Francesco Carducci.

While Florentines struggled to devise a constitution that would be satisfactory to all and Savonarolans fought to impose harsh moral legislation, Clement was preparing to take back the city. The pope had been trying for years to reintroduce Medici rule, and now he looked to Charles for aid in taking the city by force. The Florentine Republic was firmly opposed to the Spanish, reaffirming instead the city's traditional ties to France. Many in Florence hoped that with French assistance imperial troops might be still be driven from Italy; but when Francis I signed the Treaty of Cambrai in August 1529, agreeing not to intervene in Italy, it became inevitable that the emperor would attack Florence. The Florentines made preparations for their defense, strengthening fortresses in their dominion cities and building fortifications

Reformations 281

on the hills surrounding Florence. In addition to hiring 10,000 Italian mercenaries, the Republic organized a citizen militia of 10,000—one sixth of the city's population—to defend the city. When a Spanish army of around 30,000 troops appeared in 1529, the Florentines were well-prepared and fought a number of heroic battles. Eventually Spanish commanders decided, however, to starve the city out by siege rather than risk direct engagement. The ensuing ten months were devastating; nearly one-third of the population died of disease and famine. As many residents of the *contado* had taken refuge in Florence, the suffering of the civilian population inside the city was even greater. When the city surrendered in 1530, a sack was avoided, but retaliations were harsh with hundreds executed, imprisoned, or exiled.

1532 The Medici principate established

In 1531 the nineteen-year-old Alessandro de' Medici (1511–1537), generally believed to have been the son of Clement VII, was appointed ruler. By the next year, in 1532, Alessandro was named "Duke of the Florentine Republic." Though the title was ambiguous—it linked a hereditary dukedom with the Florentine Republic—the republican constitution established in 1293 was officially ended, and the priorate, which had lasted almost 250 years, was abolished. The duke himself, incompetent and debauched, was not well liked by the patricians, who went so far as to complain of him to the emperor. When the duke was murdered by his cousin Lorenzino in 1537, Florentines rejoiced, yet there was no uprising to take back the government. Florentine historian Benedetto Varchi (1503–1565) commented that "everyone shared in the general happiness, but no one did anything." Though the former republic might have been re-established at this juncture, the Florentine *popolo* and the elite distrusted one another too much to be able to unite in forming a representative government. Furthermore, the memory of the recent devastating siege was still fresh, and fear of an imperial reprisal strong. The legislative Council of Forty-Eight gathered, and after some debate, they decided to accept Medici rule as preferable to Spanish occupation. They eventually selected Alessandro's distant cousin Cosimo de' Medici (1519–1574) to be "head," (*capo e primario*), rather than "duke," of Florence.

The teenaged Cosimo becomes duke of Florence

The son of Giovanni delle Bande Nere, Cosimo was only seventeen years old at the time he assumed power. The boy had been raised in relative obscurity and no one knew much about him. He was never expected to rule independently, as his supporters, among them Guicciardini, assumed they would be able to control the teenager and shape his government. Once he was appointed, however, Cosimo astonished everyone by dismissing some of the most experienced members of government, including Guicciardini.

From the start, Cosimo, with behind-the-scenes help from his mother, Maria Salviati (1499–1543), shrewdly judged that his true power derived from the emperor, rather than from the Florentine elite. This point was driven home later that same year when, in the summer of 1537, a group of exiled Florentines who challenged the regime were crushed at the Battle of Montemurlo. The leaders of the rebellion, mostly members of Florence's noblest families, were captured, tortured, and dragged before Cosimo, his mother, and the Florentine populace assembled in the Piazza della Signoria where the rebels were publicly beheaded. Impressed with the young Medici's brutal suppression of the rebellion and loyalty to Spain, Charles V conferred the ducal title on Cosimo two months later. Recognizing that Spanish hegemony in Italy was essentially complete, throughout his career Cosimo was staunchly loyal to Charles. In 1539 Charles arranged for Cosimo to marry Eleonora of Toledo (1522–1562), the daughter of the wealthy and influential Spanish viceroy of Naples, linking the Medici even closer to Spain. Through a series of dynastic marriages, the Medici would elevate their prestige by entering the royal houses of Europe—two became queens of France, Catherine de' Medici in 1547 and Maria de' Medici in 1600, and in 1565 Cosimo's son Francesco married Johanna von Habsburg, the daughter of the German emperor. After expanding Florentine territory to encompass all of Tuscany—Florence took Siena in a terrible siege in 1557—Cosimo was named grand duke of Tuscany in 1569 by the pope. The Grand Duchy of Tuscany remained in the hands of the Medici family through the eighteenth century when the last male descendant, Grand Duke Gian Gastone de' Medici, died in 1737.

Michelangelo and the Medici, 1516–34

From early in his life, Michelangelo's career and that of the Medici were intertwined. After completing the frescoes on the ceiling of the Sistine Chapel, Michelangelo was sent by Pope Leo X de' Medici to design the façade of the family church of San Lorenzo in Florence in 1516. Michelangelo spent long months selecting and quarrying marble for this project, which was to include a multitude of sculpted figures, only to have the entire project cancelled in 1520. The pope instead directed Michelangelo to sculpt tombs in the Medici Chapel (New Sacristy) of San Lorenzo for Lorenzo the Magnificent (father of Leo X), Giuliano de' Medici (father of Cardinal Giulio, Clement VII from 1523), as well as for the recently deceased Dukes Lorenzo and Giuliano de' Medici. From 1519 through 1534 Michelangelo worked on the tomb sculptures and architecture of this chapel. Already in his paintings on the ceiling of the Sistine Chapel, the artist had begun to explore the expressive possibilities of the human form, experimenting with contorted poses and exaggerations of musculature, transcending a naturalistic representation of the body. By the time Michelangelo started work in

Figure 13.1 Michelangelo, *Night*, 1526–33, New Sacristy, Basilica of San Lorenzo, Florence

San Lorenzo, he had abandoned the classical balance evident in the *David* to achieve a mood of agitated philosophical reflection in the two pairs of reclining nude sculptures representing *Dawn and Dusk* and *Night and Day* in the New Sacristy. These allegorical figures seem to portray psychological conditions, rather than male and female bodies. The highly polished figure of *Night* appears to glimmer in the moonlight as she twists in troubled sleep, while the tensed, alert figure of *Day* beside her reclines uneasily (Figure 13.1). *Dawn* languidly greets the new day, while *Dusk* gazes downward, lost in contemplation of the oncoming darkness. Neither Christian nor classical in their inspiration, these statues seem to be a soulful expression of the artist's troubled state of mind.

Michelangelo was uncomfortable working for the Medici. Though he never forgot Lorenzo the Magnificent's generosity, the artist was devoted to the Florentine Republic. Accustomed to working for a despotic pope, Michelangelo could not have enjoyed being answerable to a series of insignificant princelings. When the Medici were overthrown in 1527, Michelangelo stopped work on San Lorenzo, and when Florence was threatened by siege, he worked to build defenses for the city. Though he resumed work after the Medici returned to power in Florence in 1531, three years later he left for Rome, leaving the Medici Chapel forever unfinished.

284 Reformations

Martin Luther: A German friar protests

After 1530, with the suppression of the Florentine Republic, Charles V's control of the peninsula was assured and he could turn his attention to pressing problems elsewhere in his vast empire, especially in Germany. When, in 1517, an Augustinian friar named Martin Luther (1483–1546) published his *Ninety-five Theses*, protesting papal abuses, the effect was electric and immediate, as printed copies spread throughout Europe. In this work he criticized the church for selling indulgences. These official documents guaranteed that a sinner whose sins had been pardoned would be released from centuries of suffering in Purgatory. To finance the construction of St. Peter's, a massive fund-raising campaign was launched, and indulgence peddlers hawked their wares throughout the cities and villages of Europe. Luther was condemning the corruption and greed of the papacy, as he would in greater detail in his 1520 work *The Babylonian Captivity of the Church*, but he was also calling into question the role of priestly intervention in salvation. Luther advocated justification by "faith alone," asserting that an individual's salvation depended on their personal relationship with God, who alone granted Grace to a sinner. Followers of Luther, known as "Protestants," came to believe not only that indulgences were worthless, but that the majority of the Sacraments administered by priests were equally unnecessary. Individual priests, who were often themselves sinful and corrupt, could not help anyone attain Grace; instead, clerical intervention was replaced by the "priesthood of all believers." Rather than passively listen to priests reciting liturgy in Latin, Luther believed that all Christians should have access to the Bible in their own language so that they could have direct access to the "word of God."

Humanist origins of the Reformation: "Christian humanism"

Much of the intellectual underpinning of the Protestant Reformation movement in northern Europe was based on the philological research of Italian humanists. The writings of the Dutch humanist Desiderius Erasmus and the movement known as Christian humanism that were so influential on Luther were inconceivable without the accomplishments of earlier Italian humanists. In 1504 Erasmus found a manuscript of Lorenzo Valla's *Annotations to the New Testament*, in which Valla argues that the Latin Bible in use at the time was full of inaccuracies (Chapter 7). So impressed was the Dutch humanist with Valla's text that he had it published the following year.

The edition of the Bible being used in Catholic churches was the Latin version known as the Vulgate, translated by St. Jerome in the early fifth century CE. Writing less than 400 years after Christ, Jerome had admitted that New Testament texts were confused and inaccurate. "If after only four hundred years the river had become so murky," commented Valla, "what need is there to marvel, if after a thousand years—for that is the amount of time that separates us from St. Jerome—that the same river, never having been purged, carries both mud and debris?" To understand exactly what the Bible said, and before it could be translated into vernacular languages, reformers needed to have accurate versions of biblical texts in their original languages. Influenced by humanists such as Valla, Erasmus learned Greek and Hebrew in order to study the Bible. He corresponded with Luther about the importance of reading the Bible in the original languages. Erasmus composed a critical edition of the New Testament with Latin and Greek texts side by side. Printed in 1516, this book was used by Luther for his own 1534 German language translation.

Catholic reformations before the Reformation

Reform in itself was not new; efforts to reform the church also had a long tradition in Italy prior to the Reformation. Before Savonarola, in his "puritan" austerity, launched his attacks on the Roman curia, before his observant Dominican predecessor Antonino Pierozzi initiated episcopal reforms, and before Francis of Assisi gave away his belongings to wander barefooted, in the eleventh century Florentine nobleman Giovanni Gualberto (c.995–1073), the founder of the Vallombrosan order, was already preaching against clerical abuses. Indeed, the tradition of reformation reaches far back; it is as old as the Christian church itself. Paul of Tarsus was the first to refer to reformation as the need to "re-form" one's soul in accordance with Christ. As early as the fourth century CE the Donatists, followers of Donatus, urged clerical reform, claiming that Sacraments administered by a corrupt priest were worthless, a charge refuted by Augustine. The Gregorian Reforms, named after Pope Gregory VII (Chapter 1) and instituted around 1050–80 CE, were intended to correct abuses among the clergy, specifically clerical marriage and the buying of church offices. The mendicant orders arose in the thirteenth century as a response to the need for reform, as did the vigorous involvement of laypeople in Italian religious life. Through their participation in tertiary orders and confraternities, which became particularly pronounced during the fourteenth and fifteenth centuries, laypeople were fulfilling important functions that the church did not adequately provide (Chapter 5).

A more direct approach to reform was taken by the fifteenth-century conciliarists who systematically attempted to initiate changes through the consensus of a broadly based group of theologians and canon lawyers (Chapter 4). However, the movement was suppressed by Renaissance popes, who viewed conciliarism as a threat to their authority. They generally avoided convening a council unless under duress. Thus, Julius II called the Fifth Lateran Council (1512–17), not so much out of a spirit of reform, but to fend off attacks that his enemy King Louis XII of France made on him at the Council of Pisa, organized in 1511. The Fifth Lateran, the last council before the Protestant Reformation, was conducted mainly during the papacy of Leo X. Two monks, Tommaso (Paolo) Giustiniani (1476–1528) and Pietro

286 *Reformations*

(Vincenzo) Querini (1478–1514), in 1513 published a pamphlet addressed to Leo X passionately urging reform of monastic orders, putting limits on papal spending, and condemning absentee bishops. Though the council issued a number of reforming decrees, the conservative attitude of the papacy was summed up in the words of Egidio da Viterbo (Giles of Viterbo 1470–1532) at the opening of the Fifth Lateran: "It is right that people be changed by religion, not religion by people." The official papal position that emerged from that council was that reform would essentially consist in reaffirming the teachings of the church and renewing its institutions without actually altering anything. Despite papal opposition, however, there were strong currents of dissatisfaction among the Italian laity, and some members of the clergy who were also clamoring for change.

The Church reacts: Catholic versus Protestant

The Catholic Church was forced to respond to the Lutheran movement under pressure from Emperor Charles V, for the Protestant revolt was tearing the empire apart. Despite Leo X's excommunication of Martin Luther in 1520, the movement continued to grow and was becoming increasingly vocal and violent. In 1524, the so-called German Peasants' War broke out, spreading through the southern and central parts of the empire. Common people were demanding not only to select their own priests and to have access to the Bible in their own language; they also refused to pay taxes, called for improved justice, and an end to serfdom. The rebellion was brutally suppressed, but in the meantime many nobles had also joined the Protestant movement, fragmenting authority within the empire. For some years Charles had watched as the situation in the German-speaking portions of his realm deteriorated; it was thus with the utmost urgency that he pressed Pope Clement to call a church council in 1530.

Not only did Clement fail to organize the promised council, delaying year after year, but he actually hastened the split between Catholic and Protestant churches by refusing the English King Henry VIII's petition to annul his marriage to Catherine of Aragon. Catherine was the aunt of Charles V, who opposed the divorce, and Clement complied with the emperor's wishes. Despite being a devout Catholic, Henry's pressing need to produce an heir won out over his obedience to the pope and caused him to break off from Rome, forming the Anglican Church in England in 1534. When Clement died that same year, never having convened a council, it would be up to his successor Pope Paul III Farnese (r.1534–49) to confront the Protestant challenge. In 1541 Paul sent the reforming Cardinal Gasparo Contarini (Chapter 8) as his representative to meet with Protestant leaders at the Diet of Regensburg (Ratisbon). A former Venetian ambassador to the empire, Contarini worked with theologians to reconcile differences between the opposing sides. Ultimately neither side accepted the compromises worked out at Regensburg; perhaps by this time positions were too deeply held, the

Reformations 287

battle lines drawn. In spite of the failure to reach an accord at Regensburg, Pope Paul III continued with the project of reform by calling a council—one of the most important in church history, with long-reaching consequences.

The Council of Trent, 1545–63

Paul III Farnese must have seemed like an unlikely individual to spearhead a bold new reform movement. Having spent a portion of his youth at Lorenzo de' Medici's palace, Paul was related to Alexander VI Borgia through his sister, who had been Borgia's mistress. Farnese greatly admired Alexander VI, who had promoted the young man's career. Paul III has been called the "last Renaissance pope," as he shared many traits with his immediate predecessors, shamelessly advancing the careers of his nephews, one of whom, in a Borgia-like move, he established as Duke of Parma. As both the beneficiary and distributor of papal largesse, Paul could hardly have been expected to crack down on church abuses such as simony and nepotism. Yet it was during his papacy that the most comprehensive reform program in Catholic history began. In 1540 the pope approved the Jesuit Order (Society of Jesus) under the leadership of Spanish nobleman Ignatius Loyola (1491–1556). The Jesuit order was structured by Loyola, a former soldier, with military discipline to carry out the reform agenda of the church; the general of the order was answerable only to the pope. Disciplined and unswervingly loyal, the Jesuits were dedicated to preaching, listening to confessions, education, and missionary work; their impact both in Europe and throughout the world would be immense. In 1542 Paul established the Roman Inquisition (Chapter 15), which along with the Jesuit order were powerful instruments for enforcing the dictates of the Council of Trent.

Paul III had pledged to call a council at the time of his election, yet it took over a decade before the group could actually meet. First, deciding on a location was complicated; many cities in Italy and Germany were proposed, but all these locations were unsatisfactory to one side or the other. Eventually the parties agreed to meet in Trent, at the time a free city within the empire, located in the far north of Italy halfway between Verona and Innsbruck. Interrupted by wars and forced to relocate on a number of occasions because of the spread of disease, the council, which stretched across three decades and four papacies, covered a broad range of topics. The meetings, in which sometimes as many as 450 delegates participated, were often stormy. The council took a two-pronged approach to reform. There were both practical issues of institutional reform within the church as well as theoretical matters of doctrine to be decided. Though certain institutional issues, such as establishing seminaries for improving the education of priests, were fairly easy to agree upon, others, touching on the privileges of the curia, were more contentious. The decision that a bishop, cardinal, or other prelate should hold no more than one benefice and that he must reside in his diocese or parish was bitterly debated before being passed.

Doctrinal issues, however, began to take precedence, as the Council of Trent responded to specific Protestant charges. Martin Luther had said that a believer could be saved "by faith alone," implying that most prayers, rituals, and veneration of holy objects had no place in religious observance. Now the delegates at Trent systematically began to examine the many beliefs and social practices, which in addition to the teachings of the Bible, had accumulated over centuries. In most of its decisions the council came down on the side of tradition. Thus it decided that saints and relics would continue to be venerated as they had been for centuries.

The Vulgate Bible: "No one is to dare or presume to reject it"

As the text of the Bible itself had come under scrutiny, the council had to establish which edition to accept as authentic. The council decided that Jerome's Vulgate version of the Bible, despite humanists' criticisms of the translation, was the appropriate one to use; once again the reason was tradition. As the text of the council's decree reads:

> The said old and vulgate edition, which, by the lengthened usage of so many years, has been approved of in the Church, [must] be, in public lectures, disputations, sermons and expositions, held as authentic; and that no one is to dare or presume to reject it under any pretext whatever.

In one stroke, the Council of Trent dismissed humanists' thorough philological research and decreed that laypeople were not to challenge the words of the Latin Bible. Any portions of Biblical texts that were confusing would be explained in sermons by a priest, who would "expound and interpret the said sacred Scripture" for the faithful.

The Sacraments and the role of the priest reaffirmed

Regarding the Sacraments, the representatives at Trent reaffirmed all seven, while the Lutherans retained only two: Baptism and the Eucharist (the Lord's Supper). Even in matters on which both sides agreed, there was a complete lack of compromise on particulars. Both Protestants and Catholics agreed that the Eucharist was the most sacred moment during the Mass, when the faithful re-enacted the moment when Christ offered the Apostles bread and wine, as his flesh and blood, participating in Christ's sacrifice. Certain Protestants insisted that members of the congregation also drink from the chalice, which was forbidden by the Catholic theologians, who claimed that only the officiating clergy ought to drink Christ's blood. Moreover, the very nature of the ceremony was contested, Protestants asserting that it was not the real body and blood that was being consumed, but that the ceremony was merely a commemoration of Christ's Passion. The Catholics insisted on their traditional position, asserted at the Fourth Lateran Council in 1215, that Christ

Reformations 289

was actually present in the Eucharist. They claimed that Transubstantiation ("change of substance") occurred at the moment that the priest elevated the Host, changing the wafer into flesh and the wine into blood.

Social consequences of Trent

Although decisions regarding abstract concepts such as Transubstantiation may seem to have little impact on people's lives, there is no denying the powerful and long-lasting social ramifications of dogma established at Trent. For instance, the Tridentine[1] decree reaffirming matrimony as a Sacrament made marriage a religious, rather than civil, union between a couple. By insisting upon a priest's officiating at the marriage ceremony, the church guaranteed that it would play an ever greater role in people's lives, as it did by increasing the emphasis on Confession. According to Catholic dogma, absolution, or forgiveness of sins, could be achieved only with the aid of a priest who listened to a Confession in which the sinner "examined himself diligently, and searched all the folds and recesses of his conscience." Confessions had previously been carried out once a year, usually at Lent, but after Trent the faithful were encouraged to confess more frequently. An event that had taken place in the semi-public setting of a corner of a church was relocated during the sixteenth century to enclosed confessional booths, where intimate details could be whispered through a grate to the priest listening on the other side. These priests were better trained, and ever on the lookout for transgressions, especially of a sexual nature. Though certain sexual sins, such as sodomy, had been vociferously condemned from the pulpit (Chapter 10) and sporadically punished, before Trent such private offences were often overlooked. Trent ended the comparatively free and easy attitude toward believers' private lives. It was now mandated that sins, which had been formerly left largely as a matter between an individual and God, had to be resolved through priestly intervention, giving the church ever greater control over men and women's actions, even in their bedrooms.

Clerical reform and full enclosure of nuns

Just as life for the laity was more strictly controlled, so too was that of the religious. The lives of priests were more closely monitored, and clerical celibacy was absolutely affirmed. The behavior of members of monastic orders came under closer scrutiny as well. Female tertiaries were now required to take full vows, and restrictions were tightened on convents: "for no nun, after her profession, shall it be lawful to go out of her convent, even for a brief period, under any pretext whatever." This decision was taken, it was

---

1 Adjective meaning "pertaining to the Council of Trent."

290   *Reformations*

argued, for the protection of the women's chastity and to correct abuses, but it limited women's participation in acts of charity in the community. All forms of popular, spontaneous piety came under scrutiny, and many practices were condemned as superstitious or inspired by the devil. Caterina of Racconigi, one of the "living saints" (Chapter 5) in 1512 was accused of witchcraft and heresy because of her prophetic visions, stigmata, and miracles she allegedly worked.[2] The era when such local holy women proliferated came to an end after the decrees of Trent. Though the church still recognized female holiness after Trent, unsubstantiated claims of working miracles were investigated and modes of spirituality that involved mystical experiences and ecstatic visions were discouraged.

The rigid Tridentine doctrines adopted by the Roman Catholic Church would have a dramatic impact on the lives of Catholics for generations to come. No aspect of social or cultural life, music, literature, science, or art would be untouched by the decisions of the Council of Trent.

Michelangelo in Rome 1534–64

When the *Last Judgment* was uncovered, Michelangelo proved not only that he had triumphed over the first artisans who had worked in the chapel, but that he also wished to triumph over himself in the vault he had made so famous ... how truly happy are those who have seen this stupendous wonder of our century ... Most happy and fortunate Paul III ... !

Giorgio Vasari, *Life of Michelangelo*

Whereas many Protestants criticized the worship of sacred images as idolatry, even destroying paintings and sculptures of Christ, the Virgin Mary, and the saints (iconoclasm), the Council of Trent reaffirmed the role of religious art to instruct and inspire the faithful. Catholic theologians were nevertheless sensitive to the critics who accused Renaissance artists of suffusing their images with pagan symbols and sensuality. When the church began to condemn the classically inspired celebration of the naked human body that figured so prominently in Renaissance art, one of the first artists to be attacked was Michelangelo.

In the year of his death, Clement VII had discussed with Michelangelo the idea of working on another large fresco project for the Sistine Chapel. When Paul III became pope, one of his first commissions was to hire the artist to paint the scene of the *Last Judgment* above the altar. To paint this fresco, the pope gave Michelangelo permission to destroy the pre-existing frescoes by Perugino on that wall, as well as two lunettes above it, previously painted by Michelangelo himself as part of the ceiling design. Though

---

2 Racconigi was successfully defended by Gianfrancesco Pico della Mirandola, author of *Strix* (Chapter 15), not to be confused with his uncle Giovanni Pico della Mirandola.

the theme of the last day, when the dead will rise from their graves and be judged, had been treated by many artists (see Chapter 1 for Giotto's *Last Judgment*), never before had it been depicted with such raw emotional power. Michelangelo covered the immense wall with depictions of mostly naked human bodies—writhing, cringing, some plunging downward, others surging upward. Everywhere is movement, panic, and anxiety, as figures of varying proportions respond to the cataclysmic event. The largest figure, dominating the upper central portion of the painting, is an impossibly muscular, nearly nude Christ. Rather than the sedate, bearded figure usually portrayed on a throne surrounded by the seated Apostles, this Christ is young and vigorous. He rises, swiveling, his right hand raised in a commanding gesture to cast down the damned, drawing the saved to him with the left, with a kind of magnetic attraction. While some familiar iconography is present—angels blowing trumpets and demons waiting below in the fiery pit—Michelangelo has stripped this scene of many of its traditional symbols. The angels have no wings; the saints have no haloes; and rather than sinners being skewered on red-hot pokers or gnawed by demons, the horror of damnation registers on an emotional level. Despite their muscularity, the hundreds of nude bodies have an oddly touching vulnerability to them; they have been stripped to expose the fragility of the human condition. The viewer's eye moves constantly between the monumental scenario of humanity's last day on earth to close-ups of individual human drama. Standing apart from the others, one man on the lower right crouches, covering a part of his face with his hand; his one visible eye gazes out in shock and despair.

Michelangelo's stature as an artist was such that he was given free rein to express his striking new vision on this wall, as he had been on the ceiling of the chapel. Between the time it was commissioned, however, and when the painting was finished in 1541, the mood in Rome had greatly changed. Because this immense fresco was painted on the wall of one of the most significant locations in Christendom—the pope's private chapel—and precisely because Michelangelo was such a prominent artist, the work drew an enormous amount of attention. Critics charged that his portrayal of the *Last Judgment* contained a number of theological inaccuracies. Others were outraged at the nudity not only of the sinners but also of the saints, some of them bent in obscene postures that violated decorum. After the Council of Trent, it was decided to hide the genitals of the figures with painted loincloths and veils. In several places, portions of plaster with the offending figures were actually gouged out and re-painted by the artist's assistants.

Fortunately, Michelangelo did not live to see his masterpiece thus vandalized. But in the later years of his life, he was affected by the prevailing spiritual mood. Over the course of his lifetime Michelangelo wrote over 300 poems. By turns philosophical, earthy, spiritual, playful, and erotic, these poems are among the most expressive in the Italian language. They also open a window into Michelangelo's feelings about his art. In a fragment from around 1552 he wrote: "In such servitude, in such tedium, and with false

292   Reformations

ideas and great danger to my soul, here am I sculpting divine things." Such was Michelangelo's deepening spiritual despair, that he could no longer find consolation in creating art. During this same period he concluded a sonnet with the words:

> Neither painting nor sculpting can calm the soul,
> Turned towards that divine love, as He opened His arms,
> To take us upon the cross in His embrace.

Aside from a number of sculptures, many left unfinished or mutilated by Michelangelo himself, the artist spent the last thirty years of his life focused mostly on architecture. His painting may have been condemned by many in Rome, but popes found Michelangelo's ability to conceive of grand projects, which promoted the glory of Rome and the papacy, too useful not to employ him. Michelangelo completed Paul III's Palazzo Farnese, begun by Antonio da Sangallo the Younger. He also designed the layout for the renovation of the Campidoglio—the civic center of Rome on the Capitoline Hill. Michelangelo designed the New Palace and the façade of the Conservator's Palace, creating a harmonious, impressive effect. And most important, he was made chief architect of St. Peter's in 1546. Although he did not live long enough to see it completed, it was Michelangelo's design that mostly prevailed in the final building (Chapter 14). For the next 300 years, hardly a dome anywhere in the world would be designed without reference to this work.

Florentine mannerism: The avant-garde art of Pontormo and Rosso

Michelangelo not only looms as an immense figure to us today; he also cast a great shadow in his own day. Considered by contemporaries to be the most talented artist alive, Michelangelo's sketches were collected by fellow artists and kept as prized trophies to be studied and copied. Those artists living in Florence during Michelangelo's last stay there (1516–34) were particularly influenced by his work. It was during this period that a new style of art was being born in Italy that has come to be known as mannerism. In the 1520s, painters and sculptors a generation younger than Michelangelo began to produce works in a startling new style that, while recognizing the achievements of High Renaissance art, deliberately upset its classical balance. Rather than idealizing nature, these edgy artists distorted and exaggerated it to heighten the emotional impact, even violating laws of gravity and perspective.

Pontormo's (Jacopo Carucci 1494–1557), *Capponi Chapel Altarpiece* (1525–28 Church of Santa Felicita, Florence; Figure 13.2), is filled with a flurry of figures, stretched and twisted in unnatural poses. Drawing the eye back and forth across the canvas are cool blue pastel tones and luminescent pinks, which heighten the sense of movement. The entire weight of the dead body is born by two precariously poised figures in the front, who stare blankly

Figure 13.2 Jacopo Pontormo, *Capponi Chapel Altarpiece*, 1525–28, Church of Santa Felicita, Florence

in anguish out of the painting as does the artist himself, in a self-portrait in the rear, righthand corner. Although there is an indication of stone in the foreground and blue sky with clouds in the back, it is impossible to tell where the figures are in space, whether they are standing on solid ground or floating. The physical instability, combined with the pained, confused expressions and dramatic gestures, create an unsettling effect. Known interchangeably by the titles *Deposition*, *Lamentation*, or *Entombment*, depending on the viewer's interpretation of the artist's narrative, even the very meaning of this crucial moment in Christ's Passion is up for grabs.

Born the same year as Pontormo, Rosso Fiorentino (Giovanni Battista di Jacopo 1494–1540) developed a distinct style that was equally revolutionary. Unlike Pontormo's work in the Capponi Chapel, the subject of his *Deposition* (1521 Pinacoteca, Volterra), is clear. However, Rosso as well, breaks away from naturalism, and has depicted the central figure of Christ's body being lowered from the cross in a livid green. An eerie light starkly illuminates the almost cubist forms of the onlookers, caught in lurching positions against an unreal backdrop. In other works, such as his *Dead Christ* (1524–57 Museum of Fine Arts, Boston), Rosso opted for a more naturalistic treatment, though the sacred theme is intermixed with eroticism, due to the sensual curve of Christ's naked body in the foreground, the smile on his face, and the attractive androgynous teenaged angels that surround him.

Though mannerism is generally associated with Florence, in other regions of Italy there were artists experimenting with the new style. The painter Francesco Mazzola (1503–1540)—known as Parmigianino because he came from Parma—adopted a similar sense of instability and distortion in his *Madonna of the Long Neck* (1534–40 Uffizi). The Madonna, whose neck, fingers, and legs are gracefully elongated, gazes down at the enormous baby splayed across her lap. The limp, naked child, whose position evokes that of the dead Christ in Michelangelo's Vatican *Pietà*, seems to be slipping downward off the eddying folds of his mother's robe. Meanwhile, the rosy cheeks and smile playing around the lips of the Virgin, her gown modeled so closely as to reveal a nipple and her navel, as well as the semi-clothed youths looking on, all add, as in Rosso's *Dead Christ*, an erotic charge to the sacred theme. Like Pontormo, Rosso Fiorentino, and other mannerists, Parmigianino was breaking with tradition and consciously experimenting with a jarring new style of painting.

The artist as courtier: Agnolo Bronzino and others

Mannerist artists were in part reacting to the art of Leonardo, Raphael, and Michelangelo. Challenged to create something different and to display an original style, they broke out in fresh new directions. At the same time, they were also producing art designed to satisfy the tastes of their patrons. And in Florence, the most important patron was the duke. Cosimo had succeeded in his *coup d'état*, and he did not want Florentines to be surrounded by works of art in the old style, like the *David*, which might inspire republican sentiments. Thus, he and the Duchess Eleonora promoted art that glorified their family; many artists produced little more than heavy-handed propaganda for Medici rule. Bartolomeo Ammanati's (1511–1592) ponderous *Neptune* (1550–75) and Baccio Bandinelli's (1488–1560) lumpy *Hercules and Cacus* (1525–34) that flank the *David* in front of the Palazzo Vecchio cannot compete with Michelangelo's masterpiece artistically, but their sheer bulk transmits a message of Medici power. Other artists patronized by the Medici dukes created works of delicacy and beauty. Cosimo commissioned

Benvenuto Cellini (1500–1571) to create his graceful bronze statue of *Perseus and Medusa* (1545–54 Loggia dei Lanzi, Florence), and later, Cosimo's son Ferdinando I had the masterpiece of the mannerist sculptor Giambologna (Giovanni da Bologna 1529–1608) placed beside it. In Giambologna's *Rape of a Sabine* (1581–83) three intertwined figures spiral impossibly upward with rhythmic movement and seemingly effortless grace.

Unlike Michelangelo, these artists were content to work under the patronage of the Medici court, and in the process, they were becoming courtiers themselves. Like his teacher Pontormo, Agnolo Bronzino (Agnolo di Cosimo Mariano di Tori 1503–1572) benefited from Medici patronage. The artist painted many refined and elegant portraits of the duke and duchess, their children, as well as courtiers. His work displays yet another side of mannerism, a self-conscious virtuosity that is an end in itself. While revealing little of the sitters' inner lives, Bronzino's portraits display an incomparable polished elegance—the artist lavishes minute attention on a swath of brocaded fabric, a piece of glinting armor, or a finger carelessly holding the place in a book—that is both aloof and arresting.

The one artist who beyond all others served the duke's grandiose ambitions was Giorgio Vasari (1511–1574). A mannerist painter and architect, Vasari filled Florentine halls and ceilings with painted representations of Cosimo's glory, designed theatrical and processional displays, and constructed important buildings for the duke. His first commission from Cosimo was to redesign the Palazzo della Signoria or Palazzo dei Priori (today known as the Palazzo Vecchio or "old palace"), as a private residence for Cosimo and his family. Vestiges of the republican government were altered by Vasari to suit the new regime; thus he converted the Salone dei Cinquecento into a grand reception hall for the duke, decorated with paintings of Florence's history and culminating in the *Apotheosis of Cosimo I* overhead, where Cosimo sits on a pile of puffy clouds being crowned by an allegorical figure representing Florence. In 1559 Vasari began work on the Uffizi (offices) for the duke as well. This building, connected to the Palazzo Vecchio, brought together into a central location all the scattered government ministries and served as the visual representation of the power concentrated under Cosimo's rule. Inspired by Michelangelo's architectural innovations, Vasari devised a new idiom for architecture.

The Lives of the Artists: Vasari invents art history

Vasari's greatest contribution to Renaissance culture was not a building or a painting, but a book. First published in 1550, and later expanded in 1568, Vasari's *The Lives of the Artists* was a pioneering work in the field of art history. In this work Vasari not only tells the stories of the lives of Italian painters, sculptors, and architects from the time of Cimabue in the thirteenth century, to his day, listing their major works, but discusses artistic style, examining how it changes and evolves over time. Despite occasional

296   Reformations

inaccuracies and a bias toward Florentine artists, Vasari laid the groundwork for modern art history; his book is still essential reading today.

Vasari devised a periodization for Italian Renaissance art, which although it has been contested, is still with us; it divides Italian art into three periods—early, middle, and high. The fourteenth century produced artists, above all Giotto, whom Vasari describes as "the first lights." The ancients were first re-born in these artists who were focused on imitating nature. They lacked, however, the rules for correct measurement, as well as a lightness of touch. The fifteenth century saw an increase in technical skills as well as gracefulness, but Vasari judges the work of quattrocento artists, such as Botticelli and Ghirlandaio, to be "*secca, cruda e tagliente*" (dry, rough, and harsh), compared with the best work of artists of his own day. It was not until his own century that the third phase, originated by Leonardo da Vinci, came into being. Vasari claims that the arts reached their perfect form in works that merged spontaneity and judgment to produce the quality of *grazia* (grace). Vasari names Raphael as the artist who possesses this quality to the highest degree. Much like Castiglione's concept of *sprezzatura*, Vasari believes that displaying too much effort destroys grace; according to him, the "excessive study" displayed in quattrocento art made it inferior to that which came after.

In addition to *grazia*, an artist must also have *invenzione*—the poetic invention to tell a story in art. *Disegno* (drawing) is equally important. Florentine artists were famed for doing careful drawings before painting, whereas Venetians laid color on the canvas and built up with it. However, even though the technical aspects of *disegno* are important—respecting perspective and the proportions of the human body—these aspects can also be moderated using *giudizio* (judgment); for measurement alone cannot produce great art. All these elements combined make up the *maniera* (style) of the artist. The one artist whom Vasari praises most highly is Michelangelo, because he possessed all the above qualities, reaching perfection in not just one, but in three art forms: painting, sculpture, and architecture.

Vasari was a good historian; he demonstrated how each era builds on the accomplishments of the last. He also attempted to show that artists from the past are not necessarily therefore inferior, as no artist can be judged separate from his age. His three-part periodization of Renaissance art, however, created difficulties. Based on a biological model, indicating a period of birth, then another of growth, and finally one of maturity, Vasari was faced with the problem of what comes after the third phase—the decline or death of art? Vasari included many contemporary artists in *The Lives*, among them his own teacher Andrea del Sarto (Andrea d'Agnolo 1486–1530). In the second edition of the book, published after the death of Michelangelo, he names various Florentine mannerists, whom he praises for their innovations. The term "mannerism" derives from the Vasarian use of the word *maniera* and the heavy emphasis Vasari places on *maniera*—on an artist developing an individual style. This individual style no longer depended on imitation, either of the ancients, or of nature. Vasari exalts the Promethean role of the artist as creative genius, setting the highest possible standard for art for generations to come.

Benvenuto Cellini's *Autobiography*: The artist invents himself

> "My lord, this Benvenuto of yours is a terrible fellow."
> "He's much more terrible than you imagine."
>
> Exchange between the Ambassador from Lucca and Duke Cosimo from Cellini's *Autobigraphy*

Because of their artistic rivalry, one contemporary who Vasari barely mentions in *The Lives* is sculptor Benvenuto Cellini—and he certainly does not refer to him as a genius. But it does not really matter, for Cellini himself informs us of his genius in his *Autobiography*. In this supreme work of Renaissance self-fashioning, Cellini presents himself as a warrior, lover, and daring artistic innovator. He describes his early years of apprenticeship as a goldsmith; his constant striving for artistic perfection; his efforts to stretch himself as a creative individual; and to prove himself in the competitive world of Italian Renaissance artists.

In the *Autobiography*, he models himself on "that great Michelangelo Buonarroti, from whom alone and from no one else I have learnt all I know." Cellini, if anything, exaggerates his own *terribilità* to heighten the comparison with the maestro. He relates frustration at being forced to make baubles, when what he yearns for is the opportunity to create an awe-inspiring sculpture. And no one has ever given a richer description of the agonies and excitement involved in giving birth to a work of art than in the passage where he describes his casting of the bronze *Perseus and Medusa* (1554, Loggia dei Lanzi, Florence). Though he served the Grand Duke of Florence, Cellini's self-representation as a god-like artist and a giver of life to inanimate metal indicates the heroic proportions the role of the artist had acquired in the Renaissance.

Considerations: The sixteenth-century reformations put in perspective

Art was simultaneously under attack and blossoming in adventurous new directions. No sooner had artists begun to acquire new respect for their profession and social standing, than the Catholic Church began to crack down on artistic freedom, censoring no less a figure than Michelangelo. However, the Catholic Church continued to promote and patronize the arts, defending the role of beautiful images in devotion, against Protestant attacks condemning religious art as idolatry.

By the mid-sixteenth century battle lines between Catholic and Protestant were drawn, though as late as the Diet of Regensburg in 1541 there had been hopes of reaching a compromise. Some spark may still have been flickering when the delegates met at the first session of the Council of Trent in 1545.

298 Reformations

However, it soon became evident that neither side was going to cede any ground. Rather than effecting a reconciliation, the Council of Trent was forever to divide Protestant from Catholic, which from this point became known as "Roman Catholic."

What was the spirit driving the Council of Trent? Did the pope ever intend to heal the rift by meeting the Protestants halfway? Under attack on many fronts, the primary concern of the papacy was to maintain its authority over the Catholic Church. Though the Council did enact many reforms, the promised reform, "in head and members," did not ultimately affect the head itself. If the church had not been forced into a defensive position by the Lutherans, would reform have taken place? Catholic historians and theologians have argued that many reforms put forward by Martin Luther had long been debated within the Catholic Church, and reform movements were already well under way when the Protestant challenge emerged. They point, for instance, to Gian Matteo Giberti (1495–1543), who was bishop of Verona between 1528 and 1543. There Giberti instituted many reforms, which anticipated Tridentine decisions. Historians aligned with this point of view prefer to call the movement the Catholic Reformation, as opposed to the Counter Reformation. Opponents argue that whatever reforms had previously been under consideration, the Lutheran attack polarized the debate and changed the focus of reform entirely. From the advent of the Protestant Reformation, it is argued, the Catholic Church took a dramatically reactionary direction that can only be termed "Counter Reformation." The lack of consensus on the terminology, which persists to this day, indicates that the controversy debated at Trent lives on.

Since this is a book about Renaissance Italy, it is not the place to discuss why or how the Protestant Reformation occurred in Germany. It is, however, important to consider why Protestantism never caught on in Italy. Why did Italians put up with the abuses that they knew existed within the church? Many Italians, not only laypeople but also churchmen such as Gasparo Contarini, were initially sympathetic to Lutheran ideas. But the Italian elite had vested interests in maintaining the status quo. There were 263 bishoprics in the Italian Peninsula, 10 in Sicily and 18 in Sardinia, compared to 131 in France and 67 in the British Isles. These bishoprics as well as the multitude of smaller benefices provided income to many Italians. Guicciardini, who made his fortune as a papal governor in the Romagna, wrote:

> I can think of no one who dislikes the ambition, avarice, and the effeminacy of priests more than I do … Nevertheless, the positions I have held under several popes has forced me, out of my own self-interest, to love their greatness. If it were not for this consideration, I would have loved Martin Luther as much as I love myself.

Aside from those, like Guicciardini, who owed their livelihood to the church, given the widespread anti-clerical sentiment that existed in Italy, why

Reformations 299

didn't Renaissance Italians become Protestants? The simplest answer to that question is that the majority of Italians did not want to relinquish tradition—the beloved images of the Madonna, the familiar stories of saints' lives, and the ceremonies that had become an intricate part of the texture of their lives. Cultural practices that have grown and developed over centuries cannot be easily uprooted, no matter what reason may argue.

Certainly, however, if an agreement on reform had been reached at Regensburg or before, much human suffering could have been avoided; not only the persecutions of the Roman Inquisition (Chapter 15) but the deaths of hundreds of thousands of people during the European religious wars of the sixteenth through seventeenth centuries might not have occurred. Whether it is called the Catholic Reformation, the Counter Reformation, or the Catholic Revival, the movement initiated at Trent by Pope Paul III would introduce a period of intolerance and repression that the greatest minds in Italy would struggle against for generations. However, the movement cannot be judged in a vacuum; it must be viewed against the Europe-wide context of intolerance and oppression during the period of the Wars of Religion. Martin Luther defended the nobles who in 1526 brutally suppressed popular rebellion in the German Peasants' War, resulting in 100,000 deaths. Luther justified the slaughter, writing:

> [the peasants] disguise their hideous, abominable sins with the Gospel, calling themselves Christian brethren; they take oaths and swear allegiance, and force people to take part in such outrages with them. They thereby become the worst blasphemers and violators of God's holy name, honoring and serving the devil, under the pretense of the Gospel; thus they deserve death in body and soul ten times over.

Luther promised that anyone who died fighting the rebellious peasants would go directly to Heaven. In Calvinist Geneva, the Spanish scientist, physician, and humanist Michael Servetus (1509–1553) was burned at the stake for his theological writings opposing the concept of the Trinity. It was John Calvin (1509–1564) himself who urged Servetus's death. The Protestant Calvin, not a Roman Catholic, wrote the following words:

> Whoever contends that wrong is done to heretics and blasphemers by inflicting punishment on them ties himself to their blasphemous crimes. Man's authority does not enter here, but God who speaks and we hear clearly what He commands for His Church for all time.

Though the Catholic Church in the sixteenth century set in motion a policy of systematic repression of free-thinking, vigorously persecuting those who resisted, it is important to remember that throughout history intolerance has never been the exclusive monopoly of any one religion. Nevertheless, it is against

300   *Reformations*

this background of religious repression that we will explore the achievements of late Italian Renaissance art, music, and science in the following chapters.

Sourcebook

Luigi Gonzaga, *Account of Charles V's Italian Sojourn and Coronation*
Niccolò Martelli, *Letter to Rugasso*
Decrees of the Council of Trent, Session XXV
Michelangelo Buonarroti, *Last Judgment*
Michelangelo Buonarroti, *Sonnets*
Lorenzo Pagni, *Letter to Pierfrancesco Riccio*
Agnolo Bronzino, *Portrait of Bia*
Giorgio Vasari, *The Life of Leonardo da Vinci*
Giorgio Vasari, *The Life of Andrea del Sarto*
Benvenuto Cellini, *Autobiography*
Benvenuto Cellini, *Perseus and Medusa*

Further reading

Assonitis, Alessio and Henk Th. Van Veen, eds. *A Companion to Cosimo I de' Medici*. Brill, 2022.
Falciani, Carlo and Antonio Natali, eds. *The Cinquecento in Florence: "Modern Manner" and Counter-Reformatio*n, Mandragora, 2017.
Hall, Marcia. *After Raphael: Painting in Central Italy in the Sixteenth Century*, Cambridge University Press, 1999.
O'Malley, John W. *Trent and All That: Renaming Catholicism in the Early Modern Era*, Harvard University Press, 2000.
Rebecchini, Guido. *The Rome of Paul III (1534–1549): Art, Ritual and Urban Renewal*, Harvey Miller, 2020.
Shearman, John. *Mannerism*, Penguin, 1967.
Wallace, William E. *Michelangelo, God's Architect: The Story of His Final Years and Greatest Masterpiece*, Princeton University Press, 2019.

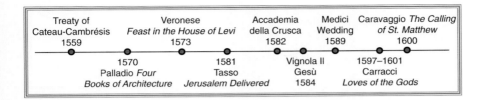

14 The "Imperial Renaissance"
Italy during the Spanish Peace

> Italy has not felt the oppression [by Spanish rule] that was feared, rather for many years now she has been enjoying even greater happiness than ever before.
> Scipione Ammirato, *Discourses on Tacitus*, 1594

In these words, historian Scipione Ammirato (1531–1601) summed up the sentiments of many who lived through this period, which some have called the *pax hispanica* (Spanish peace), comparing the peace provided by the Spanish Empire to that of the Roman Empire under the so-called *pax romana* (Chapter 1). During the second half of the sixteenth century, the entire peninsula fell under the political domination of Spain, through a complex web of alliances that tightly bound the destinies of the Italian states to the Habsburg dynasty until the nineteenth century.

The Habsburgs: A spectacular matrimonial conglomerate

In 1556 Charles V abdicated his throne in favor of his son Philip II (1527–1598). Charles at that time divided the immense territories of the Spanish Empire into two parts. As demanded by the German electors, he gave the lands of the Holy Roman Empire and the imperial title to his brother Ferdinand (1503–1564), while the larger portion including Spain, the New World, the Kingdom of the Two Sicilies, and Milan he left to his son Philip; Charles outlined strategies for governing the peninsula in his *Political Testament to Philip II*.

Charles saw to it that the Italian Peninsula became crisscrossed with a web of political obligations and family ties to the Habsburgs. Apart from the

DOI: 10.4324/9781003270362-14

302 The "Imperial Renaissance"

Map 14.1 Italy in 1559

approximately half of Italy that Spain possessed outright, the rest was effectively under Habsburg control by this time (Map 14.1). A part of imperial strategy in the peninsula was creating alliances with the Italian principates and duchies through marriage alliances, prompting historian Paula Sutter Fichtner to refer to the Habsburgs as a "spectacular matrimonial conglomerate." In addition to the duke of Florence's marriage to Eleonora of Toledo, Cosimo's son Grand Duke Francesco de' Medici was joined in marriage to Charles's niece. Guglielmo Gonzaga, duke of Mantua (1538–1587) was

The "Imperial Renaissance" 303

married in 1561 to yet another niece, as was the duke of Ferrara, Alfonso II d'Este (1533–1597) in 1565.

One state not mentioned in the emperor's testament is the Duchy of Savoy. Located in the northwestern corner of Italy, encompassing much of today's region of Piedmont and extending to Nice in southern France and up to Lake Geneva in the north, for generations Savoy–Piedmont had been in the possession of the French. It became independent in 1559, although Torino and other cities were heavily occupied by Spanish troops. The region was useful as a buffer state for Spain, upon whose support the duke of Savoy depended; his son Carlo Emanuele I (1562–1630) married the granddaughter of Charles V in 1585.

Keeping the troublesome republics subdued

Unlike the principalities, the republics could not be bound to Spain by means of dynastic marriages. The tiny republics of both Lucca and Siena were potential problems for Spain, as they were located in the strategically important region of Tuscany. Being so near to Florence, they might harbor Florentine exiles and threaten the stability of the Duchy. Siena sealed its fate in 1552 by destroying the Spanish fortress built there; the Republic was crushed by Cosimo I, and thereafter it was absorbed into the Grand Duchy of Tuscany. Lucca, on the other hand, miraculously kept to itself and maintained its independence until 1796. Genoa was by this point a republic in name alone. Over the course of its tumultuous history, Genoa had fluctuated between authoritarian and republican regimes. When in 1528 Andrea Doria (1466–1560) seized power, abandoning France as an ally in favor of Charles V, the city's fortunes became closely linked to Spain, and thereafter it played a pivotal role in the empire. Genoa lent its maritime resources to Spain, greatly increasing Spain's naval power; and because Genoa's trading in the eastern Mediterranean had been interrupted by the growing Ottoman presence there, its merchants were highly dependent on trade with the Spanish Empire for their survival. Genoese bankers in the meantime had become extremely powerful, floating loans to the Spanish government in between shipments of gold and silver from the New World.

The rule of Spanish viceroys

Philip for the most part followed his father's advice, maintaining cordial relations with the Italian states, all of whose political and economic fortunes were closely bound to Spain. The two states ruled directly by Spain—Milan and the Kingdom of Naples—the king of Spain governed through a series of viceroys. The main resistance Philip encountered in Italy came from the Neapolitans. The population of Naples surged under the Spanish and reached 100,000 by 1500; it doubled by 1550. By 1600 there were 300,000 inhabitants, making Naples, along with Paris, the most

304 The "Imperial Renaissance"

populous city in Europe. Poverty, overcrowding, and crime contributed to create a restive atmosphere among the populace, making it prone to rioting and rebellions. The Neapolitans especially resented paying taxes to finance Spain's imperial projects such as its costly wars in the Netherlands. Early in his reign, Philip had trouble from the pope, who was a Neapolitan. Paul IV Carafa (r.1555–59) waged the so-called Carafa War against Spanish domination from 1555 to 1557. The Spanish swiftly put down that rebellion and also crushed a 1585 popular revolt in Naples with exceptional brutality. An even greater threat to Spanish rule than the populace of Naples was posed by the rural landowning barons. The activities of these local nobles were restrained by encouraging them to come and live in the city where the viceroy could more easily supervise them. Swept up in the splendid court life in Naples, with its lavish celebrations and gift-giving, these noble families accumulated debts and incurred deep obligations to the Spanish crown. Spain had Naples firmly within its grasp, and Philip's subjects were always aware of the presence of the iron hand within the elegant Spanish glove.

Pax hispanica

Italy enjoyed a peace dividend as a result of the religious dissent in France; because he was embroiled in fighting French Protestant Huguenots, the king of France, Henry II (1519–1559) signed a pact with the Spanish, the Treaty of Cateau-Cambrésis in 1559, ending the Habsburg–Valois wars. While the peace lasted, the peninsula enjoyed forty years of relative tranquility under Spanish Rule, until 1598 when the French, having signed the Edict of Nantes, were free to turn their attention back to their territorial ambitions in Italy. Even the one immense military conflict that Italy engaged in during this period—the Battle of Lepanto in 1571 against the Turks—served to unify the peninsula. In 1520, soon after Charles V was crowned emperor, a powerful ruler of the Ottoman Empire had risen to power, the Sultan Suleiman the Magnificent (1494–1566) who posed an increasing threat to the West. The Holy League, organized by Pope Pius V and led by Spain, included Venice, the Kingdom of the Two Sicilies, Genoa, Tuscany, Urbino, Savoy, and Parma. The stunning victory not only raised the morale of the Italian states, but provided some economic respite from the Turks' tight grip on trade in the Mediterranean.

It was also an era of increasing prosperity and population growth throughout the peninsula. By 1595 Italy's population surpassed its levels before the calamities and returned to becoming the most densely populated country in Europe. Improved methods of farming helped feed the growing population that, despite a devastating plague in 1575 and a famine in the 1590s, reached 13 million by 1600. Italy's economy was booming as well. Cloth industries had recovered, producing greater quantities of wool and silk than ever, and trade increased. In the 1580s the Grand Duke of

The "Imperial Renaissance" 305

Tuscany opened the free port of Livorno (Leghorn); with no duty assessed on goods traded there, the port attracted shipping from all over the world. Venetian merchants enjoyed an "Indian summer" as her maritime rivals the Portuguese and the Dutch were temporarily distracted. In 1572 the Dutch rebelled against Spain and were plunged into decades of bloody conflict, while Portugal, which merged with Spain in 1580, had much of its resources diverted to pay the costs of the conflict in the Netherlands. Through the end of the century, the profitable spice trade was thus re-opened to Venice. Banking also boomed in Italy during this period; it was led by the Genoese, who four times a year held a kind of financial summit, which was attended by around 200 of the most powerful merchants and bankers from Genoa, Lucca, Florence, and Milan. On these occasions the Italian power brokers set exchange rates and transacted business, which in the peak years around 1600 amounted to the equal of the tax revenues of Spain, France, England, and Italy put together.

Learning that was not strictly academic

Throughout this period learning flourished in Italy. By 1600 there were over two dozen universities in Italy, the highest concentration anywhere in Europe, the Universities of Bologna and Padua generally acknowledged as the most excellent. The Society of Jesus provided superb instruction in the Latin humanities curriculum free of charge or at very low cost at Jesuit colleges throughout Italy. The number of Jesuit schools rose from 18 colleges in 1556 to 49 by 1600 and 111 by 1700. Education took place not just in formal school or university settings, but in largely private institutions known as academies, which sprang up all over the Italian Peninsula. Originally in 1530 about a dozen of these academies were founded in Italy, by 1600 there were over 200, and at least another 600 were founded by 1700 in over 227 locations in Italy. Like the Platonic Academy run by Marisilio Ficino (Chapter 9) these academies were intended to be intimate gatherings, similar to clubs where like-minded individuals could discuss intellectual pursuits in a relaxed, congenial atmosphere.

Organizations such as the Accademia degli Intronati, the "dazed ones" founded in Siena in 1525; Accademia degli Invaghiti, the "infatuated ones" founded in 1562 in Mantua; the Accademia dei Gelati, the "frozen ones" in Bologna in 1588 bore whimsical names, but within these semi-playful environments, humanists conducted important intellectual inquiry in the fields of literature, the arts, and the sciences. Indeed, compared to the well-defined structure at the universities, there was no clear division between the disciplines as they were treated at the academies; members shared a background in humanist learning and an overwhelming sense of curiosity. Though this approach encouraged a certain amount of dilettantism, the Italian academies also fostered shockingly original ideas and breakthrough advances, particularly in the areas of philosophy and the sciences.

306   *The "Imperial Renaissance"*

The academies also contributed to other areas of Italian culture, some assuming public functions. The Accademia della Crusca (of the chaff) was founded in Florence in 1582 to regulate usage and supervise the purity of the Italian language; La Crusca produced Europe's first dictionary in 1612. The Accademia delle Arti del Disegno was founded in Florence by Giorgio Vasari and other artists to improve training in drawing for artists, as well as to provide instruction in history and literature. Above all, it was the intention of its founders to raise the status of the artist from that of a mere craftsman to a creative intellectual. A public institution under the official auspices of Cosimo I, the academy trained many mannerist painters whose art exalted the state. Similarly, the Accademia Fiorentina (Florentine Academy) came under the wing of the grand duke from 1560 and sponsored public lectures on literature, philosophy, mathematics, and astronomy.

Print culture: Read all about it

> Since the wonderful printing press has come into being, the majority of men as well women know how to read, and what is most important is that philosophy, medicine, and all the other fields of knowledge have been translated and printed in our mother tongue.
>
> Leonardo Fioravanti, 1583

These words, taken from a book compiling tidbits of information about the natural sciences for the general public, point to another important trend in education. It was not necessary to enroll in a university or attend public lectures to learn about the latest ideas; by this time knowledge was also widely circulating even in the remotest parts of the peninsula by means of print media. In the sixteenth century more than a hundred printing presses throughout Italy were turning out low-cost printed books and pamphlets. The easy availability of printed material written in vernacular offered the urban poor and rural Italians access to new poems and stories, as well as philosophical and scientific treatises. Ideas spread throughout the peninsula, enabling even a miller in remote Friuli to acquire knowledge that was being discussed at the University of Padua (Chapter 15).

Though printed gazettes or newspapers available to a wide Italian reading public emerged in the 1640s, handwritten news reports were in use from the late fifteenth century among the elite and in government circles. Known as *avvisi*, these reports covering politics, military affairs, and gossip were often compiled by resident ambassadors at foreign courts or by independent paid observers. Rome was a center of *avvisi*, as was Venice. By the seventeenth century the grand dukes of Tuscany received regular *avvisi* from all over the world, including from such distant places as Constantinople, Flanders, Persia, Paris, Prague, and London. Then, as now, information was a precious commodity, and Italians were among the best-informed of Europeans.

The epic poetry of Torquato Tasso

The most renowned poet of this period was Torquato Tasso (1544–1595). His verse is considered, along with that of Dante, Petrarch, and Ariosto, as some of the finest ever written in the Italian language. The son of a court poet, Tasso wrote his greatest work, the epic poem *La Gerusalemme liberata* (*Jerusalem Delivered*) under the patronage of the duke of Ferrara. Like Ariosto, Tasso exalts the Este family; departing, however, from the madcap adventures of the *Orlando furioso*, Tasso set out to write a more sober epic poem, conforming to the Aristotelian unities of time, place, and action. Rather than a fantastical or mythological subject, Tasso chose to write about a historical event, the First Crusade. Written during the years 1565–75, the story of a Christian war against Muslims was highly topical, as the Ottomans had seized Malta in 1565 and the Battle of Lepanto was fought in 1571. Furthermore, the theme of a victorious church was in keeping with the militant spirit of Tridentine Catholicism. Nonetheless, within these seemingly conservative strictures, Tasso includes sorcery, an enchanted forest, and a hero smitten with a Saracen warrior maiden whom he unknowingly kills in battle. The lush descriptions of nature, the dark, mysterious atmosphere, exciting battle scenes, and unexpected plot twists made the work, first published in 1581, immensely popular throughout Europe. Tasso's epic poem strongly influenced the works of English poets Edmund Spenser and John Milton.

Women speaking out: Veronica Franco and others

Poetry of an entirely different kind was being written in Venice by Tasso's contemporary, Veronica Franco (1546–1591). Born into a respectable family of original citizens (Chapter 8) of limited means, along with her three brothers, the girl received a humanist education. When she came of age, like her mother before her, Veronica became a courtesan. It has been estimated that in 1500 the number of prostitutes in Venice was 12,000 within a total population of 100,000. Among these prostitutes, 215 of the elegant and accomplished women known as courtesans were listed in the 1570 printed *Catalogue of All the Principal and Most Honored Courtesans of Venice*; included in that list is the twenty-four-year-old Franco. A published poet, Franco used her literary talent to turn traditional Petrarchan commonplaces upside down. Here was the lovely, distant, and unattainable object of the poet's attention not only speaking for herself, but openly bragging about her own sexual availability, all in flawless metered verse. Not only did Franco challenge standard Petrarchan poetry, but in a response to a male critic who denigrated her poetry because it was written by a woman, she defended herself and women in general, in these lines:

> I do not know if you believe it to be but a slight risk
> To enter the field of combat with a woman.

308 *The "Imperial Renaissance"*

Though caught off guard at first, I warn you
… When one day we women are trained and armed,
We will be able to stand against any man,
With hands and feet, as well as hearts, like yours.

Franco is renowned for her poetry, but she was not the only female writer of the late Renaissance. It is one of the ironies of the latter part of the sixteenth century when the Catholic Church was taking ultra-conservative positions on social issues, that women began to have a powerful voice in Italian writing. Between 1580 and 1602 thirty-seven books were published by Italian women, including two feminist polemical works. Women's elevated literary profile had caused an anti-feminine backlash, and these last two books were written in their defense: Moderata Fonte's (1555–1592) *The Worth of Women*, and Lucrezia Marinella's (1571–1653) *The Nobility and Excellence of Women*, were both published in 1600, adding impassioned arguments to the *querelle des femmes*.

Buffoons, faithful shepherds, and prima donnas: Birth of Renaissance theater

In the mid-sixteenth century Italy revolutionized theater in Europe. It began when the first sprightly Harlequin took his slapstick—two pieces of wood wrapped in leather that made a loud slapping noise—and whacked the doddering Pantaloon on the backside. From the first documented performance in 1545, professional troupes of actors performing what is known as "commedia dell'arte" were traveling all over Italy by the mid-sixteenth century. A small cast of actors playing stock characters—the foolish old husband, the pompous doctor, the wily servant, the blustering captain, the handsome lover, and the pretty young wife—like jazz musicians, artfully improvised based on set themes. Their comedies were fast-moving, uproarious, vulgar, and extraordinarily popular. The craze for commedia dell'arte swept throughout Europe; it was performed everywhere for the next two centuries.

What was new and important about commedia dell'arte was first of all that it was professional theater; the name means literally "comedy of the profession" or "guild." Previously theater was the pursuit of amateurs; members of confraternities or trade guilds might act in *sacre rappresentazioni* and humanists might re-enact classical dramas. The elevation of European theater to an art form that follows rules and involves specific techniques and training dates from this period. Theater's heightened prestige brought actors, and especially actresses, both fame and notoriety. Women's increased prominence in courts and in literature was matched by their presence on stage during this time. In Renaissance tragedies, the leading female role was central—three quarters of the tragedies take their name from the heroine; and actresses playing the lead in such tragedies as Gian Giorgio Trissino's (1478–1550) *Sofonisba* delivered impassioned monologues expressing noble

sentiments. Women were featured performers in comedy as well. Isabella
Andreini (1562–1604) was the most famous actress of her time; she toured
widely with the commedia dell'arte troupe, the Gelosi, in Italy and France,
where she performed on various occasions for the king. A celebrated poet
and author of the drama *La Mirtilla* (1588), Andreini was one of the few
women to be admitted to an academy, becoming a member of the Accademia
degli Intenti in Pavia.

Another important aspect of commedia dell'arte was that, though it was
popular theater, the borders between commedia dell'arte and the so-called
commedia erudita (learned theater) were highly permeable. Because of the
many plots of both Renaissance popular and learned comedies that derived
from ancient authors such as Plautus (Titus Maccius Plautus, c. 254–184
BCE) and Terrence (Publius Terrentius, after c. 195–159 BCE), there was
clearly transmission from "high" to "low" drama, not that contemporaries necessarily made fine distinctions between the two. When Andreini
performed for the wedding celebrations of Grand Duke Ferdinando I de'
Medici to Christina of Lorraine in Florence in 1589, the troupe provided
both light comedy as well as more complex drama, including a dramatic
mad scene. Though Renaissance theater was technically divided into three
categories—comedy, tragedy, and pastoral—in actual performance there was
a great deal of mixing of genres.

In addition, the pastoral dramas favored in court theaters at the time were
tinged with seriousness. Despite their idyllic surroundings, the shepherds and
nymphs that inhabit these pastoral fantasies suffer emotional ordeals, often
risking their lives for love. *Il Pastor fido* (*The Faithful Shepherd* 1580–83) by
Battista Guarini (or Guarino 1538–1612) is the story of the shepherd Mirtillo
who nearly sacrifices his life for the lovely Amarilli. In Tasso's hit play *Aminta*
(1571), the despairing lovesick shepherd Aminta is on the brink of suicide
until Silvia agrees to return his love. Tasso was an admirer of Andreini, who
starred with the Gelosi in the opening of *Aminta*, further proof of the inter-
play between the improvised popular theater and the scripted formal dramas
of the day. It was this subtle overlapping of styles—high and low, tragic and
comic—with its focus on moral dilemmas and exploration of the psyche of
individual characters that would inspire Renaissance dramatists outside Italy
and would also carry over into a brand-new art form invented in Italy at the
turn of the century—opera.

Italian words and music come together: Madrigals, motets, and masses

Music was flourishing in Italy during this time. The stringed instruments
produced in northern Italy were among the finest in Europe, notably those
built by Andrea Amati (1505/10–1577) who was from Cremona and by
Gasparo da Salò (Gasparo Bertolotti 1540–1609) from Brescia. The lutenist
Francesco da Milano (Francesco Canova 1497–1543), known as *il Divino*
(the Divine), was a prolific composer famous for his complex polyphonic

310 The "Imperial Renaissance"

compositions. The enjoyment of polyphony extended to ensemble singing of madrigals, which caught on with the Italian public in the 1530s. The music—in which three or four vocal lines weave in and out, in turn harmonizing and then clashing in subtle dissonance—was wedded to the vernacular poetry of Petrarch, Sannazaro, Ariosto, Tasso, and Guarini to create expressive word-painting. When the poet describes the flight of birds, the notes flutter upward; when he depicts harshness or cruelty, the notes clash; and the voices move languorously when the poet sighs. This music, performed both publicly at formal court events and for private entertainment, was complex enough to be interesting, but not too difficult for trained amateurs to sing in informal gatherings for their own amusement. Songs could be sung alone or with one or more vocal parts played on guitar or lute. Greatly aided by means of printing—the first to set musical notation in moveable type was Ottaviano Petrucci in Venice in 1501—madrigals became all the rage: 2,000 collections were printed between 1530 and 1600. Among the Italian composers of madrigals were Andrea Gabrieli (*c*.1532–1585) and his nephew Giovanni Gabrieli (*c*.1553–1612); Luca Marenzio (1553–1599); the first published woman composer Maddalena Casulana (*c*.1544–1583); Luzzasco Luzzaschi (*c*.1545–1607); Carlo Gesualdo (*c*.1561–1631); and Giovanni Pierluigi da Palestrina (*c*.1525–1594).

Palestrina is better known for his sacred, rather than secular compositions; from 1551 he served as choir master of the Cappella Giulia, the choir of St. Peter's, and wrote over 104 settings of the Mass and 375 motets (polyphonic sacred vocal music). The function of music during religious services was discussed at the Council of Trent, which decreed that understandability of the words of sacred texts should not be sacrificed to complex polyphonic voicings. Rather than eliminating polyphony, however, the church's focus on music resulted in an expanded, updated repertoire. Palestrina's pared-down compositions project textual clarity, but they also have an immediacy of expression, grounded in perfect balance and restraint. In the realm of secular music as well, without entirely eliminating polyphony, composers were nevertheless exploring how to increase the expressiveness of the solo voice so as to increase dramatic impact.

This was especially true in music-drama, which played an increasingly important role in court festivities. And whereas in the previous century mostly foreign musicians, many from Flanders or France, were employed by Italian courts, by the early sixteenth century there were more Italians performing and composing. For the 1589 Medici wedding celebrations, composer Giulio Caccini (1551–1618), poet Ottavio Rinuccini (1562–1621), and others collaborated on the so-called Florentine *intermedi*. These were musical interludes accompanied by elaborate stage effects inserted between the acts of the plays. These musicians and poets who called themselves the Camerata (meaning "association" or "club") experimented in matching their words and music to enhance dramatic scenes. Particularly striking was an aria (song) with exposed solo line sung by composer Jacopo Peri (1561–1633), who just eleven years later composed the first opera, *Dafne*. Though the intent of Peri and the Camerata was to revive ancient Greek music-drama by emphasizing declamation of text, with the melodic line underneath as mere support, they opened the way for the creation of a dynamic new Italian art form (Epilogue).

Architecture: Perfection of classical forms and experimentation

Throughout Italy the second half of the Cinquecento was a time of landmark achievements in architecture. Peace and prosperity are conducive to large construction projects; painters may be able to work during times of crisis, but buildings do not go up while armies invade and destroy cities. Throughout the peninsula, edifices were being built that expressed the confidence and stability of Italy's states. Like Vasari's Uffizi complex in Florence (1560–80), which projected an aura of permanence and importance for the grand duke, Sansovino's impressive group of buildings around Piazza San Marco asserted the power of the Venetian Republic (Chapter 8). Similarly, Rome saw its biggest burst of building projects yet, at the end of the century under Pope Sixtus V Peretti (r.1585–90). In addition to restoring Rome's largest basilicas, Sixtus laid out new avenues and built fountains and aqueducts. He had ancient obelisks moved to prominent points in the city; these and ancient Roman monuments were topped with Sixtus's family insignia and Christian images, symbolically linking his papacy with the triumphs of imperial Rome.

Palladio shapes Western architecture

After the 1527 Sack of Rome, many artists and intellectuals, such as Aretino (Chapter 12) and Sansovino, had fled to the *Serenissma*, making Venice a vibrant cultural center. Venice had by this time regained her *terraferma* possessions and, having recovered from the defeat at Agnadello, Venetians were reasserting themselves on the mainland. It was at this time that an architect emerged, not from the city itself, but from the Venetian mainland, who arguably had the most powerful impact on Western architecture of any Renaissance Italian. Palladio (Andrea di Pietro, 1508–1580) was born in Padua and began his career as a stonemason. His patron, the humanist Trissino, discovered the young man's talents and educated him, bringing him to Rome on a number of occasions to study classical architecture. By the 1550s Palladio—the elegant nickname suggesting the Greek goddess of wisdom, Pallas Athena, was given to him by Trissino—was working as an architect in Vicenza and much in demand. Palladio is best known for his country villas, eighteen of which still exist today in the Veneto region. This area, whose swamps had been drained to eliminate malaria, was full of farms producing a variety of crops, including corn introduced from the New World. Noble Venetian landowners increasingly depended on the income from these properties as the Republic's maritime fortunes faded, causing them to spend

312　The "Imperial Renaissance"

Figure 14.1 Top, Andrea Palladio, *Villa La Rotonda*, 1569–80; bottom, the Pantheon originally built in 27 BCE, rebuilt 125 CE, Rome

The *"Imperial Renaissance"* 313

more time in the country. These educated patricians wanted elegant but practical country homes; the building should not merely function as the hub of a working farm, but also present a stately classical appearance. Such settings satisfied the aristocratic longing for a refined pastoral life, as promised in the paintings of Giorgione and Titian, the verse of Sannazaro and Guarini. Palladio provided his clients with dignified mansions that reposed harmoniously within their natural settings (Figure 14.1). Featuring elements of Greek and Roman architecture—temple façades, classically inspired friezes, and colonnaded covered walkways—these buildings exude balance and harmony both on the exterior and on the interior. Though imposing from the outside, the rooms of Palladio's villas are proportioned according to the rules of Vitruvius (Chapter 11), lending the interior spaces a satisfying human dimension.

In Venice he designed the majestic churches of San Giorgio Maggiore (begun 1565) and the Redentore (Church of the Redeemer, begun 1577) as well as many civic buildings, urban palazzi, and a theater in the city of Vicenza. Palladio's architectural concepts spread throughout Europe, not only by visitors who admired his work first-hand, but through books he published, the most influential of which was his *Four Books of Architecture*, published in 1570. Palladio's work was much more influential than Alberti's, not only because the printing press assured greater circulation, but because with his former training as a mason, Palladio's instructions were clearer and more practically applicable. It is impossible to over-estimate Palladio's influence on architecture over the following centuries: Inigo Jones and Christopher Wren in England, Thomas Jefferson's Monticello, plantations in the southern United States, and the Capitol building itself in Washington, D.C. (Figure 16.1), all owe an enormous debt to Palladio, whose work represents the apex of classically inspired Renaissance architecture.

Rome gloriously rebuilt

Meanwhile, in Rome, bold new architectural developments were under way. Rome had by this time recovered from the Sack; its population by 1600 would reach 100,000. There were building and restoration projects everywhere. From 1546 Michelangelo, now in his seventies, worked on St. Peter's Basilica, discarding the more restrained classical designs of his predecessor Antonio da Sangallo. Michelangelo demolished work that had already been done, replacing it with a more dramatic, upward-thrusting building; St. Peter's as we see it today largely reflects Michelangelo's design (Figure 16.1). Though Michelangelo was inspired by the classical, his designs pushed the limits of Renaissance style, leading the way to new directions in architecture. At his death in 1564 the building was still unfinished and the project continued under Giacomo Vignola (1507–1573). After Vignola's death, architect Giacomo della Porta (*c.*1540–1602) took over, finishing the dome in 1590, although he chose the elongated shape of an ogival arc over

Michelangelo's hemisphere to relieve outward pressure on the structure. The iconic shape of St. Peter's dome was later repeated in domes throughout the world not only on religious, but also civic structures, most notably the dome of the U.S. Capitol in Washington, D.C.

Nearly 200 churches in Rome were either restored or constructed during this period. The largest newly constructed church was the headquarters of the Jesuit order—the Basilica of Il Gesù, completed in 1584. The two architects who followed Michelangelo at St. Peter's—Giacomo della Porta and Giacomo da Vignola—worked on this massive church as well. Constructed along principles of the Council of Trent, Il Gesù became the model for many Catholic churches, notably the Jesuit Church of San Fedele in Milan, commissioned by Carlo Borromeo (see later in this chapter). Its design is an unlikely fusion of simplicity and grandeur intended to represent Tridentine ideals. Because the Mass had to be visible to the members of the congregation and the priest's words audible, the building was designed with a wide central nave and chapels in place of aisles. Light floods down over the altar, providing everyone with an unimpeded, dramatic view of the proceedings. The façade designed by della Porta combines the Renaissance form of Alberti's Santa Maria Novella in Florence (Chapter 4) with elements from Michelangelo's design for St. Peter's: pairs of pilasters (flat columns) and columns perched on pediments. The overall effect is imposing, both classical and dignified. With its eclectic mix of styles Il Gesù was influential on a new style of extravagant architecture just coming into style—the Baroque (Epilogue).

Venetian masters: Titian's late style, Tintoretto, and Veronese

The *pax hispanica* predictably benefited the visual arts as well. Painting flourished throughout the peninsula, and nowhere more than in Venice. Venetian Renaissance art reached its fullest blossoming in the later works of Titian and the younger artists who followed him during the second part of the Cinquecento. Titian's late style developed during the mid 1540s, when his international reputation was established. The Emperor Charles V was a great admirer and commissioned many paintings from the artist, including the 1548 equestrian portrait (Figure 12.2). Charles's son Philip II, in turn, became Titian's principal patron for the rest of the artist's career. Royal patronage brought the painter great fame and made him extremely wealthy, yet Titian never stopped innovating. In his later paintings—both erotic works on mythological themes and religious subjects—the artist employed broader, almost impressionistic brushwork. Like the impressionist painters three centuries later, Titian in his late works tried to evoke a mood, a quality of light rather than carefully reproducing details of anatomy and volumetric forms. Rather than the smooth, finished surface of his early works, Titian applied color in free brushstrokes, in places thickly smearing on the paint, in others barely daubing it on. Free to explore themes of his own choosing, Titian's later paintings often have darker, more brooding subjects. In one of his last works, *The Flaying of Marsyas* (1570s, Archepiscopal Palace, Kroměříž), painted when the artist was in his eighties, the satyr dangles upside down, as the god Apollo, who has triumphed over him in a song contest, intently strips pieces of flesh off Marsyas's body. The paint is laid on thickly, the viscous oil appearing to ooze from the canvas and the russet hues suggesting crusted blood add to the horror. The canvas is modern not only in the artist's application of paint, however; it is also a rich psychological study. The scene is a metaphor for high art triumphing over lower forms, and to the side, the artist has included a portrait of himself as Midas. The elderly Titian meditates on the determined cruelty before him, considering his own mortality, and the role of art in a brutal world.

Titian's influence on the Venetian artists of the next generation was immense; it is reflected in the works of both Paolo Veronese (Paolo Cagliari 1528–1588) and Jacopo Tintoretto (Jacopo Robusti 1519–1594). Veronese's paintings show the refined polish of Titian's earlier work, whereas inspired by the later Titian, Tintoretto attacked his canvases with dramatic, broad brushstrokes. While Veronese's canvases delight the eye with splashes of color against a serene Venetian sky, the brooding intensity of Tintoretto can inspire spiritual reflection. Between the 1540s and the 1580s, these two artists competed for important commissions, striving to outdo each other, as well as the older master. Out of this rivalry was born some of the finest art of the Renaissance.

Veronese was commissioned to decorate the walls of Palladio's Villa Barbaro as well as monastic refectories (dining halls). A popular theme for decorating the latter was the representation of Biblical feasts. Veronese painted two immense canvases depicting Biblical dining. So exuberant were these busy scenes, including dogs, parrots, halberd-carrying soldiers, and court jesters that the sacred subject is lost amidst the activity, for instance in his *Wedding Feast at Cana*, in which Christ is upstaged by an ensemble of musicians in the foreground (1562–63, Louvre; Figure 14.2). Veronese was in fact accused of impiety for depicting Christ in *The Last Supper* in the center of such a chaotic scene and called before the Inquisition (Chapter 15). The painter was reprimanded and ordered to alter the painting. Veronese solved the problem by renaming the work *The Feast at the House of Levi* (1572–3 Accademia, Venice).

After fires in 1574 and 1577 destroyed the interior of the Hall of the Great Council in the Doge's Palace, Veronese was commissioned to paint the *Apotheosis of Venice* (1582), on its ceiling, and after Veronese's death, Tintoretto painted the *Paradise* (after 1588) on the wall below. Tintoretto is best known for the immense paintings he created for Venetian confraternities. Among the canvases he painted for the Scuola of San Rocco between 1564 and 1587 is a moody atmospheric *Crucifixion* (1565). As if in a snapshot, Tintoretto's feverish painting style conveys hectic activity surrounding the solitary, immobile figure of Christ. Flashes of dramatic light pierce through

Figure 14.2 Paolo Veronese, *Wedding Feast at Cana*, detail, 1562–3, Louvre

the brooding overcast sky, nightmarishly illuminating the scene. Covering acres of canvas, several hundred of Tintoretto's works survive, including 150 portraits.

Opportunities for women artists: Sofonisba Anguissola and Lavinia Fontana

To produce canvases on such a scale, Veronese and Tintoretto had to employ large workshops of assistants. Tintoretto was assisted in his work by his son Domenico (1560–1635) and his daughter Marietta (*c.*1554–1590). Women increasingly began to assume prominence as painters in Italy during this time. Throughout the Renaissance, women were largely excluded from membership in artistic guilds and academies and they were prohibited from studying nudes, hence adequate training was difficult for women to acquire. Some, such as Tintoretto's daughter, grew up in artistic families, and their work was often absorbed into the production of their fathers' workshops. Others, like Artemisia Gentileschi (1593–after 1654), who was the daughter of painter Orazio Gentileschi (1563–1639), became famous in their own right. Sometimes women outside the major cities and even outside the artistic milieu had a better chance of achieving recognition for their work.

Born in Cremona, Sofonisba Anguissola (1532–1625) was one of a number of talented daughters of a nobleman who provided them with a teacher in painting. Sofonisba's abilities were recognized early by Michelangelo and Vasari (Figure 14.3). She came to the attention of the king of Spain and served as lady-in-waiting and painter at the Spanish court. Lavinia Fontana (1552–1614), from Bologna, was the daughter of a painter who had studied under Vasari. In her paintings, more of which survive than any other female painter before 1700, she tended away from mannerism toward a more realistic style. Fontana painted religious, historical, and mythological subjects, sometimes involving nudes, but she was most celebrated as a painter of detailed, opulent portraits of Bolognese women. She was one of the few

Figure 14.3 Sofonisba Anguissola, *Portrait of the Artist's Sister as a Nun*, 1551, City Art Gallery, Southampton

318   *The "Imperial Renaissance"*

women honored by being allowed entry into an artistic academy, the prestigious Roman Accademia di San Luca.

The anti-mannerists: Annibale, Agostino, and Ludovico Carracci

Also from Bologna was Annibale Carracci (1560–1609), who with his brother Agostino (1557–1602) and cousin Ludovico (1555–1619) founded the painting academy there, the Accademia degli Incamminati, in 1582. The Carracci family developed an "academic" style, a reaction against mannerism (Chapter 13). Their style was at once more restrained and idealized as well as naturalistic, based on classical models and the Renaissance painters, mostly Raphael. Although known for his realistic scenes from everyday life, landscapes, and religious works during his early years, Annibale's style changed when in 1595 he moved to Rome, and he increasingly adopted a more stylized classicism. Carracci's masterpiece there was his work on the ceiling of the Palazzo Farnese, the *Loves of the Gods* (1597–1601), the scale of which elicits comparisons to the Sistine chapel ceiling. Jove, Diana, Hercules, Venus, Polyphemus, and others are vibrantly and joyously represented in a series of bright, sunny tableaux celebrating erotic love. Carracci's influence was strong not only on Italian Baroque painters but also on Nicolas Poussin (1594–1665) and Peter Paul Rubens (1577–1640).

The Michelangelo from Caravaggio

Then, at the very end of a half-century of innovations and experimentation, a striking talent burst onto the artistic scene, revolutionizing painting. Born Michelangelo Merisi (1571–1610) in a town outside Milan, the painter took the name of his birthplace: Caravaggio. After apprenticing for four years in Milan with a disciple of Titian, in 1592 Caravaggio came to Rome. Caravaggio brought with him from Lombardy a very different artistic sensibility; Lombard art was more straightforward in its depiction of nature, with a directness and realism closer to northern European painting. Furthermore, Tridentine decrees regarding art were strictly applied in Milan by the reforming Archbishop Carlo Borromeo (1538–1584). Borromeo wrote a treatise setting forth guidelines on Catholic art and architecture, specifying not only that sacred art should avoid giving inappropriate pleasure, but that it should not exaggerate or "deform the human shape or represent extraneous objects … no little birds, sea, or green fields put there that might distract the viewer." In short it was forbidden to paint in the style of the mannerists.

In Rome Caravaggio made a living at first by painting in the workshops of other painters. He became known for the realism of his still lives; he created flawless paintings of fruits—luscious and gleaming in glass bowls. Eventually his work, especially the genre paintings of the mid-1590s, *The Fortuneteller* (Louvre, Paris) and *The Cardsharps* (Kimbell Art Museum,

The "Imperial Renaissance" 319

Fort Worth), brash, witty depictions of deception executed in a cold light of punctilious realism, brought him to the attention of discerning Roman art patrons. Caravaggio gained the support of one of the most influential patrons, Cardinal Francesco Maria del Monte (1549–1627), and moved into his household around 1596, where he lived for at least four years. The Venetian del Monte was highly influential in Vatican circles, at one point considered a candidate for pope. A renowned art collector, del Monte was also fascinated with the natural sciences and was a supporter of Galileo. The Cardinal's palazzo was the central meeting place for intellectuals in Rome, and it was in this permissive atmosphere, far from the restrictions of Borromean Milan, that Caravaggio painted his sensual canvases of semi-nude raven-haired boys. In *Bacchus* (1597–98 Uffizi), the heavy-lidded teen-ager with flushed cheeks and grape leaves in his hair is purported to represent the classical god, but the model leaning back on some drapery that does not quite cover a soiled cushion undermines that illusion. There is a subversive realism at work in this image of a Roman boy who, with bedsheets thrown around his shoulder to resemble a toga and dirt under his fingernails, lan-guorously holds out a delicate crystal chalice of wine toward the viewer. The over-ripe, bruised fruit in the foreground serves to heighten the sensual mood—a promise of sensory delights.

Through the cardinal's influence, Caravaggio received his first public commission for art in a Roman church, and the two large paintings he did there on the subject of St. Matthew established his fame. His painting, *The Calling of St. Matthew* (1600, San Luigi dei Francesi, Rome) was a break-through in Caravaggio's style (Figure 15.1). The painter treats the figures sitting around the table in his usual ultra-realistic manner, using common people as models. This could be a scene from a local tavern with neighbor-hood types sitting around, but for Caravaggio's exciting use of light and ges-ture that signals a mystical event is occurring. Cast almost entirely in shadow, except for light grazing the face and hand, Christ points to the tax-collector Matthew, summoning him, as illumination sweeps from right to left across the canvas. Caravaggio pioneered the dramatic, exaggerated use of chiaro-scuro known as tenebrism (from *tenebroso*, the Italian word for dark or gloomy) that would be exploited by such diverse artists as Georges de La Tour (1593–1652), Diego Velázquez (1599–1660), and Rembrandt (1606–1669). Placing figures and objects against a very dark background enabled Caravaggio not only to intensify the drama, but to impart greater realism, since such stark lighting enhances three-dimensionality.

Like the other Michelangelo, Caravaggio was an artist in whom the spir-itual and physical came into conflict; his work disturbingly transgressed borders between sacred and profane, spiritual and real. Sometimes reviled as the "anti-Michelangelo," he was accused of using a prostitute to model for a figure of the Virgin Mary, and committing other breaches of decorum. In his life, Caravaggio had a fiery disposition, which del Monte described as *stravagantissimo* (unbelievably bizarre). Constantly involved in violent

320   The "Imperial Renaissance"

altercations, the artist was brought to trial eleven times during the years 1600 to 1605 alone. Eventually he killed a man in one of these fights and had to flee Rome. He was awaiting a pardon when he died, probably of a fever, in 1610. Caravaggio blazed through the Roman art world; only eighteen years after he first arrived in Rome, the artist was dead by the age of forty. Yet in that short time, so great were the innovations he introduced, that Caravaggio has often been identified as the first "modern" painter.

Considerations: Was the late sixteenth century a *Siglo de Oro* for Italy?

Alessandro Manzoni (1785–1873), in his historical novel *I promessi sposi* (*The Betrothed*), set in 1628, portrayed an Italy crushed under oppressive Spanish overlords. Manzoni's widely read work helped inspire Italians to rise up, overthrow Austrian rule, and unify the country during the Risorgimento in the late nineteenth century. The negative image of the Spanish occupation of Italy has remained in the popular imagination, shared over the years by most historians of Italy as well. Certainly, Spanish rule in Naples was harsher than elsewhere on the peninsula; nowhere else in Italy were there the intermittent uprisings and bloody reprisals that occurred in Naples. By and large, however, Italians cooperated with the Spanish, as demonstrated by the fact that Spain maintained no more than 20,000 troops on the peninsula at any given time. In his book *Spanish Rome*, historian Thomas Dandelet provides an explanation for Spain's success in Italy, in its policy of "informal imperialism," a combination of "limited military force, constant diplomatic contact, a strong presence of Spaniards in the city, and generous foreign aid." The prevailing attitude toward the Spanish is evident in the character of the captain in commedia dell'arte spoofs, who was usually represented as a self-important, pompous Spaniard. Undoubtedly hostilities lingered from the Spanish participation in the Sack of Rome; however, there is no reason to believe that, in poking fun at the Spanish, the Italian people in general resented them more than they would any other authority figures.

This period coincides with the *Siglo de Oro*, the Spanish Golden Age, but it was also a kind of golden age for Italy. Rather than falling into a decline after the military and political defeats of the first portion of the sixteenth century, the arts continued to flourish. In the case of Venice, the High Renaissance in painting did not even reach its peak until the latter half of the century. Italian culture arguably made its widest impact on Europe during the sixteenth and seventeenth centuries; when exported throughout the world, Italian theater, poetry, music, architecture, and art were spreading the Renaissance across the continent. For most of Europe, beyond Italy, the Renaissance was only just beginning in the sixteenth century. The English Renaissance, in particular, owes a great deal to cinquecento Italian culture. Though few people today have heard of Matteo Bandello, Luigi da Porta, or Giambattista Giraldi Cinzio, the stories of these writers traveled to England, and once translated, Shakespeare used their plots for *Romeo and Juliet, Much Ado*

The "Imperial Renaissance" 321

About Nothing, Othello, Measure for Measure, and others. It is true that fewer literary works of greatness were written in Italy during the second half of the sixteenth and beginning of the seventeenth centuries than in the earlier period of the Renaissance, but that creative energy was now poured into the musical and dramatic arts, which Italians came to dominate. To argue that the Renaissance was in decline at this time is to deny the dynamic new art forms that were being born—both spoken drama and lyric opera.

Intellectual inquiry in Italy was also blossoming, encouraged by the proliferation of academies and the circulation of information in print. The press, which made it possible for women writers to be published in unprecedented numbers, and spread reproductions of Raphael and Palladio's works beyond the Alps, also promoted an interest in science. There was an explosion of printed works on scientific subjects to satisfy everyone, from the general reader to the most learned academician. The Italian academies, regardless of their silly names, fostered serious discussion in many scientific and philosophical fields that were outside the mainstream of the universities. The first dictionary, published by the Accademia della Crusca in 1612, seems a kind of premonition of the activities of the French Encyclopedists in the next century, and like those future Enlightenment intellectuals, members of the academies corresponded with like-minded members of the republic of letters. We will see in the next chapter how, out of this stimulating environment of intellectual cross-pollination, one of the greatest scientific minds of all time emerged—Galileo Galilei.

Sourcebook

Charles V, *Political Testament to Philip II*
Veronica Franco, *Capitolo; Letter to a friend*
Moderata Fonte, *The Worth of Women*
Jacopo Tintoretto, *Portrait of a Widow*
Giuseppe Pavoni, *Diary of the 1589 Wedding Festivities*
Gabriello Chiabrera, *Sonnet for Isabella Andreini*
Titian, *Letter to Philip II*
Transcript of Paolo Veronese's Trial Before the Holy Tribunal
Paolo Veronese, *Apotheosis of Venice*
Artemisia Gentileschi, *Susanna and the Elders*

Further reading

Bailey, Gauvin A. *Between Renaissance and Baroque: Jesuit Art in Rome, 1565–1610*, University of Toronto Press, 2003.
Dandelet, Thomas James. *Spanish Rome 1500–1700*, Yale University Press, 2001.
Hanlon, Gregory. *Early Modern Italy 1550–1800: Three Seasons in European History*, esp. Part I "High Summer, 1550–1620," pp. 37–176, St. Martin's Press, 2000.
Marino, John A., ed. *Early Modern Italy 1550–1796*, Oxford University Press, 2002.

322 *The "Imperial Renaissance"*

Robin, Diana. *Publishing Women: Salons, the Presses, and the Counter-Reformation in Sixteenth-century Italy*, University of Chicago Press, 2007.

Rosand, David. *Painting in Sixteenth-Century Venice: Titian, Veronese, Tintoretto* Cambridge University Press, 1997, rev. ed. of *Painting in Cinquecento Venice*, 1985.

Spike, John T. *Caravaggio*, Abbeville Press, 2001.

Testa, Simone. *Italian Academies and Their Networks, 1525–1700: From Local to Global*, Palgrave Macmillan, 2015.

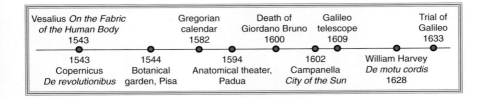

15 Celestial Revolutions
Heaven and Earth Collide at the Turn of the Seventeenth Century

Thus is the glory of God magnified and the greatness of His empire made manifest: it is glorified not with one sun, but with innumerable suns, not one earth, but ten hundred thousand I say, in an infinite number of worlds.

Giordano Bruno, *On the Infinite Universe and Worlds*, 1584

On Thursday morning in the Campo de' Fiori the wicked Dominican friar from Nola was burned alive. This most obstinate heretic, about whom we have written before, formed certain bizarre beliefs, which are against our Faith.

Avviso (News Report) from Rome, February 19, 1600

On the morning of February 17, 1600, in the midst of the papal Jubilee and as Caravaggio was putting finishing touches to *The Calling of St. Matthew* (Figure 15.1), the remains of Giordano Bruno smoldered in a pile of ashes in the piazza of the Campo de' Fiori in Rome, where the philosopher had been burned alive for heresy. Born in 1548 in Nola, a small city not far from Naples, Bruno had trained in a Dominican seminary and became a friar. Not limiting himself to the material taught there, like Ficino and Pico della Mirandola, the young man threw himself into the study of Plato, the Jewish Kabbalah, and the pseudo-Egyptian magical writings attributed to Hermes Trismegistus. For Bruno, Christianity was only one of a number of explanations for the universe. While he did not reject Christianity itself, the philosopher questioned church dogma that Mary was a virgin when she gave birth (the Virgin Birth); that God the Father, Son, and Holy Spirit were separate yet one (the Trinity), and that bread and wine during Mass

DOI: 10.4324/9781003270362-15

324 *Celestial Revolutions*

Figure 15.1 Caravaggio, *The Calling of St. Matthew*, 1600, Church of San Luigi dei Francesi, Rome

changed into the flesh and blood of Christ (Transubstantiation). This was already heretical enough, but Bruno went further. Immersing himself in ancient Epicurean philosophy (see later in this chapter) as well as writings of the Polish astronomer Copernicus, Bruno questioned prevailing Christian explanations of the nature of the universe.

For Bruno, God did not exist separately from nature, controlling it from on high, but is present everywhere and in everything (pantheism); moreover, Bruno proposed the existence of an infinite universe with a multiplicity of worlds. He expounded these, and other unorthodox ideas, at length in many printed books. It was this last belief that the church felt most undermined its foundations, for the Bible taught that Creation happened once; God created one world and its human beings, and His only son died for their sins. If there were many worlds and they were populated with other creatures, would each of them have a Christ to redeem them too?

Inquisitions

Bruno did not stop with merely suggesting alternative visions of the cosmos, but openly mocked religious beliefs, for instance in his 1584 *Spaccio della bestia trionfante* (*Expulsion of the Triumphant Beast*). For the last eight years of his life Bruno was held in prison and questioned by examiners of the court of the Holy Office of the Roman Inquisition, established by Pope Paul III in 1542. The institution itself was not new, however. Since the thirteenth century, ecclesiastical tribunals—called inquisitions, from the Latin *inquerere* (to inquire)—investigated alleged heresies, deviations from official doctrine. Derived from the Greek word for "choice," heresy was considered a willful act of subversion of Christianity and was severely punished. After the slaughter of thousands of members of the Cathar sect in southern France in the Albigensian Crusade (1209–29) failed to eradicate the heresy, Pope Gregory IX (r.1227–41) instituted a formal permanent office to root out heretics. Inquisition into heresy was carried out by church officials called inquisitors, who after extensive, detailed questioning would determine the suspect's innocence or guilt. If the individual was found guilty, he or she would be turned over to secular authorities for punishment. In 1252 Innocent IV decreed that torture could be used to extract confessions. Judicial procedure in the communes of northern Italy, by the thirteenth century, required for conviction of a crime either testimony from two eyewitnesses who concurred exactly, or the defendant's full confession. Because the former was difficult to obtain, it became common practice to use torture in civil trials to prompt confessions. Over the centuries there were various local inquisitions, among them the Spanish Inquisition, begun in 1478, infamous for the public penitential procession known as the auto-da-fé (in old Spanish, act of faith), which often ended in burning convicted heretics en masse. In 1547 the Venetian Inquisition was created, while areas ruled by Spain fell under the jurisdiction of the Spanish Inquisition, which was imposed in Sicily and Sardinia in 1500. Between 1537 and 1572, nineteen auto-da-fé were held in Palermo; hundreds were condemned and twenty-two victims were burnt at the stake. The Spanish attempted to introduce their Inquisition in the Kingdom of Naples in 1547, inciting bloody riots; eventually Naples became subject to the Roman Inquisition.

The Roman Inquisition: Myth and reality

As an instrument of repression, the Roman Inquisition was crueler, and at the same time, more merciful than is commonly imagined; though the cultural damage it caused was immeasurable, its agents inflicted less physical suffering than they are usually given credit for. The courts of the Inquisition followed due process meticulously; anonymous denunciations were not accepted; and circumstantial evidence was not considered sufficient for conviction. The use of torture was more limited than in criminal courts: it was not practiced on children, pregnant women, the elderly, or the handicapped. If a convicted heretic recanted, punishment could be relatively lenient, from performing an act of public penance, or living under house arrest, to serving time aboard a galley or several years in prison. The death sentence was reserved for obstinate heretics who refused to be reconciled with the church, and these cases were relatively few. It has been calculated that between 100 and 200 individuals were actually executed by the Roman Inquisition.

Persecution of Jews, Protestants, Muslims, and witches

The Jewish population in Italy was small, but well established, dating back to ancient Roman times; and in contrast to the Spanish Inquisition, the Roman Inquisition did not violently target Jews or Jewish sympathizers. So, after the expulsions from Spain in 1492 and Portugal in 1497, many Jews immigrated from the Iberian Peninsula to Italy. Though over the centuries Jewish communities were sometimes attacked, especially during moments of social crises, Christians and Jews generally lived side by side in Italian cities through the early sixteenth century. By that time, however, increased animosity toward other faiths was spreading: in 1541 Jews were expelled from the Kingdom of Naples, in 1569 from the Papal States (except Rome and Ancona), and in 1597 from Milan. In the rest of Italy, the official response was one of containment rather than expulsion; Jews were made to live in separate sections of cities known as ghettos. The word derives from *gheto*, which in Venetian dialect means foundry, because one was located near the Jewish neighborhood in Venice. And it was in Venice that after 1516 Jews were first required to be locked in the Ghetto at night, and forced to wear identifying badges or hats, to distinguish them from Christians when they went out in the daytime. Pope Paul IV officially endorsed this state of apartheid with his papal bull *Cum nimis absurdum* in 1555, establishing Jewish ghettos throughout Italy. One exception was the Grand Duchy of Tuscany, where in 1591 Jews in the cities of Livorno and Pisa were granted exceptional freedoms by Ferdinando I de' Medici.

Though inside the ghettos their freedom was restricted and living conditions were cramped, Jews were by and large tolerated rather than persecuted by the Roman Inquisition. The focus of the Roman Inquisition, especially initially, was on ferreting out Protestants, although in Sicily and Naples, under the direct influence of the Spanish, there were many trials of Muslims as well. The inquisitors' emphasis, however, gradually shifted to illicit magic. The *Malleus maleficarum* (*Hammer of Witches*), a manual on witchcraft by two Dominican inquisitors in Germany was first published in 1486 and went into many

Celestial Revolutions   327

reprintings, notably influencing Gianfrancesco Pico della Mirandola (1469–1533). The nephew of humanist Giovanni Pico della Mirandola (Chapter 9), Gianfrancesco in 1523 wrote a learned book in Latin arguing that satanic activity was real. *Strix* was translated into Italian in 1524 as *La Strega* (*The Witch*), and its lively dialogue form made it highly popular.

Witch-hunting became widespread in both Catholic and Protestant countries during the subsequent centuries: of the over 100,000 prosecuted, around 60,000 witches, mostly women, were burned. Sometimes the "witch-frenzy" that raged throughout Europe during the sixteenth and seventeenth centuries reached such a pitch that entire villages were wiped out. This never happened on such a scale in Italy, however, where the number of witchcraft prosecutions peaked during the time of the Italian Wars (1494–1530) and diminished thereafter. It has been observed that in Protestant countries with convents emptied, there were large populations of single, older women who were rootless, and thus a focus for misogyny and persecution, whereas in Italy they continued to live in enclosed monastic communities. Furthermore, the Roman Catholic Church was largely concerned with reigning in superstitions and magical folk practices, as decreed by the Council of Trent. Those found guilty—overwhelmingly women, but also men, including clerics—were almost never sentenced to death, a penalty reserved for rare proven cases of demonic magic, especially those involving misuse of the Eucharist. To keep such cases from developing into mass hysteria, in 1588 the Holy Office banned procedures against people accused of attending black Sabbaths and condemned excessive torture in interrogations. In this way, the Roman Inquisition actually restrained the spread of the witch craze.

The *Index of Prohibited Books*

As emphasized above, the Roman Inquisition was originally instituted as a response to the Reformation, as a means to investigate and prosecute suspected Protestants. The church managed to root out Protestantism fairly easily in Italy, and by the 1570s the focus of the Roman Inquisition shifted. Rather than exclusively seeking out invaders from outside, the Catholic Church turned its attention to rooting out heterodox beliefs from within, such as those of the Dominican friar Giordano Bruno. Dangerous new ideas circulated in books, which in little over a century since the advent of printing were widely available and covered the broadest possible range of topics. It was impossible for a preacher from his pulpit to control what people believed if they were constantly exposed to a flood of contradictory printed arguments. Thus, in 1559, Pope Paul IV Carafa established the *Index librorum prohibitorum* (list of prohibited books). Commonly referred to as the *Index of Prohibited Books*, or the *Papal Index*, this list, revised and enlarged over the course of time, included not only openly seditious works that contested official doctrine but also works that were considered even obliquely threatening to papal authority, such as Dante's *On Monarchy*, Boccaccio's *Decameron*, several of Petrarch's sonnets, Machiavelli's *The Prince*, Guicciardini's *History*

328   *Celestial Revolutions*

of Italy, and Castiglione's *The Courtier*. Vernacular translations of the Bible and unauthorized commentaries were also banned. The Catholic Church banned reading the works of over 500 authors; many books were destroyed, others printed, but with offensive passages removed. Every new book had to be submitted to the church's censors before printing. First the work would be reviewed by a theologian, who might suggest changes. If the theologian approved, the book would be marked with the words *"nihil obstat"* (Latin for "nothing stands in the way") and then passed to the bishop who would grant an official imprimatur (Latin for "let it be printed"). Anyone found reading a book without the imprimatur could be subject to examination by the Inquisition.

Even the reading material of peasants in remote regions of Italy was of interest to the Inquisition. In the 1580s a miller named Menocchio (Domenico Scandella 1532–1599)—from a mountain village in Friuli, not far from the Austrian border—came to the attention of authorities. Menocchio was denounced by the local priest who said:

> He is always arguing with one person or another, and he has the vernacular Bible and imagines that he bases his reasoning on it, and he remains obstinate in these arguments of his.[1]

In his subsequent trials it emerged that the miller possessed not only a forbidden translation of the Bible, but also an unexpurgated copy of the *Decameron*; perhaps a copy of the Koran; and a dozen or so other books on religion, history, and travel. From these books he had formed his own ideas about the world and the origins of the universe. Declaring that God was nothing but "earth, water, and air," Menocchio believed that the universe had formed out of primordial chaos like milk coagulating into cheese. Many of his pantheistic ideas resemble those of contemporary intellectuals such as Giordano Bruno; Menocchio, for instance, declared: "Everything that we see is God, and we are gods." Similarly, he denied the Virgin Birth and other doctrines. And like Bruno, Menocchio was burned at the stake.

Missionaries to the *mezzogiorno*: "The Indies down here"

As historian Carlo Ginzburg has suggested in his book *The Cheese and the Worms*, not all the ideas Menocchio developed derived from books; rather than being new, some of the miller's ideas may have been very old, holdovers from ancient folk traditions. Throughout Europe people living in rural areas may have retained pre-Christian animistic[2] beliefs and practices, but because these peasant cultures left hardly any written traces, it is impossible to ascertain the

---

1 Ginzburg, 1980, p. 4.
2 Animism is the belief in a world of spirits who exist amongst us, and that all living creatures, inanimate objects, and natural phenomena possess a soul.

exact nature of these beliefs or how widespread they were. Ironically, what we know of peasant beliefs is largely thanks to inquisitors, for under their scrutiny many unorthodox beliefs surfaced and were recorded. Contemporary Jesuits were struck by how little of Christianity had penetrated into remote regions, particularly in southern Italy. One Jesuit described shepherds in the outlying hills of Campania as "totally ignorant not only of prayers, or of the other special mysteries of the holy faith, but also of the very knowledge of God." As much as converting pagans in the East Indies (Asia) and the West Indies (the Americas), a major focus of the Jesuit order became eliminating religious heterodoxy and imposing Tridentine Catholicism in southern Italy, which was referred to as "the Indies down here." To enforce orthodox religious beliefs Spanish authorities expelled Jews and other ethnic minorities such as gypsies from their territories. They also massacred a community of thousands of Waldensians (a Christian sect founded by Peter Waldo in twelfth-century France) in Calabria in 1560–61, and in the 1590s they began to eliminate Greek rites from Calabria and Apulia. The cultural diversity for which the *mezzogiorno* had been so well known (Chapter 7) was effectively stamped out; the task of imposing "modern" Catholic belief systems on southern Italians proved much more complicated.

Religious practice in the *mezzogiorno* was not based solely on doctrine, but grew out of deep mystical currents in the culture. Like other Renaissance Italians, southerners worshipped relics and believed that saints could intercede with Christ and perform miracles (Chapter 5), none more so than San Gennaro, patron saint of Naples, whose blood is said to liquefy miraculously every year. Southerners, more than other Italians, believed that the spirit world was intrinsically linked with the world of the living, and the dead were participating in everyday events. Medicine, natural science, and religion also overlapped; when someone fell ill he or she might go to an apothecary for medicine, to a priest for an exorcism, or a wise woman for magical cures. Documented from 600 CE in the region of Apulia, tarantism was a malady that was believed to have been caused by a spider bite, from which the "tarantella" takes its name. It was "cured" through frenzied dancing, in which the dancer becomes possessed by the spirit of the tarantula, in order to expel it from his or her body. At some point, the Apostle Paul became associated with the cure of the disease, and sufferers would dance before the altar in his chapel in the Church at Galatina. This is just one example demonstrating how complex the layering of ancient animistic practices and Christian belief was in southern Italy. Tarantism ultimately proved resistant to Tridentine measures, persisting even down to the 1950s.

On a practical level it was almost impossible to exert centralized control over the church in the *mezzogiorno*. Though to impose reforms, the Council of Trent had strengthened bishops' authority, in the south it was undercut by a number of factors. The priests in the Kingdom of Naples were organized into collegiate churches in a traditional system called *ricettizia* (received into the church). Owning church property collectively, these clerics elected their

330 *Celestial Revolutions*

own superior, making them somewhat independent from the directives of a bishop. Because this system required priests to be local residents, they naturally shared many of the beliefs and superstitions of their parishioners. Thus, the Tridentine ideal of educating priests, so that they could instruct and correct the mistakes of their flocks, made little headway in the *mezzogiorno*. Furthermore, the numerous wealthy and powerful monastic institutions in the south—nearly half of Italy's monasteries and convents were located in the Kingdom of Naples and Sicily—were outside the control of the bishops. Because the *Regno* was a papal fief, religious control there was further divided between the king of Spain, who appointed the two dozen or so most influential bishops, and the pope, who selected the more than one hundred others. Because of these institutional factors as well as the geographical isolation of many of the rural people, religious reform was slow in coming to the *mezzogiorno*.

The "new philosophy": Natural philosophers reading the book of nature

> The world is the book on which Eternal Wisdom wrote its own thoughts.
> Tommaso Campanella, *Sonnet*, 1622

If it proved complicated to extirpate ideas of backward villagers, clamping down on unorthodox views of intellectuals who published books and met in academies, by comparison, was more straightforward. In 1542 the Spanish viceroy closed the Accademia Pontaniana (Chapter 7) on accusations of heresy, and several years later he shut down other academies in Naples. Despite these closures, there was a vibrant intellectual presence in the *Regno*, which continued during the second half of the Cinquecento; in addition to Bruno, two other important philosophers during this period, Bernardino Telesio (1509–1588) and Tommaso Campanella (1568–1639), came from the south, from the region of Calabria, and spent significant portions of their lives in Naples. Their field, "natural philosophy," as it was taught in Renaissance universities, encompassed all the life sciences, physical sciences, and philosophy according to the writings of the ancients, above all Aristotle. This discipline has no exact equivalent today, in our highly compartmentalized fields of knowledge. Telesio's writings, for instance, ranged over the fields of cosmology, meteorology, geology, biology, physiology, and psychology, covering such topics as dreams, colors, and ethics. In his treatise *On the Nature of Things According to Their Own Principles* (1565), he argued that true knowledge of the world comes from our senses through direct observation of nature. His works had a strong impact on both Bruno and Campanella, who shared Telesio's dislike of "bookish" science, especially of Aristotle. According to Campanella, rather than poring over books of logic, the "book of nature" ought to be studied. Like Telesio and Bruno, Campanella was open to ideas of panpsychism, writing in *On the Sense of*

Things and on Magic (1620) that "the world is a feeling animal ... whose parts partake in one and the same kind of life." While Telesio during his lifetime had managed to avoid the Inquisition—his writings were condemned posthumously in 1593—Campanella spent over thirty years in jail, where he was tortured and had to feign insanity to avoid the death sentence. Campanella nonetheless managed to produce a huge body of writings while in prison, including poetry, treatises on astrology, rhetoric, theology, and, most important, his dialog *The City of the Sun* (1602). In this enormously successful book, Campanella envisions an ideal society, a utopia, in which property is held in common, every worker's dignity respected, and all citizens enjoy liberty and justice. Given the repressive society in which he lived, Campanella's dream indeed seems to be that of a "madman."

The natural philosophy of Telesio, Bruno, and Campanella was also referred to as the "new philosophy," distinguishing it from the "old philosophy" of Aristotle. After having nurtured many of the greatest humanist thinkers of the past two centuries, the Catholic Church, guided by Tridentine policy, fell back on medieval tradition and returned to endorsing strict scholastic education. The Jesuits centered their curriculum on Aristotle and Thomas Aquinas; the teaching of Plato was officially frowned upon. Many of the more daring humanist inquiries into Neoplatonism, magic, and Kabbalah were now considered heretical. The professor Francesco Patrizi (1529–1597) who taught Plato at Ferrara and later at the University of La Sapienza in Rome was brought before the Inquisition; his *New Philosophy of the Universe*, written in 1591, was banned three years later. Yet Aristotelians were not immune from persecution either. The works of two professors of natural philosophy at the University of Padua, Jacopo Zabarella (1532–1589) and Pietro Pomponazzi (1462–1525), both Aristotelians, were denounced to the Inquisition. Pomponazzi's *On the Immortality of the Soul* was condemned because he claimed that there was no natural proof that the soul was immortal. His *On Incantations*, which cast doubt on the existence of miracles, was placed on the *Index of Prohibited Books*. Inspired by Pomponazzi, Giulio Cesare Vanini (1585–1619) in his writings expressed a purely materialistic view of the universe, asserting that supernatural phenomena are only the product of the human imagination, which is easily manipulated by religious authorities. Vanini was put to death, as was philosopher Francesco Pucci (1543–1597). Others examined by the Inquisition include the Neapolitan philosopher Giovan Battista della Porta (*c*.1535–1615), the physician and mathematician Girolamo Cardano (1501–1576), and naturalist Ulisse Aldrovandi (1522–1605).

Italian scientific revolutions

Despite growing persecution from the Catholic Church, scientific inquiry was flourishing in the Italian Peninsula during this period. The so-called Scientific Revolution in Europe was sparked by the innovative advances in the sciences

332 *Celestial Revolutions*

coming from Italy beginning in the sixteenth century. These developments were, in part, a legacy of humanism. Because humanists emphasized the study of literature and history over the medieval scholastic curriculum of logic, mathematics, and astronomy, it is often wrongly assumed that scientific inquiry declined in Italy during the Renaissance. When Petrarch ridiculed those who pompously proclaimed to know "about birds and fishes, about how many hairs in a lion's mane, how many feathers in the tail of a hawk, how elephants mate from behind and are pregnant for two years," he was not condemning science per se, but how it was currently taught in the schools, with students absurdly memorizing useless facts from outmoded texts. Indeed, humanist scrutiny of texts, such as that employed by Valla in analyzing the Donation of Constantine, encouraged the questioning of long-held basic beliefs, including scientific theories. Furthermore, among the many ancient manuscripts the humanists unearthed and retranslated were ancient Greek scientific and mathematical texts (Table 3.1). Euclid, whose works had been available through Latin translations from Arabic, began to appear in improved editions, translated directly from Greek into Latin between 1509 and 1579. Diophantus's *Mathematics* was first translated from Greek by Raffaele Bombelli (1526–1572); the mathematical works of Apollonius, Aristarchus, and Pappus and others were translated by Federico Commandino (1509–1575). Printed editions of these Latin translations circulated throughout Europe. Many of these works reached a more popular audience at home through vernacular translations, such as those of Archimedes and Euclid translated into Italian by Tartaglia (Niccolò Fontana *c.*1499–1557) in 1543.

Poggio Bracciolini's discovery in 1417 of a manuscript of the poem *De rerum natura* (*On the Nature of Things*) by Lucretius (Titus Lucretius Carus died *c.*50 BCE) contributed to some of the most important scientific and philosophic developments in early modern Europe. In this work the Roman poet expresses the theories of Epicurus (third century BCE), for whom the entire universe is constructed of miniscule atoms, which are in constant motion. Within the infinite universe, infinite worlds constantly come into being and cease to exist, while the basic elements of which it is composed are indestructible. Lucretius's account of the origins of life on Earth and his proto-Darwinian theories of a kind of natural selection also incited humanists to ever greater curiosity about natural history. Humanists read the writings of Greeks Theophrastus (*c.*371–287 BCE) and Dioscorides (*c.*40–90 CE) and the Roman Pliny the Elder (Gaius Plinius Secundus 23–79 CE) on zoology, botany, pharmacology, mineralogy, metallurgy, geography, and ethnography.

A flowering of the natural sciences

Pliny in particular, with his fanciful descriptions of exotic animals and strange peoples, came under critical scrutiny by humanists such as Venetian

Celestial Revolutions 333

Figure 15.2 Giovanna Garzoni, *Ranunculus* (*Ranunculus asiaticus* with Two Almonds and a European Carpenter Bee, *Xylocopa violacea*), *c*.1648, Uffizi. The exotic plant depicted here is from Asia, rather than America. Note the artist's attention to the plant's root structure and minute observation of detail, which might have involved the use of a lens

Ermolao Barbaro the Younger (1454–1493), who wrote *Corrections to Pliny* in 1493. The discovery of the New World with its marvelous variety of previously unknown plants and animals both confirmed the wonder inspired by the ancient Roman author and demonstrated the limitations of classical knowledge. Pliny himself would have been amazed at the unheard-of marvels arriving from the Americas. Moreover, entering Italy through connections with the Spanish court, newly discovered plants and animals meticulously depicted by artists such as Bacchiacca (Francesco Ubertini,

1494–1557), Jacopo Ligozzi (1547–1627), and Giovanna Garzoni (1600–1670) greatly contributed to the rise of a new genre of painting—the still life (Figure 15.2).

The Medici grand dukes were equally delighted by the aesthetic, as well as the culinary value of these novelties that filled their gardens and tables with turkey, squash, corn, and—especially important for Italian cuisine—tomatoes, a sample of which was presented to Cosimo I for the first time on October 31, 1548. Significantly, the grand dukes funded zoological, botanical, and pharmaceutical research as well. The effort of recording and organizing information fell to botanists such as Luca Ghini (1490–1556), Pier Andrea Mattioli (1501–1578), Andrea Cesalpino (1519–1603), Pietro Castelli (1574–1662), and Ulisse Aldrovandi (1522–1605), author of works on zoology, botany, mineralogy, and geology. Among the pharmacological properties discovered were: roughbark lignum-vitae (*guaiacum officinalis*), from Hispaniola, introduced to cure syphilis; quinine bark (*cinchona officinalis*), native to the forests of Columbia, Ecuador, Bolivia, and Peru, used for the prevention and treatment of malaria; and sarsaparilla (*smilax officinalis*), native to southern Central America and northwest South America (Honduras, Nicaragua, Costa Rica, Panama, Colombia, and Ecuador), used to treat rheumatism, fever, and scabies.

All over Italy, interest in the natural sciences was growing, both inside and outside universities, with some of the greatest advances in the sciences originating from the learned academies. The public's fascination is demonstrated by the many books printed on the topic in Italy, as well as by the founding of Europe's earliest botanical gardens. The first was established in Pisa in 1544, followed by Padua (1545), Florence (1550), Rome (1563), and Bologna (1568). Museums of natural history also emerged during this time, notably associated with the universities in Bologna, Verona, Rome, and Naples. Collecting specimens and performing experiments also became fashionable at Italian courts and in the homes of leisured nobles, where in order to be considered cultured, it was essential to be well-versed in the latest scientific developments. A favorite pastime among the wealthy was to collect natural objects to keep in "cabinets of curiosities"; in such a room the shelves would be piled with fossils, shells, corals, gems, Egyptian mummified cats, bizarrely twisted roots, and crystals, while a stuffed toucan or iguana might dangle overhead. Though nowadays accumulating such things may seem like the behavior of eccentric amateur hobbyists, in the sixteenth and seventeenth centuries such activities were not considered odd, and there was not always a clear division between amateur and professional seekers of knowledge. Recognized experts, though, were in great demand; there were potentially rich rewards for the naturalist who could add some new wonder to a princely collection, or who, by dedicating a book of cutting-edge research could contribute to his patron's prestige.

The sciences put to work: Engineers and artists go to war

Beyond observation of curiosities in the natural world, science also had practical applications in engineering. The Medici grand dukes and other monarchs needed people who could use a surveyor's compass to lay out new streets for urban renewal projects, to operate pumps for draining malarial swamps, and to erect cranes for raising monuments in the ruler's honor. Books such as Guidobaldo del Monte's (1545–1607) *Mechanics* printed in 1577 and Agostino Ramelli's (1531–1600) *Various and Ingenious Machines* printed in 1588 are testaments to Italians' proficiency with the technological applications of mathematics. The mathematician Girolamo Cardano (1501–1576), author of the fundamental algebra treatise *Ars magna*, and his student Ludovico Ferrari (1522–1565) often worked in surveying or cartography. Moreover, artists and mathematicians sometimes collaborated: Leonardo da Vinci provided the illustrations for *Divina proportione*, a book by mathematician Luca Pacioli (1445–1517). Pacioli's *Summa de arithmetica, geometrica, proportioni et proportionalita* (1494) was, in turn, inspired by his studies with painter Piero della Francesca. Piero was himself a mathematician and author of works on geometry, arithmetic, and algebra: *Libellus de Quinque Corporibus Regularibus* (*Book of the Five Regular Solids*), *Trattato d'Abaco* (*Abacus Treatise*), and *De Prospectiva Pingendi* (*On Perspective for Painting*). And mathematician Paolo Toscanelli was influential on the work of both Alberti and Brunelleschi (Chapter 3).

The so-called "military revolution" of the sixteenth century, which laid the foundation of the success of the West in conquering the New World and beyond, was due in large part to the Italian advances in art, architecture, and technology during the Renaissance. The increasing use of gunpowder meant there was a need to create fortifications that would withstand heavy artillery attacks. Known as "*la trace italienne*," the angular bastion developed by Italian military architects over the years 1450–1520 became the gold standard for fortress design across Europe. Italians were known as specialists in all the military sciences during this time: in the 1490s Francesco di Giorgio Martini (1439–1501) wrote his *Treatise on Civil and Military Engineering*, and Vannoccio Biringuccio (1480–1537) wrote the first treatise on chemical metallurgy describing the forging of metals, *Pirotechnia* (published 1540). Among thirty-four works concerning military engineering published in Europe between 1554 and 1600, twenty-six were Italian. The need for precision in surveying territory and calculating the trajectories of cannon balls motivated no less a figure than Galileo to develop practical instruments such as the geometric and military compass and to study the velocity and parabolic paths of projectiles.

Furthermore, Renaissance artists were drawn into military pursuits as well. Sculptors' expertise in casting large bronze statues, such as Cellini's *Perseus*, lent itself to constructing canons. Built to endure intense heat and repeated explosions, these canons were sturdy, the barrels often intricately decorated

336 *Celestial Revolutions*

with artistic motifs. Ironically, bronze sculptures were not infrequently melted down to be converted into such weaponry. Renowned across the continent for its production of exquisite weapons, as well as armor, Milan was where the Missaglia family and especially one of their descendants, Filippo Negroli (*c.*1510–1579) produced the most sumptuous, sought-after armor in Europe. In addition to Leonardo's offer to design military machines for Ludovico Sforza (Chapter 10), the artist also collaborated with Machiavelli on a number of engineering projects including a plan to divert the course of the Arno River in 1503 when Florence was at war with Pisa. Although that plan was never carried out, the overhead maps of the Chiana Valley and the town of Imola that Leonardo produced while he was briefly employed by Cesare Borgia combine both technical innovation and artistic expertise. In the Map Room (Guardaroba) of Florence's Palazzo Vecchio, Egnazio Danti (Pellegrino Rainaldi Danti 1536–1586) and Stefano Bonsignori (d.1589) created fifty-three stunning paintings for Cosimo I, which accurately depict an atlas of the entire known world, the first of its kind. While through the medium of print, books such as *Navigations and Travels* (*Navigazione e viaggi* 1550–59) by geographers Giovanni Battista Ramusio (1485–1557) and Antonio Pigafetta (1480–1531) described voyages of exploration, numerous cartographic woodcuts and engravings produced by Giacomo Gastaldi (1500–1566), Paolo Forlani (fl. 1560–74), and Giovanni Camocio (fl.1552–74), were renowned across Europe for their combination of artistry and scientific measurement.

Anatomy: Physicians and artists look inside the human body

Art and practical science are also wedded in the great advances in knowledge of anatomy that took place during this time. Medicine was making enormous strides toward becoming an empirical science in Italy during the sixteenth century. Just as Pliny was being challenged by new discoveries in the natural sciences, Galen was losing ground as a medical authority. Faith in Galen had already been shaken by the arrival of syphilis, a "new" disease not mentioned by the ancient Greek writer. Now there was also concrete proof that his anatomy was mistaken, as discovered by the Flemish physician and anatomist Andreas Vesalius (1514–1564), who studied and later taught at the University of Padua. Though the anatomists Alessandro Achillini (1463–1512), Iacopo Barigazzi (Berengario da Carpi 1460–1530), and others made advances, none were as thorough as Vesalius, who revolutionized the field. His encyclopedic work *On the Fabric of the Human Body* (1543), illustrated with engravings from Titian's workshop, also underlines the links between art and science. Renaissance artists had long been dissecting corpses to gain a fuller understanding of the human body, epitomized in Leonardo's beautiful and minutely detailed anatomical drawings. Gabriele Falloppio (1523–1562), known for the fallopian tubes named after him, Bartolomeo Eustachi

Figure 15.3 Anatomical theater, built in 1594, Palazzo Bo, Padua. This is the anatomical theater in Padua, which could hold up to 240 spectators. Attended by both medical students, as well as local dignitaries and the general public, dissections would take place over the course of several weeks, during the winter months. There was often musical accompaniment

(1510–1574), after whom the eustachian tubes are named, and Giovanni Battista Canani (or Canano 1515–1579), who published a major work on musculature, are several anatomists who followed Vesalius. Girolamo Fabrici (or Fabrizio) d'Acquapendente (c.1533–1619) was a physician and professor of anatomy at the University of Padua, where he was responsible for establishing the first permanent anatomical theater in 1584 (Figure 15.3). Fabrici was a pioneer in embryology and also studied the folds that function as valves inside the veins. His student, the Englishman William Harvey (1578–1657), built on this research to discover the circulation of blood (*De Motu Cordis*, 1628).

Astrology, astronomy, cosmology: The sixteenth-century view from Earth

Despite the many advances in the natural sciences, medicine, mathematics, and engineering in Italy during this time, this period is most noted for startling new developments in astronomy and cosmology, though their origins are complex. As historian Paula Findlen has observed, "old and new, sacred and

338   *Celestial Revolutions*

secular, occult and scientific, professional and amateur systems of knowledge could and did coexist in the sixteenth and seventeenth centuries."[3] Nowhere is this better demonstrated than in the fields of astronomy and astrology, which were largely interchangeable in the sixteenth century. Throughout the Renaissance various forms of magic were considered valid sources of knowledge, and as long as the object was not to harm anyone (so-called "Black Magic" was forbidden) the Church did not object. The practice of "natural magic" was widespread—from intellectuals who studied the occult numerical combinations of the Kabbalah to unlock the secrets of the universe to peasants who consulted almanacs to know the most auspicious astrological date to plant their crops. Many individuals dabbled in alchemy, trying to transmute the properties of matter, and monarchs and popes regularly had their horoscopes cast.

Throughout the Renaissance, astrology in particular was a highly regarded "science." The revival of interest in classical mythology and the many artistic depictions of stories of the gods and goddesses who gave the planets their names brought the night sky vividly to life for Renaissance Italians. Much of the research in astronomy during the sixteenth century was conducted with the aim of making astrological predictions, based on the movement of the planets, more accurate, as well as aiding in navigation. Astrology and astronomy hence were closely linked, and because they required precise calculations, astrology and astronomy were taught alongside mathematics at Renaissance universities, sometimes all three subjects by the same professor. All three were equally recognized fields, but as they were mere tools used for calculating, these were considered beneath the discipline of natural philosophy. Odd as it may seem to us today, questions about the cosmos were not left to the astronomers, but dealt with by professors of natural philosophy who lectured on Aristotle.

The accepted cosmology as taught in the universities in the Renaissance was the geocentric model: Earth was at the center of the universe, with the Sun and planets revolving around it; beyond these "wandering stars", in the highest heavens were the "fixed stars." Ancient Greek philosophers held that the heavenly bodies moved in perfect circles; for everything about the heavens was perfect, in contrast to our imperfect world below. Aristotle in *On the Heavens* and in his *Physics* distinguished between the earthly or "sublunary" (literally "beneath the Moon") region and the heavens. Earth was a place where things changed and decayed, whereas the heavens were immutable and perfect. Everything in the sublunary realm was composed of four elements: earth, air, water, and fire. On the other hand, the heavenly bodies were not made of material substances, but of ether, also known as quintessence, meaning literally the "fifth element." In *Paradiso* Dante describes Earth as

---

3 Findlen, *Possessing Nature*, p.10.

encircled by rings of concentric crystalline spheres of the heavens, beyond which is the empyrean, where God, the angels, and elect dwell.

Measuring the heavens: Mathematicians invade outer space

There were problems with the geocentric system, however, noted already by the Greeks, who observed that the heavenly bodies appeared to speed up, slow down, stop, or change direction as they "circled around Earth." To fit these erratic movements into perfectly circular orbits, the astronomer Claudius Ptolemy (fl. 150 CE) designed a complex system of constructions—the eccentric, the epicycle, and the equant—to explain these phenomena. The Ptolemaic solution "fixed" the problem to a point, but as measurements became more precise, astronomers noted inaccuracies and observed that some of the rotations were slightly off-center. Furthermore, many astronomers, as well as philosophers, were disturbed by the inelegance of Ptolemy's system and sought a simpler explanation for the working of the universe.

The answer came from a Polish mathematician and astronomer who simply moved heaven and earth. Nicholas Copernicus (1473–1543), who had studied at the University of Bologna, published *De revolutionibus orbium coelestium* in 1543; in this book, he proposed a convincing solution to the problem of the rotations of the planets by placing not Earth, but the Sun at the center, and all the planets circling around (heliocentrism) (Map 15.1). Though Copernicus's work was widely read and discussed, displacing the earth from its immobile place at the center of the universe was too unsettling for most to accept. Apart from being counterintuitive—we are unable to feel any evidence of its rotation—Earth moving along with the other planets around the Sun contradicted certain passages in the Bible, and thus was considered heretical. Yet Copernicus's mathematical calculations were so precise that they were widely used even by the Catholic commission established at the Council of Trent in 1563 to reform the calendar. Due to the imprecision of the Julian calendar, in use since the time of Julius Caesar, moveable feast days, such as Easter, calculated by the phases of the Moon, were falling later with each year. A team of astronomers in Rome, headed by Jesuit mathematician and astronomer Christopher Clavius (1538–1612), applied rigorous astronomical observations and mathematical calculations to devise the Gregorian calendar, named after Pope Gregory XIII Boncompagni (r.1572–85), who approved it in 1582.

Everyone, it seemed, was looking up toward the heavens, when in 1572 a supernova appeared in the skies, followed in 1577 by an extremely bright comet. How could a new star appear if the heavens were unchangeable? And if a comet blazed through the perfect realm above the Moon, would it not shatter the crystalline heavens? Thanks to the precision instruments he developed, Danish astronomer Tycho Brahe (1546–1601) shattered the spheres himself by proving that these celestial events took place far above the Moon. Johannes Kepler (1571–1630), the German astronomer and

340 *Celestial Revolutions*

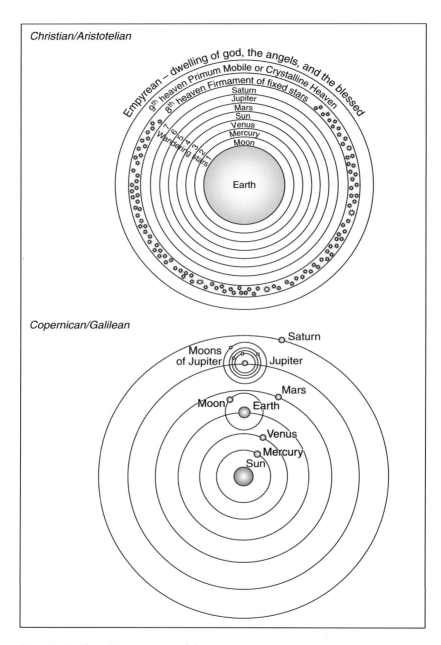

Map 15.1 Changing concepts of the cosmos

mathematician who had trained with Brahe, observed the elliptical orbit of the planets and introduced the concept that physical laws functioned in the heavens. The astronomers had now firmly entered the field of cosmology, and yet still the majority refused to accept the heliocentric model that some astronomers were supporting; Brahe himself rejected it and devised a model of his own in which all the planets revolved around the Sun, except Earth, which remained immobile. It would take much more to unseat the paradigm of the Earth-centered universe; it would take an individual of uncommon creative genius who could engineer better tools for observing and measuring the heavens, know how to interpret those measurements, and communicate his findings to the public.

Galileo and the "new science"

> Philosophy is written in this enormous book that is continuously open before our eyes—I mean the universe—but it cannot be understood if one does not first learn the language and know the characters in which it is written. It is written in the language of mathematics, its characters are triangles, circles, and other geometric figures, without which it is impossible to understand even a word of it; without these one is hopelessly lost in a dark labyrinth.
>
> Galileo, *The Assayer*

Galileo Galilei (1564–1642) was a multifaceted Renaissance genius on the scale of Leonardo and Michelangelo. Also a Tuscan, Galileo was born in Pisa and raised in the late cinquecento atmosphere of scientific and philosophical inquiry, surrounded by the arts. His father Vincenzo Galilei (c.1520–1591) was a renowned musician and composer, who taught the boy to play the lute; throughout his life Galileo turned to music for solace in difficult times. Galileo also learned drawing and participated in the artistic community in Florence, maintaining friendships with painters such as Lodovico Cardi (il Cigoli 1559–1613) and Artemisia Gentileschi. Delighting especially in the wild poetic romps of Ariosto and the twists of Dante's vigorous imagination, he sometimes lectured on literature at the Florentine Academy. Over the course of his life Galileo wrote poetry and published scientific works in an expressive Tuscan prose style that was not only understandable, but engaging reading for the common layperson. Though as a young man he was sent to the university to study medicine, Galileo had a hard time limiting himself to one discipline; besides, his analytical mind preferred ranging through the complexities of mathematics. He studied privately with Ostilio Ricci (1540–1603), court mathematician to the grand duke of Tuscany, and in 1585 he left the University of Pisa, never finishing his degree.

With the tools provided by the mechanics of Archimedes and geometry of Euclid, Galileo began to unlock the secrets of physics. He pioneered modern

342   *Celestial Revolutions*

scientific method, which, because of its emphasis on experimentation, was called by his followers "experimental philosophy." Scientific method begins with close observation of a natural phenomenon and the formulation of a tentative assumption, called a "hypothesis" to explain it. The truth of the hypothesis is then tested through a series of experiments. If the hypothesis is true, experiments will result according to predictions, and the hypothesis can be adopted as theory. If it is false, the hypothesis must be rejected or modified, and the process of observation and experimentation starts again. Galileo's experiments always involved precise, well-documented measurements and findings that could be repeated. He insisted on the necessity of keeping an open mind, being guided by reason and sense experience, but never being limited by them. Like Leonardo who found fossils of sea creatures buried in the ground in the Apennine Mountains and hypothesized that the region had once been under the sea, a seemingly absurd yet, as it turned out, true proposition, Galileo recognized that human knowledge is limited and the scientist must always ask new questions and seek new answers.

When he was only twenty-two, Galileo wrote a short work explaining one of his inventions for measuring the volume of metals in water to determine the gold or silver content. This early work already displays Galileo's interests in both the abstract and the practical in science, as well as his technician's attention to precision-measuring instruments. Supporting himself by giving private lessons in mathematics, the young scientist was in need of a secure salary to continue his research. Within the scientific community of Tuscany Galileo's brilliance was beginning to attract attention, and in 1589 Galileo was appointed professor of mathematics at the University of Pisa, through the intervention of mathematician Guidobaldo del Monte (1547–1607). It was a humble, low-paid position, but it allowed Galileo to pursue his studies in the physics of movement. Whether he ever performed the famous experiment of dropping two unequal weights from the top of the Leaning Tower of Pisa is debated, but through experimentation he did refute Aristotle's claim that a heavy object fell to the ground faster than a light object of the same material. By measuring the velocity of falling objects, the swing of a pendulum, and the descent of a ball on an inclined plane, Galileo was able to discern laws of physical motion and inertia. Natural philosophers such as Campanella had wanted to "read the book of nature," but it was Galileo who introduced the language of mathematics into his "new science" that made this possible.

Galileo takes a spyglass and turns it into a telescope

Oh my dear Kepler, I wish we could laugh together at people's remarkable stupidity. The principal professor of philosophy here stubbornly refuses to look at the Moon, the planets, and my telescope, even though I have asked him a thousand times.

Galileo, *Letter to Kepler*, August 19, 1610

Celestial Revolutions 343

In 1592 Galileo was appointed chair of mathematics at the prestigious University of Padua. Under the dominion of nearby Venice, the most tolerant state in Italy, Padua enjoyed an exciting atmosphere of intellectual freedom. During his eighteen years in Padua, Galileo met and exchanged ideas with some of the most original thinkers of his day. He also encountered resistance from intractable colleagues, but their arguments only energized his creative genius. In Padua, when he was not teaching mathematics, mechanics, astronomy, or military engineering, Galileo carried out most of his research that created the groundwork for modern physics, although he did not publish his findings until several decades later in his masterpiece *Two New Sciences* (1638). He put this work aside, however, when a series of events led him from studying earthly movement to make new discoveries in the heavens.

Throughout his years in Padua, Galileo's interest in designing precision scientific instruments never waned. Instruments such as his pendulum clock were crucial for Galileo's study of the mechanics of motion and could also have market value. Similarly practical was the geometric and military compass he developed in 1597 and sold with an accompanying manual. These devices brought monetary rewards and brought their inventor to the attention of powerful patrons. On the strength of the latter invention, Galileo was appointed tutor to the teenager who later became Grand Duke Cosimo II (1590–1621). In early 1609, while still employed at Padua by the Republic of Venice, Galileo learned that a Dutchman had designed a spyglass. As the name implies, the device was useful for spying on enemies, and Galileo immediately recognized its potential usefulness for the Venetian state. Having studied the principles of optics, Galileo applied himself to fitting a long tube with two spectacle lenses, one convex and the other concave, and refined the instrument until in August he was able to present the Doge of Venice with an "eyecane" (*cannocchiale*), as he first called it—an instrument sixteen times more powerful than the Dutch spyglass. The Venetian Senate immediately doubled his salary and awarded Galileo a lifetime tenured teaching position at Padua.

The telescope, as it later came to be called, was initially considered useful primarily as an instrument of military intelligence; by using it, troops could be spotted or an approaching ship seen two hours before it could be sighted by the naked eye. Rather than train his own telescope on the horizon, however, Galileo pointed it up at the sky. All astronomical observations until this point had been done with the naked eye, so when he first looked up at the heavens through his telescope, Galileo saw things that literally no human had ever seen before. He could see that the Milky Way, which had formerly appeared as a celestial mist, was in reality composed of a myriad of individual stars and that the smooth, apparently perfect surface of the Moon was irregular, composed of mountains and craters. He observed sunspots and the phases of the planet Venus. He also discovered that the planet Jupiter was encircled with moons of its own.

The *Starry Messenger*: The Medici become moons and the scientist becomes a star

Galileo hastened to record these startling new discoveries, which he published in January 1610, in a work entitled *Sidereus nuncius*. The title means *Starry Messenger* in Latin, the language in which Galileo chose to write this book, so that it could be read and understood throughout Europe. He illustrated it with his precise drawings of the pock-marked Moon and the orbit of the four satellites around Jupiter. He named these satellites "the Medicean Stars," and he dedicated the book to his former pupil, now Grand Duke Cosimo II de' Medici. Along with the telescope, the book was a sensation, and its author became a celebrity. Like modern-day researchers, Galileo needed to drum up funding; he proved to be an adept courtier, sending telescopes as gifts to influential people and devising "parlor tricks" to be performed with his equipment to stir their interest. Galileo capitalized on his fame by requesting a position as "chief mathematician and philosopher" to the grand duke of Tuscany, which he was granted. In addition to a large salary, Galileo was exempted from teaching anyone but members of the grand ducal family. The scientist immediately resigned his position at the University of Padua and moved back to his native Tuscany in the fall of 1610. The next year Galileo visited Rome, where he was greeted triumphantly by Clavius and the other Jesuit mathematicians at the Roman College. Everywhere in Rome the astronomer was feted, and he met with high-ranking cardinals and the pope himself. At this time Galileo was inducted into the Accademia dei Lincei in Rome. The academy printed a number of his works, but more importantly, among the learned seekers of knowledge he met there, Galileo developed significant personal and professional connections that he maintained throughout his life. In 1611 it would be humanists at the Accademia dei Lincei who named his invention: they coined the word *telescopio* by combining the Greek *tele* "from a distance" and *skopeo* "I see."

With celebrity, however, also came exposure to criticism. Like Michelangelo, whose *Last Judgment* had become a target for zealous extremists, Galileo's discoveries in the following years came under increasing attacks from conservative churchmen and Aristotelians, as well as from envious courtiers. Galileo responded to those who criticized his theories or doubted his observations by refuting their arguments with humor and sometimes with biting sarcasm. Some of the accusations were easy to laugh off, such as the people who claimed that the moons of Jupiter were painted inside the lens of the telescope, while others were more insidious, charging Galileo with heresy. His observations of the phases of Venus and the orbits of the other planets around the Sun had convinced Galileo that Copernicus's model was the correct one. Though the official position of the Catholic Church on Copernicus was at this point still somewhat ambiguous, it was risky to endorse heliocentrism. It was acceptable to use the heliocentric model for

Celestial Revolutions   345

calculations, but it was forbidden to state that the Sun was at the center of the universe. Emboldened by his supporters and secure in the position he held with the grand duke, Galileo embraced Copernicanism openly for the first time in print in 1613 in his *Letter on Sunspots*.

The conflict between the new science and religion

> It is the intention of the Holy Spirit to teach us how to go to heaven, not how heaven goes.
>
> Cardinal Baronius, cited by Galileo in *Letter to the Grand Duchess Christina*

As the frequency and virulence of attacks on supporters of Copernican theory increased, Galileo became anxious to address his opponents openly. In 1615 he wrote the *Letter to the Grand Duchess Christina*, an eloquent defense of science as a system of knowledge distinct from the claims of religion. At a dinner party, the dowager grand duchess of Tuscany had raised some questions with one of Galileo's supporters about the theological implications of Copernicus's system. Galileo felt that the time was ripe to address the issue head-on. In this letter, Galileo declares that he believes "the Sun remains motionless in the center of the revolution of the celestial orbs, while Earth rotating on its axis, revolves around the Sun." Because his knowledge is based on reason, sensory observation, and measurement, he cannot deny this belief; once demonstrated, scientific fact is not subject to interpretation. Even if he is silenced, Galileo adds, to eradicate heliocentrism "it would be necessary to prohibit, not only Copernicus's book and the writings of other authors who agree with his theory, but to outlaw the entire science of astronomy, indeed to forbid men from looking up at the sky."

The Bible's truth is more complex, argues Galileo. Biblical texts are written in a sometimes obscure language with passages that are seemingly contradictory. These must be carefully interpreted by theologians, who do not ignore or prohibit scientific discoveries but reconcile scientific truths with Christian scripture. Galileo urges people to "seek the incontrovertible sense of the Bible with the assistance of demonstrated truth"; he emphasizes that scientific knowledge can only strengthen faith. Galileo furthermore warns that the church should not "flash her sword merely because she has the power to do so." He argues that, because the theory of heliocentrism is gaining ground, it would be a mistake "to ban Copernicus now that through many observations the many readers of his work daily reveal the truth of his doctrine." If the already embattled Catholic Church defends bad science, when those theories are disproved, the church will inevitably lose authority. The church ought to stay away from scientific judgments entirely, concerning itself only with matters that affect salvation, writes Galileo, citing Saints Augustine, Jerome, and Aquinas.

346 *Celestial Revolutions*

Copies of this letter circulated widely, but rather than resolve the issue, Galileo's trespassing into the realm of theology inflamed his attackers. They did not resent the suggestion of hidden meanings behind Biblical passages; theologians had employed exegesis, the technique of textual analysis to interpret scripture, since the Middle Ages to make sense of difficult sacred writings. What angered the theologians is that a mathematician should lecture them on Biblical meaning. Galileo's opponents now vehemently asserted that if the Bible said that Joshua made the Sun stand still as it moved through the sky, it meant literally that Earth is immobile and the Sun moves. It is one of the ironies of the battle between the church and Galileo that Galileo's attackers found themselves in a defensive position and were forced to adopt a literal reading of scripture akin to fundamentalism, which was foreign to the scholarly methods of the Catholic Church.

Galileo followed up the letter with a visit to Rome to confront his opponents, though he was advised that this might be dangerous. In Rome, in early 1616, he met with top Vatican officials including Cardinal Roberto Bellarmino (or Bellarmine 1542–1621). The Jesuit inquisitor responsible for Giordano Bruno's conviction, Bellarmino had been keeping an eye on Galileo since at least as early as 1611, when several professors at the University of Padua were being investigated. Bellarmino warned Galileo not to endorse Copernican views, which were coming under increased scrutiny by the Roman Inquisition. In March 1616, with the approval of Pope Paul V Borghese (r.1605–21), all books advocating Copernicanism were placed on the *Papal Index*.

Recognizing the risk he was running, out of prudence Galileo avoided the subject of Copernicanism, until 1623, when the Florentine humanist Maffeo Barberini was elected Pope Urban VIII (r.1623–44). Twelve years earlier Galileo had met then Cardinal Barberini, who was impressed with the scientist and supported him in intellectual debates. When discussing Copernicus, Barberini had warned Galileo, however, only to accept heliocentrism as a "hypothesis," not as established fact. To Galileo, the election of the sympathetic Barberini indicated that it was the right time to re-open the discussion, and in 1625 Galileo began writing his *Dialogue Concerning the Two Chief World Systems, Ptolemaic and Copernican*. When it was finished, Galileo went through all the official channels and made adjustments to the text to receive the imprimatur, and he succeeded in having it published in February 1632. In August, the Holy Office suddenly stopped bookstores in Rome from selling the book, and in October Galileo was ordered to come to Rome to stand trial before the Roman Inquisition. Ferdinando II de' Medici (r.1621–70), who had succeeded Cosimo II as grand duke of Tuscany, tried to prevent the nearly seventy-year old scientist from being extradited, but Ferdinando was warned that if he did not co-operate, officers from the Vatican would arrest Galileo and take him away in chains. To avoid this intervention and rather than risk the pope's anger, the grand duke duly gave in and turned Galileo over to Rome.

Celestial Revolutions   347

The trial of the century: Galileo before the Inquisition in 1633

> [the Church] can forbid men to write, but it cannot make the earth either stand still or move, nor keep God and nature from revealing from time to time in thousands of ways its hidden secrets.
>
> Benedictine Friar and Scientist Benedetto Castelli (1578–1643)

Like many Renaissance works of literature, Galileo's book is written in the form of a dialogue. Galileo chose a literary genre that was enjoyable and accessible to the educated reading public, but also one in which the author could put words in his characters' mouths, disassociating himself from controversial views. There are three characters in the *Dialogue Concerning the Two Chief World Systems*: a learned scientist named Salviati; an inquisitive, intelligent nobleman named Sagredo; and a simplistic old-fashioned Aristotelian named appropriately, Simplicio. The former two are based on actual men whom Galileo had known, and the third was a fictional persona, put there to repeat commonly held beliefs, each of which is deftly refuted. The pope was enraged when he felt he recognized some of his own arguments in the mouth of Simplicio, and Galileo's enemies at the Vatican were eager to encourage the pope in this supposition. Feeling himself mocked, the pope went from being the scientist's admirer to becoming his fiercest enemy. Furthermore, Urban was under political pressure to crack down on heresy. The Spanish, angered by his support of the French and their Protestant allies in the Thirty Years' War, were talking about calling a church council to test Urban's orthodoxy. Much was at stake for the pope in this trial, but even more for the future of scientific inquiry in Catholic Italy.

When the trial began on April 12, 1633, Galileo was accused of disobeying an order given in 1616 not to advocate Copernicanism. The circumstances surrounding the trial were complex, and even today there is much that remains unclear about the nature of the charges against Galileo. Historian Pietro Redondi has suggested that Galileo's support of atomism was the true cause of his trial. Atomism, the theory that all matter is composed of tiny, indivisible particles, was considered a heresy against the doctrine of Transubstantiation; Redondi believes that Urban may have actually used the Copernicanism as a smokescreen to protect Galileo from more serious charges. Nevertheless, when charged with endorsing the Copernican view, the scientist defended himself by claiming that in the *Dialogue* he did not promote Copernicanism, but had treated it solely as a hypothesis. If Galileo thought that he could mask his views through the witty sallies of the character Salviati in his *Dialogue*, he was wrong. The inquisitors read and understood the work as a very thinly veiled polemic in favor of Copernicanism, which it was, and they were not amused. After repeated examination and threatened with torture, Galileo was advised to make a full confession of guilt and to perform an official recantation of his formerly held heretical beliefs. On June 1633 the most celebrated scientific

348   *Celestial Revolutions*

genius of his age, now a frail old man, went down on his knees in front of the gathering of cardinals and recited: "I abjure, curse, and detest the aforesaid errors and heresies."

Considerations: What would the ancient Greeks and Romans have said?

An aged Galileo was taken into custody and lived out his life under house arrest in Arcetri just outside Florence. Though he had officially retracted his belief in Copernicanism before the inquisitors, his ideas could not be silenced. In 1636 he completed his great work *Two New Sciences*, that laid the groundwork for a new physics; the manuscript had to be smuggled out of Italy, and it was published in Leiden two years later. The many books that he wrote on astronomy, mechanics, and physics electrified thinkers across Europe, and Galileo's life marked a pivotal moment in the intellectual history of Italy. Born the same year Michelangelo died, Galileo died in 1642, a year before Isaac Newton's birth. A new age was beginning, one in which, rather than looking backward to the classical past for answers, humankind, confident of its own abilities, was looking forward.

In the words of poet Alessandro Tassoni in 1620:

What did the Greeks and Romans ever invent that can be compared to the printing press ... the compass and nautical chart ...? If the Romans gloried to have brought their troops across the ocean to the Isle of Britain ... what glory is due to the one who taught the Portuguese to navigate to an unknown pole, from one horizon to the other? ... What invention so tremendous was ever imagined that could equal our artilleries? ... What would the Greeks and Romans have said of our most ingenious invention of the wheel clock, that perpetually turning, strikes and shows the hours, as well as the motion of the planets? Recently invented in Flanders and perfected in Italy, the telescope alone—with which things that are fifteen or twenty miles away can be seen as if they are before you, discovering stars which were invisible in the heavens—by far surpasses any inventions discovered by Greeks or Romans in the entire course of their famous age.

Sourcebook

Giordano Bruno, *Expulsion of the Triumphant Beast*
Ferdinando I de' Medici, *Livornine Charter*
Gianfrancesco Pico della Mirandola, *The Witch*
Tommaso Campanella, *The City of the Sun*
Ulisse Aldrovandi, *Discourse on Nature*; *Letter to Francesco I*
Galileo Galilei, *Parable of the Sounds*; *Notes on De phaenomenis*
Galileo Galilei, *Ink and Wash Drawing of Moon*
Lodovico Cigoli, *The Virgin of the Immaculate Conception*

Further reading

Findlen, Paula. *Possessing Nature: Museums, Collecting, and Scientific Culture in Early Modern Italy*, University of California Press, 1995.

Gentilcore, David. *From Bishop to Witch: The System of the Sacred in Early Modern Terra d'Otranto*, Manchester University Press, 1992.

Ginzburg, Carlo. *The Cheese and the Worms*, trans. John and Anne Tedeschi, Johns Hopkins University Press, 1980.

Heilbron, John. *Galileo*, Oxford University Press, 2010.

Herzig, Tamar. "Witchcraft Prosecutions in Italy," in *The Oxford Handbook of Witchcraft in Early Modern Europe and Colonial America*, ed. Brian P. Levack, Oxford University Press, 2013, pp. 249–67.

Muir, Edward. *The Culture Wars of the Late Renaissance: Skeptics, Libertines, and Opera*, Harvard University Press, 2007.

Redondi , Pietro. *Galileo: Heretic,* trans. by Raymond Rosenthal, Princeton University Press, 1987.

Tedeschi, John. *The Prosecution of Heresy: Collected Studies on the Inquisition in Early Modern Italy*, Medieval & Renaissance Texts & Studies, 1991.

Epilogue
The End of the Renaissance?

Though science in Italy did not die with Galileo—his student Evangelista Torricelli (1608–1647) and astronomer Giovanni Alfonso Borelli (1608–1679) carried on his research—the message sent by Galileo's trial made it clear that Italy was not a safe or productive place to do controversial research, at least in cosmology. Francesco de Sanctis in his *History of Italian Literature* (1870) writes of the "disastrous consequences" of the Council of Trent, after which, "deprived of any freedom to write, to speak and even to think … Italy was turned into the most wretched of all western nations."

Politically, as well, Italy was descending once again into turmoil. In an eerie déjà vu of the calamities of the past century, in the early 1600s hostilities broke out between the principalities of Savoy and Mantua, which, because of their strategic locations, drew in French, Spanish, and imperial forces. Carlo Emanuele, Duke of Savoy, with grandiose dreams of expansion, sided now with Spain, now with France to increase his territory, and caused the two powers, in 1613, to fight the first war in Italian territory since the Peace of Cateau-Cambrésis in 1559. In 1618 the Thirty Years' War began, pitting the empire and Spain against rebels in German-speaking lands as well as the Netherlands, England, and eventually France. Since Spanish access to the Netherlands by sea was cut off by the English and Dutch, the Alpine pass known as the Valtellina in northwestern Lombardy became vitally important to Spanish interests as a route to the Netherlands. This region was controlled by Protestants, so the Spanish encouraged the local Catholic population to rebel, massacring hundreds in the 1620 *sacro macello* (holy slaughter). When the last duke of Mantua died without an heir, there was a power-grab for the Duchy, culminating in a horrific three-day sack of Mantua by imperial troops in 1630. In 1629 a devastating epidemic of plague had broken out in northern Italy and, spread by the movement of troops, continued through 1630, thereafter engulfing the entire peninsula. Even before the plague, Italy had been falling into an economic depression—she was unable to compete with textiles produced in England, the Thirty Years' War caused Italy's export markets to dry up, and Spain squeezed the country ever more tightly for funds needed to continue that war—but now as the plague raged, poverty

DOI: 10.4324/9781003270362-16

and famine became widespread throughout Italy. The disease had not yet run its course before yet another natural catastrophe hit. On December 16, 1631, the volcano Mount Vesuvius erupted, carpeting southern Europe in ash, burying entire villages, and killing several thousand people.

Physically worn down by war, disease, and poverty, and intellectually crushed by an oppressive theocracy, the Italians had finally run out of energy. The Renaissance in Italy was over.

Or was it?

Venice had always maintained an independent, at times antagonistic, relationship with the Roman Church. When Venice passed laws limiting lands owned by the Church in the *terraferma* in 1606, the pope imposed a papal interdict on the Republic. Venice defied this interdict, refused to publish it, and expelled any priests who refused to say Mass; the Jesuits were among those ejected from Venice. By means of diplomacy the interdict was eventually lifted, though Venice never admitted any guilt, nor were the Jesuits permitted to return. Because of Venice's defiant attitude toward the papacy, had Galileo remained in Padua, under the jurisdiction of the Republic, rather than returned to Florence, in all probability he would never have ended up in the hands of the Roman Inquisition. His friends, the natural philosophers Paolo Sarpi (1552–1623) and Cesare Cremonini (1550–1631) who both lived in Venetian territory, were wanted by the Inquisition, yet the Republic never turned either of them over.

The Venetian Republic became a haven for freethinkers. Aristotelian philosophers at the University of Padua flirted with heresy by embracing a materialist view of the universe and denying the immortality of the soul. Venice's academies were the most daring in Italy, above all the Accademia degli Incogniti (active 1630–60). Many of its members embraced atheism and sexual freedom. Known as "libertines," these learned freethinkers were forerunners of the Enlightenment philosophes; the discussions that took place in their academy prefigured those in the salons of Paris a century later. They published works that were openly critical of the church, including writings by the dissident nun Arcangela Tarabotti (1604–1652).

The academy also gave its support to a brand-new art form—opera. Opera had been invented by a group known as the Florentine Camerata, of which Galileo's father Vincenzo Galilei was a member. Their first productions were self-conscious efforts to revive what Renaissance music theorists imagined classical Greek music drama to have been. The earliest operas performed in Florence were Iacopo Peri's *Dafne*, in 1598 and his *Euridice* in 1600. Francesca Caccini (1587–*c*.1645) composed numerous of these music dramas for the Medici court in collaboration with librettist Michelangelo Buonarroti the Younger (grand-nephew of the artist 1568–1646). Though born in the Grand Duchy of Tuscany, the new art form matured in the Republic of Venice. Without a royal court as patron, opera in Venice responded directly to the public's taste. Originally opera was performed at Carnival time (the forty days leading to Lent), a part of the transgressive entertainment

352 *Epilogue*

permitted during that season. So popular was the new art form that it became year-round entertainment in Venice, where the first public opera theater was established in 1637; by 1700 there were sixteen opera houses in the city. Audiences were thrilled by the stories of heroes and heroines of classical antiquity enhanced by vocal pyrotechnics and cleverly engineered stage machinery to create special effects. Among the first operatic masterpieces, *The Coronation of Poppea*, written by Claudio Monteverdi (1567–1643) was given its debut in Venice in 1642. Eventually opera spread throughout the whole Italian Peninsula and became the rage in all of Europe. Italian virtuoso singers, instrumentalists, and composers were the toast of European courts. The Florentine-born Lully (Giovanni Battista Lulli 1632–1687) was court composer to Louis XIV. Opera's popularity was such that non-Italian composers Gluck, Handel, and Mozart all wrote Italian operas to satisfy public demand. Though the Catholic Church did not approve of the erotic plots of these exuberant secular music dramas and tried to limit their performances to Carnival season, it was impossible to suppress them entirely. Rather, the church seized on the public's passion for opera and developed a parallel form of sacred music drama, known as oratorio. Emerging around 1600, the oratorio was so-named because it was often performed in an oratory or prayer hall, often of a confraternity. The oratorio, which employed a number of soloists, musicians, and sometimes a chorus in the manner of an opera, but without scenery or costumes, went on to have enormous success throughout Europe, in both Catholic and Protestant countries; the most famous oratorio is George Frideric Handel's *Messiah* (1741). Just as Italy had led the way in spoken theater with commedia dell'arte, now she was foremost in music drama, both secular and sacred. The same critic De Sanctis wrote: "As literature was dying ... music was being born."

These are all developments of what is known as the Baroque era, a period in music from around 1580 to 1750, in art and architecture from roughly 1600 to 1750. This is a period that is generally considered beyond the confines of the Renaissance, and yet there is no clear break between Renaissance art and culture and that of the Baroque. The vigor of Caravaggio's style was carried on by his followers, known as Caravaggisti, most notably the painters Orazio Gentileschi and his daughter Artemisia. Painters who followed in Carracci's footsteps included Guido Reni (1575–1642), Guercino (Giovanni Francesco Barbieri 1591–1666), and Domenichino (Domenico Zampieri 1581–1641). Architecture and urban planning in Rome continued to surge forward in the seventeenth century as well. St. Peter's Basilica was finally completed and consecrated in 1626 under Pope Urban VIII. Gian Lorenzo Bernini (1598–1680), called by art historian Howard Hibbard "the last of the dazzling universal geniuses who had made Italy the artistic and intellectual center of Europe for more than three hundred years," was a sculptor, architect, and city planner who worked closely with Pope Alexander VII Chigi (r.1655–67) to remake the face of Rome. From painter and architect Pietro da Cortona's (1596–1669) histrionic façades to architect Francesco Borromini's

Epilogue 353

Figure 16.1 Top, Michelangelo Buonarroti, et al. St. Peter's Basilica, Vatican; bottom, Thomas U. Walter, et al. United States Capitol Building, Washington D.C.

354   *Epilogue*

(1599–1667) extravagantly undulating inventions, the lush, audacious style of the Baroque was suddenly everywhere in Rome.

The vigor had not gone out of the arts in Italy, but more and more it was exported. The effervescent new style in art, architecture, and music that originated in Italy soon took hold in every part of Europe and throughout the world. The question should not be "When did the Renaissance end?" but rather "Has the Renaissance ended?" The cultural movement that began in Italy in the thirteenth century spread beyond the confines of the Italian boot. Absolutist monarchs throughout Europe would go to sleep at night under ceilings painted with rosy cherubs and smiling fleshy goddesses and pray in chapels of ornate gilt. Their courtiers, while dancing to the minuets of Corelli or Scarlatti, would strive to mimic the nonchalant grace described by Castiglione. With the Enlightenment, philosophers believed reason and scientific observation, pioneered by Galileo, would lead to unlocking the secrets of nature. The words of Voltaire (1694–1778): "*Écrasez l'infâme!*" (crush the loathsome thing) sound very much like an echo of Giordano Bruno's appeal for reason to triumph over superstition. Likewise, it was reason, not religion, they believed should determine politics, as outlined by Machiavelli, and the old regime founded on the divine right of kings was overthrown. In the American colonies the Founding Fathers would debate what form the new republic should take, settling on a mixed government modeled on that of Venice. And, like the majority of modern states today, the United States is governed by a set of legal codes based on Roman Law, which was first reintroduced in the Renaissance republics. Moreover, post offices, city halls, and public buildings the world over are designed according to Palladian proportions, their capitols surmounted with domes inspired by the one Michelangelo designed for St. Peter's. Everywhere students who study literature and history in a humanities curriculum, learning the critical thinking skills to become active, well-informed citizens, are fulfilling the dreams of the humanists Bruni and Salutati.

The Renaissance is dead. Long live the Renaissance!

Figure credits

Cover: Domenico Ghirlandaio, *Visitation*, detail. Zip Lexing/Alamy Stock Photo R88PR7

1.1	Giotto, *The Visitation*. Artefact / Alamy Stock Photo 2F4WWDM	19
1.2	Pisano, *Massacre of the Innocents*, Pistoia. Sailko, Wikipedia Commons	21
2.1	Simone Martini, *Annunciation*, detail, Uffizi, Peter Barritt/ Alamy Stock Photo JH1XWM	38
2.2	Lorenzetti, *Effects of Good Government*, Siena. Heritage Image Partnership Ltd/Alamy Stock Photo DE78X2	39
3.1	Ghiberti, *Isaac and Esau*, Opera del Duomo, restored. Wikipedia Commons	60
3.2	Donatello, *St. George*, Bargello. Rufus46, Wikipedia Commons	62
3.3	Brunelleschi, photo of Cupola, Florence. Wikipedia Commons	64
3.4	Masaccio, *Distribution of Alms and the Death of Ananias*, Brancacci Chapel. The Picture Art Collection/Alamy Stock Photo MPA3YM	66
4.1	Fra Angelico, *St. Lawrence Distributes Alms*, Chapel of Nicholas V, Vatican. ART Collection/Alamy Stock Photo HKK9NE	84
4.2	Alberti, photo of Façade of Santa Maria Novella, Florence. Amada44, Wikipedia Commons	88
5.1	*Adimari Wedding Cassone*. The Picture Art Collection/ Alamy Stock Photo MWY829	103
5.2	Domenico Ghirlandaio, *Birth of John the Baptist*, Cappella Tornabuoni. Artefact/Alamy Stock Photo 2G2GGPK	110
5.3	Piero della Francesca, *Madonna del Parto*. Rita Guglielmi/ Alamy Stock Photo 2J82FAK	112
6.1	Giovannino de' Grassi, *Visconti Book of Hours*, BNCF Banco Rari 397	124

356 Figure credits

6.2 Gozzoli, *Procession of the Magi*, detail, Palazzo Medici. AKG Images — 135

7.1 Cappella Palatina, Norman Palace, Palermo photo. kabaeh49, Wikipedia Commons — 145

7.2 Antonello da Messina, *Virgin Annunciate*, Palermo. Photo Scala, Florence — 154

8.1 Carpaccio, *Hunting on the Lagoon*, Getty. The J. Paul Getty Museum, Los Angeles, 79.PB.72. 103REK Getty Museum — 163

8.2 Giovanni Bellini, *Portrait of Doge Loredan*, National Gallery. IanDagnall Computing/Alamy Stock Photo M398JJ — 174

8.3 Sansovino, photo of Loggetta. Joanbanjo, Wikipedia Commons — 185

9.1 Botticelli, *Young Man with Medal of Cosimo de' Medici*, Uffizi. Art Library/Alamy Stock Photo M43TW7 — 191

9.2 Verrocchio, *Christ and St. Thomas*. Orsanmichele/Ministry of Culture — 204

9.3 Photo of Palazzo Strozzi. AGF Srl/Alamy Stock Photo FA7DT1 — 207

10.1 Giorgione, *The Tempest*. The Picture Art Collection / Alamy Stock Photo MYWJT0 — 217

10.2 Signorelli, *Rule of the Antichrist*, detail, Orvieto. Wojciech Stróżyk/Alamy Stock Photo 2A4W3CN — 222

11.1 Leonardo, *Vitruvian Man*. Tuul and Bruno Morandi/Alamy Stock Photo 2FXA1XA — 240

11.2 Mantegna, *Camera degli Sposi*, Mantua. Hemis/Alamy Stock Photo R7KBBB — 243

11.3 Giuliano da Maiano, Intarsia, Studiolo, Urbino. VTR/Alamy Stock Photo 2B8FCY7 — 245

11.4 Giorgione/Titian, *Sleeping Venus*, Gemäldegalerie, Dresden. IanDagnall Computing/Alamy Stock Photo 2FA04PY — 247

12.1 Raphael, *Portrait of Pope Leo X with Cardinals Giulio de' Medici and Luigi de' Rossi*, Uffizi, incamerastock/Alamy Stock Photo WWWN4M — 263

12.2 Titian, *Equestrian Portrait of Charles V*, Prado. — 269

13.1 Michelangelo, *Night*, New Sacristy, San Lorenzo. George M. Groutas, Wikipedia Commons. — 283

13.2 Pontormo, *Capponi Chapel Altarpiece*, Church of Santa Felicita, Florence. ART Collection/Alamy Stock Photo HM2FN4 — 293

14.1 Top: Palladio, photo of Villa La Rotonda. Flavio Vallenari/ iStock 525455177; bottom: photo of Pantheon, Rome. Xantana/iStock 493907838. — 312

14.2 Veronese, *Wedding Feast at Cana*, detail, Louvre. Art Collection 2/Alamy Stock Photo HR2BET — 316

14.3 Sofonisba Anguissola, *Portrait of the Artist's Sister as a Nun*, City Art Gallery, Southampton. Southampton City Art Gallery/Bridgeman Images SOU79749 — 317

Figure credits   357

15.1   Caravaggio, *The Calling of St. Matthew*, Church of San
Luigi dei Francesi. Niday Picture Library/Alamy Stock Photo
M0EWB9   324
15.2   Giovanna Garzoni, *Ranunculus asiaticus with Two Almonds
and a Hymenopteran*, Uffizi. Alinari Archives, Florence—
Reproduced with the permission of Ministero per i Beni e le
Attività Culturali/Bridgeman Images 3573682   333
15.3   Anatomical theater, Palazzo Bo, Padua. REDA & CO srl/
Alamy Stock Photo A4A86K   337
16.1   Top: Michelangelo et al. St. Peter's, Vatican, adisa/iStock
498123530; bottom: photo of Capitol, Washington D.C.
Martin Falbisoner, Wikipedia Commons   353

Index

Note: Footnoes are indicated by the page number followed by "n". Entries in *italics* denote figures.

Aachen 5
abacus, teaching of 53, 182, 335
  see also accounting; mathematics
Abulafia, David 148, 159
academies 305–6, 316, 321, 323,
  330, 334, 351; Accademia degli
  Incamminati 318; degli Incogniti
  351; degli Intronati 305; degli
  Invaghiti 305; dei Gelati 305;
  dei Lincei 344; del Disegno 303;
  della Crusca 306, 321; di San Luca
  318; Fiorentina 306; Pontaniana
  156, 330
Academy, Plato's 193
Academy, Platonic of Ficino *see* Platonic
  Academy
Acciaiuoli, Agnolo 189
accoppiatori see Florence, Republic
accounting, double-entry
  bookkeeping 28, 53
Achillini, Alessandro 336
Aetna, Mount *see* Etna
Agatha, St (Sant'Agata) 96
Agnadello, Battle of 160, 214, 226,
  246, 311
Agnolo di Tura 27, 30
Agricola, Alexander 153
Agrigento 12, 140, 142
Al-Idrisi (geographer) 169
Al-Wazzan, al-Hassan (Leo Africanus)
  262, 278
Alaric 3
Alberti family 127, 130
Alberti, Leon Battista, 63, 85–9, 91,
  92, 94, 193, 242; *On the Art of
  Building* (*De re aedificatoria*) 87; *On*

the Family (*I Libri della famiglia*)
  94, 105; *On Painting* (*Della pittura*)
  87; Palazzo Rucellai *see* Florence,
  buildings; Santa Maria Novella *see*
  Florence, churches and monasteries
Albret, Charlotte d' 223
alchemy 146, 338
Aldine Press *see* Manuzio, Aldo
Aldrovandi, Ulisse 331, 334, 348
Alexander III, Pope (r.1159–81) 8
Alexander V, antipope (r.1409–10) 81
Alexander VI, Pope *see* Borgia, Rodrigo
Alexander VII Chigi, Pope 352
Alfonso "the Magnanimous", King of
  Aragon and Naples 139, 149–58
Alfonso II, king of Naples 153, 213,
  215
Alighieri *see* Dante
Alps 6, 8, 146, 161, 177, 215, 216, 321
alum 190, 256
Amati, Andrea 309
Ambrose of Milan, St 120, 133
Ambrosian Republic *see* Milan
America, "New World" 237, 259–60,
  262, 301, 303, 311, 329, 333–34, 354
Ammanati, Bartolomeo 294
Ammirato, Scipione 301
Anagni 74, 80
anatomy 203, 239, 241, 314,
  323, 336–37
Ancona 12, 26, 56, 168, 326
Andrea da Firenze (Andrea Bonaiuti) 40
Andrea del Sarto 296, 300
Andrea Pisano (Andrea d'Ugolino da
  Pontedera) 20, 59
Andreini, Isabella 275, 309, 321

Index 359

Angelico, Fra (Giovanni da Fiesole) *84,*
85, 134, 137, 222
Angevins *see* Anjou
Anglican Church 286
Anguissola, Sofonisba 316–17; *Portrait*
of the Artist's Sister 317
animism 328–29
Anjou (Angevin dynasty) 28, 148–51,
158, 200, 213 *see also individual*
names of rulers
Annunciation (Simone Martini) *38,* 77
Annunciation feast day celebrated 196;
theme in art 38, 93, 111–12,
154–55, 258
anticlericalism 16, 29, 77, 94–95, 113,
232–33, 298
antipopes *see* papacy
Antonello da Messina 153–55, 184;
Virgin Annunciate 154
Antoniazzo Romano 111
Antoninus, St (Antonino Pierozzi,
archbishop of Florence) 98, 285
Apelles 236
Apostles' Creed (Nicene Creed) 157
apothecary *see* pharmacists,
pharmacology
Apulia (Puglia, region) 144–45, 168,
225, 329
Aquileia 161–12, 165, 167
Aquinas, Thomas, St 22, 331, 345
Arabs 5, 143–45, 148, 260; cartography
167; language 146, 175; medicine;
numerals 146; philosophy 209; poetry
143–44; translations of classic authors
56, 332
Aragon *see* Spain
Archimedes 57, 140, 332, 341
architect, changing role of 20, 87,
89; architecture: Byzantine 145,
184; Gothic 22, 63, 88, 123, 145,
161, 184–85; *see* Greek, ancient;
Renaissance 134, 135, 185,
201, 244, 252, 256, 292, 295,
311–14, 352; Roman *see* Rome,
ancient; Romanesque 184; military
architecture *see* warfare *see also*
individual architects, buildings,
cities
Arengo 170–71 *see also* Venice,
government
Aretino, Pietro 257, 274–75, 278, 311
Arezzo 12, 47, 52
Argyropoulos, John 192
aria 310

Ariosto, Ludovico 194, 243, 275, 276,
278, 307, 310, 341
Aristotle 22, 32, 45, 56, 57, 136, 235,
307, 330, 338, 340, 347, 351
arms and armor *see* warfare
Arnold of Brescia 72
Arnolfo di Cambio 20
arrabiati 220 *see also* Savonarola
Arras 153
Arsenale, arsenalotti see Venice
art history 295–97
artistic techniques: chiaroscuro 66, 239,
319; contrapposto 61, 249; *disegno*
296; fresco 65n; intarsia 244, *245;*
paints (tempera versus oil) 153, 184,
202, 238; perspective 19, 38, 59, 64,
65, 87, 184, 292, 296, 335; *poesia*
(visual poetry) 246–47; *sfumato* 239;
tenebrism 319; trompe-l'oeil 242
see also anatomy
Assisi 38, 123
Assisi, St Francis of *see* Francis of
Assisi, St
astrology 146, 193, 331; related to
astronomy 337–38
astronomy 306, 332, 339–48 *see also*
individual astronomers
Athens, ancient 189, 193; *School of*
Athens (painting by Raphael) 255
atomism, atoms 332, 347
Augustine of Hippo, St 1, 22, 285, 345
Augustinian monastic order 29,
98, 284
Aurispa, Giovanni 156
auto da fé 325
Avignon 38, 47, 48, 80; "Babylonian
Captivity", use of term; papacy at
75–79; 81, 99, 127
aviso, avvisi (pl.) 306, 323

Bacchiacca (Francesco Ubertini) 334
Baia 141
Bandinelli, Baccio 294
banks, banking 9, 11, 12, 13, 16, 24,
28, 83, 149, 305 *see also* Medici bank
Baptism 95n, 288; *Baptism of Christ*
(Verrocchio) 203–4
Barbaro, Ermolao, the Younger 333
Barbaro, Francesco 105, 114, 182
Barbarossa, Frederick *see* Frederick I
Hohenstauffen, Holy Roman Emperor
Bardi, company and family 24, 28,
29, 102; Bardi Chapel, Santa Croce,
Florence 18

360   *Index*

Barigazzi, Iacopo (Berengario da Carpi) 336
baroni (barons) *see* Rome, medieval
Baroque style 314, 318, 35, 54
Bartolo da Sassoferrato 72
Barzizza, Gasparino 86, 123, 156, 182
Basel *see* Councils of the Church
beatification *see* saints
Beatrice ("Bice") Portinari 14, 15, 101–2
Beatrice, Countess of Tuscany 45n
Beccadelli, Antonio *see* Panormita
Belcari, Feo 196
Belgium *see* Flanders; Low Countries
Bellarmino (Bellarmine), Roberto 346
Bellini, Giovanni 183–84, 247; family 183, 242; *Portrait of Doge Loredan 174*
Bembo, Pietro 182, 256, 272, 276
Benedetto da Maiano 208
Benedict XIII, antipope 81
Benedict XVI, Pope 74n
Benedict of Nursia, St 143; Benedictine order 98
benefices 47n, 86n, 215, 287, 298
Benincasa, Caterina (St. Catherine of Siena) 79, 98–99, 113, 114
Benjamin of Tudela 145, 159
Bergamo 12, 117, 177
Bernard of Chartres 45
Bernardino of Siena, St 97, 101, 113–14
Bernini, Gian Lorenzo 352
Berruguete, Pedro 244
Bertolotti, Gasparo 309
Bible 46, 70, 74, 96, 101, 218, 325; church bans vernacular translations 328; Erasmus and Luther 284–85, 286; in Galileo controversy 339, 345–46; Jerome's Vulgate 155, 288; *see also* humanism, Christian; Valla, Lorenzo
Biondo, Flavio 86
Biringuccio, Vannoccio 335
Birth of John the Baptist (Ghirlandaio) *110*
bishops 4, 70, 167n, 287, 328, 330; bishoprics 71, 77, 215, 298 *see also names of individuals*
Black Death (plague) 23–32, 36–37, 43, 49, 96, 149; effect on art 39–40; impact on population 23, 25, 178; Justinianic Plague 25, 139, 143; names for 25; quarantine measures 31–32, 122; recurrent outbreaks 79, 220, 237, 304, 350; *Yersinia pestis* 25

bocca di leone see Venice
Boccaccio, Giovanni 27–31, 41, 55, 95, 149
Boccanegra (family) 119
Bologna 12, 78, 79, 117, 122, 123, 217; painters 317, 318; University of 43, 45, 47, 85, 86, 215, 305, 334, 339 *see also* Aldrovandi
Bombelli, Raffaele 332
bonfire of the vanities *see* Savonarola
Boniface IX, Pope 81
Boniface VIII, Pope (Benedetto Caetani) 12, 16, 17, 69, 73–74, 91, 98, 234
Borelli, Giovanni Alfonso 350
Borgia (de Borja) family: Alonso (Calixtus III, Pope) 151, 215; Cesare (Duke Valentino) 91, 223–25, 228, 230–31, 232, 235, 241, 244, 253, 254, 272, 336; Jofrè 215; Lucrezia 215; Rodrigo (Alexander VI, Pope) 212, 215–17, 220, 222, 225, 232, 287
Borro, Gasparino 58
Borromeo, Carlo, 314, 318–19
Borromini, Francesco 354
botany 239, 332–34
Botticelli, Sandro 196, 203, 205, 210, 220, 222, 236, 239, 244, 250, 254, 296; *Portrait of Young Man with the Medal of Cosimo de' Medici 191, 192*
Bracciolini *see* Poggio Bracciolini 56, 86, 133
Brahe, Tycho 339
Bramante, Donato 237, 251–52, 254, 255, 257
Brancaleone degli Andalò 73
Brentano, Robert 70, 93
Brescia 12, 125, 177, 309
Bronzino, Agnolo 294–95, 300
Brown, Peter 1, 96, 114
Bruges 129, 175
Brunelleschi, Filippo 59, 62–65, 69, 87, 89, 133, 335; Cupola of Santa Maria del Fiore *64*
Bruni, Leonardo 56, 68, 133, 156, 354
Bruno, Giordano 323–25, 327, 328, 330–31, 348
Bucintoro 180
Bonsignori, Stefano 336
Buffalmacco *Triumph of Death* 40
Buonarroti *see* Michelangelo
Burckhardt, Jacob 45n, 91
Byzantine art 18, 37, 145, 184

Index 361

Byzantine Empire 71, 78, 142–43, 145, 164, 167–70 *see also individual emperors and* Constantinople, Ravenna

Cabala *see* Kabbalah
cabinets of curiosities 334
Caccini, Francesca 351
Caccini, Giulio 310
Caesar, Julius 56, 72, 90, 141, 250, 251, 339
Caetani, Benedetto *see* Boniface VIII, Pope
Calabria (region) 145, 153, 329, 330
calendar reform *see* Gregory XIII, Pope
Calendimaggio (May Day) 197
Calimala Guild 33, 59
Calixtus III, Pope *see* Borgia, Alonso
Calvin, John 299
Camaldolese order 98, 183
Cambrai, League of (1508) 225; Treaty of (1529) 280
Camera degli Sposi (*Camera Picta*), Mantua *see* Mantegna
Camerata, Florentine 310–11, 351
Camerino 224, 226
Campanella, Tommaso 323, 330–31, 342, 348
Campania 141, 150, 157, 329
Canal, Martin da 175
Canani, Giovanni Battista 337
canon law *see* law
canonization *see* Catholic Church
Canossa, Castle of 8, 69
Canova, Francesco (da Milano) 309
Canzoniere see Petrarch
capitano del popolo see Florence, Republic
Capponi, Niccolò 280
Capri 141
Capua 12, 224
Carafa War 304
Carafa, Giovanni Pietro *see* Paul IV, Pope
Caravaggio, Michelangelo Merisi da 318–20, 323; *The Calling of St. Matthew* 324 Caravaggisti 352
Cardano, Girolamo 331, 335
cardinals 76, 78, 134, 251, 280, 344, 348; College of 80–81, 82, 91, 215, 225, 265 *see also names of individuals*
Carducci, Francesco 280
Carlo Emanuele I, Duke 303

Carmelite order 98; Carmine Church (Santa Maria del Carmine), Florence 65, 111
Carnival 181, 197, 351, 352
Carpaccio, Vittore 183–84; *Hunting in the Lagoon 163*
Carracci family of painters: Agostino; Annibale; Ludovico 318
Carrara (family) 119
Carthage 140, 142
Carthusian order 98; Certosa di Pavia 123
cartography 86, 167, 169, 183, 260, 335, 336
Cassiodorus, Magnus Aurelius 162–64, 170, 186
cassone 205; Cassone Adimari *see* Scheggia
Castellani, Castellano 196
Castelli, Benedetto 347
Castelli, Pietro 334
Castiglionchio, Lapo da 85
Castiglione, Baldassarre 270–74, 276–77, 278, 354
Castile (region) 80, 81, 149, 261 *see also* Isabella of
Castracani (family) 119
Casulana, Maddalena 310
Catalan, Catalonia 150, 215
Catasto (Florentine tax) 43, 53, 106, 109, 114
Cateau-Cambrésis, Treaty of 301, 304, 350
Cathars 325
Catherine of Aragon, Queen (wife of Henry VIII Tudor) 286
Catherine of Siena, St. *see* Benincasa, Caterina
Catholic Church: definition 82n; Sacraments 74n, 95n, 199n, 284, 285, 288 *see also* Baptism; Bible; bishops; cardinals; confession; Councils of the Church; Eucharist; excommunication; heresy; interdict; monastic orders, monasticism; papacy, papal; penance; saints; tertiaries (Third Order); theology; transubstantiation (doctrine)
Cattaneo, Simonetta 195
Cavalca, Domenico 96
Celestine V, Pope 73
celibacy, clerical 47, 289
Cellini, Benvenuto 279, 295, 297, 300
Cennini, Cennino 33, 59, 68

362 Index

Cereta, Laura 58, 68
Cerretani, Bartolomeo 216
Cesalpino, Andrea 334
Champagne (region) 13, 122, 164, 176
chancellor of Florence 56: Bruni,
  Leonardo 55–56, 133; Salutati,
  Colluccio 55–56; papal, chancery
  85–86, 89; Venetian 179, 182
Charlemagne 4–5, 71, 120, 126, 186,
  194, 195
Charles of Anjou, King of Sicily 147–8
Charles of Calabria 130
Charles V Habsburg, Holy Roman
  Emperor and King of Spain 3, 257,
  259, 261, 262, 264, 265, 267, 270,
  276, 279, 282, 286, 304; *Equestrian
  Portrait* (Titian) 248, 269, 314;
  Political Testament to Philip II
  301–303, 321
Charles VIII Valois, King of France
  213–16, 221, 222
Charles III, Duke of Bourbon 266
Chaucer, Geoffrey 28
chiaroscuro *see* artistic techniques
Chigi, Agostino 256, 275
children 107, 112; abandoned
  (foundlings) 28, 30, 63, 109, 111;
  education 43, 51–53, 58, 105–6,
  107, 109; illegitimacy 94, 104,
  109; childhood mortality rates
  see demographics
Chiusi 123
chivalry, chivalric romances 54, 152,
  194, 272, 275
Christianity, early 3–4 *see also* martyrs
Christina (Cristina or Christine) of
  Lorraine (grand duchess of Tuscany)
  309, 345
Christine de Pizan (or Pisan) 274
Christmas 5, 95, 181, 219, 220
Christus, Petrus 154
church and state, separation of 5, 17,
  21–22 *see also* Investiture Conflict
Chrysoloras, Emmanuel (or Manuel)
  56, 123
Cicero, Marcus Tullius 21, 47, 55, 75,
  140, 209, 230
Cielo d'Alcamo 146
Cimabue 18, 295
Cino da Pistoia 28
Ciompi Rebellion 32–34, 127, 128,
  178, 280
Cistercian order 98

claustration 107, 289
Clavius, Christopher 339, 344
Clement III, Pope 72
Clement V, Pope 16, 75, 78
Clement VI, Pope 75
Clement VII, Pope (Giulio di Giuliano
  de' Medici) 259, 264–66, 270, 279,
  280, 281, 282, 290
Clement VII, antipope (Robert of
  Geneva) 81
Clermont 169
clientelism 130–31, 190
cloister 107
Cognac, League of (1526) 259, 265
Cohn, Samuel Kline Jr. 42, 113
coins, coinage 1, 13, 31, 72
Cola di Rienzo 75–76, 91
Colet, John 193
Colomba da Rieti, Blessed 100
Colombini, Giovanni, Blessed 100–1
Colonna family 73; Giovanni, Cardinal
  48, 69; Vittoria 270–71, 275, 278
Columbus, Christopher (Cristoforo
  Colombo) 260, 278
Commandino, Federico 332
commedia dell'arte 33n, 308–9, 320
Commercial Revolution 5–6, 24,
  45, 120
Commynes, Philippe de 216
compagnacci see Savonarola
Compagni, Dino 11
conclave 91 *see also* cardinals, papacy
Condivi, Ascanio 248
condotta 36, 223, 266; *condottiero* (or
  condottiere; pl: *condottieri*) 36, 79,
  125, 132, 190, 242, 244, 266, 272
confession: confessional booths 289;
  in legal procedure 325; as religious
  rite 74n, 98, 289
confraternities 96–97, 109, 196, 200,
  285, 308; Confraternity of the Magi
  135–36 *see also* Venice, *scuole*
consiliar movement *see* Councils of
  the Church
Constance of Aragon
  (Hohenstauffen) 148
Constance, Peace of (1183) 8 *see also*
  Councils of the Church
Constantine, Emperor 1, 3 *see also*
  Donation of Constantine
Constantinople 3, 5, 12, 71, 166, 169,
  182, 306; conquest by Turks (1453)
  132, 178, 260; siege and sack of in

Fourth Crusade (1204) 160, 169–70; *see also* Byzantine Empire; Great Schism *and individual emperors*

Constitutions of Melfi 146 *see also* Frederick II

contado (countryside) 11, 34–36, 39, 119, 125, 177–78, 199, 281

Contarini, Gasparo 186, 187, 286, 298

Conte di Virtù *see* Visconti, Giangaleazzo

contrapposto *see* artistic techniques

convents, female *see* nuns, nunneries

Conventual versus Observant friars *see* monastic orders, monasticism

conversa, converse (pl.) 107

Copernicus, Nicholas 323, 324, 339, 344, 345, 346

Corpus Iuris Civilis see law, Roman

Cortona 12, 123

Cortona, Margaret of *see* Margaret of Cortona, St

Cortona, Pietro da 352

Coryat, Thomas 160

cosmology, cosmos 325, 330, 337–38, 340, 341 *see also* astronomy

Cossa, Baldassare *see* John XXIII

Cossa, Francesco del 243, 258

Councils of the Church: Basel 80, 82, 90, 151; Constance 69, 80, 81

Counter Reformation *see* Reformation, Catholic

courtesans *see* sex trade

Cremona 12, 125, 225, 309, 317

Cremonini, Cesare 351

Cristoforo di Geremia 152

Croce, Benedetto 158

Cronaca (Simone del Pollaiuolo) 208

crusades 6, 214; Albigensian Crusade (1209–29) 325; First Crusade (1096–99) 1, 169, 307; Fourth Crusade (1202–04) 169–70, 187; Sixth Crusade (1228–29) 147

Daddi, Bernardo 37

da Milano, Francesco *see* Canova, Francesco

d'Aragona, Tullia 275

da Salò, Gasparo *see* Bertolotti, Gasparo

da Vinci, Leonardo *see* Leonardo da Vinci

Dalmau, Luis 153

Dalmatia 168, 169, 214, 216

Dandelet, Thomas 320, 321

Dandolo, Enrico, Doge 169–70, 187

Dante Alighieri 13–19, 21–22, 29, 33, 36, 47, 74, 91, 94, 101–2, 118, 146, 179, 195, 307, 327, 338–39, 341; *Inferno* 15, 17–18, 22, 46, 54, 73, 78, 156, 177, 230, 235; *Purgatory* 15

Danti, Ignazio (or Egnazio) 336

Datini, Francesco di Marco 68, 95; Margherita 68

De Sanctis, Francesco 350, 352

Dean, Trevor 22, 118

Decembrio, Pier Candido 123, 137

Decembrio, Uberto 123

Defensor pacis see Marsilius of Padua

del Monte, Francesco Maria, Cardinal 319

del Monte, Guidobaldo 342

della Porta, Giacomo 313, 314

della Porta, Giovan Battista 331

della Rovere (family) 119; Francesco *see* Sixtus, IV; Francesco Maria (duke of Urbino) 263, 266, 272; Giuliano *see* Julius II

della Scala (family) 119

della Torre, Filippo 120

Demeter 139

democracy 2, 21, 131, 137, 170, 186, 235

demographics: childhood mortality 26, 108, 109; Italian cities (*c.* 1300) 12; Italy (before and after 1348) 23; Italy (1520s) 237; Italy (1600) 304; life expectancy 26; Naples (1500–1550) 303; population, Commercial Revolution and 6, 24; Rome, ancient and medieval 70; Rome (1400) 83; Rome (1600) 313; Venice (14th–16th centuries) 178

desco da parto 205

Dionigi da Borgo San Sepolcro 29

Dioscorides 57, 332

Distribution of Alms and the Death of Ananias (Masaccio) 66

Divine Comedy see Dante

doge *see* Venice, government *see also individual names*

Doge Loredan (Bellini) *174*

Domenichino 352

Domenici, Giovanni 97–98

Dominican order 13, 16, 85, 97, 98, 99, 100, 209, 218, 221, 323, 326, 327; Observants 97, 218, 285

364   *Index*

Domenico di Bartolo 111
Donatello (Donato di Niccolò di Betto
    Bardi) 59, 60–62, 69, 87, 127, 134;
    St. George 34, 43, 61, *62*
Donati (family) 11; Gemma 102;
    Lucrezia 194
Donation of Constantine 7, 71, 157,
    159, 332 *see also* Valla, Lorenzo
Donatists, Donatism 95, 285
Doria, Andrea 303
double-entry bookkeeping *see*
    accounting
dowries *see* marriage customs
Duccio di Buoninsegna 37, 38
Du Fay, Guillaume 133
Durling, Robert 102

Eastern Church 71, 82n, 167 *see also*
    Great Schism
education *see* abacus schools; children;
    humanism; humanities curriculum;
    literacy; nuns, education
Effects of Good Government
    (Lorenzetti) *39*
Egidio da Viterbo 286
Egypt 2, 100, 144, 147, 166
Eight Saints, War of the 79–80
Eleonora of Aragon (duchess of
    Ferrara) 244
Eleonora of Toledo, (duchess of
    Florence) 282, 302
Empedocles (philosopher) 140
engineers, engineering 20, 62–63,
    183, 239, 241, 335, 336, 337, 341;
    military engineering *see* warfare
    see also names of individuals
England 6, 12, 13, 24, 34, 74, 81, 90,
    119, 158, 175, 270, 305, 313, 320,
    350; Church of 286; English Peasants'
    Revolt 23, 32; English poetry and
    drama 50, 51, 196, 307, 320–21
Enlightenment 210, 235, 321, 351, 354
Epicurus, Epicureanism 156, 324, 332
    see also Lucretius
Equicola, Mario 242
Erasmus, Desiderius 157, 284–5
d'Este (family) 119, 262, 275, 307;
    Alfonso 266; Alfonso II 303; Beatrice
    242; Borso 243; Ercole 243; Isabella
    242–43, 256, 258
Etna, Mount (volcano) *see* Sicily, places
Eucharist 95n, 288–89, 327 *see also*
    Transubstantiation

Euclid 57, 63, 255, 332, 341
Eugenius III, Pope 72
Eugenius IV, Pope 82, 83–5, 86, 87, 90,
    128, 131, 133, 150, 251
Eustachi, Bartolomeo 336–37
excommunication 8, 74, 74n, 79, 122,
    147, 199, 220, 224, 225–26, 286
exegesis 346 *see also* theology

Fabrici (or Fabrizio) d'Acquapendente,
    Girolamo 337
Falier, Marino, Doge 173
Falloppio, Gabriele 336
Fano 12, 223, 226
Fedele, Cassandra 58, 68
Federigo, King of Naples 224
feminism male gaze 102, 113, 246–47;
    misogyny 327; *querelle des femmes*
    58, 274, 308 *see also* women
Ferdinand I of Aragon (Antequera),
    King of Aragon and Sicily 149
Ferdinand I von Habsburg, Holy Roman
    Emperor 301
Ferdinand II of Aragon, King of Spain
    223, 264
Ferrante (Ferdinand) I, King of Naples
    150, 151–53, 158, 198, 199–200, 213
Ferrara 12, 79, 119, 122, 164, 182,
    201, 218, 225, 241–44, 263, 266,
    275, 280, 303, 307, 331; Council of
    Ferrara *see* Councils of the Church
    see also Este family
Ferrara-Florence 69, 82, 132, 134, 192;
    Fifth Lateran 285–86; Pavia 82; Pisa
    81, 285; Trent 95, 279, 287–91,
    297–98, 300, 307, 310, 314, 318,
    327, 329, 330, 339, 350
Ferrari, Ludovico 335
feudalism 5–6, 21, 145
Fiamma, Gabrielle 166
Fibonacci, Leonardo 146
Ficino, Marsilio 188, 192–94, 209, 210,
    220, 264, 305, 323
Filarete (Antonio Averlino) 83–84
Filelfo, Francesco 90
Findlen, Paula 337–38, 349
flagellants 27; flagellation 97, 100
Flanders 24, 164, 175, 176, 306, 348;
    Flemish music 152, 201, 310; painting
    153, 202 *see also names of individual*
    composers and artists
Florence, buildings: Orsanmichele
    (oratory and civic granary) 34, 61,

62, 204; Ospedale degli Innocenti (foundling home) 63, 94, 109; Palazzo Medici 134, *135*, 207, 248; Palazzo Rucellai 88–89, 207; Palazzo della Signoria (also called Palazzo dei Priori, Palazzo Vecchio) 10, 34, 58, 196, 199; Palazzo Strozzi *207*, 207–8; private 88n, 206–8; Salone dei Cinquecento 250, 295; towers 9, 10

Florence, Cathedral complex: Baptistry of San Giovanni 20, 59, *60*, 62, 127; Campanile 20; cupola *64*; Opera del Duomo 62; Santa Maria del Fiore (Duomo) 13

Florence, churches and monasteries: Basilica of San Lorenzo 64, 133–34 New Sacristy (Medici Chapel) 282, *283*; Brancacci Chapel, Santa Maria del Carmine 65, *66*, 111; Convent of San Marco 85, 93, 135–36, 218, 221 library 133; Santa Croce, Pazzi Chapel 264; Santa Felicita: Church of Santa Maria Novella, 13; façade 87, *88*, 231, 314; Tornabuoni Chapel *110*, 111; Santa Trinita 202, 206; Santo Spirito 64

Florence, economy: guilds 9, 32–34, 59, 61; wool industry 13, 16, 34, 62, 63, 304 *see also* banks, banking

Florence, festivals, celebrations: 195, 196–7; public spaces: Loggia dei Lanzi 295, 297; Piazza Santa Trinita 306; Piazza della Signoria 221, 306

Florence, Medici principate (1531–1737) 281–82 *see also individual names of dukes, grand dukes*

Florence, Republic of: *accoppiatori* 131, 190; *capitano del popolo* 10; Council of Forty-Eight (legislative group) 281; criminal justice, law 10, 14, 32, 36, 44, 118, 127, 198; denunciation (*tamburro*) 173; Great Council 187, 219; Ordinances of Justice 10; *primo popolo* 9–10; siege of (1529–30) 280–81; Signoria (priorate) 10, 127, 220, 221, 281; standardbearer of justice (*gonfaloniere di giustizia*) 10, 131, 227 *see also* Soderini, Piero

Florentine Platonism 56, 192, 248

Florentine Studio 43, 45, 56, 192

florin *see* coins, coinage

Fontana, Lavinia 316–17

Fonte, Moderata 275, 321

Forlì 12, 223, 226

fortuna (fortune) 230–31, 234–35, 264

Forum *see* Rome (ancient)

Fra Angelico (Beato Angelico) *see* Angelico, Fra

Fra Mauro *see* Mauro, Fra

France 5, 6, 24, 29, 34, 48, 72, 73–74, 75, 77, 78, 81, 90, 122, 124, 144, 152, 153, 158, 164, 169, 200, 227, 228, 241, 259, 264, 265, 266, 270, 274, 276, 280, 282, 285, 298, 303, 304, 305, 309, 310, 325, 329, 350; invasion of Italy (1494) 213–217; invasion of Italy (1499) 221–23; size of (1515) 262 *see also individual monarchs*

Francia 5

Francigena, Via 6, 7, 13

Francis I Valois, King of France 241, 259, 262, 265, 280

Francis of Assisi, St. 16, 18, 22, 94, 95, 184, 285

Franciscan Order 13, 97, 98, 100, 101, 221; Spirituals 97

Franco, Veronica 275, 307–8, 321

Franks 5, 142, 166

Fraticelli 97n

Frederick I "Barbarossa" Hohenstaufen, Holy Roman Emperor 8

Frederick II "stupor mundi" Hohenstaufen, Holy Roman Emperor and King of Sicily 139, 146–47, 148, 158, 253

"French disease" *see* syphilis

fresco *see* art, painting techniques

friars *see* mendicant orders

Friuli 121, 177, 306, 328

frottole see theater

Frundsberg, Georg von 266–67

Gabrieli, Andrea 310

Gabrieli, Giovanni 310

Gaddi, Taddeo 37, 39

Gaiseric 143

Galatina 329

Galen, Galenic medicine 32, 58, 235, 336

Galilei, Galileo 92, 183, 235, 239, 257, 319, 321, 335, 341–48, 350, 351, 354

Galilei, Vincenzo 341, 351

Gallerani, Cecilia 239, 258

Gambara, Veronica 275

366 *Index*

Garibaldi, Giuseppe 91
Gastaldi, Giacomo 336
Gaza, Theodore 156
Gelosi (comedy troupe) 309
gender roles in Italian courts 273–75
Geneva 299, 303
Gennaro, St 329
Genoa 25, 116, 119, 122, 148, 150, 161, 175, 177, 260, 303, 305
Gentileschi, Artemisia 316, 321, 341, 352
Gentileschi, Orazio 316, 352
geocentrism *see* astronomy; cosmology
George of Trebizond 156
George, St. 167; *St. George* (statue by Donatello) 34, 61, *62*
German Peasants' War 286, 299
gerontocracy 174
Gesualdo, Carlo 310
Gesuati order 100
ghetto *see* Jews
Ghibellines 11–12, 14, 38, 119, 170
Ghiberti, Lorenzo 43, *59*, *60*, 68, 83, 87
Ghini, Luca 334
Ghirlandaio, Davide 205
Ghirlandaio, Domenico *110*, 111, 202, 205–206, 239, 248, 254, 296
Giambologna (Giovanni da Bologna) 295
Giberti, Gian Matteo 298
Ginzburg, Carlo 328, 349
Giordano da Rivalto 97
Giorgione (Zorzi da Castelfranco) 246–47, 248, 257, 313; *Sleeping Venus* (with Titian) 247; *The Tempest* *217*, *218*, 237
Giotto di Bondone 18, 22, 37, 41, 54, 65, 67, 121, 149, 206, 291, 296; Scrovegni (Arena) Chapel 18–20, 111; *Visitation 19*
Giovanetti, Matteo 77
Giovanni di Balduccio 121
Giovanni Pisano 20; *Massacre of the Innocents 21*
Giuliano da Maiano 153, 208, 244; *Intarsia Representing Bookshelves, Lute, and Sword 245*
Giulio Romano 256, 257
Giustiniani, Tommaso 285
Goes, Hugo van der 202
Golden Book *see* Venice, government
gondolas, gondoliers *see* Venice

gonfaloniere di giustizia see Florence, Republic
Gonzaga (family) 119, 242, 270; Elisabetta 272; Federico II 266, 274; Francesco II 242, 270; Guglielmo 302; Ludovico III 242, *243*; Luigi 300
Gorgias (rhetorician) 140
Gothic style in art, architecture 20, 22, 63, 64, 88, 123, 145, 160, 184, 185
Goths 1, 3, 141, 143, 161, 210
Gozzoli, Benozzo 134; *Journey of the Magi 135*
Gradenigo, Pietro, Doge 172, 173
Grafton, Anthony 92, 93
Granada, Treaty of 224, 227
Grassi, Giovanni de' 123, *124*
grazia (grace) 271, 276, 296
Greek, ancient: architecture 140, 313; culture 139–40, 348; language 44, 56, 182; medicine *see* Galen; music drama 311; philosophy *see* Florentine Platonism; rediscovery of texts 57; *School of Athens* (painting by Raphael) 255; scientific and mathematical texts 332; teachers *see* Argyropoulos; Chrysoloras; *and individual ancient Greeks*
Greenblatt, Stephen 92
Gregorian chant 152
Gregory I "the Great", Pope 71
Gregory IX, Pope 147, 325
Gregory VII, Pope 8; Gregorian Reforms 285
Gregory XII, Pope 81
Gregory XIII, Pope 339; Gregorian Calendar 323
Grosseto 123
Gualberto, Giovanni 285
Guarini, Battista 309, 310, 313
Guarino Guarini (Guarino of Verona) 182
Guelfs 11, 14, 18, 38, 119, 170
Guercino 352
Guglielmo Monaco 152
Guicciardini, Francesco 212–13, 225, 236, 259, 260, 264–65, 266, 267, 271, 277, 278, 280, 281, 289, 327
Guido delle Colonne 146
guilds in Florence 32–34, 59, 61–63, 89, 106, 127, 128, 202; in Venice 172, 181; use of the term "*arte*" for professional associations 33, 308
see also individual guilds, Orsanmichele

Index   367

Guiscard, Robert (de Hauteville) 144–45, 167, 169
Gutenberg, Johannes 182
gypsies 329

Habsburg (dynasty) 303
  see also individual rulers
Hades 139
Handel, George Frideric 352
Harvey, William 323, 337
Hawkwood, John 36, 79
Hay, Denys 95
Hebrew language 143, 146, 157, 158, 285 *see also* Jews, Jewish culture
heliocentrism *see* astronomy; cosmology
Henry II Valois, king of France 304
Henry IV, Holy Roman Emperor 8, 69
Henry VII of Luxembourg, Holy Roman Emperor 17, 91
Henry VIII Tudor, King of England 286
Herculaneum 141
heresy: accusations of 95, 224, 290, 323, 330–31, 344; atomism 347; defined 325; denying immortality of the soul 351; denying doctrine of the Trinity 299 *see also* Cathars; Donatists; Epicureans; Fraticelli; inquisitions
Herlihy, David 37; Klapisch-Zuber 114
Hermes Trismegistus 323
  see also magic
Hibbard, Howard 352
holy days 196 *see also* Annunciation; Ascension; Christmas; Easter; Epiphany; Lent; Pentecost
Holy League (1510) 227; Holy League (1571) *see* Lepanto, Battle of
Holy Roman Empire 7, 261; Holy Roman Emperor 5, 8 *see also individual names*
Homer 57, 139, 140
Honorius III, Pope 206
Huguenots 304
humanism 37, 44–47, 54–59, 67, 85–86, 88–89, 123, 133, 155–57, 182–83; Christian (Evangelical) 156–57, 158, 284–85; civic 55–56, 250; humanist education (*studia humanitatis*) 45, 54–55, 67 *see also individual names of humanists*
humanities curriculum 67, 305, 354
Hundred Years' War 23, 24, 214

Ibn Hamdìs (poet) 143, 144
Ibn Sab'in (philosopher) 146
iconoclasm 290
Imola 12, 198, 223, 226, 336
Index of Prohibited Books (Index librorum prohibitorum or *Papal Index)* 327–28, 346
indulgences 78, 82, 284
Inferno see Dante Alighieri
Innocent II, Pope 72
Innocent III, Pope 71, 72, 73, 147
Innocent IV, Pope 147, 325
Innocent VII, Pope 81
Innocent VIII, Pope 215
inquisitions 97n, 157; defined 325; Roman 17, 287, 299, 325–26, 327–28, 331, 346–47, 351; Spanish 325, 326; Venetian 315, 325
intarsia *see* artistic techniques
interdict: Florence (1478) 199–200; Florence (1497) 220; papal defined 199n; Venice (1606) 351; War of Eight Saints (1375–78) 79
interiority 49–51
Investiture Conflict 8, 17, 72
Isaach, Heinrich 201
Isabella of Aragon (daughter of Alfonso II) 213
Isabella I of Castile, Queen 149
Istria 161
Italian language (*volgare*) 14, 53–54; vernacular education, literature, literacy 29, 50–54, 58, 192, 194–95, 210, 310, 332 *see also* Accademia della Crusca; Pietro Bembo; Tuscan dialect

Jacob and Esau (Ghiberti) 60, 83
Jacomart, Jaime 153
Jacopo de Voragine 96
Jacquerie 32, 33
Jefferson, Thomas 313
Jerome, St (San Girolamo) 1, 3, 154, 155, 284, 288, 345
Jerusalem 70, 74, 147, 169, 170; "New Jerusalem" *see* Savonarola
Jesuit order (Society of Jesus) 287, 305, 314, 329, 339, 344, 346
Jews, Jewish culture 27, 29, 67, 94, 143, 148, 150, 160, 326, 329
  see also Hebrew language; Kabbalah, Maimonedes

368 *Index*

Johanna von Habsburg, (Giovanna
d'Austria), Grand Duchess of
Tuscany 282
John V Palaeologus, Byzantine
Emperor 78
John XXIII (Baldassare Cossa), antipope
81, 127
John the Baptist, St (San Giovanni
Battista) 166, 196; *Birth of John the
Baptist* (Ghirlandaio) *110*
John the Evangelist, St (San Giovanni
Evangelista) 65
Jones, Inigo 313
Joos van Gent 244
Jove 46, 318
Jubilee, papal 74, 223, 323
Judea 3
Judges and Notaries' Guild, Florence 44
Julius II (Giuliano della Rovere), Pope
212, 215, 225–27, 250–53, 257, 262,
270, 285
jurisprudence *see* law
Justinian, Emperor 25, 44, 143
Justinianic Code *see* law
Justinianic Plague *see* Black Death

Kabbalah 193, 209, 323, 331, 338
Kepler, Johannes 339, 343
Koran 328

Landino, Cristoforo 193
Landsknechts (lansquenets) 266
Lane, Frederic 179, 187
latifundium, latifundia (pl.) 140,
141, 145
Latin 2, 5, 13, 28, 29, 43–46, 48, 49,
50, 51, 53, 58, 75, 86, 90, 156, 182,
195, 241, 242, 244, 251, 262, 270,
305, 344; Bible in Latin 155, 284–85,
288; Latin translations of Greek texts
56, 146, 192–93, 332
Latini, Brunetto 54
Laura (beloved of Petrarch) 48, 50,
51, 101–2
Laurana, Luciano 244
laurel 49, 51, 102
Laurentian Library (Biblioteca Medicea
Laurenziana) *see* libraries
law 9, 10, 44, 47, 56, 86, 90, 122, 146,
181, 264; canon (church) 28, 81, 156,
215; Roman law 44–45, 354; torture
used by civil courts 221, 228, 325;
by Inquisition 326, 327, 331, 349

Lawrence, St (San Lorenzo) *St.
Lawrence Distributes Alms* (Fra
Angelico) *84*, *85*
League of Venice (1495) 216
Lefèvre d'Etaples, Jacques 193
Legnano, Battle of 1, 8, 120
Lent 181, 197, 289, 351
Lentini (town in Sicily) 140
Lentini, Giacomo da 146, 159
Leo I "the Great", Pope 71
Leo IV, Pope 83
Leo III, Pope 5, 69, 71
Leo X (Giovanni di Lorenzo de'
Medici), Pope 212, 228, 229, 255,
262–64, 265, 266, 270, 282, 286;
Portrait (Raphael) *263*, 265
Leone Africano (Leo Africanus)
see Al-Wazzan, al-Hassan
Leonardo da Vinci 92, 199, 204, 237,
247, 248, 250, 252, 254, 255, 257,
258, 277, 294, 296, 335, 336, 341,
342; in Milan 239–41; *Mona Lisa* (*La
Gioconda*) 239; notebooks 199, 237,
239; *Vitruvian Man* 237, *240*, 241
Leonine City *see* Vatican
Lepanto, Battle of (1571) 304, 307
lepers 27
LeRoy Ladurrie, Emmanuel 35
Lewkenor, Lewis 186
libraries 47, 49, 56, 155–56, 210,
244; Laurentian (Biblioteca Medicea
Laurenziana), Florence 133; San
Marco, Florence 135–36; Marciana,
Venice 185; Vatican 85, 255
Lippi, Filippino 202, 203, 220, 239, 250
Lippi, Filippo 111, 134, 203
literacy 53, 54, 94, 113, 114, 182
Livorno (Leghorn) 305, 326
Livy (Titus Livius) 21, 75, 155;
Machiavelli, *Discourses on* 231–33,
236
Lombard League 8, 120
Lombards (Longobards) 5, 71, 120,
142, 143, 162; Lombardy (region)
120, 121, 123, 132, 143, 157, 222,
223, 265, 266, 318, 350
see also Milan
London 25, 53, 109n, 193, 306
Lorenzetti, Ambrogio 38–39, *39*, 111
Lorenzetti, Pietro 38, 111
Loschi, Antonio 123, 137
Louis XII, King of France 221–223, 227
Louis XIV, King of France 352

Index 369

Lovati, Lovato 44
Low Countries 133, 153, 261, 262
  see also Flanders
Loyola, Ignatius, St 287
Lucca 12, 32, 43, 100, 116, 123, 130,
  214, 280, 303, 305
Lucia Broccadelli da Narni, Blessed 100
Lucius II, Pope 72
Lucretius (Titus Lucretius Carus) 43, 57,
  332 see also Epicurus, Epicureanism
Lucy, St (Santa Lucia) 96
Lully, Jean-Baptiste de (Giovanni
  Battista Lulli) 352
Luther, Martin 232, 257, 279, 284–86,
  288, 299
Lutherans, Lutheranism 266, 268, 269,
  270, 286, 288, 298
Luxembourg see Low Countries
Luzzaschi, Luzzasco 310

Machiavelli, Niccolò 91, 122, 137,
  212–13, 220, 221, 224, 223–36, 237,
  257, 264, 265, 271, 273, 276–77,
  280, 327, 336, 354
Macinghi Strozzi, Alessandra 105–6,
  114, 207
Madonna, the see Mary, Virgin;
  Madonna del Parto (Piero della
  Francesca) 111, 112
madrigal 201, 309–10
Maecenas, Gaius Cilnius 209
Magi (Three Kings) 135–36; Procession
  of the Magi (Gozzoli) 134, 135
magic 193, 195, 275, 323, 326, 327,
  329, 331, 338 see also witches,
  witchcraft
Magna Graecia 140, 141
magnates 8–10, 73, 126 see also popolo
magnificence 136, 158, 201–2, 224, 244
Maimonides 146
Mainardi, Bastiano 205
malaria 78, 106, 152, 225, 311,
  334, 335
Malatesta (family) 119; Sigismondo 135
Malta 307
mannerism 292–96; 306; reactions
  against 317, 318
Mantegna, Andrea 183, 237, 241–42;
  Camera Picta (Camera degli
  Sposi) 243
Mantellate see Tertiaries
Mantua 119, 122, 225, 241–2;
  266, 270, 274, 280, 302, 305,

350; Churches of San Sebastiano,
  Sant'Andrea 242 see also Camera
  degli Sposi; Gonzaga
Manuzio, Aldo (Aldus Manutius)
  160, 182
mapmaking see cartography
Marenzio, Luca 310
Margaret of Cortona, St 98, 99
Marie Antoinette 276
Marinella, Lucrezia 308
Mark the Evangelist, St, patron
  of Venice 166–67; statue by
  Donatello 34, 61
marriage customs 104; Florentine
  dowry fund 104; manuals 105, 114;
  religious attitudes towards 99, 101,
  289 see also women, widows
Marsilius of Padua (Marsilio
  Mainardini) 17, 22, 44
Martin V, Pope 81–83, 150, 251
Martini, Francesco di Giorgio 335
Martini, Simone 38, 77;
  Annunciation 38
martyrs see saints
Mary Magdalene, St 101, 153, 247,
  258
Mary the Egyptian, St 100
Mary, Virgin (mother of Jesus) 38,
  111, 112, 155, 196, 249, 254, 299;
  Virgin Annunciate (Antonello da
  Messina) 154
Masaccio (Tommaso di Giovanni di
  Simone Guidi) 41, 43, 59, 65–67, 87,
  111; Distribution of Alms and the
  Death of Ananias 66
Masolino da Panicale 65, 83
Massacre of the Innocents (Giovanni
  Pisano) 21, 22
mathematics 63, 65, 89, 140, 306,
  332, 335, 337, 339, 341, 344; in
  university curricula 85, 332, 338,
  342, 343 see also individual names of
  mathematicians
Matilda, Countess of Tuscany 8
Mattioli, Pier Andrea 334
Mauro, Fra 183
Mazzoni, Guido 153
Medicean Stars see Galileo
Medici bank 127–31, 192, 198; Chapel
  see Florence, Basilica of San Lorenzo;
  family's origins 9, 119, 126–27;
  Palace (Palazzo Medici) see Florence,
  buildings; supporters 126n; 219, 233,

370   Index

250, 264; villas 134, 191, 199
see also Poggio a Caiano
Medici, Alessandro de', Duke 281
Medici, Catherine de', Queen of
France 282
Medici, Cosimo de' "the Elder" 128,
130–36, 137, 155, 189, 191, 192,
207, 218
Medici, Cosimo I de', Grand Duke
281–82, 294–295, 297, 303, 306,
334, 336
Medici, Cosimo II de', Grand Duke 343,
344, 346
Medici, Ferdinando I de', Grand Duke
295, 309, 326, 348
Medici, Ferdinando II de', Grand
Duke 346
Medici, Foligno di Conte de' 127
Medici, Francesco I de', Grand
Duke 302
Medici, Gian Gastone de', Grand
Duke 282
Medici, Giovanni de' (delle Bande
Nere) 266
Medici, Giovanni di Bicci de' 127, 128
Medici, Giovanni di Lorenzo de'
see Leo X, Pope
Medici, Giuliano de' (brother of
Lorenzo the Magnificent) 191, 192,
195, 199, 265, 282
Medici, Giuliano di Lorenzo de'
(1479–1516, son of Lorenzo the
Magnificent) Duke of Nemours)
229, 282
Medici, Giulio di Giuliano de'
see Clement VII, Pope
Medici, Lorenzo de' "the Magnificent"
151, 188–201, 206, 208, 209, 210,
213, 218, 244, 248, 260, 282
Medici, Lorenzo di Piero de' (1492–
1519) Duke of Urbino 229, 263,
280, 282
Medici, Maria de', Queen of France 282
Medici, Piero de' "the Gouty" 136, 188
Medici, Piero di Lorenzo de' (son of
Lorenzo the Magnificent) 213,
216–17, 228
Medici, Vieri di Cambio de' 127
medicine 143, 306, 329, 336, 337,
341 *see also* anatomy; Black Death;
Galen; Hippocrates; pharmacology;
Physicians' and Pharmacists' Guild;
quarantine

Mediterranean Sea, region 2, 13, 25,
132, 140, 142, 149, 161, 168, 169,
170, 177, 259, 260, 303, 304
Melozzo da Forlì 210, 244
mendicant orders *see* monastic orders
Menocchio (Domenico Scandella) 328
metallurgy 332, 335
mezzadria 35
Michelangelo Buonarroti 22, 59, 92,
248–51, 255, 276, 294, 295, 296,
297, 298, 317, 319, 341; *David* 61,
249–250; *Last Judgment* 290–91,
344; Medici Chapel, San Lorenzo
282–83; *Night* 283; poetry 291–92;
Sistine Ceiling 253–54, 257; St. Peter's
292, 313, 314, *353*
Michelozzo di Bartolomeo 115, 127,
133, 134, 135
Michiel, Vitale II, Doge 171
Milan 8, 12, 31, 55, 61, 79, 100, 117,
120–26, 132, 137, 150, 161, 164,
177, 189, 190, 198, 199, 200, 213,
214, 215, 216, 221–23, 225, 227,
230, 238–40, 244, 266, 270, 305,
326, 336; Ambrosian Republic
124–25, 132; capital of western
Roman Empire 119–120; commune,
early 120; French rule of 252,
262, 263, 264; Spanish rule of
279, 301, 302, 303 *see also* Sforza,
Visconti
Milan artists 121, 239–41, 318, 319;
architecture: Castello Sforzesco 126;
Duomo 40, 115, 123; San Fedele
314; San Gottardo 121; Santa Maria
Presso Satiro 252; Santa Maria
delle Grazie 252; armorers 336;
humanism 123
mendicant orders *see* monastic orders,
monasticism
military architecture, engineering *see*
warfare
Milton, John 307
Minta, Stephen 50, 68
Missaglia family of armorers 336
Modena 122, 214, 243, 262, 264
monastic orders, monasticism:
Conventual versus Observant 97–98;
friars 98; mendicant orders 16, 97,
98, 100, 285 *see also* nuns, nunneries;
tertiaries (Third Order); *and names of
individual monastic orders*
Montaperti, Battle of 38

monte delle doti see marriage, dowries
Montecassino 142, 143, 158
Montefeltro (family) 119, 244; Federico da 190, 244, 255; Guidobaldo da 224, 270, 272
Montefeltro Malatesta, Battista 58
Montemurlo, Battle of 282
Monteverdi, Claudio 352
Monticello 313
Montpellier 47
Morelli, Giovanni di Pagolo 54, 68
mosaics 83, 141, 145, 183, 184
motet 133, 201, 310
Mugello 126, 131, 134
Muhammad 144
Muir, Edward 186, 187, 349
multiplicity of worlds 324
Murano island, glassmakers *see* Venice
music *see* aria; Camerata, Florentine; Flanders; madrigals; motets; opera; oratorio; patrons, music; polyphony; *and individual composers*
musical instruments 146, 309
Muslims 143–44, 145, 148, 169
  see also Arabs; Koran; Muhammad; *Reconquista*; Turks *and individual names*
Mussato, Albertino 44
Mussolini, Benito 91
mythology, pagan 29, 46, 51, 139, 195, 203, 205, 246, 256, 314, 318, 338
  see also names of individual gods and goddesses

Naples 139; ancient and medieval 141–43; French seizure of 217, 222–24; Kingdom of, under Angevins 132, 149; under Aragonese 50, 158–59, 199–200, 213–15; Spanish rule 225, 227, 282, 303–4, 320, 325, 326 *see also* Anjou; Aragon; Granada, Treaty of; Papal States, Naples as papal fief; *and names of individual rulers*
Naples: architecture: Castel Nuovo 152; art 153–55; humanism, 155–58; music 152–53, 201, 243; religious practices 329–330; university 146, 334
Naples, Bay of 139, 141, 142
natural philosophy 330–31, 338
navigation 183, 260, 336, 338, 348
Negroli, Filippo 336

Neoplatonism 92n, 208, 209, 331 *see also* Ficino, Florentine Platonism, Plato
Netherlands 5, 152, 153, 158, 244, 284, 304, 305, 343, 350 *see also* Flanders; Low Countries
New World *see* America
Niccoli, Niccolò 56, 133
Nicholas III, Pope 16
Nicholas V, Pope 83, 84, 85, 87, 89, 90, 91, 128, 251, 252
Nicholas of Bari, St 96, 167
Nicola Pisano 20
Nogarola, Angela, Ginevra, Isotta 58
Normans 139, 144–46, 148, 167, 169, 216
notaries 10, 33, 36, 44, 54, 77, 146, 179
nuns, nunneries (female convents) 98, 101, 107–8, 113, 196, 197, 224, 268, 317, 327, 330, 351; education, 58, 107; forced monachization 108
  see also monasticism, tertiaries

Odysseus 139
oligarchy 2, 34, 137, 173, 189, 219
opera (music drama) 309, 311, 321, 352–53
oratorio 352
Orcagna 40
Ordinances of Justice *see* Florence, Republic
Orlando (legendary knight of Charlemagne) 197, 275, 307
orphans, abandoned children 97, 109, 111 *see also* Florence, *Ospedale degli Innocenti*
Orsini (family) 73; Clarice 189; Rinaldo 198
Orvieto 12, 40, 279
Ottoman Empire, Ottomans *see* Turks
Oxford 45

Pacioli, Luca 335
Padua 119, 161, 177, 182, 227, 334; anatomical theater 323, 337; humanism 44, 86, 182; University of 182, 183, 305, 306, 311, 331, 336–37, 343, 344, 346, 351
  see also Giotto, Scrovegni Chapel; Marsilius of
Palazzo dei Priori (Palazzo Vecchio) *see* Florence, buildings

372 Index

Palermo 12, 155, 325; Cappella Palatina, Norman Palace *145*; medieval Jewish community in 145, 159 *see also* Sicilian Vespers
Palestrina, Giovanni Pierluigi da 310
Palladio, Andrea 160, 185, 301, 311–13; Villa la Rotonda *312*
Palmieri, Matteo 105
Panormita (Antonio Beccadelli) 155–56
Pantheon *312 see also* Rome, ancient
papacy, papal 5, 69, 70–74; 80–85, 92 antipopes 6, 71, 79, 90, 127, 151; Apostolic Camera 76; chancery 85–86, 156; conclave 91n; curia 73; dispensation 222; *Index see Index of Prohibited Books*; nuncio 269, 270; tithes 77–78, 256 *see also* Avignon, papacy at; church and state, separation of; Guelfs; Eight Saints, War of; Investiture Conflict; Medici bank; Rome, Vatican (Holy See)
papal bulls 74n, 76, 86n; *Clericis laicos* (1294) 74; *Cum nimis absurdum* (1555) 326; *Execrabilis* (1459) 90; *Periculoso* (1298) 98; *Unam sanctam* (1302) 74, 93, 234; bull of excommunication *see* excommunication
Papal States (Patrimony of St. Peter) 71, 77–78, 79, 83, 122, 147, 198, 223, 225, 226, 262, 302, 326; Kingdom of Naples as papal fief 150, 224, 330 *see also* Donation of Constantine
Paradiso see Dante
Parenti, Marco 189
parlatory 107
Parliament, Great Britain 187
Parma 12, 78, 263, 264, 287, 304
Parmigianino (Francesco Mazzola) 294
Parthenope 139
Pasquino, pasquinades 256, 258, 262
Patrimony of St. Peter *see* Papal States
Patrizi, Francesco 331
patronage, patrons 136, 158, 202, 206, 209–10, 238, 239, 241, 253; of architecture 87, 88, 92, 133, 152, 153, 251, 311; the arts 59, 119, 134, 146, 149, 183, 184, 242, 251, 294–95, 314; humanist studies 123, 155–56; literature 146, 149, 276, 307; manuscripts 133, 243; music 133, 152, 201, 243, 263; sciences 335, 344 *see also individual patrons*

Paul II, Pope 151
Paul III Farnese, Pope 286–87, 290, 292, 299
Paul IV Carafa, Pope 304, 326, 327
Paul V Borghese, Pope 346
Paul of Tarsus (Apostle), St 285
Pavia 12, 120, 122, 125, 164, 309; Battle of (1525) 259, 265; Certosa (charterhouse) 123; University of 123, 156; *see* Councils of the Church, Pavia
pax romana see Rome, ancient
Pazzi Conspiracy 188, 198–99
Peloponnesian War 57, 140, 277
penance 74n, 95, 326 *see also* Sacraments
Penn, William 187
Pepin, King of Italy 166
Pepoli (family) 119
Pergusa, Lake *see* Sicily
Persephone 139
Peri, Jacopo 310–11
Perugia 12, 32. 79, 123
Perugino (Pietro Vannucci) 239, 254, 290
Peruzzi, Baldassare 256
Peruzzi (company, family) 9, 24
Peter III, King of Aragon and Sicily 148
Peter (Apostle), St 70–71, 81, 92, 166, 252
Petrarch (Francesco Petrarca) 47–51, 55, 67, 69, 70, 75–76, 77, 91, 94, 121, 307, 332; *Ascent of Ventoux* 48, 68; sonnets (*Canzoniere*) 50–51, 68, 102, 146, 310, 327 *see also* Laura
Petrucci, Ottaviano 310
pharmacists, pharmacology 33, 53, 107, 183, 329, 332, 334 *see also* medicine
Philip II Habsburg, King of Spain 278, 301, 314, 321
Philip IV "the Fair", King of France 24, 73–4
philology 46, 157, 288
philosophy *see names of individual philosophers*: Aristotle; Epicurus; Ficino; Florentine Platonism; Lucretius; Pico della Mirandola; Plato *see also* natural philosophy
Phoenicians 140
Physicians and Pharmacists' Guild 33
Piacenza 12, 78, 119, 125, 156, 263
piagnoni see Savonarola

Piccolomini, Aenea Silvio *see* Pius II, Pope
Pico della Mirandola, Giovanni 158, 193, 209, 210, 219, 220, 235, 241, 323, 327
Pico della Mirandola, Gianfrancesco (or Giovanni Francesco) 290n, 327, 349
Piedmont (region) 123, 303 *see also* Savoy
Pier della Vigna 146
Piero della Francesca 244, 335: *Madonna del Parto* 111, *112*
Piero di Cosimo (painter) 250
Pierozzi, Antonino *see* Antoninus, St.
Pietrasanta 253
pilgrims, pilgrimage 6, 7, 13, 74, 75, 83, 195, 223
Pinturicchio (Bernardino di Betto) 254
Pinzochere see tertiaries
Pisa 6, 11, 12, 20, 79, 123, 161, 169, 198, 199, 217, 326, 334; Baptistry 20; Camposanto 40; Florence, at war with 130, 227, 228, 336; Leaning Tower 342; University of 341, 342 *see also* Councils of the Church
Pisanello (Antonio Pisano) 152
Pisano, Andrea, Giovanni, Nicola *see* Andrea, Giovanni, Nicola
Pitti, Luca 189
Pius II (Aeneas Silvius Piccolomini), Pope 69, 89–91, 92, 93, 128, 131, 151, 177, 180, 244, 251
Pius III, Pope 225
Pizan (Pisan), Christine de, 274
plague *see* Black Death
Plato 57, 192–93, 209, 255, 323, 331 *see also* Florentine Platonism; Marsilio Ficino; Neoplatonism
Platonic Academy founded by Ficino 193, 305
Plautus 309
Pliny the Elder 332, 333, 336
podestà 9–10, 118, 175
poesia (visual poetry) 246
poet laureate 49
poetry 14, 29, 54, 144, 210, 307; carnival songs 197; drama in verse 196, 309; epic 29, 48, 194, 195, 275, 307; Latin 44, 48; pastoral 275; sonnets 50, 51, 146; *terza rima* 14; troubadour 13, 146 *see also names of individual poets*; Orlando; *sacre rappresentazioni*

Poggio a Caiano 201
Poggio Bracciolini, Gian Francesco 56, 86, 133
Poliziano, Angelo 193, 195, 206, 209, 210
Pollaiuolo, Antonio del, Piero del 203
Polyphemus (Cyclops) 139, 318
polyphony 133, 152, 158, 243, 309–310
Pompeii 141
Pomponazzi, Pietro 331
Pontano, Giovanni 155
Pontormo, Jacopo da 279, 292–94, 295; Capponi Chapel Altarpiece *293*
Pontremoli 125
popes see *names of individual popes see also* papacy
popolo 8–10, 32, 73, 119, 120, 172, 179, 219, 281
population statistics *see* demographics
Portugal 144, 260, 305, 326
Poussin, Nicolas 318
Prato 47, 53, 79, 111, 203, 228
Presley, Elvis 51
print, printing 306, 321, 348; books 256, 271, 332, 336; engravings of art 203, 256; maps and atlases 336; newspapers 306; sheet music 310; papal censorship of 327–28; presses in Rome 256; Venice 182, 310
promissione see Venice, government
prostitution *see* sex trade
Protestant, Protestantism *see* Reformation, Protestant
Provence 47, 146, 147
Ptolemy, Claudius 57, 339, 346
Pucci, Francesco 331
Pulci, Antonia *see* Tanini Pulci, Antonia
Pulci (family) Bernardo 194, 196; Luca 194; Luigi 194–95, 196, 197
Punic Wars 140
Purgatory 284 *see also* Dante, *Purgatorio*
Pythagoras 65

quarantine *see* Black Death
Quintilian (Marcus Fabius Quintilianus) 54
Quinzani, Stefana, Blessed 100
Querini family 173
Querini, Pietro (Vincenzo) 286

Ragusa (Dubrovnic) 26, 33
Raimondi, Marcantonio 256

374   *Index*

Ramelli, Agostino 335
Ramusio, Giovanni Battista 336
Raphael (Raffaello Santi) 251, 254–56,
257, 258, 271, 276, 277, 294, 296,
318, 321; *Portrait of Baldassarre
Castiglione* 272, 278; *Portrait of Pope
Leo X* 263, 265
Ravenna 12, 14, 164, 165
Reconquista (1492) 260
Redondi, Pietro 347, 349
Reformation, Catholic (or Counter)
285–87, 298–99 *see also* Council of
Trent; *Index of Prohibited Books*;
Inquisition, Roman
Reformation, Protestant 82n, 92, 157,
235, 253, 286 *see also* Anglican
Church; Calvin; humanism, Christian;
iconoclasm; indulgences; Luther;
Regensburg, Diet of
Regensburg (Ratisbon), Diet of 286–87,
297, 299
Reggio 243, 262, 264
Regno di Napoli see Naples, Kingdom of
relics *see* saints
Reni, Guido 352
Renzo da Ceri (Lorenzo Anguillara or
Orsini) 367
res publica see Rome, ancient Republic
rhetoric 54–55, 58, 86, 270
Riario (family) 119; Girolamo,
Pietro198
Ricci, Ostilio 341
ricettizia 329
ricordi, ricordanze (memoirs) 54,
189, 201
Rimini 119, 135, 223
Rinaldo d'Aquino 146
Rinuccini, Ottavio 310
Risorgimento 276, 320
Robert "the Wise" of Anjou, King of
Naples 28, 49, 139, 149, 158
Rogier van der Weyden 153, 154
Roland (legendary knight of
Charlemagne) *see* Orlando
Romagna (region) 79, 119, 123, 197,
223, 225, 231, 262, 264, 266
Roman College (*Collegio Romano*) *see*
Jesuit order
Rome (ancient) 1–4, 20, 21, 47, 61,
75, 119–120, 141, 209, 230,
250–51, 254, 311, 348; Colosseum
2, 70, 89; consuls 2, 6; Diocletian
3, 120; Baths of 69; Eastern Roman

Empire *see* Byzantine Empire; Forum
2, 70; Pantheon 63, 70, 252, 256,
312; *pax romana* 2, 301; Republic 44,
56, 76, 128; Senate 2, 55, 72; roads 2,
4; Trajan's column 70, 84
Rome (Medieval and Renaissance)
baroni 73, 75, 76; commune 72–73,
83; Great Council 267; La Sapienza,
university of 331; Lateran, Apostolic
Palace 73, 83; *rioni* 267; Sack of,
(1527) 212, 237, 267–270, 272, 278;
Via Papale 250
Rome, churches: Il Gesù 301, 314; St.
John Lateran (San Giovanni Laterano)
83; San Luigi dei Francesi 319, 324;
St. Paul's Outside the Walls (San
Paolo Fuori le Mura) 83; Santa Maria
Maggiore 83; Santa Maria sopra
Minerva 111; Tempietto 252
Rome, places: Capitoline Hill 251, 292;
Castel Sant'Angelo (Mausoleum of
Hadrian) 70, 268, 280; Palace of the
Campidoglio 292; Palazzo Farnese
292, 318; Ponte Sisto 251; Piazza
Navona 256; Senators' Palace 251;
Villa Farnesina 256
Rome, Vatican (Leonine City) 83;
Chapel of Nicholas V *84*, 85; Cortile
del Belvedere 251, 254, 258; Library
85; Sistine Chapel 22, 200, 237,
253–54, 257, 282, 290–92, 318;
St. Peter's Basilica 252; Stanza della
Segnatura 255, 257; Swiss Guard 268
see also papacy
Romulus (founder of Rome) 2
Romulus Augustus (Augustulus),
Emperor 4
Rosso Fiorentino 294
Rousseau, Jean-Jacques 276
Rubens, Peter Paul 318
Rucellai, Giovanni di Paolo 88, 206;
Palazzo Rucellai *see* Florence,
buildings

sacre rappresentazioni (sacred dramas)
96, 196, 200, 308
saints 54, 95–96, 98–101; beatification
85n, 102; canonization 85n, 98,
101; cults of saints 101; ex voto 96;
hagiographies (biographies of saints)
96, 101, 299; martyrs 4, 70, 96, 252;
patron saints 61, 96, 155, 166–67,
184, 196, 206, 329; relics 96, 166,

269, 288, 329; reliquaries 96 *see also names of individual saints*
Salernitano, Masuccio 156
Salerno 12; medical school 143, university 53
Salutati, Coluccio 55–56, 354
Salviati, Francesco, Archbishop of Pisa 198, 199
Salviati, Maria 282
San Gimignano (Tuscan town) 9
San Marino, Republic of 116n
Sangallo (family), Antonio da 250; Antonio da (the Younger) 292, 313; Giuliano da 201, 207, 208, 250
Sannazaro, Jacopo 156, 275–76, 310, 313
Sano di Pietro 101
Sansovino (Jacopo Tatti) 185, 311; Loggetta *186*
Saracens 143, 275, 307
Sardinia 26, 149, 151, 298, 325
Sarpi, Paolo 351
Sassetti, Francesco 206
Savelli family 73
Savonarola, Girolamo 94, 98, 187, 209, 212, 218–21, 227, 235, 236; 248–49, 280, 285
Savoy 303, 304, 350
Scheggia, (Giovanni di Ser Giovanni) *Adimari Wedding Cassone 103*
Schism, Great (1054) 71, 82, 82n, 145, 167
Schism, Western (1378–1417) 79–81
scholasticism *see* universities, scholastic curriculum
science 182–83, 239, 257, 305, 306, 331–339, 341–48, 350; scientific method 342 *see also* natural philosophy *and individual branches of science*
Scot, Michael 146
Scotti (family) 119
Scrovegni, Enrico 18, 136, 206; Scrovegni Chapel *see* Padua
Scuola di San Giobbe *see* Venice, scuole
sculpture 20–21, 60–62, 153, 185, 203–4, 248, 249–50, 253, 256, 282–83, 295, 352; ancient 61, 84, 205, 251, 254 *see also names of individual sculptors*
Scylla and Charbidis *see* Strait of Messina
Sebastian, St (San Sebastiano) 96, 184

Sebastiano del Piombo 256, 257
Segesta 140
"self-fashioning" 92, 113, 209, 235, 297
Selinunte 140
Sensa see Venice
serrata see Venice, government
Servetus, Michael 299
sex trade: courtesans161, 247, 274–75, 307; prostitutes, prostitution 27, 37, 109, 113, 307; public brothels 109
Sforza (family) 119; Caterina 223, 228; Francesco Duke of Milan 115, 119, 125–26, 132, 137, 151, 188, 230; Francesco II, Duke of Milan (r.1521–24) 264, 279; Galeazzo Maria, Duke of Milan 135, 190, 198, 199, 210; Ludovico ("il Moro"), Duke of Milan 213–15, 221, 223, 237, 238, 239, 244, 252, 257, 258, 270, 336; Massimiliano Maria, Duke of Milan (r.1513–15) 262, 263
sfumato see artistic techniques
Shakespeare, William 8, 14, 51, 186, 235, 320–21
sharecropping *see mezzadria*
Sicily 139–51, 153–55, 157–58, 298, 325, 326, 330; Accademia degli Intronati 305; Hospital (Ospedale di Santa Maria della Scala) 99, 111; painting 37–39; Piazza del Campo 101; Sicilian School of poetry 50, 146, 159; Siena 12, 27, 32, 38, 79, 100, 109, 116, 123, 256, 282, 303; University of 90 *see also* Catherine of; Bernardino of
signore, signori (pl.) 9, 37, 83, 115, 119, 130, 136–37, 152, 158, 238; signoria (signorial government) 37, 116, 118, 125, 130, 137; Signoria (priorate) *see* Florence, Republic
Signorelli, Luca, *Rule of the Antichrist* 222
simony 16, 78, 287
single-point perspective *see* artistic techniques
Sinigaglia (or Senigallia) 224, 226
Siracusa (Syracuse) 12, 140, 144
Sistine Chapel *see* Rome, Vatican
Sixtus IV Pope (Francesco della Rovere) 197–98, 200, 210, 251, 254
Sixtus V Peretti, Pope 251, 311
slavery 109, 148, 175

376 Index

Soderini, Niccolò 189
Soderini, Piero 212, 227–28, 233, 234
Sodoma (Giovanni Antonio Bazzi) 256
sodomy 220, 289
sonnets, sonnet form *see* poetry
Sorrento 141
Spain: kingdom unified (1469) 149,
 260; *Reconquista* (1492) 260; *Siglo
 de Oro* 320; Spanish control of
 Duchy of Milan 301–2; of southern
 Italy 148, 149–56, 158, 223, 227;
 Spanish Empire 260, 262, 301;
 Spanish Inquisition 325, 326;;
 Spanish viceroys 149, 279, 303–4
 see also names of individual rulers
Sparta 140
Spenser, Edmund 307
Spoleto 12, 123
sprezzatura see Castiglione, *The Courtier*
Squarcialupi, Antonio 201
Stampa, Gaspara 275, 278
standardbearer of justice *see* Florence,
 Republic
Stefano Protonotaro 146
Strait of Messina 139, 148
Strozzi (family) Strozzi, Alessandra *see*
 Macinghi Strozzi, Alessandra; Filippo
 207–8; Matteo 105; Palazzo Strozzi
 see Florence, buildings
studia humanitatis see humanism
studiolo 113, 242, 244, 245
Suleiman the Magnificent 304
sumptuary laws 15
Swiss Federation 227
syncretism 46
syphilis ("French disease") 41, 237,
 334, 336

tamburro see Florence, crime,
 denunciation of
Tanini Pulci, Antonia 196, 210
tapestries 105, 153, 176, 264
Tarabotti, Arcangela 351
Tarantism 329
Tartaglia (Niccolò Fontana) 332
Tasso, Torquato 194, 275, 307,
 309, 310
Tassoni, Alessandro 348
taxation 10, 33, 73–74, 76, 79, 122,
 125, 131, 144, 147, 148, 150,
 169, 179, 227, 286, 304, 305;
 tax collectors 77, 149, 256, 319
 see also Catasto, tithes

Telesio, Bernardino 330–31
tempera *see* art, painting techniques
terraferma 164, 177 *see also* Venice,
 mainland possession
Terrence 309
terribilità 225, 253, 297
tertiaries (Third Order) 98, 99, 100,
 285, 289
theater 181, 197, 254, 262, 295,
 299, 308, 309, 310–11; *commedia
 erudita* (learned theater) 309 *see also*
 commedia dell'arte; *frottole*; opera;
 sacre rappresentazioni
Theodore, St 167
Theodoric, King of the Ostrogoths 143
theology 13, 22, 157, 186, 218, 255,
 331, 345; use of exegesis 346; as
 "Queen of the Sciences" in scholastic
 curriculum 46 *see also names of
 theologians*
Theophrastus 57, 332
Thomas (Apostle), St *Christ and St.
 Thomas* (Verrocchio) 204, 204–5
Thirty Years' War 347, 350
Thucydides 30, 57, 277
Tiepolo (family) 173
Tinctoris, Johannes 152
Tintoretto, Jacopo 315–16, 321;
 Domenico 316; Marietta 316
tithes 77, 86n
Titian (Tiziano Vecellio) 246–48, 257,
 258, 313, 314–15, 318, 321, 336;
 Sleeping Venus 247; *Equestrian
 Portrait of Charles V 269*
Tivoli 72
Torcello *see* Venice
Torino 303
Tornabuoni, Lucrezia 194, 208
Torricelli, Evangelista 350
torture *see* law
Toscanelli, Paolo 63, 335
towers in medieval cities 9–10, 69, 73
transubstantiation (doctrine) 289,
 324, 347
Trajan, Emperor 70, 84, 152
Traversari, Ambrogio 133
Trent *see* Councils of the Church
Treviso 12, 177
Tridentine art *see* Councils of the
 Church, Trent
Trinacria 140
Trinity (doctrine) 299, 323; *Trinity*
 (Masaccio) 43, 65, 206

Index   377

Trissino, Gian Giorgio 311
troubadours 13, 146, 195
Tuchman, Barbara 24
Turks 132, 143, 160, 168, 169, 177,
  199, 227, 260, 280, 303, 304;
  Ottoman Empire 178, 200, 302, 304
  see also Constantinople, conquest;
  Lepanto, Battle of
Tuscan dialect 14, 54, 146, 195, 272
  see also Italian language
Tuscany (region) 190, 198, 200, 214,
  223, 280; Grand Duchy of 282, 303,
  305, 306, 326, 344 *see also individual*
  names of grand dukes

Uccello, Paolo 36, 134, 244
Unam sanctam (papal bull) *see*
  Boniface VIII
United States Capitol, Washington D.C.
  313, 314, *353*; Constitution 187
universities 45, 52, 305, 321, 330,
  334, 338; scholastic curriculum 37,
  45–46, 48, 331, 332 *see also* Bologna;
  Florence (Studio); Naples; Oxford;
  Padua; Paris; Pavia; Pisa; Rome;
  Salerno; Siena; Verona
Urban II, Pope 169
Urban IV, Pope 72
Urban V, Pope 78–79
Urban VI, Pope 80
Urban VIII Barberini, Pope 346,
  347, 354
Urbino 119, 214, 224, 226, 241, 244,
  254, 263, 266, 270, 304; court of,
  described by Castiglione 271–73:
  Studiolo, Palazzo Ducale *245 see also*
  individual dukes
usury 15, 18, 127 *see also* banking

Valdés, Alfonso de 270
Valentini da Udine, Elena 100
Valentino, Count *see* Borgia, Cesare
Valla, Lorenzo 156–57, 159, 284,
  285, 332
Vallombrosan order 98, 285
Valois (dynasty) 259, 304; Isabelle de
  122; *see individual kings*
Valtellina 350
Van Eyck, Jan 153, 154
Vandals (tribe) 4, 141, 143
Vanini, Giulio Cesare 331
Varano, Costanza 58
Varchi, Benedetto 281

Vasari, Giorgio 306; architecture and
  painting of 295, 311; *Lives of the*
  Artists 22, 203, 239, 248, 253, 257,
  279, 290, 295–97, 300, 317
Vasco da Gama 259, 260
Veneto (region) 121, 123, 185, 311; as
  Roman province of Venetia et Histria
  161, 162 *see also terraferma*
Veneziano, Domenico 134
Venice 6, 7, 12, 125, 128, 131, 132,
  160–87, 199, 200, 223, 225–227,
  260, 262, 266, 276, 280, 304, 305,
  311, 351, 352 *see also* Agnadello,
  Chioggia, League of Venice
Venice, art architecture 184–85,
  311–13; painting 155, 183–84; *217,*
  245–48; 314–16, 320 *see also names*
  of individual artists
Venice, economy 175–77; glass industry
  179–80; guilds 172, 181; mercantile
  origins 164, 165; printing 182, 310;
  shipbuilding 164, 175, 179, 183; silk
  industry 171, 179
Venice, government 116, 170–75, 186,
  187; *Arengo* 170; Chancery 179;
  Council of the *Sapienti* 171; Council
  of Forty 171; Council of Ten; 173
  doge 160, 170, 173–75, 179, 180,
  183, 187; doge's *promissione* 171,
  175, 187; *Doge Loredan* (Bellini)
  174; Great Council 179; mixed
  constitution 186; *Savi di Terra Ferma*
  177; *serrata* 160, 172–73 *see also*
  names of individual doges
Venice, places Arsenal (*Arsenale*)
  175–77, 185; Doge's Palace (Palazzo
  Ducale*)*; canals 160, 178, 181;
  Lagoon 161, *163*; 167, 178, 179,
  180, 183; Lazzaretto 32; Logetta 185;
  mainland possessions (*terraferma*)
  125, 164, 177–78, 182, 183, 226,
  245, 311; Marciana Library 185;
  Murano Island 179, 180; Redentore
  (church) 313; Rialto 162, 166, 184;
  St. Mark's Basilica (San Marco) 166,
  170, 184; San Giorgio Maggiore
  (church) 313; Torcello Island 162,
  165; Zecca (Mint) 185 *see also*
  Aquilea, Istria, Padua, Veneto
Venice, social world of, 178–82;
  arsenalotti (Arsenal workers) 179,
  180, 181; *cittadini originarii* (original
  citizens) 178–79; courtesans *see* sex

378   *Index*

trade; education 51, 182; festivals 180–81; *ghetto* 326; Golden Book 173; gondoliers 160, 179, 181; humanists 58, 156, 182 *see also names of individuals*; myth of Venice 167, 186; *scuole* 133–34
Ventoux, Mount *see* Petrarch
Venus, goddess 205, 210, 247, 256, 318; planet 340, 343, 344
Vergerio the elder, Pier Paolo 123
Verona 12, 32, 58, 78, 119, 164, 177, 182, 298; University of 335
Veronese, Paolo 301, 315–16, 321; *Wedding Feast at Cana 316*
Verrocchio, Andrea del 110, 196, 203–4; *Christ and St. Thomas 204*
Vesalius, Andreas 323, 336, 337
Vespasiano da Bisticci 136, 137, 155
Vespucci, Amerigo 260, 278
Vespucci, Marco 195
Vesuvius, Mount (volcano) 139, 141, 351
Vettori, Francesco 229, 234
Vicenza 12, 177, 311, 313
Vikings 5, 144
Villa Casale *see* Sicily, places
Villani, Giovanni 23, 24, 27, 53
Villani, Matteo 27, 32
Virgil (Publius Vergilius Maro) 15, 16, 46, 48, 102n, 235
virtù 122, 230–231, 273
Visconti (family) 55, 115, 119, 120, 123, 125; Azzone 121; Bernabò 115, 122; Bianca Maria, Duchess 125, 126; Filippo Maria, Duke 123, 124, 125, 132, 137, 150; Galeazzo II 121, 122; Giangaleazzo, Duke 91, 121, 122–123, 124, 126, 177; Gianmaria, Duke 123; Giovanni 121; Matteo 120, 121; Matteo II 121; Ottone 120, 121; Valentina 221
Visitation (Giotto) 19
Vitruvian Man (Leonardo) 239–41, *240*
Vitruvius 87, 241, 252, 313

volgare (vernacular) *see* Italian language
Voltaire (François Marie Arouet) 354
Volterra 12, 190, 198, 199, 294

Waldensians 329
Walter of Brienne 130
warfare armor, armorers 34, 336; citizen militias 10, 36, 130, 228, 267, 268, 281; fortresses 334; gunpowder 268, 334; mercenary soldiers 79, 82, 125, 144, 262 *see also condottieri*; military engineering 223, 238, 241, 335, 343; weaponry 216, 239, 336 *see also individual battles, sieges, wars, uprisings*
Wars of Religion, European 299
Wickham, Chris 11, 22
William of Apulia 144
witches, witchcraft 67, 290, 326–27, 348 *see also* magic
women: childbirth 96, 102, 108, 110, 205; women's mortality in 106, 111; court ladies 273–74; domestic work 105, 108, 111; female artists 316–18, 321, 333–334; humanists 58, 68; writers 194, 196, 208, 210, 274, 275, 278, 309, 351; pregnancy 108, 109, 111–12, 326; religious devotion 101; wet nurses 108, 110, 111; widowhood 105–7, 321 *see also* children; feminism; marriage; nuns; saints; sex trade; slavery; tertiaries; witches
World War II 41, 158
Wren, Christopher 313

Xenophon 56, 57

yersinia pestis see Black Death

Zabarella, Jacopo 331
Zara 168, 169, 170, 176
Zoroastrianism 209